MW00752122

Also by Sean Smith

SEAN SMITH

KIM

DEY ST.
AN IMPRINT OF WILLIAM MORROW *PUBLISHERS*

DEY ST.

KIM KARDASHIAN. Copyright © 2015 by Sean Smith. All rights reserved. Printed in the United States of America. No part of this book may be used or reproduced in any manner whatsoever without written permission except in the case of brief quotations embodied in critical articles and reviews. For information address HarperCollins Publishers, 195 Broadway, New York, NY 10007.

HarperCollins books may be purchased for educational, business, or sales promotional use. For information please e-mail the Special Markets Department at SPsales@harpercollins.com.

FIRST U.S. EDITION

Library of Congress Cataloging-in-Publication Data has been applied for.

ISBN 978-0-06-244390-8

15 16 17 18 19 OV/RRD 10 9 8 7 6 5 4 3 2 1

To Rodney and Nicky

CONTENTS

PART THREE: KIM KARDASHIAN WEST

INTRODUCTION
A DAY IN CALABASAS, 4 JUNE 2015

It's a scorchingly hot Thursday in Calabasas. A helpful guy in the sushi bar told me it was 100 degrees outside. In the middle of the day, even the shade is too warm. The old cliché that you could fry an egg on the pavement certainly applies; in fact, you could cook a full English breakfast. No wonder you are unlikely to see Kim Kardashian West in her new custom-designed silver Rolls-Royce Phantom before the sun has cooled in the late afternoon or early evening.

Calabasas is in what's known in Los Angeles as 'The Valley'. More accurately, this is the San Fernando Valley or the West Valley. Locals reckon it's at least 10 degrees warmer here than in the fashionable beach areas of Santa Monica, Venice and Malibu. Calabasas, though, is becoming just as desirable, thanks to an influx of the rich and famous who realise a 40-minute crawl along the Ventura Freeway (Route 101) is a small price to pay for getting so much more bang for your buck. A $1 million property here might cost $10 million in Beverly Hills. That value for money won't last forever. The Kardashians have made Calabasas famous, thanks to their reality show and the number of times they are photographed apparently living their lives in a normal way.

Other than Kim and her family, the most famous current resident is probably Drake, the phenomenally successful Canadian rapper, who immortalised the place in his song '2 On/Thotful': 'Crib in Calabasas man I call that shit the safe house. Thirty minutes from LA man the shit is way out.'

Local legend has it that Calabasas owes its unusual name to an incident in 1824. A rancher from Oxnard, 60 miles north, was on his way to Los Angeles when he crashed his wagon, spilling a load of pumpkins along the track. The next spring, hundreds of pumpkins or gourds started to grow by the road-side. As a result, the area was called Las Calabasas – the place where the pumpkins fell – after the Spanish word for pump-kin, *calabaza*.

Technically, Calabasas is a city that became part of Los Angeles County in 1991. It doesn't feel remotely like Los Angeles here. The great Hollywood stars of the past didn't live in Calabasas. Instead, they came to work here, although some would take Valley vacations away from the bustle of LA.

In 1935, Warner Brothers bought an estate near Calabasas Creek, which became known as the Warner Bros Ranch. Many classic films were shot there: in *The Adventures of Robin Hood*, starring Errol Flynn, the dusty terrain doubled for Sherwood Forest. Flynn travelled out to the Valley to shoot a number of movies, including the Western *Santa Fe Trail*, which co-starred a future President of the United States, Ronald Reagan. The Hollywood great, Gary Cooper, won an Oscar for his portrayal of Sergeant York fighting in the (Calabasas) trenches in the story of the First World War hero. Most famously, *Casablanca*, the wartime romance that features on almost every list of all-time best movies, was partly shot at the ranch.

Nowadays, classic movies have given way to reality shows, although the Valley has also long been a favoured setting for porn flicks. *Keeping Up with the Kardashians* is by no means the first reality show to be shot at a house in Calabasas. The best known was probably *Newlyweds: Nick and Jessica*, which began in 2003 and followed the embryonic marriage of boy band vocalist Nick Lachey and the blonde bombshell singer Jessica Simpson. The dumb blonde antics of Jessica were quite amusing, but the show had nowhere to go after three seasons, when she filed for divorce. Real life ruined the reality show.

The Kardashians aren't seen in town as much these days, especially after moving their boutique, DASH, to West Hollywood in 2012. The original store, I discover, was in a small parade in Park Granada, just across the road from a large shopping complex called The Commons, the central point of Calabasas. A few years ago, the Kardashians were genuinely out and about every day, as they sought to build their business before the store became little more than a film location. It was pleasant enough, but nothing special – the sort of place you might find in a thousand small towns across America.

In the Shibuya sushi bar, a few yards down from DASH, they used to see the Kardashians every other day. The Kardashian women have always tried to keep their voluptuous figures in check by eating healthily. The chef preparing my tasty lunch of seared toro and peppered tuna at the counter told me that Kim had been to the restaurant lots of times, but Kanye West had joined her on only one occasion.

Shibuya is small and fills up quite easily, so when Kim and Kanye turned up on an evening in late April, they were made to wait in line and sat on a bench outside for half an hour until a table became available. Kim had just appeared on the talk show *Jimmy Kimmel Live!* and this proved to be a convenient photo opportunity on their way home. A photographer was able to shoot some very clear shots. Kanye looked miserable and scowled, as he always does for the cameras. Kim, elegantly made up and revealing her considerable cleavage, smiled happily.

Kim always favours the house sushi roll when she visits Shibuya. In actual fact, they had no need to stop off at all, because they employ a full-time chef. My own chef was not so absorbed in news of the Kardashians. He was extremely interested in Manchester United, however, and dreams of the day when Wayne Rooney pops in for a sashimi snack.

In and around the exclusive little shops, ice cream parlours and health food stores, you are far more likely to see Kim's younger half-sisters, Kendall and Kylie Jenner, who, as teenagers do, prefer to hang out in the mall with their friends than in the fur-lined prison of their gated community.

Round the corner for coffee at the Blue Table deli, a young woman, who was working in Calabasas while she waited for her break as a singer, told me that she had seen Scott Disick the day before. The long-standing boyfriend of Kim's sister Kourtney, and the father of her children, has become a well-known face from his regular appearances on the TV show. 'What does he actually do?' asked my companion. I had to admit I had no idea and made a mental note to find out.

Having celebrities pop in does wonders for local trade. A few hundred yards away, in yet another shopping centre, El Camino, is a 'homey café for health-conscious bites' called Health Nut, which has become celebrated as the place where the Kardashian girls buy the salads they are always munching on TV. I pop in to grab a takeaway of Kim's favourite salad, whatever that might be.

'No problem,' said the man at the counter, bashing my order into the till and taking the money.

'What's in it?' I asked.

'No idea,' he responded smilingly. 'I just hit a button marked "Kardashian".'

It turns out to be a pretty dull chicken salad with a pleasant tangy dressing – nothing the chef couldn't run up in five minutes at home.

For a while, the Kardashians had a major rival as the most famous faces in the neighbourhood when Justin Bieber bought a house in a gated Calabasas community called The Oaks for $6.5 million in 2012. These days it's a Kardashian enclave. Justin tired of life in the suburbs after two years and sold his five-bedroom mansion, complete with pool, hot tub, movie theatre and skateboard ramp, at a $1 million profit to Kim's sister Khloé. She can easily walk round to see their elder sister Kourtney, who also lives there.

Khloé's mansion is relatively ordinary compared to the extraordinary palatial luxury enjoyed by Drake. He is one of the biggest stars in the US, although he has yet to cross the Atlantic with similar success. His best-known British hit was as the featured artist on Rihanna's number one 'What's My Name?'.

He lives in an outrageously opulent home in Hidden Hills, which was originally on the market for $27 million in 2009, but he was able to pick it up for the knockdown price of $8 million after the property market collapsed. It has a cinema, wine cellar, stables, volleyball court, Olympic-sized pool, stables, wet-room bar and so on. Drake once sang on a number called 'Versace' by the hip-hop group Migos: 'This is a gated community, please get the fuck off the property.' He may rap the language of the street, but I don't suppose he wants to live anywhere near one.

Hidden Hills is the gated community that attracted Kris and Bruce Jenner when they were looking to move from Beverly Hills while Kim and her siblings were still at school. Kris was first introduced to the neighbourhood by a friend after her marriage to Kim's father, Robert Kardashian, had collapsed.

There's rumoured to be more money in Hidden Hills than in Bel Air. Kim and Kanye have now bought an estate there with an estimated value of $20 million. I heard they are going to turn it into a palace and it's going to make Drake's property seem like a terrace.

It's supremely ironic that gated communities don't just keep the public out, they fence the residents in. You can't get past the guards without an appointment or, it seems, an E! Entertainment Television identification badge. At least for the famous people who live here, it means the paparazzi aren't looking over the garden fence.

Hidden Hills has a number of entrances and exits, so the photographers split up and wait at each one. Kim will leave eventually, but they won't know in advance which exit she is going to use. When she is spotted, the photographer stationed at that particular gate texts everyone else that she is on the move. By clubbing together in this way, they ensure that they all have the opportunity to get a picture. It is reminiscent of the days when squadrons of paparazzi used to hang around outside Kensington Palace in the hope that Princess Diana would go out. A Kim picture guarantees a sale in much the same way as one of the adored royal icon did.

I popped into a hotel in Calabasas to ask for some directions and told the receptionist, probably a resting actress, that I was writing a book about Kim Kardashian. She volunteered, 'I don't really like her. I don't see what her point is.' It reminded me of local hostility against Britney Spears when I visited McComb, Mississippi, where she was born. Perhaps it's the way people always feel about the most famous face in their midst.

I enjoyed my day in Calabasas, but I needed to beat the traffic on the freeway to return to downtown Los Angeles and civilisation. Before I left, there was time to ask an elegant woman shopping for clothes in a boutique very similar to DASH what she thought of the Kardashians: 'You don't get anywhere in that family without a vagina. Bruce has realised that ...'

PART ONE

KIMBERLY

1

MOTHER ARMENIA

Kim Kardashian West demonstrated to the world the global power of her celebrity when she arrived at the Armenian Memorial Complex in that obscure country's capital of Yerevan in April 2015. The pictures of her, solemnly carrying a bunch of bright red tulips that matched the colour of her dazzling jumpsuit, went round the world.

After she had laid the tribute at the eternal flame, bedlam broke out as TV cameramen and photographers – and the public brandishing phones – battled for pictures of Kim and her family. It had been the same story ever since she had touched down in Mother Armenia, as she calls the land of her ancestors.

'Armenia, we are here!!!!!' She posted to her then 30 million Instagram followers when she arrived. 'We are so grateful to be here and start this journey of a lifetime. Thank you to everyone who greeted us. I can't wait to explore our country and have some yummy food!'

On the flight from Los Angeles International Airport (LAX), Kim had slept completely hidden from prying eyes by a blanket. She always does this on planes so nobody can snap an unglamorous shot of her snoring with her mouth open. They flew the last part of their journey economy class, much to the amazement of other passengers.

When she arrived, she appeared completely refreshed, in ripped white jeans and a tight white top, although she hid her eyes behind a huge pair of sunglasses, in case the ravages of jet lag had caught her before her make-up artist, who always travels with her, could step in.

The visit saw Kim, and her younger sister Khloé, give an object lesson in how to combine glamour with tasteful respect. For their audience with the prime minister, they wore figure-hugging outfits that showed off all their curves. Kim chose beige and combined it with killer heels. Yet for their trip to the sacred Geghard Monastery, a World Heritage Site, she chose understated black.

Kanye West was on hand to secure his wife's veil affectionately, although her wardrobe assistant took over to make the necessary adjustments for the perfect picture. Arguably, Kim has never looked lovelier than in this respectful homage to the country's tradition. She looked very Armenian, with her coal-black eyes, long black hair and curvaceous silhouette.

This was Kim's first visit to the land of her father's family. Inevitably, there was nothing low key about it, especially as the plan was to feature her journey to the homeland in her long-running reality show, *Keeping Up with the Kardashians*. The television crew from E! tried to look as inconspicuous as possible – as if carrying around a large boom microphone were the most natural thing in Armenia.

A stills man from the Splash News & Pictures Agency, Brian Prahl, a sort of unofficial official photographer at the court of Queen Kim, travelled with them to record the trip, ensuring that the pictures taken were pin sharp and of the highest quality. Brian did his job well and everyone looked their best.

Wherever she went, the streets were lined with hundreds of people anxious to get a glimpse of her or, most prized of all, a selfie with the most photographed woman in the world. It was like a boisterous royal tour, with Kanye and Kim in the role of Prince William and 'Princess Kate'. Their little daughter, North, captured hearts with an array of cute expressions, just as the baby Prince George had on his first overseas trip to Australia a year earlier.

Even Kanye broke into the occasional smile, usually when playing with North. He stayed a pace behind his wife, much in the manner of William with Kate, or Prince Philip accompanying the Queen. The men understand that they are not the focus of attention on these occasions.

Kanye did have his moment in the spotlight, however, when he gave an 'impromptu' concert for thousands of excited Armenians and was able to display some rock 'n' roll behaviour by jumping fully clothed into Yerevan's romantic-sounding Swan Lake. Apparently, he made the decision to go out and sing for the people only that night, although it's doubtful if his Armenian security detail would have allowed such spontaneity. It proved to be good fun.

He had just started singing 'Good Life', when he took everyone by surprise by leaping into the water, which, a little undramatically, only came up to his knees. He managed to get his microphone wet, which brought the song to an abrupt halt. That didn't bother his audience, who began to jump in and splash around as well. Kim, who, dressed in sweats, was looking about as casual as she ever gets, explained that he wanted to be closer to the fans on the other side of the lake. 'It was an exciting, crazy night!' she said. After he had been firmly helped out of the water by guards, Kanye sang another five songs: 'Stronger', 'Jesus Walks', 'Power', 'Touch the Sky' and 'All of the Lights'.

His escapade lightened the mood of what could have been a very sombre few days. Despite the excitement her journey to Armenia generated, there was a serious point to it all. Kim wanted to draw attention to what many – and certainly all of the Kardashians – regard as the first modern genocide.

She had flown in just before the one hundredth anniversary, on 24 April, of the slaughter of more than 1.5 million Christian Armenians by Muslim Ottoman Turks. It preceded the Holocaust in Nazi Germany by a generation, but became a footnote in the history of the twentieth century, scarcely covered in school history lessons. Kim was determined to change that. She blogged, 'Every year, I honour the memory of the martyrs who were killed during the 1915 Armenian Genocide.'

This didn't sound like the sort of issue that might concern a woman posting selfies to her Instagram followers or sharing information online about her favourite salad or how to bleach your eyebrows. She explained, 'So many people have come to me and said, "I had no idea there was a genocide." There aren't that many Armenians in this business. We have this spotlight to bring attention to it, so why would we just sit back? I will continue to ask the questions and fight for the genocide to be recognised for what it was.' There are a few household names from Armenia: Cher, Andre Agassi and the popular French singer Charles Aznavour were three of the best known before the Kardashians became so famous.

Not only is their country a fleeting presence in history lessons, it doesn't feature largely in geography classes either. The Republic of Armenia is a landlocked, mountainous country wedged between the Black Sea and the Caspian Sea. Turkey is to the west, Georgia to the north, Azerbaijan to the east and Iran to the south. Since it achieved independence from the Soviet Union in 1991, Armenia has relied on tourism to the beautiful country to bolster a struggling economy still reliant on Russian gas. An estimated third of the 3 million-strong population live in poverty.

The premier, Hovik Abrahamyan, welcomed Kim and Khloé with open arms, realising they were putting Armenia on the map for millions of people around the world. The sisters were joined by two previously unheralded Armenian cousins, Kourtni and Kara Kardashian, who hadn't shared the limelight with their famous American relatives until now.

Prime Minister Abrahamyan praised the Kardashian contribution to the 'international recognition and condemnation of the Armenian genocide'. Kim, in turn, repeated her pledge to campaign for worldwide acknowledgement of the atrocity.

She apologised for not being able to speak Armenian and said she and her sisters were intent on learning the language, which doesn't feature in the curriculum of the exclusive private schools of Beverly Hills and Bel Air. Even her father, Robert Kardashian, so proud of his heritage, wasn't a fluent speaker.

Kim's efforts to reveal a more serious side to her public image received an unexpected boost when Pope Francis condemned the cruelty of the genocide during a service at St Peter's in Rome. Many commentators acknowledged that the combination of Kim Kardashian and the Pope was a PR disaster for Turkey.

After the family left Armenia, there was one more important stop to make before they flew home. They travelled to Jerusalem for North to be baptised into the Armenian Apostolic Church. The hour-long ceremony at the Cathedral of St James in the Old City was conducted in both Armenian and English, and ended with North being anointed on the head with holy water.

Kim followed the custom of these occasions by wearing a striped wraparound floor-length dress and flat shoes and covering her head with a white shawl. Kanye looked relaxed and happy in white trousers and sweater. North, in a white christening gown, went to sleep. It had been a long trip for a little girl but, as a reward, she was treated to a day out in Disneyland on her second birthday in June.

The 'state visit' to Armenia was a triumph for Kim, although her one disappointment came when President Obama failed to use the 'g word' (genocide) in a speech marking the anniversary. He couldn't risk antagonising Turkey, an important ally in the ongoing fight against terrorism. Kim, who doesn't blame modern-day Turkish people, observed, 'It's very disappointing he hasn't used it as a president. We thought it would happen this year. I feel like we're close ...'

When she had first arrived in Armenia, Kim made a point of saying that her father and his parents, now all dead, would have been hugely proud of the visit and what she was trying to achieve. Like her, they had been born in the United States. It was the previous generation of Kardashians, Kim's great-grandparents, who preserved the family line by fleeing Armenia just before the mass slaughter of their countrymen.

In leaving the remote village of Karakale, where the family originated, they were heeding an extraordinary warning made by an illiterate and sickly boy who had visions about the future. Efim Klubnikin predicted, 'Those who believe in this [prophecy] will go to a far land, while the unbelievers will remain in place. Our people will go on a long journey over the great and deep waters.'

Although he made the prophecy first as an 11-year-old boy in the 1850s, he repeated his warning 50 years later, just in time for some 2,000 Armenians to leave before the nation's holocaust. Kim's forebears were among the lucky ones. Accounts testify that 'every soul' in Karakale was murdered. The village is now an entirely Muslim settlement, near the city of Kars, in the harsh, snow-covered environment of eastern Turkey.

In an extraordinary twist, Klubnikin urged his 'believers' not just to flee to the United States, but to settle specifically in Los Angeles. Kim's great-grandparents sailed independently to a new life, and met and fell in love on the boat from Germany. They were among some of the last to flee, not setting sail until 1913.

At the time of the massacres, Armenia was still in Russia. The First Republic of Armenia was formed in 1918 and became a founding member of the Soviet Union four years later. Strictly speaking, the Kardashian ancestors were of

Russian–Armenian stock and the family name was Kardashcoff, which doesn't trip off the tongue as well as Kardashian, although they could still have called their famous boutique DASH.

By the end of the First World War, the Kardashian family was beginning to establish itself at the centre of the new Armenian community in Los Angeles. Many had settled in a poor, slum-like neighbourhood known as 'The Flats' in Boyle Heights, East LA. The area was a gateway to the city for newcomers, and one that they aspired to leave. The Kardashians were no exception.

The displacement of some of a nation's finest men and women bred great spirit and a desire for achievement. Friendships forged in adverse circumstances would last a life-time, binding successful Armenian families together. A fierce loyalty was the hallmark of the community.

The rise in fortunes of the Kardashians began with a rubbish collection business and moved on to hog-farming. From there, it was a natural progression to opening a slaughterhouse for meat processing, as an outlet for their livestock concern. The Great Western Meat Packing Company started up in 1933 in the city of Vernon, 5 miles south of downtown LA. It's a very unprepossessing, almost exclusively industrial area, full of warehouses and plants – and slaughterhouses. Vernon is not a place where you would want to live.

Arthur Kardashian, Kim's grandfather, was born in Los Angeles in 1918 and married her beautiful grandmother, Helen Arakelian, who was a year older, when he was 20. He took over the family business with his brother Bob when their father retired and built it into one of the most successful

Southern Californian enterprises, with a turnover of more than $100 million.

Art and Helen became pillars of a new prosperous Armenian community, settling in the affluent suburb of Baldwin Hills, a million miles away from The Flats. Former California Senator Walter Karabian, a frequent guest, described their home as 'beautiful' and 'upscale'. In the space of a generation, the Kardashians had risen from hard-working immigrants to millionaires. They possessed an ideology of success and how to achieve it that they would pass on to their children and grandchildren.

Kim adored her grandparents. Particularly, she was close to Helen, who died, aged 90, in 2008. 'Nana was seriously so much fun,' she said. 'She was your typical Armenian grand-mother and always cooking the best Armenian meals. Our favourite when we visited was a breakfast dish called *beeshee*, which is a pancake topped with lots of sugar.' Her grand-parents eventually retired to Indian Wells, near Palm Springs, where they originally had a holiday home. When Helen died, she and Art had been married for 70 years.

The biggest influence in Kim's life was her beloved father, Robert Kardashian, who was born in Baldwin Hills in 1944. She observed, 'My father always taught us never to forget where we came from. We grew up learning so much about our Armenian ancestors that we will teach to our own kids one day.' She is clearly giving North a head start in that regard.

2

TOWER OF STRENGTH

———————

Robert Kardashian is a name that sounds as if it belongs to a very serious person. In reality, Bob, or Bobby as he was known, was funny and fun-seeking, a young man with a reputation as a practical joker, who never wanted to be tied to the family meat-packing business. It didn't suit his style at all. He would leave that responsibility to his elder brother, Thomas, known as Tommy, who was four years his senior. An elder sister, Barbara, pursued a successful career as a dentist.

He followed them both to USC – the University of Southern California – in Los Angeles where he studied business administration from 1962 until 1966 and, like his brother, was the senior manager of the student American football team, the formidable USC Trojans. Both brothers were keen on sport, particularly football, and could play to a high, if not professional, standard.

Robert decided to continue his education at the University of San Diego, where he graduated in 1969 with a law degree. Tommy observed that his younger brother went to law school to avoid going into the family business. The elder Kardashian already had a Rolls-Royce and Robert was determined that he would have one too. On his return to Los Angeles, aged 25, he joined the firm of two USC law graduates, Richard Eamer and John Bedrosian. After two years, he became a named partner in Eamer, Bedrosian and Kardashian of Beverly Hills.

Bedrosian, a fellow 'hye' (the Armenian word for an Armenian), developed the firm's interest in healthcare, while Robert found entertainment law more to his taste. One of his friends, George Mason, who founded the Armenian newspaper *The California Courier*, observed, 'He's not the kind of man who wants to be chained to a desk and take a briefcase full of work home with him every night.'

If Robert had stuck with his partners, he would have ended up considerably wealthier. They established National Medical Enterprises, which became one of the top healthcare providers in the US before it was sold in the 1990s. As a result, they moved into the realms of the super-rich.

Robert, though, enjoyed the world of celebrity more than the boardroom. He met the man who would change the future for him and his family on a tennis court in Beverly Hills one Sunday morning in the spring of 1970. A game of doubles was set up by the maître d' at the Luau, which was a popular local place for young playboys on the prowl.

Robert and his brother Tommy were a formidable pairing, but they were concerned they had met their match in O. J. Simpson and Al Cowlings. These two had both won sporting scholarships to USC, but did not enrol there until after the Kardashians had left. Orenthal James Simpson, known as 'The Juice', was the most famous college footballer in the US and the winner of the prestigious Heisman Trophy as the most outstanding player of the year. In UK terms, it would be the equivalent of discovering that your weekend tennis game was against David Beckham.

O. J. was already a celebrity. Robert and Tommy were well known in the fashionable bars and restaurants of Hollywood, but they mixed more with professional people. O. J. would change that.

To their surprise, experience narrowly won the day for the Kardashian brothers. The four all became friends and the one-off game became a weekly ritual. Robert and O. J. got on particularly well, despite their very different backgrounds. O. J. had been brought up in a poor area of San Francisco, belonged to a street gang and served time in a youth detention centre. When he moved from college into the professional game, he became one of the most sought-after names in the celebrity world and, by 1971, was said to have earned enough money from endorsements to retire.

Robert recognised the selling potential of his new friend. O. J. would be perfect as the public face of some business ventures. Robert had the ideas and O. J. had the fame, and together they started several stores and restaurants.

They both still had a strong affinity with USC and one of their more successful enterprises was a fashion boutique on the campus called jag O. J. – a play on the popular student cocktail of orange juice and Jägermeister. It sold top-of-the-range jeans and casual wear and they made a tidy profit when they sold the shop after a couple of years.

One of Robert's policies where his start-ups were concerned was not to hang on to a business for too long, whether it was successful or not. He formed a corporation with O. J. called

Juice Inc. and opened a frozen yoghurt shop in Westwood Village, which they called Joy and, once again, sold after a couple of years.

The association with O. J. opened up a new world for Robert Kardashian and his brother. They moved into a house in Deep Canyon Drive, Beverly Hills, which they turned into a bachelor's playground. O. J. was always around, helping to attract a constant stream of guests for tennis and pool parties. In the mid-seventies, he even stayed with the brothers for six months during an off-season as the star running back of the Buffalo Bills. There were three Rolls-Royces parked in the driveway then. Robert had finally acquired one – and he was still in his twenties. O. J. also rented space in Robert's offices to oversee his growing business concerns away from football. Robert's legal secretary, Cathy Ronda, became O. J.'s personal assistant. The connection between the two men was a very strong one.

Robert wanted to pursue interests in music, one of his great loves. His fortunes were transformed in 1973, when he set up a magazine, *Radio & Records*, with his brother Tommy and a new partner, Robert Wilson, who had many music contacts. They had spotted a gap in the market for a weekly trade publication for radio and the music industry in general. At least a third of the pages were charts and statistics. Record company executives could see what radio stations in Alabama or Iowa were playing that week. The idea was to turn it into something that was an essential read for anyone working in the world of music and, to that end, it succeeded brilliantly. It became widely known as *R&R*, a sister to the famous *Billboard*, and an industry bible.

Eventually, the success of this and some of the ventures with O. J. allowed Robert to reduce his law commitments until, in 1979, he was able to stop practising altogether. By that time, he had fallen in love.

When Robert George Kardashian met Kristen Mary Houghton, he was a lawyer, an entrepreneur and a very eligible bachelor living in Los Angeles. She was an 18-year-old girl from San Diego growing accustomed to the finer things in life, thanks to a relationship with a professional golfer 12 years her senior.

They bumped into each other at the renowned Del Mar Thoroughbred racetrack, which boasted the famous slogan 'Where the Turf Meets the Surf'. In the summer months, Hollywood stars would mingle with the cream of moneyed society in a beautiful setting by the ocean. A consortium of famous actors from the golden age, including Gary Cooper and Oliver Hardy of Laurel and Hardy, had clubbed together to build the course. They were led by Bing Crosby, who was on the gate greeting racegoers when it opened in 1937.

The meeting in July was a little like Royal Ascot, in that the wealthy and well-connected would travel from San Diego, 20 miles south, or Los Angeles, 100 miles to the north, to be seen and to show off their new hats. It was definitely a place to interest an aspiring socialite.

According to Kris, Robert barrelled up to her outside the exclusive Turf Club and said that she was someone he knew, even though he kept getting her name wrong, insisting she was called Janet. She thought he bore a striking resemblance to the pop singer Tony Orlando, who memorably sang 'Tie a

Yellow Ribbon Round the Ole Oak Tree'. With his big, heavy moustache and slick black disco hair, he might also have been mistaken for a seventies porn star. She was a shapely brunette with great sex appeal. She had oomph.

He persisted with his corny chat-up lines and asked for her phone number, which she refused to give him. He trailed after her for the rest of the day and even introduced her to his elder brother Tommy, who was with him that afternoon. Naturally, her reluctance to give him her number lit the blue touch paper of his enthusiasm. At the time, she thought he was too old, although, at 30, he was four months younger than her boyfriend.

In her autobiography, she refers to the golfer only as Anthony. That wasn't his name, of course. Much later, he was revealed to be a forgotten, if handsome, face on the PGA tour called Cesar Sanudo, who was from a modest Mexican family. He had been a caddie before graduating to playing golf himself. He was on the tour for 14 years at a time when great names like Jack Nicklaus, Arnold Palmer and Tom Watson ruled the fairways. The irrepressible 'Super Mex', Lee Trevino, was one of his best friends on tour.

Although Cesar won only one tournament, the 1970 Azalea Open Invitational at the Cape Fear Country Club in North Carolina, he was a popular figure, always at ease with ordinary golfers and film stars like Bob Hope and Clint Eastwood. He also played golf with presidents, including Richard Nixon, Gerald Ford and George Bush, Sr.

After they started dating, when she was just 17, he gave Kris the perfect introduction to the world of celebrity, and took her to golf tournaments all over the world. His brother Carlos maintained that it was Cesar who provided Kris with the connections she was able to use throughout her life.

Cesar installed his teenage girlfriend in his townhouse near the ocean in Mission Beach, an area of San Diego rather similar to Malibu or Santa Monica. Kris moved in, with her best friend from high school, Debbie Mungle, for company, as Cesar spent so much time on the road at golf tournaments. It wasn't Beverly Hills, but it was a step in the right direction.

Kris may not have enjoyed the privileged upbringing that plenty of money gave Robert Kardashian, but she was comfortably middle class. Her father, Robert Houghton, had a good job as an engineer with the now defunct aircraft company Convair in San Diego. Her grandparents ran a candle store called Candelabra in fashionable La Jolla and her mother, Mary Jo, was their part-time assistant. When she was old enough to be a help and not a hindrance, Kris worked in the back room too.

Kris paid tribute to her grandmother in her autobiography *Kris Jenner … and All Things Kardashian*. She 'taught me the value of hard work', she explained. That ethic is very much in keeping with the philosophy of Robert Kardashian and one that they passed on to their children, especially Kim.

Her childhood, however, was very different from Robert Kardashian's. His parents were married for 70 years, but Kris's parents split up when she was seven. It was a traumatic time for Kris and her four-year-old sister Karen. Mary Jo had to sell the family home and go out to work full time. Eventually, Kris's mother met a reformed alcoholic called Harry Shannon, who gave up booze for life when they married. Kris loved Harry's entrepreneurial spirit and thought he was a 'great guy'.

Mary Jo believed in bringing up her daughters to follow strict household rules, but that didn't stop her from agreeing to let her eldest go to Hawaii with Debbie to watch a golf tournament, which is where she met Cesar. Robert Kardashian didn't know at first that, while he was pursuing her, Kris had accepted her boyfriend's proposal of marriage.

Robert wasn't the least put off by her initial refusal to give him her phone number. He promptly found it via a friend who worked for the telephone company and boldly rang her up. She explained to *E!* that despite her initial hesitation and annoyance at his perseverance, they eventually realised there was a spark between them.

The path of true love didn't run smoothly. On their very first date to the movies, they went back to the house she shared with Cesar, who was away playing in a golf tournament – or so she thought. Just as they were getting down to things in the bedroom, the door burst open and in charged Cesar. He made sure that Robert didn't hang around to chat. Kris maintains they were still in their clothes. Cesar's brother verified that they were discovered in the bedroom. He alleges that his brother was suspicious of Kris and had deliberately missed the cut in the tournament so that he would be home early. If that were the case, then his suspicions were confirmed, and it marked the beginning of the end of their relationship.

As well as the problems in her love life, Kris had to deal with a family tragedy that year, 1975. Her father, with whom she had been enjoying a much better relationship in recent years, was killed in a road accident in Mexico at the age of 42. The evening before he planned to marry for the second time, he was driving his Porsche when he hit a truck head on. Kim never knew her maternal grandfather.

Two decades later, *Star* magazine in the US ran a story that Bob Houghton had been an alcoholic and had been drinking margaritas on the night of the crash. A girlfriend after his divorce, Leslie Johnson Leech, claimed, 'I broke up with him because of his drinking.'

Kris and Cesar didn't split immediately and technically remained engaged for a few more months. The end occurred with a counter allegation of cheating, which gave Kris the opportunity to leave her golfer once and for all. Cesar became a club professional in El Cajon, a suburb of San Diego, when he quit the main tour, but resumed tournament golf on the seniors' circuit when he was over 50. He never spoke about Kris while he was alive, although his brother revealed some salacious details after his death in 2011. She has never responded, preferring her first serious lover to remain enigmatically as Anthony.

She didn't waste any time and rushed into the arms of Robert, who was living the high life in his swanky new home in Deep Canyon Drive. She was trading up. He was clearly besotted with Kris and proposed within three weeks of her finally ditching Cesar. After she turned down his first proposal, Kris decided she needed her independence and wanted to see more of the world, so she trained as a flight attendant with American Airlines.

Robert responded to her rejection by dating Priscilla Presley, the ex-wife of 'The King', who was still alive and the biggest star in the world. He didn't just phone her up and ask her out. Her best friend, Joan Esposito, was dating and would eventually marry his brother Tommy, so it wasn't too surprising when Robert and Priscilla got together.

Joan was a former Miss Missouri who had been married to Joe Esposito, the larger-than-life road manager for Elvis. She forged a bond with Priscilla when they were both part of the mad Elvis world in the mid-sixties. Joanie, as she was known in those days, was a Vegas showgirl called Joan Roberts when she married Joe. As a couple, they went everywhere with Elvis and Priscilla. Joe was best man when the Presleys married at the Aladdin Hotel in Las Vegas and Joanie was matron of honour. Both women settled in Los Angeles in the early seventies after their marriages ended.

The Kardashians were very popular. Susan Stafford, the original host of the game show *Wheel of Fortune*, described her friends Tommy and Joan as 'decent and terrific people'. More interestingly, Susan had no idea that Robert Kardashian, fun and sociable, would eventually become famous in his own right. She observed, 'The longer you are in Hollywood, you find yourself rubbing shoulders with people who become headline news.' That would be particularly true of Kim Kardashian and her extraordinary family. Hollywood is indeed a very small world.

Fortunately for the history of the Kardashian clan, Robert's dalliance with Priscilla was short-lived, although he did move into her house on Summit Drive for a short time. When it ended, Robert resumed his pursuit of the woman with whom he was clearly very much in love.

After completing her training, Kris was based in New York, but flew the route to Los Angeles every week. Robert, always dapper and expensively dressed, would meet her at LAX in his

Rolls-Royce and whisk her back to the house, where they would play tennis or relax by the pool. He kept two Rollers in the garage now: one black and one white (and a convertible Mercedes for sunny days).

Robert could easily have continued living the life of the Hollywood playboy, but he was determined to marry Kris. He introduced her proudly to his close-knit family and friends, like O. J. Simpson and Al Cowlings.

Kris tells an amusing story of how she and Robert joined O. J. and the Bond actress Maud Adams on a trip to the Montreal Olympics in 1976. By now O. J. was even more famous, thanks to a blossoming movie career, with roles in *The Klansman* and the blockbuster *The Towering Inferno*. Everybody recognised him wherever he went, but nobody, including Kris, had a clue who Bruce Jenner was … until he won the decathlon gold medal.

Eventually Robert and Kris married at the Westwood United Methodist Church on Wilshire Boulevard in July 1978, five years after their encounter at the racetrack. It was a big, opulent wedding with a reception for 300 at the Bel-Air Country Club. Tommy was best man, O. J. was the principal usher and the massive Al Cowlings, known as A. C., was ring-bearer. Her younger sister Karen was the maid of honour.

Kris returned from an idyllic honeymoon in Europe, free from her job as an air hostess, happy and pregnant. She would later observe, 'The Armenian women watched and counted the weeks until I gave birth to make sure I wasn't pregnant before I got married.'

To the relief of the matrons, she wasn't, and gave birth to her first child, Kourtney Mary, on 18 April 1979. She was

23. At 24, she had her second. She had conceived again on a skiing trip to the fashionable resort of Aspen, Colorado, with O. J. and his new beautiful blonde girlfriend, Nicole Brown.

Kimberly Noel Kardashian was born in Los Angeles on 21 October 1980.

It was time for the growing family of four to move to a house of their own. With perfect timing, in 1979, Robert pulled off his biggest business deal to date, when *Radio & Records* was sold for an estimated $12.5 million. He was thought to have made about $3 million on the deal – a sum worth $10.5 million in today's money. Unsurprisingly, he stopped working as an attorney and relinquished his licence to practise law.

As a result of his windfall, he was able to buy a dream home four miles away. Tower Lane is a cul de sac that is so private it contains only three massive, luxurious mansions. 9920 Tower Lane would be the house where Kim and her siblings would enjoy an idyllic childhood. All three properties were behind massive iron gates to avoid the prying eyes of star-hungry sightseers.

Nobody knew who the Kardashians were at this point, of course, although they soon became renowned for throwing the best parties in the neighbourhood. The mansion had a large swimming pool, a tennis court, a Jacuzzi and a bar by the pool. To buy it in 2015 would cost something like $6 million. There was nothing a thousand other homes in the gilded nirvana of Beverly Hills didn't enjoy. A housekeeper took care of the shopping and the washing, allowing Kim's mother the time to go out to lunch with her friends. Uncle O. J. would stop by every week to play tennis, and there would always be a big barbecue for friends and family at weekends.

As there were so few houses in their little enclave, they decided to call theirs Tower Lane, the same name as the street, so Kim was brought up in Tower Lane, Tower Lane, which must have confused the postman. Anybody who found themselves wandering up Tower Lane would have been looking for a glimpse of either Madonna or Bruce Springsteen, who occupied the other houses during the 1980s. Bruce made it his permanent home, while Madonna was just renting for a short time. This is Los Angeles, however, so you would never walk, even to chat to a neighbour like the famous talk show host Jay Leno, who lived in the next road. The drive at the Kardashian house was almost too long to walk in any case.

It was a paradise for the little girls, and their early lives were recorded on video by a doting father keen not to miss a second of his children growing up. He called his second daughter Kimbo, or by the pet name of Joge, although she never knew why. In Armenian, the word means 'imagine'. Kim was a very sweet and pretty child, as the countless home movies show. She and her elder sister Kourtney were so close together in age that they tended to wear the same outfits and often resembled twins. Even though there was plenty of space, the two sisters shared a bedroom, which meant that they forged a special bond and became a clique of two.

There were cats and dogs, rabbits and birds, and lots of dressing up. The two cats were called Coco and Chanel, an amusing tribute to the queen of French fashion, Coco Chanel. Among the pack of dogs was Valentina, a little Bichon Frisé who, the sisters recalled in *Kardashian Konfidential*, died after eating some poison. Kourtney and Kim cried their eyes out.

Having two babies by the age of 24 didn't stop Kris from having two more by the time she was 30. Khloé Alexandra was born on 27 June 1984, and a longed-for son arrived on 17 March 1987. In the best Armenian tradition, he was called Robert Arthur, after his father and grandfather respectively. Just as Kourtney and Kim were particularly close growing up, Khloé and Robert Jr likewise played together – although the youngest daughter was regarded as a personal plaything by her two elder sisters.

If the children tired of their wonderland at home, there were always the annual vacations to look forward to: a spring break at Robert's parents' holiday home in Indian Wells, skiing in Colorado every autumn to celebrate Thanksgiving and, in between, a trip to Mexico or, if they were very lucky, to Hawaii.

One of the most important aspects of Robert Kardashian was the strength of his religious beliefs, a product of his Armenian Christian roots. He would meticulously say his prayers every morning by his bedside. He would also say grace before meals in their sumptuous dining room and often carried a Bible with him. Traditional bedtime stories for kids would be mixed with the occasional tale from his Bible. He was very keen for his family to follow his beliefs. The importance of worship, a strong spiritual bond and the belief that marriage was sacred would come to be supremely ironic in a family culture in which adultery and broken marriages became the rule rather than the exception.

The leading light in the religious community that Robert and Kris were drawn to was the famous fifties singer Pat

Boone, who would host weekly Bible studies for like-minded neighbours, including Doris Day, Priscilla Presley and the Kardashians, at his luxurious mansion. Boone was well known for baptising some 250 people in his swimming pool.

They didn't go in for any of that in the Kardashian pool, although friends were always welcome to drop in for a swimming lesson. That circle of friends widened naturally when Kourtney and Kim went to school, first to the Beverly Hills Presbyterian Preschool in Rodeo Drive, and then to the ultra exclusive Buckley School in Sherman Oaks, where today it would cost between $33,000 and $39,000 a year to send your child.

Kim would forge some long-standing friendships with schoolmates, who included Paris Hilton, Nicole Richie, fashion designer Nikki Lund, Kimberly Stewart, the daughter of Rod Stewart and Alana Hamilton, and T. J. Jackson, the nephew of Michael Jackson. Her best friend, however, is Allison Azoff, who has never sought fame outside her privileged world.

Allison is the daughter of Irving Azoff, one of the biggest names in American music. In 2012, he was named the most powerful person in the music business by *Billboard* magazine. While best known as the boss of Live Nation, Azoff has also managed the affairs of a string of famous artists, including The Eagles, Christina Aguilera, Maroon 5 and, most aptly, as far as Kim is concerned, Kanye West. Irving and Kanye were brought together by Kris, who has been best friends with Irving's wife Shelli for more than 30 years.

The Azoffs and the Kardashians lived near each other in Beverly Hills, so it seemed natural that their children would grow up together, spending time at each other's houses. Kim used to enjoy exploring Shelli's wardrobe and jewellery box, in particular, and trying on her diamond rings for size.

Kim has always been respectful of Allison's desire to keep a low profile and the pair are seldom pictured together, even though they still speak all the time. Kim often says that she and Allison 'met the day I was born' and leaves it at that. Other friendships with equally famous people may receive far more publicity, but Allison is her oldest and dearest.

This rarefied upbringing relied on Robert continuing to make plenty of money without having to go back to the meat-packing business. Not all of his investments went as well as *Radio & Records*. Irving Azoff observed, 'Some have and some haven't been successful. But he's real dependable and honest and quite an entrepreneur.'

The Kardashian family were firmly entrenched in Beverly Hills society. They were established in the pool and party circuit, with four lovely children and all the trappings that success could bring. This happiness didn't last. In 1990, the Kardashians' world fell apart.

3

A COMPLICATED AFFAIR

The Kardashian family always ate dinner together, even when the children were young. After prayers, Robert would go round the table for 'The Peak and the Pit'. Everyone in turn had to declare the highlight and lowlight of their day. When Kim revealed on television that they used to do this, it was copied in homes around the country.

On one particular day in 1990, there were no peaks. That was when Robert and Kris sat them down and explained quietly that they were getting a divorce. Robert Jr was only two, so he wasn't involved, but the three girls were in floods of tears. Their parents tried hard not to reveal the true extent of their own anguish.

They wanted to cause as little disruption as possible to their children's lives, having vowed that their welfare would remain the most important consideration and they would try to act as normally as possibly. That was easier said than done: divorce papers would later make clear just how upset Kim had been by the course of events.

Robert was completely devastated. Kris had been having a tempestuous two-year affair with a younger man called Todd Waterman, a very fit and handsome footballer with a soccer team called LA Heat. She was 33 and he was 10 years her junior.

He had spotted her first in a photo at a friend's house in Beverly Hills and liked what he saw. She evidently felt the same way when they got together during a night out with friends. Their versions of events are different. She says they kissed for the first time in the hall closet of her friend's house. He says they had sex for the first time in said closet, adding, gallantly, that it was 'magical'.

They both agree that they subsequently had a lot of sex. In her memoir, Kris, who once again gives her former lover a false name – this time Ryan – recalls less coyly that they had 'wild' sex in almost every imaginable location: tennis court, pool house, garage, back seat of the car and up and down the stairs. 'Sex everywhere, all the time,' she added.

Todd confirms that the sex was adventurous, both outdoors and indoors. 'We were pretty prolific,' he remembered with understatement. His memory failed him when he was asked if they had made love in the marital bed at Tower Lane. He did say he was sure they'd had sex in the house, but he didn't recall anything specific.

They were clearly very much in love and, as sometimes happens in those circumstances, they became foolhardy and indiscreet. Todd was like a trophy boyfriend, always on Kris's arm at celebrity parties and barbecues. She was behaving like a woman obsessed. She was seeing so much of Todd, even taking a skiing holiday with him, that his mother Ilza thought Kris and

Robert were already separated: 'She wouldn't talk about her husband with me. If she did, I would have said, "What are you doing coming after my young son, with all these kids?"'

Not surprisingly, Robert became suspicious. He kept seeing Todd in the company of his wife, especially at the house, where they would play tennis together. Todd amusingly recalled that on one occasion Robert decided to umpire their game and kept calling foot faults against him.

More seriously, Robert hired a private detective to follow his wife to the modest apartment in Studio City, which she and Todd were using as a love nest. The inevitable clash with Robert is another incident that the two lovers remember differently. She recalled that it was in a restaurant in Beverly Hills, where they were having a cosy breakfast together. Todd said they were pulling out of his garage in an open-topped Jeep, when Robert dashed up in a convertible Mercedes, jumped out and started swinging a golf club at the back of the car. Todd was all in favour of stopping and confronting Robert, but Kris was worried that her distraught husband might have a gun, so the two vehicles set off on a high-speed car chase through Beverly Hills, which ended when Todd swerved into another road.

Todd, who only came forward in 2012 after he featured as Ryan in Kris's book, was concerned for his personal safety, especially after a phone call he claims he received from O. J. Simpson warning him to stay away from Kris. O. J. apparently invited Todd over to his house to discuss things further – an invitation he had no trouble turning down.

One of the cruel ironies of the affair was that Kris paid for almost everything. But she, by her own admission, had no money. She was using credit cards that were paid for by her husband. The first thing Robert did on discovering the affair and deciding on a divorce was to cancel all of Kris's credit cards. The financial implications would eventually lead to bitter and acrimonious divorce proceedings.

The whole sorry saga was shaping up like a bad episode of *Dynasty* (or a good one, depending on whether you were living it or just watching). To her credit, Kris hasn't tried to justify her behaviour other than to acknowledge how unbearably miserable she had become in her marriage. The shattering effect her affair had on her family, particularly the two eldest girls, became clear when divorce papers were revealed in *Star* magazine in the US and published in America and the UK.

The most heartbreaking incident occurred in May 1990, when Kimberly, as they called her then, found her mother crying after a 'brutal' conversation with Robert. He was so emotionally distraught by what was happening that he would call Kris some horrible names whenever they tried to speak to one another. In her statement, Kris said, 'She became so upset I had a difficult time getting her to her [school] carpool on time.' She added that Kim called twice that afternoon begging her to come home. Clearly the young girl was worried that her mother was going to leave them.

Khloé, being that much younger than her sisters, seemed fine with Todd and would happily sit in the back seat of the car if he was going out to lunch with her mother. He thought she was smart and 'just the cutest kid'.

Robert moved out of Tower Lane, leaving Kris to manage on her own. In the divorce papers, her sworn statement details what she termed was a 'luxury lifestyle'. The mortgage payment on the house alone was $15,000 a month and then there were wages for the gardener, a maid and a housekeeper, as well as $800 a month to pay for the children's clothing and $2,000 a month for herself. Credit card debts on various store cards had grown to more than $21,000.

The unhappiness that both Robert and Kris were feeling didn't end with her sailing off into the sunset with Todd – far from it. At first, they carried on in much the same way. If Robert was looking after the children at the weekend, she would drift over to the apartment in Studio City to see Todd. Reading between the lines of her account, the enormity of what she had done – giving up what was so important to her life, the privilege and luxury of what Robert provided in Beverly Hills, for sex in a tiny bachelor flat – began to affect her.

She finally realised she had made a 'ginormous' mistake when she arrived at Todd's apartment unexpectedly and discovered him in bed with a girl he had met in a bar. It was, apparently, a one-night stand. 'I think I got busted,' recalled Todd 20 years later, although he didn't remember the exact circumstances.

Though they split up soon after, there is little doubt that they genuinely cared for one another. Todd told the *Daily Mail* that he was heartbroken when their relationship ended, but he knew that it would never have worked in the long term. He observed, 'Sometimes you stop something not because you stop caring, but because it isn't practical.' At that point in his career, he couldn't give Kris anything like the life she was used to and that was before you factored in the age difference. They both ended up with nothing to show for the pain and the passion.

It wouldn't be the last time Kris enjoyed the obvious benefits of a younger male companion, but she vowed that never again would she be so vulnerable financially. It was a lesson she vigorously taught her children – Kim in particular.

Both Todd and Kris have since regretted the heartache their relationship caused Robert and the children. Todd could see how badly Kourtney, the eldest, was affected. She struggled to accept what had happened and certainly didn't want anyone to replace her dad. It may or may not have affected her attitude to marriage but, at 36, she has yet to say, 'I do'. Kim, on the other hand, appeared to deal with it more easily, but had married three times by the age of 33.

She has said that at the time she was more troubled by the size of her growing breasts, and would sit in the bathtub praying to God that they wouldn't get any bigger. For a girl in the fourth grade, who had only just turned 10, one can understand her embarrassment, especially at school, where there was always some wise guy kid happy to twang the strap of her training bra. It didn't help that her big sister would tease her mercilessly. The bath prayer didn't work. She was a C cup at the age of 13.

More serious were the health concerns of their beloved grandmothers. Both Robert and Kris's mothers faced grave problems that weren't helped by the cataclysmic events in their children's lives. Helen Kardashian had a stress-related stroke and Mary Jo Shannon was battling cancer. Fortunately, they both pulled through and the grandkids had many more happy times with them.

Just when it seemed that things couldn't get any worse for Kris or her children, she went on a blind date that changed her life. The meeting with former Olympic champion Bruce Jenner was arranged by one of her close friends, Candace Garvey. She was the wife of Steve Garvey, one of the superstar baseball players with the Los Angeles Dodgers, known during his career as 'Mr Clean'. Steve and Bruce were on the celebrity sporting circuit together. They were always bumping into each other at the various tennis, golf or fishing tournaments they were forever being invited to.

Candace obviously thought, quite rightly, that Bruce needed smartening up and that the fashion-conscious Kris Kardashian would be a perfect match. Bruce wasn't so sure, until he discovered his date had four children, just like he did.

They met for the first time at the Riviera Country Club, where Bruce was playing in a golf tournament. He was immediately smitten by his vivacious companion, who was a good listener. The casual meeting led to dinner that first night, with Bruce pouring his heart out. 'I'm 40 years old,' he told her, 'and I've never been in love.'

4

THE WORLD'S
GREATEST ATHLETE

———

Rather like her mother in 1976, Kim had no idea who Bruce Jenner was. He was just suddenly there. She was still in the fourth grade at school and had to do a project on someone famous. She was asking Kris whom she thought she should do, when Bruce interrupted her and said, 'Why don't you do me?'

Kim replied, innocently, 'Well, who are you?' He had to explain to her that he was an Olympic decathlon champion.

Her project was a resounding success, especially when the man himself went along to the school. She pictured him taking part in all 10 events. Unsurprisingly, she got an A, which was unusual for Kim. Kourtney was acknowledged as the brighter of the two, while Kim was a steady B sort of student.

William Bruce Jenner came into the lives of the Kardashian family like a whirlwind. He was an action man who could ski, drive racing cars and power boats, play golf, water ski and, of course, run and jump. He was fearless.

It hadn't always been like that. He was shy and suffered from poor self-esteem growing up in small-town suburbia in New

York State. Nobody realised back then that he had dyslexia, and believed him to be either lazy or stupid – he was neither.

He was eight years old, a solitary child with few friends, when he started sneaking into the rooms of his mother and two elder sisters to try on their clothes. He was a boy, still in short pants, and he had no real awareness of what he was feeling or why he was fascinated by female clothing. He just knew it made him feel good. Instead of retreating more into his own private world of self-doubt, Bruce was able to find acceptance when it was discovered that he was a superb sportsman. He acknowledges simply, 'Sports saved my life.'

Bruce was the third of four children in a comfortable, middle-class household. He was born on 28 October 1949 in the town of Mount Kisco, a little over 40 miles north of New York City in Westchester County. He described his mother Esther as an 'all-American mom and housewife'. His father Bill was a tree surgeon who had competed in the US Army Olympics in Nuremberg in 1945 and won a silver medal in the 100-yard dash. Bruce was well built as a toddler and his proud dad called him Bruiser. Young William was generally known by his second name to avoid confusion with his father.

As a small boy, it was his dyslexia, rather than gender issues, which was the most obviously troubling. Not unusually for the 1950s, his learning disability wasn't diagnosed. As a result, his schooldays were 'torturous'. He even had his eyes tested, because it was feared his inability to read properly might stem from problems with his vision.

Bruce explained to *Ability* magazine, 'If you are dyslexic, your eyes work fine, your brain works fine, but there is a little short circuit that goes between the eye and the brain.' His undiagnosed problem ruined his self-confidence: 'My biggest fear was going to school. I thought everybody else was doing better than I was. I'd look around at my peers, and everyone else could do the simple process of reading. I was afraid the teacher was going to make me read in front of class. There was always the fear that everyone would find out I was a dummy.' Bruce had no enthusiasm for school and the teachers thought he was just a daydreamer.

When he was 11, in the fifth grade, a teacher set up a game in which everyone had to run around some chairs and back. The idea was to see who had the fastest time. It was Bruce. He was the swiftest in the whole school.

From that moment on, his life changed. Here was something he could excel at and receive a slap on the back from his fellow pupils at the quaintly named Sleepy Hollow Middle School. The village of the same name is famously the setting for Washington Irving's short story 'The Legend of Sleepy Hollow'. The author lived in nearby Tarrytown, as did the Jenner family. Nowadays, Sleepy Hollow is even better known for the television series that is set in the village and is, very loosely, a modern update of the original fantasy of the headless horseman.

When Bruce was a freshman at the Sleepy Hollow High School, aged 15, he asked the captain of the football team, known as the Headless Horsemen, for some help with punting the ball. Within an hour, Bruce was kicking it as far as his coach was. The young Bruce was extraordinarily gifted as a sportsman.

His family moved to Connecticut when Bruce was 16. They built a house on Lake Zoar, where they all could enjoy their passion for water skiing. Bruce was so good that he won the Eastern Regional Water Ski Championships and competed in the Nationals in 1966. At the local Newtown High School in Sandy Hook, he excelled in basketball, track and field and American football, and became all-state pole vault and high jump champion. He was unashamedly what Americans call a jock – a muscular athlete, usually good looking, whose life revolves around sports and girls and who is always one of the most popular guys in school.

Aged 18, Bruce was named the MVP (Most Valuable Player) in the track squad and the basketball team. He played both running back and quarterback in the school football team. His coach, Peter Kohut, recognised that he was an outstanding athlete: 'He was a good kid, came to practice every day, seemed like he was always in good condition.'

At this stage of his life, Bruce was a very clean-cut young man – the sort of suitor who was bound to impress your mother. Nobody knew that behind the masculine exterior beat the heart and mind of a man who was more female than male.

Bruce was never going to be a great scholar, but he did win a football scholarship to a small college called Graceland in Lamoni, Iowa. Any hopes of becoming a professional foot-baller were soon dashed by a knee injury in his first year. That turned out to be a blessing in disguise, because the athletics director, L. D. Weldon, recognised his potential and persuaded him to put all his energies into the decathlon. Bruce needed an operation to repair his damaged knee in early 1969, but when he was fully recovered, he abandoned football and became a full-time athlete, reluctantly also giving up water skiing.

Weldon was one of the most respected coaches in the country, whose CV, crucially, included training Jack Parker, who won the bronze medal in the decathlon at the Berlin Olympics in 1936. He was an acknowledged expert in the multi-event discipline and encouraged Bruce to train hard.

Success was almost immediate. Jenner broke the Graceland decathlon record at his very first try at the 10 events. At his first open meeting, he placed sixth in the prestigious Drake Relays in Des Moines, the state capital. The following year, he returned to win the competition. In 1972, he came from nowhere to place third in the Olympic Trials, earning himself selection for the US team that travelled to Munich for the summer games. He could finish only tenth, but the promise was there. He had four years to fulfil his destiny.

Bruce was still at college in 1972 when he married his girlfriend, Chrystie Crownover, a minister's daughter from Washington State. She had no idea, when they became man and wife, of the internal struggles her new husband had faced all his life. During their first year of marriage, she became the first person he confided in. She recalled, 'He told me he always wanted to be a woman. Understandably, I was speechless. It was hard to wrap your head around it because he was such a manly man.'

His confession didn't harm their marriage. In some ways, his revelation brought them closer together, as sharing a secret sometimes can. In her eyes, he remained a real guy, who was, quite simply, her hero.

After graduation, the couple moved to California, where the training facilities and the climate were better suited to an athlete with his eye on Olympic gold. Chrystie worked as an air hostess for United Airlines to support them, because in those days the Olympics were strictly for amateurs. She was entitled to free plane tickets, which were a godsend for Bruce, as it gave him the means to travel to athletics meetings all over the world. Today sport is a professional career and Bruce Jenner, an all-American hero, would have been a multi-millionaire, travelling first class around the world.

Chrystie was by his side when he flew to Montreal for the 1976 Olympics. He was the current world record holder and favourite to win. He was in second place after day one, but came charging through to claim the gold. He embraced his young wife, wrapped himself in the American flag and, for a fleeting moment, was the most famous man in the world. Now he needed to make some money.

Frank Litsky of the *New York Times* famously wrote of his triumph: 'Bruce Jenner of San Jose, California, wants to be a movie or television star. After his record-breaking victory in the Olympic decathlon, he probably can be anything he wants.' He wanted to be a woman and that was one thing he couldn't be … then. Instead, he immediately retired from athletics.

Just when it seemed nothing could interrupt a happy future, tragedy struck the Jenner family. His younger brother Burt died in a car crash. Bruce was visiting his parents' home in Connecticut and during his stay was loaned a Porsche by a local car dealer. Eighteen-year-old Burt volunteered to fill her up with petrol, but ended up crashing into a telegraph pole. He died in hospital, along with his young girlfriend, who had skipped school to go for a ride in the top-of-the-range sports car.

Bruce named his first child Burt in honour of his much-loved brother. His son was born in 1978, six years after he and Chrystie were married. Sadly, the cracks had already begun to appear in their relationship. Faced with a future that did not contain eight hours of athletics practice a day, the reality of Bruce's gender dysphoria – the technical term for his gender identity crisis – was making him unhappy and discontented with his situation.

He and Chrystie separated for the first time the following year, and he met the woman who would eventually become his second wife at a celebrity tennis tournament. It was held at the Playboy Mansion in upmarket Holmby Hills, LA, where he had been staying temporarily. Bruce won the tournament and the beautiful Linda Thompson presented him with the trophy.

She provided another bizarre link with Elvis Presley in the Kardashian family saga. His relationship with her was probably the most important Elvis had after Priscilla. She was a 5ft 9in willowy blonde, who was the reigning Miss Tennessee when she met The King. He moved her into Graceland, his famous mansion near Memphis, in 1972, and she was with him for four years.

Linda had been a speech and drama major at MSU (Memphis State University) and, by all accounts, was the brightest of Elvis's women. She was popular with the notorious Memphis Mafia – the entourage who seemed to be ever present with Elvis – and she had looked after him well. Marty Lacker, the unofficial foreman of the group, explained, 'She was like a mother, a sister, a wife, a lover, and a nurse.'

Elvis had bought an apartment for her in Santa Monica so she could pursue her acting ambitions. After he died in 1977, she became a regular member of the cast of a variety show called *Hee Haw* as a singer of country music.

Bruce was immediately struck by Linda's statuesque presence. He told her he and Chrystie were separated and they hit it off right away. He was uncertain about his future, however, and briefly reconciled with his wife. After Chrystie fell pregnant, he wanted her to have an abortion, because their marriage had failed. He told *Playboy* magazine in July 1980, one month after the birth, 'My first reaction was that I didn't want it.'

Initially, Chrystie went along with his wishes, and even paid for an abortion, but changed her mind after a conversation with a friend made her realise she didn't want to go through with the termination. She said at the time, 'I thought, "What an idiot I am." I wanted the baby very, very much. But I was conditioned to make decisions that were best for him [Bruce]. It was totally my choice to have the baby.'

Bruce now says he too rejected the idea of an abortion, but when Cassandra, his eldest daughter, was born, he was in the middle of divorce proceedings and sitting in a hotel room far away in Kansas City. In his famous ground-breaking interview with *Vanity Fair* in July 2015, he told Buzz Bissinger that he wasn't present at the birth: 'Under the circumstances I could not even see myself being there.'

Instead, he resumed his relationship with Linda. They married soon afterwards, in January 1981, in a beautiful setting overlooking the Pacific Ocean in Hawaii at the beachfront house of Allan Carr, the producer of *Can't Stop the Music.*

Bruce's son Burt was best man, even though he was only two, and spent the entire ceremony tugging at his father's sleeve, saying, 'I want up.' Linda walked down the 'aisle' to the sound of Elvis singing 'Hawaiian Wedding Song'. It was very romantic.

At the time, Linda was already three months pregnant with their first child, Brandon, who was born the following June. Fortunately, she got on well with Bruce's older children, both of whom came to the hospital to visit their new brother.

Linda and Bruce became fixtures on the celebrity circuit around Los Angeles, making friends with stars like Michael Jackson, Lionel Richie and Sugar Ray Leonard, who would later feature in the Kardashian story. They appeared on the front cover of *Playgirl* magazine in May 1982: she revealed an impressive cleavage; he showed a lot of chest hair.

The cover headline on the article read 'The Fall and Rise of an American Hero'. This bolstered the Bruce Jenner image of a man fighting against the disadvantages of life, including dyslexia. His story was one of triumph over adversity and was a considerable money-spinner during his years as a media personality and motivational speaker. It was an image he later promoted in his 1996 book *Finding the Champion Within*.

At no stage did he reveal to his audience his real struggle within. He would bounce on stage, all vigour and enthusiasm, wearing a pair of silk panties underneath his three-piece suit. Bruce, it appeared, was a master of living up to an image created for the general public. It wasn't real.

The offers flooded in after the Olympics and soon Bruce was a very wealthy young man. He appeared on all the top talk shows, including *The Tonight Show starring Johnny Carson* and *The Merv Griffin Show*. He became a well-known face on sports programmes, at one time co-presenting the popular *Wide World of Sports*.

He also revealed an entrepreneurial streak that would later fit in very well with the Kardashian flair for business. Their philosophy is all about making the most of every opportunity. Bruce bought his first plane in 1978 and started Bruce Jenner Aviation, which sells aircraft supplies.

He was marketed as a personality much more than the usual famous sportsman. He became the spokesperson and face on the packet of the iconic cereal Wheaties, the 'breakfast of champions', and a million families breakfasted with Bruce on the kitchen counter every day for years.

His acting ambitions didn't reach the hoped-for heights, however. He wasn't going to be the next James Bond any time soon. He tried out for the *Superman* movie, but the role went to Christopher Reeve.

He ended up in *Can't Stop the Music*, a musical comedy based on the New York disco group Village People. Kris Jenner refers to it as *Can't Stand the Music*. The film cost $20 million to make and returned $2 million at the box office. It was the first winner of the Golden Raspberry Award (Razzie) for Worst Picture. Bruce was nominated as Worst Actor, but the judges decided Neil Diamond deserved the award for *The Jazz Singer*.

On one level, the film could be viewed as compulsive viewing. Bruce plays a sober-suited lawyer who undergoes a transformation when he becomes involved in the world of the Village People and ends up dancing down the street in a crop top and cut-off denim shorts. If it were released today, as a snapshot of the age, *Can't Stop the Music* would probably be hailed as a must-see, glorious camp classic.

Bruce's acting career stalled at the first hurdle and didn't much improve with a guest-starring role in the popular motorcycle cop series *CHiPS*. He played Officer Steve McLeish, who took over from the lead, Frank Poncherello (Erik Estrada), for six weeks. He started off as a movie star and became 'made for TV' in the space of a year.

Bruce and Linda, meanwhile, shared an idyllic life by the ocean in Malibu, strolling along the beach together at sunset, playing sports, going to all the best parties and welcoming another son, Brody, into the world on 21 August 1983. Nothing could upset their happiness – or so Linda thought.

Just after New Year 1985, Bruce sat his beautiful wife down and told her his secret. It wasn't a confession she could ignore. The first time round with Chrystie, Bruce had been fairly light and matter of fact about things; this was far more serious and heartfelt. 'I have lived in the wrong skin, the wrong body, my whole life. It is a living hell for me, and I really feel that I would like to move forward with the process of becoming a woman, the woman I have always been inside.'

The couple tried therapy, but the counsellor confirmed that there was no cure or fix for what Bruce was going through. Linda would later write movingly that the enormity of what she had been told 'broke her heart into a million pieces'.

While Linda began the painful process of ending her marriage, Bruce began gender reassignment treatment for the first time. He had always hated his 'ski jump' nose, so a touch of plastic surgery to remove the bump and make it more feminine was a good start. He also had painful electrolysis treatment to remove his masculine beard and chest hair.

He started injecting female hormones, which led to him growing breasts. They weren't Kim Kardashian-sized or anything like that, but when his young sons saw him in the shower one day, they told their mother, 'Daddy has boobs!' She tried to explain it away, saying that his well-muscled body had turned to fat now that he wasn't training. Linda told the *Huffington Post* that she didn't reveal the truth about their father until her sons were 31 and 29 respectively. She had sought to protect them – and him.

Bruce, by his own admission, went on a downward spiral in the late eighties. He and Linda were divorced rapidly in 1985 and he found it difficult to cope on his own. He was living by himself in a one-bedroom house in Malibu, with no real close friends. His work had dried up. When he met Kris Kardashian, he had $200 in the bank and debts, he estimated, of $300,000. His clothes were old and worn, his house was a tip and he seemed to spend half his life in his grubby van. She needed to sort him out. She would give him her love and the energy to re-establish himself with the American public.

For his part, he decided to put his gender reassignment treatment on the back burner and stop taking the hormones. He couldn't go further at that point, because he feared the effect his transformation might have on his young children.

5

DOPE ON A ROPE

Kim wanted to be a housewife when she grew up. She was a sweet and thoughtful little girl who dreamed of being not Madonna, but a wife and mother, and maybe a grandmother one day, just like her nanas whom she adored. 'I always thought I would have lots of kids. Be getting up going to the gym every morning – super early. Coming home, making breakfast for everyone. Packing lunches and driving the kids to school.' It must have been very bewildering for a girl who wanted to play happy families to witness what was going on within her own home.

It wasn't long before Bruce was practically living at Tower Lane. The mansion was much more comfortable than his Malibu home. Robert Kardashian wasn't especially pleased by the turn of events. He blinked and his wife was having an affair with Todd. He blinked again and Bruce Jenner was sitting on his sofa.

Todd alleged that at this point he was still involved with Kris: 'I wouldn't say we were dating ... she was still coming over to the apartment and we were still sleeping together when she had started dating Bruce.'

Todd found the situation troubling. It began 'messing with his head', as he puts it. Kris has never commented on his allegation, but described in her book how he arrived at Tower Lane one night and caused a scene. He subsequently moved to London to forget her and later became a successful animator.

Financially, things improved for Kris when Robert agreed to a monthly settlement, but the divorce trauma was ongoing. In the divorce papers, Robert commented on her new relationship:'My children are exposed to another man living with their mother. I believe that is inappropriate …'

The arguments, which were inevitably about money, and who was finally going to get Tower Lane, were apparently ended when Bruce and Robert thrashed things out over dinner. Kris gave up any claim on the house and settled in Malibu with Bruce. She observed, 'There was a period of a couple of years where it was really ugly and hard and you didn't want the kids to take sides.'

By the time the divorce was made final in March 1991, Kris and Bruce had been engaged for four months. They were married four weeks later, on 21 April 1991. Kim was 10 and a half.

Bruce had managed to persuade his own children's nanny, Pam Behan, a student from a small town in Minnesota, to leave his ex-wife Linda's house and go to live with his new family. Pam adored Bruce, her first platonic male friend. Only in Los Angeles could the attractive new nanny be enjoying a fling with Sylvester Stallone.

Linda Thompson had previously been dating the star of *Rocky* and *Rambo*, but had moved on to the multimillionaire music producer David Foster. They eventually married and formed a formidable songwriting partnership, writing, among others, 'I Have Nothing' for Whitney Houston and 'Tell Him', a hit for Barbra Streisand and Celine Dion.

Pam was responsible for making sure Kris's daughters didn't get chocolate down their pristine white dresses before the wedding ceremony. Bruce's eldest daughter Cassandra, known to everyone as Casey, was also a bridesmaid and, like the others, wore a garland of white and pink flowers in her hair. His three sons, and three-year-old Robert Jr, looked dashing in black tuxedos and pale pink bow-ties that matched the groom's. Only Kourtney, still missing her dad, looked slightly uncomfortable about the happy family day out, She did, however, manage a weak smile for the wedding pictures.

Kris and Bruce were married in the garden of the Bel Air home of Terry and Jane Semel. He was the boss of Warner Bros, and subsequently chairman of Yahoo! This was the orbit of extreme wealth and influence the Kardashians already inhabited. In the world of the Kardashians and Jenners, everyone is a 'dear friend', but the generosity of the Semels was obvious.

After the divorce, relations between Robert and Kris settled down for the sake of the children. Kourtney still had a problem with Bruce taking her father's place, but they saw plenty of Robert. He had moved back into Tower Lane and was in charge every other weekend, a time when he played the devoted dad.

Robert tried to keep everything as normal as possible. As always, he took the children to church at weekends and, if they were with him during the week, he made sure he drove them to school. He was very popular with Kim's friends and would entertain them with a variety of spoonerisms – if he was going to take a shower, he would tell them he needed to 'shake a tower' – the sort of harmless sense of humour he had always had.

Nikki Lund, whom he insisted on calling Dicky, recalled that Robert was always stricter than Kris: 'He was a fun kind of guy, but he had a responsibility as a man to daughters as beautiful as these. He would take us to church. He prayed and read the Bible. He was a really good dad. Kim was a sensitive girl and definitely spiritual.'

Robert gave Kim a Bible, which he signed, and it became her most treasured possession. The word Bible is one of her favourite expressions, said at the end of a sentence to indicate that she swears it's true. She, Nikki and her other friends were young Christian girls, although they possibly liked church more because they could wear jeans there on a Sunday.

Kim was one of those girls who could fit into any group. She had her circle of friends, like Kimberly Stewart and Nikki Lund, but she was equally as happy mixing with Kourtney's group – the nerds, as she called them. With her closest pals, she devised a special sign language that they all learned so they could 'talk' about people who were in the room or class with them. Nikki recalled, 'It was a way of being in a group. It was our little thing. We were obsessed with it.'

Kim was becoming fascinated by clothes. She and Kourtney barely had time for breakfast in the mornings, because it took them so long to get ready. They would grab a vanilla sandwich cookie on the way to Pam's car for the morning school run from Malibu to Beverly Hills. Pam, who wrote a book called *Malibu Nanny*, was thrilled to discover the house they were then living in used to be home to Sean Penn when he was courting Madonna.

Kourtney was definitely the boss, perhaps because she was older and a little brighter; certainly, she was the fastest reader in the household. The two sisters used to play fashion games together. One favourite, at least with Kourtney, was when she pretended to be the leading fashion designer Donna Karan, creator of the DKNY label, and poor Kim was her beleaguered assistant. Kourtney used it as a means to make fun of her. Kim recalled, 'She would just make me do anything she said. She would do it on purpose and embarrass me in front of her friends.' Despite the natural sibling rivalry, the two girls were very close.

At their new home, they had use of the obligatory pool and Jacuzzi, as well as a magnificent view of the ocean from the patio. Kim preferred to spend a lot of her free time in her room, however, indulging her passion for making things, particularly jewellery. She had every conceivable size, shape and colour of bead and would carefully sort and select them to make the right necklace, earrings or bracelet.

One of the jobs of the nanny was to make sure the children were tucked up comfortably in bed at night. Kim would often talk in her sleep. Sometimes she would even have a conversation with Pam, even though she was in a deep slumber. On one occasion, she shouted out, 'There's an elephant on my desk.' Pam told her to get it off the desk, whereupon Kim, still fast asleep, replied, 'Help me. Help me. Get it off.' Pam had to leave the room before her laughter woke up her young charge.

Kim may have been a quiet girl when she was 10, but she had blossomed into a much livelier teenager by the time of her eighth-grade graduation from her junior school El Rodeo in Whittier Drive, Beverly Hills, in 1994. She was filmed at the party afterwards by another student eager to make a movie of the night. There's always one home-movie maker who wants to be the next Spielberg.

The already curvy 13-year-old Kim is excited and enjoying herself, dancing madly, in a white blouse, perfect make-up and a shorter than usual bob haircut. She is talking straight to the camera, 'Is anyone getting a tape of this? I hope you do, because when you see me when I'm famous and old, you're gonna remember me as this beautiful little girl.'

She continues to lark about as the cameraman starts to walk away: 'Excuse me, are you leaving? My name's Kim Kardashian. I'm the dopest of the ropest person in this class. I'm dope on a rope.' When someone off camera interrupts, 'Define "dope", Kim', she answers, 'Dope is Kim.' She seems to be displaying a confidence she says she never had as a girl. She ends the clip by comparing herself to a classmate: 'I'm more popular than she is ... everyone loves me. I'm so popular and everyone loves me ...'

She's just a schoolgirl having fun on a big night out, but it's interesting that she should be using 'dope' as hip-hop slang for excellent or wonderful. Perhaps she picked it up from her first serious boyfriend, Michael Jackson's nephew T. J.

From a young age, Kim preferred black men. She wasn't brought up in the Deep South like Britney Spears, where racism was still rife. This was Beverly Hills, where black families had just as much money and prestige. Lionel Richie and Sugar

Ray Leonard were good friends and neighbours of the family. Lionel was the father of Nicole Richie, whom Kim was at school with. Sugar Ray was so close to the Kardashians that he was Khloé's godfather. Most of the Jackson clan lived in the area. And there was Uncle O. J., too, of course. He lived on North Rockingham Avenue, in exclusive Brentwood, with his wife Nicole, whom he had married in 1985. The sociable Nicole had become very much part of Kris's wide circle.

By 1994, the Kardashian family had undergone much change. Kourtney had started high school at an all-girl Catholic school called Marymount, on Sunset Boulevard, and Kim would be joining her at the start of the next academic year. Kris and Bruce had decided that travelling to and from Malibu was becoming too much of a logistical challenge and had rented a house in Benedict Canyon.

The most dramatic change was that Kim's father had a new woman in his life. He had sold Tower Lane and leased an enormous 15-room house 10 miles away, in the pretty suburb of Encino. He was making a fresh start with his fiancée, Denice Shakarian Halicki, a graceful blonde, who wore very short skirts and was generally described as a 'knockout'. She also happened to drive a Rolls-Royce, which had been left to her by her late husband. She was Armenian on her father's side, but didn't have the exotic features of the Kardashians. Instead, she had inherited her Norwegian mother's looks. When she was 16, there had been talk of an arranged marriage, but that had come to nothing and she was able to pursue a career as a model and actress.

In 1983, she met Toby Halicki, who had become a multi-millionaire thanks to his stunningly successful cult film *Gone in 60 Seconds*. He was a larger-than-life character, one of 13 children, who, in a great Hollywood story, came to Los Angeles, aged 15, with nothing but an extensive knowledge of automobiles and the salvage business that his family ran in New York.

His hit movie cost under $100,000 to make, but grossed more than $40 million at the box office. There was little in the way of a script, but there were lots of cars. For the film's finale, Toby performed an amazing 39-metre jump, which resulted in him compacting 10 vertebrae and walking with a permanent limp.

He married Denice in May 1989, just before starting work on the sequel *Gone in 60 Seconds 2*. She was to be one of the stars, while he would again write, direct and perform most of the stunts. He had already bought 400 cars to be sacrificed in an orgy of vehicle destruction. He was preparing for a stunt during filming near Buffalo, New York, when a telegraph pole snapped and fell on him, killing him instantly. They had been married for three months.

Denice met Robert Kardashian through mutual Armenian connections, and they helped each other at a difficult time in their personal lives. Her late husband's considerable fortune was tied up in probate for many years and she went to Robert for legal advice. She wasn't the super-rich widow many might have assumed she was – at least not then. She had a traditional Christian upbringing and the couple shared a strong religious connection.

While relations had improved a little with his ex-wife, it wasn't a case of coffee mornings and trips to the beach together. It was awkward, especially if Bruce was around.

When Robert went to their house to pick up the children, the two youngest, Khloé and Robert Jr, would be waiting outside. He would then honk the horn, which was the signal for Kourtney and Kim to run out of the house to join them.

The journey back to Encino took no more than 30 minutes. The new house was on Mandalay Drive, in a very quiet neighbourhood with manicured lawns and his and her luxury limousines in the driveway. While it didn't have the extreme privacy of a gated community, the residents kept to themselves and tended to live in the same house for many years. It was very comfortable, but you were only likely to speak to your neighbours if you met them while you were collecting your letters from the mailbox.

Robert suggested that Kourtney and Kim might like to spend more time at his house, as the peaceful surroundings might be better suited to the serious study he wanted for his daughters. Kourtney was particularly keen, as she was still reluctant to accept Bruce. Kim wanted to stay close to her sister, and both girls enjoyed Denice's company.

The new house was just a short 10-minute drive from Uncle O. J.'s mansion in Brentwood, but Robert had seen his old friend only twice in two years. O. J. put in an appearance at a surprise fiftieth birthday that Denice had thrown for Robert in February 1994, and gave him an autographed football jersey. They also bumped into each other by accident in Palisades Park in Santa Monica in May, when they were both playing with their children. Robert was throwing a baseball with his son, while O. J. was helping his daughter Sydney practice her basketball skills. The two children knew each other well and were happy to pass the time together while the two men chatted on the grass about their troubles with women.

Their mutual business interests had dwindled, mainly through lack of success. In the 1980s, O.J. had joined Robert in a venture called Concert Cinema, which screened music videos in cinemas before the main feature. It was early days for MTV, but demonstrated how Robert thought ahead. In this case, what was clearly a good idea proved too expensive to run, and after a year they closed the business without making a profit.

The blossoming friendship between Kris and Nicole had made it difficult for the two men to remain buddies. O.J. and Nicole had struggled with marital problems, which culminated in their divorce in 1992, after seven years of marriage and two children together. Nobody knew that their strife included domestic violence.

Since his divorce from Kris, Robert's social circle had inevitably changed. O.J. was more likely to bump into Bruce Jenner on the celebrity circuit, although, as a football hero and movie star, O.J. was still far more famous than the former Olympic champion. Surprisingly, Robert didn't even know that Nicole was living in a condo in Bundy Drive, Brentwood.

The morning of 13 June 1994 started like any other for Robert Kardashian. As he always did, he said his prayers and then worked out for 30 minutes before starting work in his large office in the house. He no longer kept any business premises. Just after 10 a.m., the phone rang. It was Shelli Azoff, buzzing with the story that Nicole had been killed. She had just found out about it at the hairdresser's, so the whole world, except Robert, had heard the bombshell news. He phoned

Kris and discovered it was true. His ex-wife had been due to lunch with her friend that very day.

Without being asked, Robert rallied round his friend of 23 years. He invited O.J. to stay in his home to escape the media storm that inevitably exploded around the murder. It transpired that Nicole had suffered horrendous stabbing injuries, including one violent open wound that exposed the larynx and spinal chord. A local waiter and aspiring actor called Ron Goldman was also found dead outside the home on Bundy.

Four days after the murders, Robert had to stop his friend from killing himself, when he found O.J. in the bedroom with a gun. He told him, 'You can't. This is my daughter's bedroom.' Both Kourtney and Kim were staying in the house, but neither registered the magnitude of what was going on.

A warrant was issued for O.J.'s arrest and his chief lawyer, Robert Shapiro, was told his client needed to turn himself in at a police station. Shapiro had co-opted Robert on to the team, realising that Bobby, as O.J. still called him, had a special relationship with Simpson and would be useful to him. It also meant that they would now be protected by attorney–client privilege. Robert would need to reactivate his law licence, which he had allowed to lapse.

He was still concerned that his friend was going to end his life after O. J. disappeared from his house when he was supposed to be leaving for the station. He had apparently made a run for it in a white Ford Bronco driven by his buddy Al Cowlings. It became the most famous and bizarre slow-speed car chase in history, as a flotilla of police vehicles, with more than 20 helicopters soaring overheard, followed them down Interstate 405 at 35 miles an hour. The police didn't want to intercept the 4 X 4 because O. J., who was lying low on the back seat, reportedly had a gun and they wanted to avoid a violent end. Thousands lined the route and stood on overpasses to cheer him. Eventually, after 90 minutes, he gave himself up outside his Rockingham home. Millions watched on television, mesmerized by what they were seeing. It was described by one lawyer as 'the day Los Angeles stopped'.

Meanwhile, Robert was in front of the TV cameras for the very first time, reading a handwritten document that O. J. had left at the house. It was his suicide note to the world. Robert, in his steady deep voice, read the letter in front of more than 100 members of the media: '… Don't feel sorry for me. I've had a great life, made great friends. Please think of the real O. J. and not this lost person. Thank you for making my life special …'

This was the exact moment when life changed for the Kardashians. Now the media were shouting out and asking Robert how he spelled his surname. They mostly got it wrong. Kim and her siblings became the children of the famous lawyer Robert Kardashian. He would sit beside O. J. Simpson throughout the 'trial of the century'. O. J.'s confidante and erstwhile manager, Norman Pardo, observed drily, 'The Kardashians would be nothing without O. J. Simpson.'

6

NEVERLAND

Incredibly, 10 weeks after the grisly killing of Nicole Brown Simpson, Kim's life was rocked by another violent murder, which affected her just as deeply at the time.

All the Kardashian children grew up with the music of Michael Jackson blaring out from the sound system at the parties and barbecues their parents had. Robert Kardashian liked doo-wop, but this failed to impress his offspring. Kim enjoyed the music of all the Jacksons, but Janet Jackson was definitely her favourite in her youth. It was the next generation of the famous family with whom she came into contact, however, simply by moving in the same circles in Beverly Hills.

Kim was 13 when she started dating T. J. Jackson, the youngest son of Tito Jackson. The initials stand for Tito Joe, after his father and grandfather. They had met first of all at the Buckley School, but kept bumping into each other at parties. He was two years older than Kim, but she was a precocious young teenager.

T. J.'s father was the third oldest of the 10 Jackson children. When he was 18, he married Delores 'Dee Dee' Martes. She had been born in New York City to Dominican parents, but as a girl moved to LA, where she met Tito at Fairfax High School in West Hollywood. They married at the height of the Jackson 5 success in 1972 and had three sons, Taj, Taryll and T. J.

Despite the family's enormous wealth and fame, Dee Dee was determined that her three sons would have a normal childhood. Tito observed, 'She saw what the Jacksons had to endure to be successful.' All three boys attended the Buckley School, where they excelled more in sports than music. They were good looking and well liked. Their mother adored her sons, whom she called the three Ts. Even after their parents divorced in 1993, the family remained close. Despite their regular upbringing, the boys couldn't wait to follow in their famous family's footsteps.

Their Uncle Michael doted on his three nephews and was a frequent visitor, acting almost as a third parent and giving them advice about enjoying the best years of their lives. They witnessed him being besieged by fans after one concert. He turned to the boys and said, 'Are you sure you want to do this?' Of course they were. They called themselves, naturally enough, 3T and set about recording their debut album with their father as their manager. T. J. had just turned 16. It was very exciting for Kim to have a boyfriend who was going to be a pop star.

On 27 August 1994, the brothers received an early morning call from the daughter of their mother's new boyfriend, telling them she had been in an accident. They were about to head off to the studio, but instead they rushed to the hospital in Inglewood, where she had been taken, to discover that she was already dead. Dee Dee was 39.

Initially, it was assumed the death was accidental. The boyfriend, a businessman called Donald Bohana, told police that they had been swimming that night at his house in Ladera Heights. He had popped inside briefly and when he returned Dee Dee was at the bottom of the pool. Her sons were suspicious of this explanation, as they were well aware that their mother couldn't swim and would never go near water.

Their misgivings proved entirely correct, when a coroner's report found that the numerous cuts, scratches and bruises on her body suggested 'blunt force traumatic injuries' and a non-accidental 'assisted drowning'. The Jackson family, unhappy with the lack of action from the district attorney's office, filed a wrongful death lawsuit against Bohana a year after the dreadful news.

The suit detailed 58 injuries Dee Dee had suffered, including fingernail gouges to her breasts. Tito explained, 'It's plain to see that it was more than a simple drowning. My sons came to me and said, "Dad, don't let him get away with this."' The action speculated that there had been a row over money, in which Dee Dee had refused to help Bohana, who had massive debts and had filed for bankruptcy.

The lawsuit alleged that Bohana assaulted Jackson over a four-hour period and killed her by holding her head under water in the swimming pool. He then dialled 911 and told an emergency operator that someone had fallen into his pool.

The Jacksons would have to wait until 1997 for the case to come to criminal trial in the Los Angeles Superior Court. Bohana was found guilty of second-degree murder and sentenced to 15 years to life in prison. Tito added, 'She was just a well-caring mother, and these kids were actually robbed of something that nothing can bring back.'

For her part, Kim was a 13-year-old trying to cope with a grieving boyfriend and a father desperately trying to help Uncle O. J., who would soon be standing trial for the murder of one of her mother's best friends, Auntie Nicole. It was a grim welcome to an adult world.

Dee Dee's tragedy brought T. J. and Kim closer together. He was polite, respectful and softly spoken. Her parents liked him very much, although her father warned her about the perils of interracial dating, even in a place as broad-minded as Beverly Hills: 'He explained to me that he's had a lot of interracial friends, and it might not be the easiest relationship. He said I should prepare myself for people to say things to me.'

One of the perks of dating a member of the Jackson clan came when Kim celebrated her fourteenth birthday in October 1994. The party was held at Neverland, Michael Jackson's famous 3,000-acre ranch near Santa Barbara, about 100 miles north of Los Angeles. Even though she was growing up as a privileged youngster in Beverly Hills, where birthdays and holidays were celebrated with no expense spared, this was something entirely different and totally thrilling. Michael Jackson's indulgent folly was a children's paradise – no wonder her friends were keen to join her. T. J. and his brothers were also there, while Kris and Bruce drove everyone and joined in the fun.

The amusement park was accessed from the main house by the Neverland Express, the ranch's own bright red train. Michael called the steam engine Katherine after his mother.

Kim and her friends rode on the Ferris wheel, a carousel, a wave-swinger, a super-slide and a host of roller-coasters. The private zoo contained giraffes and parrots, alpacas and elephants. It was Michael Jackson's fantasy world made real. He had missed out on a proper childhood because of the demands of recording and touring when he was a small boy. He never enjoyed Christmas or birthdays the way ordinary children might. He explained, 'I wanted to have a place that I could create everything I never had as a child.'

Kim loved it. She recalled, 'When you drove up, there were baby elephants and chimpanzees in overalls, and there were all the rides. It was everything you can possibly imagine. The memories I have from that place will last for the rest of my life.'

Although she would meet Michael many times, he wasn't at the party. He had spent a year dealing with an accusation of sexually abusing a 13-year-old boy, so perhaps it might not have been the most tactful move to have played host at a fourteenth birthday party full of excited children.

He had married Lisa Marie Presley the previous June in what would prove to be a short-lived marriage. Ironically, they had been in negotiations to be the stars of the reality show *Newlyweds*, which was eventually made by Nick Lachey and Jessica Simpson.

Neverland provided a perfect birthday party for Kim and one she still talks about: 'It was just me and my friends. It was something I'll never forget.' Disappointingly, her father wasn't there to enjoy it with her. Instead, he bought her a course of make-up lessons, which probably proved more worthwhile in the long run.

Great days like the Neverland excursion strengthened her blossoming relationship with T. J. Kim enjoyed being in a settled relationship, despite being so young. T. J. even moved in with Kris and Bruce for a short time, while he was coming to terms with what had happened.

After they had been going out for a year or so, she approached her mother to discuss birth control. She told Oprah Winfrey, 'When I did want to have sex for the first time, I was almost 15.' Kris, who was heavily pregnant with her fifth child, was supportive and understanding when Kim told her she was going to sleep with her boyfriend. Kim continued, 'She was like, "This is what we're going to do, we're gonna put you on birth control" and she was really open and honest with me.'

T. J. has remained gallant about what happened between him and his girlfriend, thus ensuring he remains welcome in the Kardashian household. All he has said is: 'We became extra close when my mom passed away. She dropped everything to be with me.'

3T eventually finished recording their first album, entitled *Brotherhood*, which proved to be a much bigger hit in Europe than in the US. It reached number 11 in the UK charts and a single from it, 'Anything', only just missed out on the top spot. They may not have been superstars, but Kim Kardashian, a high school teenager, was dating a member of a boy band. Her classmates were hugely envious.

From being a popular, if rather anonymous, girl at school, Kim was becoming far better known. Not only was she going out with one of the Jacksons, but her father was on television every single day when the trial of the century began on

24 January 1995. It transfixed a nation and caused a huge division within her family.

On the one hand, her mother was convinced of O. J.'s guilt and was happy to voice that opinion. Her father, meanwhile, was standing by his old friend. Kris observed how confused her children were because their parents were on different sides of 'a crazy situation'.

The scale of public interest was enormous. While he was remanded in jail, O. J. was getting an estimated 3,500 letters of support a day. An estimated 95 million people had watched the notorious slow-motion car chase. The *Washington Post* reported, 'No one as well known and celebrated as Simpson has ever been charged with such a crime in the history of this country.'

Centre stage was Robert Kardashian, described by the newspapers as O. J.'s 'personal attorney', who sat by his side in court every day. Even before the trial began, the news programmes would feature his regular visits to O. J. in jail. When Robert went to eat out at a fashionable Beverly Hills restaurant like Spago, the room went silent and everyone turned round to stare, as if Tom Cruise had just walked in. He was happy to chat to well-wishers and the curious. One night someone asked him what O. J.'s jail cell was like. 'It's a seven-by nine-foot cage,' he replied.

Before the ordeal of the trial took hold, Kim's father seemed in good spirits about the case. At one of his parties in Encino, he asked guests if they wanted to see how O. J. slipped out of the house for the now famous drive. He nodded at Al Cowlings, who ambled out of the party, got into his white Ford Bronco and drove off.

Explaining to his children what was happening to Uncle O. J. was more problematic, especially as both Kris and Bruce openly discussed his guilt. He had to fall back on the old 'innocent until proven guilty' line. He was at least encouraged by his daughters wanting to write to the man with whom they had spent many happy days and holidays. Kim supported her father. She confirmed, 'I definitely took my dad's side. We just always thought my dad was the smartest person in the world, and he really believed in his friend.'

Robert, by all accounts, was aware of the business opportunities that might accrue from the notoriety of the case. He helped to secure a £1 million advance for O. J.'s book, *I Want to Tell You*, which was published three days after the trial began. O. J. ostensibly wrote the book for two reasons – financial benefit and a desire to respond to the 300,000 letters he had received since his arrest. He wrote, 'I want to state unequivocally that I did not commit these horrible crimes. I loved Nicole. I could never do such a thing.'

He certainly needed the money. When he and Nicole divorced in 1992, he was earning $1 million a year. Now he faced ruin, whatever the trial verdict, and still had to pay $15,000 a day to his defence team. Only Robert was giving his services for free.

At least Kim's father never had to give evidence at the trial, protected by attorney–client privilege. The prosecution had been desperate to question him about O. J.'s garment bag, which he was seen carrying on the day of the murders.

The Kardashians were as divided inside the courtroom as they were outside. Kim and Kourtney were caught in the middle of a difficult situation: 'Kourtney and I would go to the trial with my dad and we'd sit on his side and I remember looking over and my mom was on the other side sitting next to Nicole's parents, and it was so much tension.' The girls were worried that their mom would be mad at them for sitting with their dad.

Any good humour Robert may have brought to the saga soon left him as the days turned into months. One of the first casualties was his wedding plans with Denice. They were put on hold because of the demands of the case. Eventually, they split up. She has never spoken of the exact reasons, although she may well have been uneasy at the depth of his involvement in the trial and just wanted to get on with her life.

Instead, while Robert was at the Los Angeles courtroom every day of 1995, she set about reviving her late husband's last project, the sequel to *Gone in 60 Seconds*. The new film, which had the hugely successful producer Jerry Bruckheimer and Disney on board, eventually came to screens in 2000 and starred Nicholas Cage, with Angelina Jolie in the role that Denice would have played. It turned into more of a remake than a sequel, but still it returned over £237 million at the box office.

The evening before the trial began, Robert drove over to his ex-wife's house to give her a letter he had written to her and his children, in which he explained why he had made such an enormous commitment to Uncle O.J. She quoted the letter in full in her memoir.

Robert, clearly under enormous strain, recognised how the tragedy had invaded their privacy and that the division in the family was very sad. He said he valued his family above all else and that their lives were far more important than this one case. 'My life will never be the same,' he wrote emotionally.

Kris was expecting to give evidence about the domestic violence she knew about in the Simpson household. In the end, she wasn't called, as the prosecution decided, probably wrongly, that it would have an adverse influence on the jury. She did talk to reporters, however, revealing that Nicole knew she was in danger long before she died.

Kris spent her entire pregnancy absorbed in the case, either watching it on television or attending in person with Bruce. Some of the aspects of the case will never be forgotten, including the bloody glove the prosecution made O. J. try on, only to discover it didn't fit. 'If it doesn't fit, you must acquit,' said his lead defender, the renowned black attorney Johnny Cochran, who introduced the alleged racism of the LAPD so skilfully into the defence arguments.

The world awaited the verdict on 3 October 1995. Robert and Johnny had been to visit O. J. in jail and they had prayed together. The jury spent less than four hours reaching its conclusion and, genuinely, nobody knew what might happen. They ruled 'not guilty' on both counts of murder.

Robert looked stunned and bewildered, as if he couldn't believe what he was hearing; he didn't even smile. O. J. slapped him on the back. Johnny Cochran was elated and slapped O. J. on the back. While the formalities were being concluded, Robert took off his glasses and wiped his eyes.

His children were at school. He had seen little of them during the last few months, as he was concerned for their safety at his house, which was receiving a great deal of public attention. He was incensed when someone scrawled 'nigger-lover' on his car. They had spent the time at Kris and Bruce's house and Robert did his best to get there at weekends. Robert and Bruce would discuss the situation, keen for the family not to be torn apart.

When Kim, Kourtney and Khloé got home on the day of the verdict, Bruce, who had always believed O. J. to be guilty, was still watching it unfold on TV. He recalled, 'They came in and said, "Ah, I told you he didn't do it!"' Bruce asked them to sit down while he explained something to them: 'Look, just because he got a not guilty verdict doesn't mean he didn't do it and I just don't want to hear his name any more.'

Robert never expressed any opinion about O. J.'s innocence until he was interviewed by Barbara Walters a year later and admitted he did have doubts: 'The blood evidence is the biggest thorn in my side that causes me the greatest problems. So I struggle with the blood evidence.'

Robert helped the renowned writer Lawrence Schiller with his classic book *American Tragedy*, co-written by *Time* magazine reporter James Willwerth, which provided the inside story of the defence team during the trial. According to Dominick Dunne of *Vanity Fair*, he received a 'substantial proportion' of Schiller's fee. There were also rumours that Robert was the source of many post-trial stories about O. J.

He had to piece his life back together. When Denice left, she had taken all the furniture and the television sets. They were hers to begin with, but the house was literally empty without her. She had only kind words to say about her former fiancé, however. 'O. J. used Robert,' she said. 'Robert went over to the house on Rockingham as soon as he heard about the murders, like any friend would, and O. J. used him from then on. It's been terrible for Robert. His friends have left him.'

Robert's relationship with O. J. was never the same again. A friendship that could have lasted a lifetime vanished in 10 months inside a crowded courtroom. Schiller and Willwerth wrote, presumably with Robert's blessing, that the doubts would never leave him. He also realised that for years his friend had kept his troubled life with Nicole from him. He had seen them have only one argument the whole time he had known them. He went to the victory party at Rockingham, but barely saw O. J. again after that.

The epic case wasn't finished. A civil action was launched by the families of both victims against O. J. for the unlawful killing of Nicole and Ron Goldman. They won the case and were awarded $33.5 million in compensation and damages. This time, the events that took place over five months in a Santa Monica courthouse weren't televised. Robert was required to give a deposition for the court, although what he was able to say was still heavily governed by attorney–client privilege. He was able to comment on Nicole for the first time: 'She was kind. She was sweet. I loved Nicole. She was a fun person ... She was a good wife and an excellent mother.'

The house on North Rockingham Drive, where O. J. had lived for 20 years, was sold for close to $4 million and was promptly demolished by the new owner, an investment banker. The former sports star moved to Miami to start a new life. In December 2008, he was found guilty of 12 felonies as a result of an armed robbery and kidnapping at a Las Vegas hotel-casino. He received a minimum sentence of nine years and a maximum of 27. Robert Kardashian wouldn't live to see his friend sent down.

The murder trial never goes away. It is part of American history, a modern legend. Kim is asked about it at some point during most interviews. She has become adept at avoiding it, like a politician swerving an awkward question. She simply acknowledges that it was the 'biggest struggle' within her family apart from her parents' divorce: 'It's the biggest separation my family's had, so why even bring it up.' She was asked about it yet again by *Rolling Stone* magazine in July 2015. 'It's weird,' she said. 'I try not to think about it.'

THE REAL WORLD

———

Having a steady boyfriend meant that Kim wasn't prone to sneaking into unsuitable nightclubs as a teenager. While her more spirited friends may have been up for an adventure, Kimmy, as she was generally known, wasn't a party girl during high school. She had a large social circle and they could usually be found hanging out at each other's extremely nice houses.

She was happy with T. J., although she could have had her pick of the boys. She always had great sex appeal and was a very pretty girl – almost innocently so. The nanny, Pam Behan, remarked that she didn't let the many compliments she received go to her head. She was never conceited about her looks. Pam observed, 'She knows she is beautiful because everyone tells her she is beautiful. Yet she maintains her sweetness.'

Although unpleasant adult troubles intruded, in the form of her parents' ugly divorce, the O. J. Simpson furore and the murder of her boyfriend's mother, she was able to enjoy being a teenage girl without going off the rails. Her great friend

Nikki Lund recalled, 'We made little coffee cakes and painted our nails and talked about our next diet.'

The girls tried every diet going. They sampled the popular Atkins and South Beach Diets. They also took over the kitchen to cook up vast quantities of cabbage soup when that was the latest weight-loss fad.

After Kim started dating, she became aware that all the popular girls around her seemed to be skinny and blonde. She was the anti-blonde – petite, buxom, bottom-heavy and bothered by the female Armenian characteristic of too much dark body hair. From the age of 13, Kim was a regular visitor to the beauty salon for her bikini wax.

Her schoolgirl hero wasn't a string-bean runway model, but J.Lo, the shapely Hispanic actress and singer. From the mid-nineties onwards, Jennifer Lopez was in possession of the most photographed and appreciated bum in the world.

Like all teenagers, Kim had many favourites. As well as Jennifer Lopez and Janet Jackson, she followed leading R & B artists, including Babyface, Mary J. Blige and the vocal group Jodeci. She had a special affection for the Spice Girls, who brought 'girl power' to Marymount. She was 16 when they burst onto the music scene in the US with their breakthrough number one, 'Wannabe', in February 1997. That year, their debut album, *Spice*, was the world's biggest seller.

Kim was an admirer of Victoria Beckham and her image as Posh Spice. One friend confided, 'She liked the idea of being posh and she thought Victoria was the prettiest Spice Girl.' Kim wore her hair then in a shortish bob like Posh and tried to do her make-up to imitate the well-known sultry pout.

Occasionally, her school would have an 'off day', when you could ditch the school uniform for a day and dress as you please. Kim and her friends would go as the Spice Girls. She had a short-sleeved leather dress with a slit up the side that mirrored the sort of outfit that the chic and fashionable Posh would wear. The girls would each be a different character and spend hours getting ready. They enjoyed dressing up and playing their parts more than the music, although it was good fun to practise 'Wannabe' or 'Spice Up Your Life' in front of the mirror. They were never brave enough to give a *Stars in Their Eyes* type of performance in public.

For her sixteenth birthday, Kim was given a new white BMW 318 saloon. It was a rite of passage for each of the sisters to be given a car on reaching the age when they could start driving. Their father would often produce contracts for his children to sign to ensure they understood the meaning of responsibility. While it was his way of having fun with his kids, it did have a serious purpose. The car contract was no exception.

Four days after her birthday, Robert produced the document. In it, he calls himself her 'wonderful and kind' father. Kimberly, as she was referred to, had to agree to drive her younger sister and brother to their activities, run errands for her dad, not talk back to her mother or father, ensure that she maintained a good grade average at Marymount, not take drugs, smoke cigarettes or marijuana or get drunk.

She was one of the few girls at her school who didn't have a credit card for her personal use. For her car, however, her father provided her with a gas-only one for Standard Oil, so she could fill up with petrol whenever she needed it. It was in the contract that she had to keep up the payments on the card. She also had to agree to wash the car once a week. Last, but by no means least, she was responsible for all repairs. She explained, 'If I crashed it, I had to be responsible for paying for it.'

The contract was more an indication of her father's affection than anything else. He even states in paragraph seven of the agreement that 'your dad loves you very much'. It was something lovely and precious between a father and his daughter. Kim, who pranged the car almost immediately, didn't see it that way.

She was crawling along in bumper-to-bumper traffic, when she dropped her lipstick, reached down to pick it up and rear-ended the car in front. She recalled, 'I tapped someone. It was so not a big deal, but I had to pay for it.' It didn't help that the driver of the other vehicle saw the name Kardashian on her documents and realised she must be the daughter of O. J. Simpson's lawyer. 'They sued me for a lot of money.'

As a result of the mishap, Kim needed to find a Saturday job to help pay for things. She was strolling through the centre of Encino on a day off from school, when she saw that a local boutique called Body was looking for a part-time shop assistant. 'It was the coolest clothing store in the Valley,' recalled Kim proudly. She loved being around the latest fashions and would often go to the store after school to work for an extra hour or two before heading back to her father's house.

In pre-mobile phone days, all the schoolchildren had beepers with different coloured cases that would clip onto a belt or a bag. A beeper was a pager that they would carry to keep in touch with their parents or, more usually, their friends. Kim would change her colour every weekend. She was keen to make small fashion statements even then, and would disappear to her room to devise different coloured headbands. She used fish wire to sew on flowers and made sure they matched her eyeliner and the colour of the top she was wearing. Her parent's entrepreneurial character rubbed off on her, because, as well as wearing the accessories herself, she would hawk them round little boutiques in Hollywood, trying to sell some for a few dollars. Her job meant she was in retail; her little sideline was her start in business.

Kourtney had moved into her dad's full time, because the quiet atmosphere there was much more conducive to studying, which she needed to do to realise her ambition of going to university. Kim didn't harbour such aspirations, preferring to spend her evenings talking for hours on the phone to her friends rather than with her nose in a schoolbook. She was happy to stay over at her dad's to keep her sister company, especially as life at Kris and Bruce's house had become chaotic with the arrival of their baby half-sisters.

Kris had given birth to their first child, Kendall, on 3 November 1995. They gave her the second name of Nicole to honour the memory of Nicole Brown Simpson. Yet another daughter, Kylie Kristen Jenner, was born on 10 August 1997. It was all a bit much for the two older girls.

Staying at Robert's became even more practical when Kris and Bruce decided they needed to move from the house in Benedict Canyon, because it was too small for their growing family. They were still renting, and Kris was determined that they should have a place of own. They found their next house purely by chance. She had been invited to lunch by a friend who lived in Hidden Hills in Calabasas, which, in Beverly Hills terms, was the sticks. Kris didn't even know how to get there, other than it was a long drive out on the Ventura Freeway. Once there, of course, she fell in love with its tranquillity and privacy. She talked Bruce round with the promise that he would still be able to play golf. Together they found a house that required a lot of work, but it was the start of her family's love affair with the little-known community.

Thanks to the impetus Kris gave him, Bruce's career was again moving forward. To a large extent, Robert Kardashian hadn't needed Kris in his working life. He had been content for her to raise his children in a traditional family unit. Bruce and Kris worked as a team. As well as overseeing the proper marketing of his motivational speech, 'Finding the Champion Within', they produced an infomercial for a line of stair-climbers and a keep-fit video, which showed Bruce coaching Kris. Their business prospects hadn't been harmed by her involvement in the O. J. Simpson trial, although that was the last thing on their minds at the time.

Kim wasn't half-hearted about working out. For her, any pain was always worth it. She enthusiastically joined in the craze for Tae-Bo that swept through her circle of friends. They all had the video on how best to perform the aerobic exercise and would work out at each other's spacious homes. The name Tae-Bo is a blend of taekwondo and boxing. It's a sort of martial arts dancing and great fun to do, as well as good exercise.

Kim, like many teenagers, was swayed by what was 'in' and popular at school. They all watched *Melrose Place* so they could talk about it the next day. The popular prime-time soap followed the lives of young men and women living in an apartment complex in West Hollywood. It was the follow-on series from the hugely popular *Beverly Hills, 90210*, another Aaron Spelling-produced programme. Coincidentally, Kim was actually at El Rodeo School, which has a 90210 postcode, when that show aired.

Even though she was only 11 when it finished, she also liked *The Golden Girls*, which she watched as reruns. Another favourite sitcom was *Growing Pains*, which featured a teenage Leonardo DiCaprio in an early role. It was the story of a family of two parents and four children and followed the dramas of their everyday lives.

The most inspiring film for Kim was the cult success *Clueless*, because she loved the fashions and decided she was going to be the main character, Cher Horowitz, played by Alicia Silverstone. 'I literally had at least 10 of the outfits Cher had,' she confessed. In the film, the heroine is a rich and privileged girl living in a Beverly Hills mansion, like Kim was, and her father is a lawyer.

The show that had by far the most significant influence on Kim began broadcasting on MTV in 1992. It was called *The Real World* and is widely acknowledged to be the model for the modern reality shows that followed, including *Keeping Up with the Kardashians*. It is no surprise to learn that the production company Bunim/Murray is responsible for both programmes. They also produced *The Simple Life*, with Paris Hilton and Nicole Richie.

In the show, a group of seven or eight young adults are selected to share a house and interact – or, more precisely, fall out – with each other. It's a simple formula that has worked well over the years, from *Big Brother* to the Kardashian block-buster. It has always been hugely popular with a teenage audience in the US. Its themes include plenty of dysfunctional behaviour, addiction, drunkenness, eating disorders, sexuality, racism, politics, religion and, of course, an on-screen wedding or two – all the ingredients of classic reality television are here. Kim loved it.

Jonathan Murray explained the thinking behind the ground-breaking show: 'We've always been interested in what the people across the street were doing. We're gossips. So, at the very beginning of *Real World*, it was like being a fly on the wall watching these people lead their lives.'

He is most proud of the storyline in the third series that featured a gay man, Pedro Zamora, who was dying from AIDS. His inclusion brought the subject of HIV into millions of living rooms around the country. Even President Clinton told Jonathan that Pedro's story made more of a difference than anything he could do from the Oval Office. The producer recalled proudly, 'We got to deliver to our viewers entertaining television but also television that actually changed their lives.' When Pedro died, the audience felt they had lost someone they knew. It demonstrated the positive effect reality TV could have. During its first season, an article in the *New York Times* said: 'The series has been steadily evolving into the year's most riveting series, a compelling portrait of twenty-somethings grappling with the nineties.'

It's easy to see how *The Real World* came to represent the standard to which other reality shows aspire. Kim Kardashian, watching in her father's house in Encino, was so hooked on the show that she abandoned her ambition to be a housewife with a large family. Instead, she wanted to be on *The Real World*.

A more pressing concern was the realisation that her elder sister was going away to college. Kourtney was accepted by Southern Methodist University in Dallas, Texas, to study communications and journalism. It was not a happy time. She was homesick, and her family back in Los Angeles, particularly Kim, missed her terribly. After sticking with it for two years, she transferred to the University of Arizona, where she had many friends. Her new course of theatre studies suited her creative side much more. Part of the major involved acting classes and being filmed – skills that would serve her well in the future.

Kourtney persuaded Kim to live full time with their father, who would have been on his own when his eldest daughter left. Kim enjoyed the settled nature of being in Encino. As well as working at Body, she started helping out at her father's business, which was called Movie Tunes, Inc. It was proving to be another success story.

The company provided music for cinemas, fulfilling a need for both movie theatres and record companies wishing to increase exposure for their performers. Originally, artists used Movie Tunes, Inc. as an outlet when they were unable to secure the radio airplay they wanted, usually because they were considered past their sell-by date. By the time Kim came on board, however, bigger stars, including the Spice Girls and Janet Jackson, were involved. Her job was principally to answer the telephones, do the filing and help burn the CDs.

Each month, Movie Tunes, Inc. produced a 14-song, hour-long music show for cinemas, which, according to Robert, reached more than 75 million theatregoers. The captive audience that had come out to watch a film was encouraged to buy a disc of the music from a concession stand. Robert had identified another essential marketing tool for the music business, just as he had done 20 years earlier with *Radio & Records*.

Her work experience was preparing Kim for life after Marymount. Before she left high school, when she was 17, her parents had to write a letter with advice about her future. They both said very similar things about demanding respect and being respectful in return, treating others how you would want to be treated, having a strong head and not succumbing to peer pressure. Robert's phrase was the most memorable: 'Know your self-worth.' It could have come from one of Bruce's motivational speeches. Always the doting father, Robert couldn't resist adding that she should know what a pretty girl she was.

She looked forward to her senior prom. She managed to persuade her father that she needed a dress by her then favourite designer, Mark Wong Nark. She still loves his dresses. This one was white and floor length, with a square neckline and a slit up the front. T. J. was on hand to accompany her, looking immaculate and suave in a black tuxedo. Kim wore her hair up and the two of them looked like a very glamorous young Hollywood couple, which, of course, they were. They even managed two of the cheesiest grins for the official photographer, revealing pearly smiles that even the most expensive Beverly Hills dentist would have been proud of. They looked very happy together.

Sadly, however, they broke up soon afterwards. The relationship had been winding down, as the demands of touring with

3T took T. J. away more and more. He remained popular with Kim's family, though. In the very small world they inhabited, the Kardashians didn't sever links with the Jackson clan. In fact, Kourtney started dating T. J.'s elder brother, Taryll.

Kim, meanwhile, was soon to make a dramatic life choice. She would leave the safe cocoon of her Beverly Hills upbringing in favour of the real world.

PART TWO

KIM KARDASHIAN

MRS THOMAS

Kim looked at pictures of interracial couples in the teen magazines she bought as a schoolgirl and thought they looked cute together. Very occasionally she has gone out with white guys. When she was 19, for instance, she went on one date with the actor and former child star Joey Lawrence, but it was nothing. She knew from an early age the type she liked and has never made a secret of her attraction to black men.

Damon Thomas wasn't cute. He was flash and edgy and came into her life like a whirlwind the moment he walked into Body one Saturday afternoon. He was much cooler than the safe celebrities of Beverly Hills with whom she had grown up. He was 10 years older than her, for a start, and that was flattering.

In 1999, Damon was a record producer going places. He told Kim that he had just started a production team called The Underdogs and that he personally worked with Babyface. That got her attention, because Kenneth 'Babyface' Edmonds was one of her favourite artists and wrote some of the most memorable songs of her teenage years, including the Boyz II Men classics 'End of the Road' and 'I'll Make Love to You'.

He helped Damon learn about production, while they worked together on a number of songs, including co-writing and producing 'These Are the Times', which was a top five *Billboard* R & B chart hit for the vocal group Dru Hill in the autumn of 1998, and 'Never Gonna Let You Go', which made number one in the same chart for the singer Faith Evans in 1999.

Less auspiciously, Damon had a run-in with the rapper Dr Dre (Andre Young). The two had apparently got into a fight at an apartment in Woodland Hills, just up from Calabasas. Dr Dre faced assault charges after Damon suffered a broken jaw in the row. A spokesman for the city attorney said 'the incident stems from an inappropriate remark that Mr Thomas had made to Mr Young's girlfriend.' Dr Dre subsequently was fined $10,000 and sentenced to 90 days' house arrest.

For The Underdogs project, Damon teamed up with former college basketball player Harvey Mason, Jr, who had spent a lifetime among the musical elite of Los Angeles. His father, Harvey Sr, was a jazz drummer who played with outstanding performers, including Herbie Hancock and Quincy Jones. He used to take his son along to recordings.

While Damon was a protégé of Babyface, Harvey Jr was working with another leading producer, Rodney Jerkins, and his Darkchild crew on projects involving Whitney Houston, Michael Jackson and Toni Braxton.

When Damon and Harvey decided to work together, they were a dream team. They joined forces initially to write a track called 'I Like Them Girls', which they went on to produce for the album *2000 Watts* for the male model-turned-singer Tyrese.

There's no doubt that Kim found Damon exciting, especially as she had lived a comparatively sheltered life and was, after all, a Catholic schoolgirl. She had been a big fan of 'N Sync at school, and this new man in her life was actually friends with Justin Timberlake. He was also writing a song for Pink, one of the hottest new acts. T. J. was lovely, but Damon was different. He was a man making his way in the world purely on the basis of his talent.

She was swept away by it all and decided to leave the comfort of her father's house and move in with Damon. He had an apartment in Romar Street, Northridge – a Valley neighbourhood that wasn't the least bit fashionable and was even more remote than Calabasas. Neither of her parents knew she was sharing her new home with a boyfriend, although Kris was suspicious when Kim arrived in Hidden Hills one day behind the wheel of a top-of-the-range Jaguar sports car. How on earth could she afford that while she was still working at Body? Kris even phoned up Robert to find out if he had anything to do with it. She didn't know that her daughter was involved with a music high-flyer.

Damon took Kim to Justin's twentieth birthday party in Las Vegas in January 2000. While they were there, it seemed like the perfect time to get married. She became Kimberly Thomas on 22 January 2000. It wasn't the fairy-tale Beverly Hills wedding Robert Kardashian or Kris Jenner had wanted for their beautiful daughter. Their own big day had been perfect and, naturally, they hoped for something similar for Kim. As it turned out, Robert Kardashian would never have the opportunity to walk any of his daughters down the aisle.

Kim didn't know how to tell her family, so she didn't. Instead, Mrs Thomas returned to Northridge and kept her secret for three months. She did tell her friends, however, and swore them to secrecy. That didn't work, because one of them rang Kourtney to tell her the news. She went online and found her younger sister's marriage certificate from Vegas. Kourtney did what any big sister would do in these circumstances – she told her mother.

Kris rallied round. She may not have been happy about the situation, but she wasn't a hypocrite. After all, she had been younger than Kim when she became engaged for the first time, and she was only 22 when she got married.

Kim's father wasn't as philosophical about the situation. He refused to speak to his daughter, perhaps more through disappointment than anger. When he finally met Damon, he didn't like him and he didn't care for the relationship. He would have preferred her to have waited and, according to friends, was happy to tell her what he thought. He didn't want her to be with Damon. He wasn't as understanding as her mother.

Kris reveals in her memoir how, when she first met him, she tore into Damon for taking advantage of her teenage daughter, but she accepted they were married and did her best to include Damon in family gatherings. He remained a bit of an outsider, however. In her book, he isn't even afforded the privilege of a pseudonym. He isn't named at all. He is just 'the husband'.

Kim gave up her job at Body less than two months after her marriage. She would later state, in an astonishing court declaration, that she did so because Damon told her to. 'He said that he did not want me to have contact with my old boyfriends, who would be able to reach me at the clothing store. He said that he wanted to know where I was at all times.'

If all the allegations in the divorce papers are to be believed, this was the start of an unhappy period in Kim's life. She claimed that Damon preferred her to stay at home and wanted her to prepare meals for him, even if he arrived home at 4.30 in the morning after a long session in the studio.

Damon, she alleged in August 2003, wouldn't allow her to leave the house unless he knew exactly when and where she was going. She claimed that she couldn't go to the mall by herself, or dine with friends she had known since she was a child and that he even tried to poison her mind against her family, calling her mother and sisters 'evil'. She said, 'Damon decided what we would do and when we would do it. He was very much the "King of the Castle".'

Now that she no longer had her wage from Body, she needed to find other ways of supplementing the income she had from helping her father at Movie Tunes, Inc. Working in the boutique had given her the opportunity to meet clients whom she could advise on their wardrobe choices. It was an upmarket store, so customers invariably had some money to spend and were happy to pay Kim extra for her help. That revenue was now lost as well.

She needed to find something she could do at home or a sideline she could work on during the quieter moments at her father's office. It was while there that she started taking an interest in eBay. The ubiquitous online auction site seems to have been around for many years, but it only launched in September 1995. Kim spotted its potential. Arguably, the most useful attribute she inherited from her mother and father was their entrepreneurial spirit – the ability to identify a way to earn money and to exploit the opportunity fully.

She was a huge fan of Manolo Blahnik shoes. They were the must-have fashion footwear for celebrities and well-off women. Their appeal greatly increased when they featured heavily in *Sex and the City*. In the third series, broadcast in the autumn of 2000, the lead character Carrie Bradshaw, played by Sarah Jessica Parker, is mugged for her pair of Manolos, as they are popularly known.

Kim became aware of them when J.Lo wore them. She still absolutely adored J.Lo and couldn't stop singing her break-through hit 'If You Had My Love' around the house and in the car. She checked with a store and they had five pairs similar to the ones J.Lo sported, but they were $700 each.

She did what any young entrepreneur would do under these circumstances. She borrowed the money from her father, who, as usual, demanded that she sign a contract agreeing to repay the money with interest. She bought all five pairs and then put them up for sale on eBay. It was her first real business success. Each pair sold for $2,500; altogether, she made a profit of $9,000. From that moment on, if there was anything in her wardrobe that she wasn't wearing, she would sell it on eBay. She was very unsentimental about it.

Meanwhile, her husband's fortunes were also on the up. The new millennium began the golden years for Damon and The Underdogs. They produced many tracks for Tyrese and old friends, such as Babyface and Brian McKnight, but also branched out to a more mainstream audience, by working with Lionel Richie and with Victoria Beckham on her solo album. Most of their recordings for Kim's teenage favourite ended up as B-sides to singles, but one track, 'Girlfriend', made the final cut. The album wasn't the success everyone had hoped for, though.

Much more successful was a collaboration with Justin Timberlake. The singer was passionate about basketball and had idolised Michael Jordan growing up in Tennessee, so he formed an easy friendship with Harvey Mason, who had played practically at professional level. Brian McKnight, one of the smoothest R & B vocalists, was also mad about basketball, so recording often took a back seat while the four friends went outside to shoot hoops.

The Underdogs wrote and produced 'Still on My Brain' for Justin's debut album, *Justified*. It was a slow and soulful number about lost love. Beautifully sung, it is a stand-out track and one that hasn't dated. While, as fans thought, the song might be about Justin's break with Britney Spears, it could just as easily reflect any painful split.

In her divorce papers, Kim claimed that an appalling incident occurred on a day when she and Damon were going skydiving with Justin. She alleged: 'Before we left our home, Damon hit me in the face and cut my lip open. I fell onto the bed frame and banged my knee hard. I was limping when we went skydiving.'

Her declaration states that Damon started hitting her a few months into their marriage. She points out that she is 5ft 3in tall and weighs 107 pounds. Damon, she says, is 5ft 10in and 175 pounds. In one incident at her mother's house, she claimed that he became angry after learning she had paged someone on her beeper: 'I told him the name of the friend. He became enraged and punched me in the face. My face was bruised and swollen as a result. I thought about calling the police, but was afraid and decided not to do so.'

It was a relief for everyone when they separated in early 2003. After she was no longer living with Damon, she claimed she experienced the worst of his violence against her. She recalled in the papers how she went back to the house to collect some personal items on the night before the rest of her belongings were due to be moved. She described what alleg-edly happened when she went into the bathroom to collect some toiletries: 'Damon screamed that I should get out of his bathroom immediately. He came at me and slammed me against the closet wall. He held me up against the wall with his hands around my neck and threatened to choke me. He then took one hand and punched the wall right next to my head.

'He then grabbed me by my hair and told me to get out. He put one hand against my back and pushed me up the stairs (the front door is on the ground level and the bedroom is one level below ground). At the top of the stairs, he threw me across the room and I hit my head against the front door. I got up and ran out of the house. I was frightened.'

Kim has never repeated these allegations in public or in interviews. They weren't included in Kris Jenner's book or in *Kardashian Konfidential*. For his part, Damon emphatically and vehemently denied these incidents ever took place. He told *In Touch* magazine, 'It's just absolutely not true.' He pointed out that she had never filed a restraining order or a protective order against him throughout their marriage, and accused her of using the alleged abuse as a bargaining chip in their divorce battle.

Damon actually sued Kim for divorce. He did so, he said, because she was unfaithful to him with 'multiple guys'. She, in turn, denied this allegation. Clearly, there were many areas of dispute as the divorce took its course. One of them was the story of her liposuction.

Kim said she had lipo, which cost $3,650, because Damon wanted her to be 'perfect'. He countered that she wanted him to pay for that and for additional work. Damon said he bought her clothes to fit her new shapelier outline. He said he was happy to pay for them – until he saw a picture on the cover of a magazine of her with another man, which showed her wearing the very clothes he had paid for. Damon observed, 'It was not, as a husband, anything you wanted to see.'

The date in question was the dancer and choreographer Cris Judd, who, in a curious twist, used to be married to Kim's idol, Jennifer Lopez. They had wed in Calabasas in 2001 and divorced after less than a year.

For the most part, Damon has remained silent about his marriage to Kim and what he thought of his ex-wife, even though he has had some very negative press coverage. Some years later, however, in 2010, he gave an interview to *In Touch* in response to the divorce papers being made public. He was very outspoken, claiming she was jealous and competitive with her sisters and desperate to be famous. He called her, unflatteringly, a 'fame-whore'.

It really is a case of whom to believe in an acrimonious split. When the divorce was made final, Damon was ordered to pay Kim $56,000, which was by no means a large sum. There wasn't much left after she settled the debt she had run up on her credit cards of $40,000. Fortunately, he agreed to cover her legal fees, totalling $20,000. Of more importance to her than money at this point, however, were the precious possessions which she had left behind at Damon's house: an inscribed Bible from her father, a signed Manolo Blahnik book, her high school yearbooks and about a hundred other books that made up her library.

Her financial concerns were insignificant next to Damon's, which included a tax liability of more than $700,000. His career continued its upward path, though. In 2003, when his private life was in turmoil, The Underdogs signed a deal with the legendary Clive Davis at J Records to start a new label, Underdog Entertainment. This was big news in the music business. Damon gushed, 'Clive has a true love for artists and their music, and that is exciting to us.'

The rise of The Underdogs culminated in 2006, when Damon and Harvey produced the soundtrack for the Oscar-winning film *Dreamgirls*, loosely based on the early days of The Supremes. Two of the big ballad tracks became modern classics: 'Listen' by Beyoncé and Jennifer Hudson's powerful 'And I'm Telling You I'm Not Going'. Damon and Harvey won a Black Reel Award for the soundtrack and derived enormous kudos from their work.

Only Harvey seemed to kick on after this triumph, however. He formed Harvey Mason Media in 2008, has won six Grammys and is a major success story. His website's online biography of his career and achievements doesn't mention Thomas's contribution.

Damon hasn't done as well financially in recent years, filing for bankruptcy in 2012. The documents revealed he owed more than $3.5 million, mainly in back taxes. His principal asset was a Lamborghini worth $170,000. Damon still works at Harvey Mason's studios on Vineland Avenue, North Hollywood, but has been living more modestly in Northridge.

One thing is sure about Kim's first marriage: it wasn't a happy one for either of them. Perhaps Kim was indulging in some teenage rebellion a little later than most young people. She demonstrated for the first, but not the last, time that she possessed a strong will and that if she wanted to do something, then she would press ahead and do it.

In 2015, blissfully married to Kanye West, she looked back on her first attempt and told the TV host Matt Lauer, 'You think you know so much about love when you're young and you look back later and probably realise it is not what you thought it was.'

9

THE DEATH OF
ROBERT KARDASHIAN

While Kim was involved in her bitter divorce, she received some awful news. Her father, Robert Kardashian, was dying. It came as a terrible shock to all the family when, in July 2003, he told them that he had oesophageal cancer. The oesophagus, or food pipe, is the tube that carries food from your mouth to your stomach. He had suffered badly over the years with severe acid indigestion and was forever taking antacids to relieve his discomfort. His cancer had already advanced to Stage IV, which meant that it had spread to other organs in his body, leaving little room for hope.

Grimly, his illness wasn't the only one casting a shadow over the family that summer. Kim's maternal grandfather, Harry Shannon, was in hospital in San Diego and sinking fast. Kris Jenner's 78-year-old stepfather, whom she affectionately called Dad, was admitted after a car accident. Tragically, he caught a staph infection and never made it home. Robert managed to travel to San Diego for the funeral, but it would be his last trip.

Robert's private life since the O. J. Simpson trial had been interesting, to say the least. Out of the blue, he had married a woman called Jan Ashley in November 1998. Jan, who lived nearby in Encino, had no children and they got married so they could have a child together. Robert wasn't the sort of man who would contemplate such a thing outside marriage.

According to divorce papers he filed the following May, he couldn't go through with it: 'Approximately two months after our marriage, I changed my mind. I decided that since I already had four biological children, I did not wish to have any more. The respondent [Ashley] and I both entered into this marriage with the expectation of having a child together. I am the one who changed my mind.'

It was a most curious episode in Robert Kardashian's life. Much later, Jan would put the blame for the demise of her short-lived marriage firmly on the shoulders of his children, who she claimed were after him for 'money, money, money'. She didn't look back on her time as Mrs Kardashian with great joy. 'It took me about one day to get over it,' she said.

Robert moved to Lake Encino Drive, another smart street in Encino. The house, on a corner and with no view, was nothing like the best in the neighbourhood. It was still a desirable property, just not in the same league as Tower Lane. He began dating an elegant blonde woman called Ellen Pearson, who was involved in real estate. They had started seeing each other in 1998, but had split up before he became involved with Jan. After meeting again at a party in December 1999, they resumed their relationship. Robert bought a second house near his parents in Indian Wells and the couple divided their time between the two homes.

They became engaged in 2002, and planned their wedding for the following year. They decided to have a honeymoon before getting married and enjoyed an idyllic holiday in Italy in May and June 2003. On their return, they thought they had plenty of time to finish the preparations for the big day at Hotel Bel-Air on 5 August 2003. On a weekend visit to Indian Wells in early June, however, Robert complained of stomach pains and decided he needed to see a doctor. A few weeks later, on 11 July, he was given the bleak diagnosis and told his family. Ellen recalled, 'He was a religious man. He was not at all concerned about passing, because he believed in God. He just hadn't wanted to go so soon.'

His deterioration was rapid and the wedding had to be cancelled. He could eat very little and was losing a lot of weight. Kim did her best by going to the house and making him his favourite Cream of Wheat, a type of porridge that is popular in the US. Robert liked his served especially sweet, so Kim would always sprinkle a layer of sugar in the bowl before she stirred in the cereal. It was something she had enjoyed preparing for her father when she was a little girl and here she was, a 22-year-old woman, trying to do something nice for her dad before he died.

Robert was well enough to marry Ellen at the house in Encino on 27 July. His four children were there, as were his brother Tommy, sister Barbara and Ellen's daughter April. Understandably, it was a very small affair, with a subdued celebration in the garden afterwards.

The circumstances of Robert's demise set off a decade and more of feuding between stepmother and children, with allegations and counterclaims flying all over the place concerning the access the children had to their father in his dying days. They now seem to have settled their legal issues.

Ellen became the second person Kris Jenner couldn't bring herself to name in her autobiography, calling her 'a woman he had only been dating a short time'.

Robert Kardashian passed away on 30 September 2003. He was 59. The funeral at the Inglewood Park Cemetery was standing room only, as his many friends gathered to pay their respects. Kim gave an address, which, unused to public speaking, she found very hard. Afterwards, everyone went back to the Bel-Air Country Club, which, by grim coincidence, had been the venue for the reception when he had married Kris. Al Cowlings was there, but O. J. Simpson didn't attend, which was probably a good thing. He would have been the focus of attention rather than the celebration of Robert's life.

O. J. had tried to reach Robert on the phone before he died, despite the two not having spoken for years. He was gracious about his former friend after his death: 'It's shocking when a friend close to you passes. I loved Bobby. We had one disagreement over the years, about a book he did for money. He explained it to me. I understood it, and we put it aside. Bob was there when I needed him most.'

The newspaper obituaries, unsurprisingly, focused on Robert's involvement in the O. J. Simpson trial. The *New York Times* spelled it out in its headline: 'Robert Kardashian, a lawyer for O. J. Simpson, dies at 59'. His family barely received a mention in the article. The *Guardian* pointed out that few would have heard of Robert if he had not sat beside O. J. throughout the trial. Until she found fame in her own right, Kim was frequently described as the daughter of O. J. Simpson's lawyer.

One of the issues that has caused much subsequent speculation is how much money Robert had and what his children actually inherited. He had made a considerable amount from the sale of *Radio & Records*, but that had been nearly 25 years before and since then he had provided an extravagant lifestyle for his family.

There is no doubt that Kim and her siblings were indulged and spoiled as children. They admit it themselves. By Beverly Hills standards, they were comfortably off, but not particularly wealthy. According to Jan Ashley, they weren't rich. She maintained, 'He didn't have any money. He always pretended he had money.'

Ellen maintained that he had large mortgages on the two properties in Encino and Indian Wells. She became president of Movie Tunes, Inc., which was now based on Ventura Boulevard in Studio City. Financial difficulties, however, led to her filing for Chapter 7 bankruptcy in 2010. The house in Indian Wells was repossessed by the bank and sold. The Encino house was also sold. She began working for a real estate company called Western Resources Title as part of their sales force based in San Diego. She hasn't remarried and still calls herself Mrs Ellen Kardashian. She remembers Robert fondly: 'He had a lot of dignity, a great outlook on life and a fantastic sense of humour. We were very much in love.'

Details of Robert's will weren't made public, although apparently there was an insurance policy that would benefit his children in due course. They were also left 'his personal tangible and intangible property', a clause that would be contentious in a future vicious legal action between Ellen and the Kardashian children.

Robert's daughters reacted in different ways to the shock of his death. Kourtney joined her mother in a new venture. For years they had talked of running their own store and now was the perfect time to focus on something new and take their minds off a miserable year. They opened a children's boutique called Smooch in the centre of Calabasas. Kris had been helping to run a similar shop, which had been the family business for 30 years, while Harry was ill and that had inspired her to open her own.

Kourtney relished the opportunity and threw herself into running everything. Her life revolved around it: 'I used to work in the store all day, every day, stay hours after closing and was obsessed with it. Smooch was my baby ... in a weird way, the store really helped me deal with my father's death ... I put my feelings into the store!'

Khloé, aged 19, wasn't as fortunate. She was so upset that she had found it too difficult to visit her ailing father. The emotional stress caused her hair to fall out and she had to wear wigs, extensions and hats until it grew back. She started drinking too much and spent most nights going to clubs with an unsuitable crowd. She was very unhappy.

Kim planned a holiday in Mexico for her twenty-third birthday in October 2003. She needed to relax and get away from her troubles. The night before she flew, she made a sex tape with her boyfriend that would have an extraordinary effect on her future.

All three of his daughters saw Robert Kardashian as the greatest influence on their lives. They try hard to keep his memory alive by marking special occasions throughout the year, including the anniversary of his birthday or his passing, or Father's Day. On his birthday, they return to his favourite Armenian restaurant in Hollywood, called Carousel. He used to take his family there for special celebrations so they could sample the authentic, unpretentious food. Kim usually ate chicken, although she was also partial to the feta cheese appetiser.

Sadly, Robert Kardashian didn't live to see the birth of his grandchildren, nor did he witness what would have been one of his proudest days – when his only son, Robert Jr, graduated from USC, his old alma mater, with a degree in business in 2009. His ex-wife Kris Jenner observed, 'The one regret, if I had to do it over, was divorcing Robert Kardashian.'

To mark the fifth anniversary of her father's death, Kim posted a touching eulogy on her website. His absence has somehow made his presence in their lives greater. She said he was watching over and protecting them: 'There isn't a day that goes by when I don't think about him or wish he were here.' She concluded simply, 'I love you, Dad.'

10

QUEEN OF THE
CLOSET SCENE

Kim's new boyfriend was a handsome young rapper and actor called William Ray Norwood, Jr, known as Ray J. They were introduced by his sister, Brandy, a very popular singer and TV actress, at a party in early 2003. As far as he was concerned, Kim was a married woman and off limits, but there was an instant attraction between the two. It wasn't long before they couldn't keep their hands off one another.

Ray J would later reveal that Kim left Damon for him as soon as they started having sex and said their passion for each other was intense. Wild and extreme sexual chemistry, according to the indiscreet Ray J, was a big part of their relationship: 'We were like animals, sexually free to try anything.'

Ray J and his sister were from McComb, Mississippi, the Southern town where Britney Spears was born and went to school. They were unlikely ever to have bumped into her though, because the area was notoriously racist and, historically, a stronghold for the Ku Klux Klan.

They escaped that prejudice when their parents moved to Carson, California, 13 miles south of downtown Los Angeles.

Their father was the gospel singer Willie Norwood, and both children learned much of their vocal technique from listening to their father sing in church. He wasn't the only musical one in the family – the rap superstar Snoop Dogg is a first cousin (his mother Beverly is also from McComb). From a young age, the Norwood children were involved in the performing arts.

Brandy, who is two years older than her brother, made her television debut, aged 14, in 1993 and signed with Atlantic Records the same year. Kim's husband, Damon, featured on her first, eponymously titled album, playing piano and keyboards. He also co-wrote and produced two tracks, 'I'm Yours' and 'Love Is on My Side', which he composed with Robin Thicke, who would become a household name 20 years later, thanks to the song 'Blurred Lines'. Harvey Mason, Jr worked on her second album, *Never Say Never*, so both Underdogs knew her well. She was very much part of the new wave of young black talent sweeping the music business.

Ray J always seemed to be hanging on to his sister's coat-tails, a pace behind. He had a record deal at 14, but was dropped by Elektra Records after just one album. His sister's career continued to prosper, however, with the success of 'The Boy Is Mine', her 1998 duet with Monica. It was the bestselling single of the year, with sales of 2.6 million.

Kim worked for Brandy after meeting her through Damon. She had realised that she couldn't make a living buying and selling her own possessions on eBay, and had displayed early business acumen by expanding into closet organising and personal styling. Progress was slow. At first, she would take every opportunity to go through the things her friends no longer had a use for, advising them which items they could sell and then splitting the profits with them.

She took her business a step further one day when she was visiting the Pacific Palisades home of Sugar Ray Leonard and his second wife, Bernadette. Sugar Ray had been a family friend of her father since before she was born and was also a long-standing friend of Bruce Jenner. They had both won gold medals at the Montreal Olympics and Ray, too, had subsequently carved out a career as a motivational speaker.

Bernadette had a massive closet, as big as a bedroom, which was seriously disorganised. Kim explained, 'I said to her, "You really need to clean out your closet." Well, we spent the whole night doing that.' She persuaded Bernadette that it would be far better to sell the thousands of dollars of designer clothing on eBay than to throw away the expensive dresses and accessories. It was the start of the next stage of her career.

She became 'Queen of the Closet Scene' when Bernadette started recommending Kim's skill to her friends. Kim used her own seller's account, and photographed every article so that it looked its best. She would write little paragraphs describing the items, so she had the best chance of selling every single thing. This wasn't an idle pursuit; it was work and it was supplying her with an income. Kim was very methodical and precise. She had never been a teenage girl whose bedroom was a mess of clothes. She liked everything to be clean and tidy, labelled and folded.

Although she was incredibly well organised, she could still be endearingly dippy. She was thrilled when she could afford to buy her own Range Rover. She had a new mobile to put into the middle console in the car as well, and she bedazzled the cell so it would stand out. Unfortunately, she put so much decoration on the phone that, when she came to slot it into the console, it didn't fit.

She had discovered a niche market. Soon, big names, like Cindy Crawford and Serena Williams, Rob Lowe and the acclaimed saxophone player Kenny G, were taking advantage of her services. Kim was learning very quickly that it was all about connections in Los Angeles. If you didn't make enough of them at school, then it helped to be with someone who had them. Her mother was an accomplished networker from the moment she moved to LA, and Kim was keen to follow her example.

Working for Brandy as a personal stylist was another step forward, although it wasn't entirely glamorous. She still had to go and pick up the dry cleaning if there was a specific outfit she was recommending her client to wear. Brandy had seen her name on a worst-dressed list, which wasn't the best news for someone in demand on the red carpet, and had asked Kim for fashion advice.

The singer had branched out into the world of reality television in a way that Kim hadn't seen before. The great majority of reality shows seemed to be about putting real people – usually celebrities – into unreal situations. That was not the premise of *Brandy: Special Delivery*, which ran on MTV for four episodes in June and July 2002. Brandy was expecting her first child with her then husband and producer Robert 'Big Bert' Smith – although he later revealed they were never officially married. The show linked things that were going on during the pregnancy with events in her professional life. She shops, she goes to parenting classes, she appears on TV, she discusses pregnancy with her mum, she is in the recording studio, she has an ultrasound of the baby, she enjoys a baby shower and she has a photography session. Ray J wasn't forgotten, and appeared in a couple of episodes. After Brandy gave birth to a daughter, Sy'rai, there was nowhere for the series to go.

For Kim Kardashian, it was an eye-opener. Here was someone she knew turning her life into entertainment. Throughout her career, Kim has done very little that could be described as original, but she is unsurpassed at absorbing influences and making sure she does it bigger and better.

Kim was warmly accepted into Paris Hilton's entourage when she was hired to sort out the dressing room and closet in her Spanish-style townhouse in North Kings Road, just below Sunset Strip in West Hollywood. Kim had a growing reputation as the best person for this kind of job. Organising Paris's wardrobe was quite a task, because it was so big. It was rather like refitting and restocking a boutique.

Paris Hilton was a phenomenon. She was by no means the first person to be famous for being famous, but she maximised the celebrity of her name and turned it into a huge money-spinner for herself. Kim had known her first in preschool. When the two became friends again after Kim's marriage split, she was able to watch and learn from a master.

Superficially, at least, the two women couldn't have been more different. The tall, willowy, blonde Paris Whitney Hilton was born into a level of American high society that was a division above the relatively new money of the Kardashians. The surname Hilton was one of the most famous in the US, mentioned in the same breath as Getty or Rockefeller. Her great-grandfather, Conrad Hilton, who founded the Hilton hotel chain, was married to Zsa Zsa Gabor; her great-uncle, Conrad 'Nicky' Hilton, Jr, was one of the husbands of Elizabeth Taylor.

She is the eldest child of real-estate developer Richard Hilton and actress-socialite Kathy Richards. She was always introduced back then as the heir to a $360-million fortune, but, in fact, she was one of multiple heirs. She spent her childhood moving between the couple's many five-star luxury homes, which included mansions in The Hamptons and Bel Air, as well as a suite in the Waldorf Astoria hotel in Manhattan. Her family was huge. She is the eldest of four children, with a younger sister and two brothers. She had 10 cousins on her mother's side, and her father had seven siblings. Christmas, Halloween and Easter were big family events, with her father on hand to record everything lovingly on video – just as in the Kardashian household.

Paris began modelling as a child and was given the nickname 'Star' by her mother. In 2000, while Kim was settling down to domestic life as a married woman, Paris signed a contract with Trump Model Management in New York. Donald Trump is a friend of her father. She had already become a fixture in the gossip columns, thanks to a romance with Leonardo DiCaprio. The renowned 'Page Six' of the *New York Post* seemed to have a Paris story every day. A controversial feature in *Vanity Fair*, with eye-catching pictures by David LaChapelle of her in hot pants, with younger sister Nicky, enhanced the impression that everyone was talking about her. It was an early example for Kim of how a photograph was the most effective way of obtaining publicity.

The voracious daily coverage of the glamorous life of Paris Hilton was an example of how publicity, both good and bad, would lead to more publicity and thereby increase one's fame. In many ways, it was a template for turning oneself into a brand that Kim would have been foolish not to try to emulate, Paris was so successful at it.

In 2003, she signed with the Fox television network to star in a new reality show with her sister Nicky called *The Simple Life*. The idea was to inject humour into the reality television genre by taking the two socialites out of their comfort zone of designer dresses and credit cards and putting them to work on a farm in Arkansas, a state in the Deep South. Paris had, of course, never worked a day in her life. The idea was inspired by an old sixties sitcom called *Green Acres*, which starred Eddie Albert and Eva Gabor.

The head of casting at Fox, Sharon Klein, explained, 'They wanted to see stilettos in shit.' Sharon was impressed with Paris, whom she found funny, genuine and not at all stupid: 'She was in her own reality and not embarrassed to talk about it. There was a sweetness about her.'

The show was scheduled to begin in December 2003. On 5 November, the 'Page Six' column revealed that there was an explicit sex tape involving Paris in circulation. She had made it in May 2001 with her then boyfriend Rick Salomon. He, apparently, was in the habit of filming himself having sex with his girlfriends, and Paris was no exception. This one wasn't going to win any Oscars, although it was shot in a realistic, grainy black–and–white mode, or night vision.

Salomon, it transpired, was a handsome character, who made his living as a professional poker player after giving up a career as a teenage drug dealer. He admitted, 'In my teens, I dealt in drugs big time.' After Paris, he married Shannen Doherty, one of the stars of *Beverly Hills, 90210*. They had apparently been dating for just two days before becoming husband and wife. The marriage was annulled after nine months, and Shannen reflected, 'I haven't made the best choices in men.' He also enjoyed hot-tub parties with Pamela Anderson, whom he married in 2007 and again in 2014. Salomon is one of the bad boys women love.

There is no doubt that the video, though rampantly exhibitionist, was originally made for personal consumption. The dialogue, such as it is, was too embarrassing to have been planned. Paris told Rick to say he loved her and wanted to kiss her; he just wanted to take off her pants.

Salomon offered the tape for sale on his personal website for $50 a time and then negotiated a distribution deal with Red Light District Video. He is said to have made millions from it. After many legal proceedings and lawsuits from both of them, Paris was reported to have settled for $400,000, plus a share of the profits, and to have given most of the money to charity. She had no further contact with him. He continued to prosper, however. When he played in the 2014 World Series of Poker, he won $2.8 million.

Her then media consultant, the much-respected Elliot Mintz, observed that it was a terrible experience for Paris. 'It's something that will always be a footnote to her life. She was wounded and then took a deep breath and then moved forward. She did not allow it to stop her, which is saying more than most of us could say if a personal video tape that we recorded with somebody of that nature suddenly was available around the country. So nothing to be proud of, but the true measure of a woman or a man is how well they can adapt to something that occurs in their life and move forward, which I think she did with grace.'

Paris handled the situation with good humour in public. Three days after the premiere of her reality show, she appeared on the fabled *Saturday Night Live* in a sketch of double entendres with the comedian and presenter Jimmy Fallon. He asked her, 'Is the Paris Hilton roomy?' She replied, 'It might be for you, but most people find it very comfortable.'

The press storm surrounding the sex tape was very welcome publicity for *The Simple Life*. Her sister Nicky had dropped out, apparently not relishing the prospect of the full glare of public attention, so her place was taken by Nicole Richie, the adopted daughter of Lionel Richie.

The interesting aspect of *The Simple Life* as a reality show is that there was nothing real about it. Paris and Nicole were placed in a situation that they would never have come across in their lives. It was completely fabricated. It was, in effect, a situation comedy with them playing themselves or, more precisely, a version of themselves. In these programmes, the participants are creating on-screen personas. Paris Hilton is a far more sophisticated woman than the clueless heroine of this series.

She was certainly smart enough to understand that she could use its popularity to increase the profile of her brand as Paris Hilton. She signed a music contract with Warner Bros and started recording an album in 2004. She produced a best-selling book, *Confessions of an Heiress: A Tongue-in-Chic Peek*

Behind the Pose, which featured countless photographs of Paris fashions, recollections of childhood and helpful hints on how to behave.

She appeared in acting roles in several popular television series, including *The O.C.*, *Veronica Mars* and *Las Vegas*. She also made some forgettable films, such as *The Hillz*. The publicity poster for the film naturally featured Paris, as she was by far the most famous person in it. She even won an award for the horror movie *House of Wax* – the Teen Choice Award for best scream scene.

She launched her own fragrance and line of jewellery, and was earning hundreds of thousands of dollars in personal appearances. As an example of how to maximise a brand, Kim couldn't have had a better one. Elliot Mintz observed, 'There is no question that she was influenced by Paris. Her eyes were open, her ears were open, but that is a lot different from saying she made a conscious effort to imitate Paris. I don't think there was an agenda. She observed the phenomena happening to Paris at the time.' In the future, it would certainly be extraordinary how many aspects of the Kim Kardashian story would mirror the celebrity branding of Paris Hilton, whether consciously or unconsciously.

Paris adopted Kim as her companion for nights out to the fashionable clubs of Los Angeles. Nobody knew who Kim was – she was just referred to by Paris as 'my friend' and that is how everyone regarded her. She even appeared fleetingly in *The Simple Life*.

They have a boring conversation inside Paris's closet about an outfit that she might wear to visit India – her 'if-I-ever-go-to-India outfit'.

LEFT & BELOW: The young Kim Kardashian grew up happily in the rich and privileged world of Beverly Hills. Here she is sharing carefree moments with close friend Nikki Lund.

BOTTOM: Her family remained close after her mother remarried. From left to right: younger sister Khloé, older sister Kourtney, stepfather Bruce Jenner, mother Kris, Robert Jr and Kim.

Bruce already had four children of his own, so there were now eight youngsters and two adults to fit into family portraits. Kim is far right.

Salad days ... Newly married in 1991, Kris and Bruce were keen to promote keeping fit and eating healthily.

ABOVE: An Easter-egg hunt in Mexico, 1994. It was the last vacation with
'Uncle O. J.' Simpson and his wife Nicole (pictured together in the back row).
She was murdered two months later. Kim is front right.

RIGHT: Kim's father, Robert
Kardashian, became famous
defending O. J. at his murder
trial. At O. J.'s house after
the 'not guilty' verdict, they
still had plenty to talk about.

LEFT: Now a celebrity,
Robert arrives for the
Grammy Awards with his
then fiancée, Denice Halicki.

LEFT: Kim's first husband, Damon Thomas (pictured in shades with business partner Harvey Mason, Jr), was a cool record producer, but their Vegas marriage didn't prove to be happy ever after.

BELOW: Kim made *that* sex tape with hip-hop artist Ray J in 2003, and they were still together when they went to a fashion launch in March 2006.

ABOVE: Multi-talented TV host Nick Cannon was good fun for a couple of months. They strike a pose at a party for Kanye West at a New York restaurant in September 2006.

ABOVE: American football star Reggie Bush looked like he might be husband number two when they watched a basketball game in New Orleans in January 2010 ... But the couple split after dating for two and a half years.

LEFT: Paris Hilton was an old school friend whom Kim went to work for when she was a celebrity stylist. They both loved shopping and made sure their handbags were large enough.

ABOVE: Three of these celebrities took part in notorious sex tapes – Kim, her boyfriend at the time, Ray J, and Paris Hilton. Tennis great Serena Williams, a close friend of Kim's, is the odd one out.

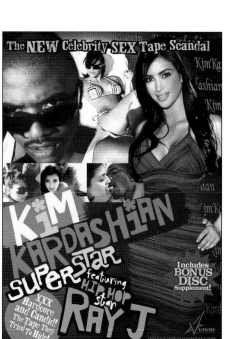

LEFT: The sex tape that launched a multi-million-dollar fortune. 'Kim Kardashian Superstar' was a premature description back in 2007, but not today.

Kim poses with her little sisters, Kylie (left) and Kendall Jenner, at a launch in October 2007 for *Keeping Up with the Kardashians* at the Chapter 8 restaurant in Agoura Hills, California.

My, how you've grown! Kendall and Kylie tower over Kim when they watch the MTV Awards together at The Forum in Inglewood, August 2014.

TOP LEFT: Kim is happy to be asked to the annual *Teen Vogue* Young Hollywood party at the Sunset Tower Hotel, Los Angeles in September 2006. She loved the grown-up magazine and this was the next best thing to being at one of its big fashion events.

TOP RIGHT: Kim looks gorgeous and almost demure in front of her first *Playboy* cover at a celebration party at the Retreat Club, New York, in November 2007. Not quite *Vogue* though ...

LEFT: Kim is serious and seriously chic at the inaugural Vogue Paris Foundation Gala at the Palais Galliera in July 2015 ... well it is *Vogue!*

The essential Kim Kardashian ...

Kim: You're not allowed to show any of your hair.

Paris: Are you allowed to have blonde hair? If you travel there, do you really have to do this?

Kim: I think so or you'll get shot.

An urban myth grew up that Paris Hilton ordered Kim Kardashian to 'clean out my closet'. Paris probably did ask Kim to clean out her closet at some point – after all, that was what she was originally paying her for – just not on film.

Elliot met Kim in the closet one day when Paris was trying on clothes to decide what to wear. He saw Kim at the house frequently and then she started to go out with them in the evenings. The old school friends were clearly pals, but Kim was always careful to get in the car after Paris and enter buildings a step behind her.

Elliot was very impressed by Kim, who was completely different to many of the entourage. 'She was low maintenance and undemanding. She was gracious. She was extremely polite. She was somewhat reserved. She would never create an embarrassment. She was not a drinker or substance abuser. She never got into arguments or quarrels with other people.

'She was also very punctual. If we were all going to some location at 10 p.m., then she would be at that spot at 10 p.m. If I told everyone that we were leaving in 10 minutes to avoid our car being followed by the press – perhaps at a service entrance – then Kim would be there 9 minutes and 50 seconds later.'

It's easy to understand why Kim was so well liked. She was the nice best friend in a movie, who was never going to embarrass the star – in this case, Paris Hilton. She wasn't the person handing out business cards or collecting them. This was her first exposure to a bona fide celebrity world and all its accompanying madness. She didn't reach into her handbag on evenings out, take out a Filofax and write notes.

If you look at many of the things she later attempted, they were tried first by Paris, with varying degrees of success. Elliot maintained, 'Paris is the mother of reality television. She created it.' It would be fair to say that *The Simple Life* brought the reality genre into the mainstream. It ran for five series, three with Fox and then two with E! before it was cancelled in July 2007.

The producer, Jonathan Murray, who would later be the man silently pulling the strings on *Keeping Up with the Kardashians*, wasn't entirely happy about his former show. 'With Paris and Nicole, we never reached the point where they would just trust us to shoot. It often felt like they were doing the light, fluffy story on our show, and then there would be this whole other story about them in the tabloids. For viewers, it began to feel like they got the truth from the tabloids rather than from the show.' Reading between the lines, it would seem that Murray was looking for a show that the public thought was more genuine.

11

VIVID IMAGINATION

With Smooch proving to be a success, Kourtney decided she wanted to expand and open another store – this time for grown-up women. She asked Khloé if she would like to be involved and her sister jumped at the opportunity. At first, they decided not to include Kim, who seemed busy with her own life and would have little time to help. Her work with Brandy and Paris was going well and she was trying to enhance her reputation as a personal stylist. She was also having her fair share of problems with Ray J.

Kim was offended that her sisters didn't appear to want her in their new venture and told them so. For the sake of family harmony, they invited her to join them. Her first priority, however, was making a name for herself. She opened a Myspace profile, using the sobriquet Princess Kimberly. She acquired 856 friends on the now outdated social networking site. Her mini bio read: 'I'm a Princess and you're not, so there.' She listed 'My Daddy' as her hero. It was an early, if underdeveloped, recognition that social networking was a vital ingredient in self-promotion.

Kourtney and Khloé basically ran the shop without her. When they found the premises around the corner from Smooch, they dragooned Bruce to do the shop-fitting and transform the place into the chic boutique they had in mind. They decided to call it DASH.

All the girls helped with choosing stock, but it was Khloé who took on the day-to-day running of the store, while Kourtney continued to look after Smooch. Kim would bring her friends and those employing her as a stylist to DASH and encourage them to buy clothes. It was an astute move, because she earned something from both ends of the deal.

Indirectly, the store led to her final breakup with Ray J. After nearly three years together, their relationship was going through a particularly rocky patch towards the end of 2005 and into 2006. Ray described what happened in a book called *Death of the Cheating Man: What Every Woman Must Know About Men Who Stray*, a collaboration with lifestyle guru Maxwell Billieon. Ray related how he suspected her of playing away, but was so caught up in his own straying that he didn't care. He said there had been a breakdown in trust and she seemed to be checking up on him at every opportunity: 'She literally thought I was cheating with every girl I ran across.'

He complained that 'KK' – as he referred to her in the book – seemed to know every time a girl called for him or left a voicemail message. It later dawned on him that she must have been checking his phone. He confessed, 'I used sex with other women to dull the pain and ease my conscience.'

The most dramatic incident came when he flew in from New York on Kim's twenty-fifth birthday. He'd planned to meet up with another woman before he went home to his girlfriend. When he landed, he discovered there was a message on his phone from Kim, who was far from happy: 'I know you're back in LA, you piece of shit!' she shouted, before telling him she never wanted to see or talk to him ever again. Ray went off to have 'fantastic' sex with the other woman before trotting home, where he patched things up, at least temporarily.

Then Kim fell out with Brandy over money. Ray didn't go into any details – it wasn't relevant to a discussion on cheating – but later Brandy's mother, Sonja Norwood, filed a lawsuit against Kim and her siblings for running up credit card charges without permission. Sonja alleged that in 2004 Kim had been authorised to make one purchase only on the Norwood American Express card in her capacity as Brandy's stylist. She claimed that Kim made unauthorised purchases and passed the card number on to her brother and sisters, who then also made unauthorised purchases, including items from their two stores, DASH and Smooch. The suit alleged the total amount charged was $120,636. Sonja was asking for the return of the money plus 10 per cent interest.

The Kardashians issued a statement: 'The charges against the Kardashians are meritless. Both Kim and Khloé were employed by the Norwoods and never used their credit cards without express authorisation. The Kardashian family looks forward to proving the absurdity of these claims in court.' Mrs Norwood, who told *People* magazine that the Kardashians had reneged on a promise to repay the debt, was also looking forward to her day in court.

In the event, neither party got their wish and the case was dismissed with prejudice, which meant that it couldn't be appealed or filed again. It was over permanently. Media reports described it as an 'apparent settlement', but the details remained confidential. Neither the Norwoods nor the Kardashians have subsequently commented on the lawsuit. Brandy and Kim are no longer friends and the singer was stony-faced when asked about Kim in a television interview in 2014.

Once she and Ray J were no longer an item, Kim was free to date whomever she chose. She couldn't help but notice that anyone Paris went out with was snapped by the paparazzi and appeared all over the magazines as a result. Such publicity would be gold dust for both her and, just as importantly, DASH.

In May 2006, she went to the movie *The Da Vinci Code* in Calabasas one afternoon with Nick Lachey at a time when his divorce from Jessica Simpson was going through. When they came out, there was a mass of photographers waiting to record the event. Nick was very unimpressed and would later imply that it was Kim who tipped them off. When he was asked if those shots sparked the start of her rise to stardom, he replied, 'That's one way to interpret it.'

He continued, 'Let's just say this. We went to a movie. No one followed us there. Somehow, mysteriously, when we left, there were 30 photographers waiting outside.' He added, 'There are certain ways to play this game, and some people play it well.'

The *New York Daily News* quoted a friend saying, 'She wanted to get her photo in the magazines and knew being seen next to Nick would be big news, since he had just ended his marriage. She was in communication with editors at the celebrity weeklies and provided them with details of the date to guarantee her spot in the limelight.'

Kim herself admitted that the date with Nick was her first taste of being the centre of attention. She said that people were curious about who he was with. The liaison with Nick Lachey, who wasn't really Kim's type, amounted to exactly nothing, but did get her name into the media. By itself, it wouldn't be enough to change things. It was just a brick in the wall at this stage.

The following night, Kim was with Paris as usual. The two of them went to their crowd's usual hangout, the Hyde nightclub on Sunset. In *Kardashian Konfidential*, she recalled that for the first time, as they arrived, the paparazzi shouted her name instead of her celebrity friend's. Paris may not have been best pleased at her companion stealing the show. Certainly, their friendship began to cool as Kim became better known.

Paris was already a paparazzi favourite before her sex tape was released, but there is little doubt that *1 Night in Paris* greatly enhanced her fame. Kim, too, had a sex tape, which, as Nick Lachey would say later, 'was already in the can'.

The pornography grapevine was aware that there was a new sex tape being offered around in the winter of 2006. Kim heard about it as well, but didn't believe the rumours. She even gave an interview to *Complex* magazine – her first front cover – in which she denied the existence of any tape. On her way back from a trip to New York, she took a call from Kourtney, who told her that the sex tape she had made with Ray J was now in the public domain.

The first thing she did was to go round to her mother's house and tell her everything. She broke down in floods of tears as she came clean about the existence of the tape – a startling confession from a young woman who neither drank nor did drugs, but tended to be impetuous where men were concerned. Kim was devastated that her most intimate moments with the boyfriend she loved might be seen by the whole world.

Kris Jenner was mortified when she realised the graphic nature of the tape: 'I cried myself to sleep. I don't think anything can prepare you for something like that when it comes to your daughter. I had to go into a room and cry for a couple of days and say, "OK, pull yourself to-fucking-gether!"'

They decided they needed to handle the situation – to try and gain some control over what was happening. It was the only sensible thing to do. They learned the tape was now in the hands of a company called Vivid Entertainment, one of the leading distributors of pornography in the US. Steve Hirsch, the Vivid chairman, announced the forthcoming release of the tape in February 2007. He said, 'We are comfortable we have the legal right to distribute this video no matter what others may say.'

Kim countered by telling the media of her intention to sue Vivid. She said, 'Everyone is pretty disappointed and very confused as to what's going on and who's behind this. We're just going to get to the bottom of this and do whatever we have to do to stop it.'

When the story appeared in *E! News*, Kim was described as one of Paris Hilton's closest friends, a socialite and the daughter of O. J. Simpson's defence attorney, Robert Kardashian, a stylist and fashion designer, and the stepdaughter of Bruce Jenner. It mentioned that she co-owned the boutique DASH in Calabasas. She was also going to be in an advertising campaign for the high-end clothing line Christopher Brian Apparel, it said. The 'actor-rapper' Ray J only merited a sentence, in which we learned he was the brother of Brandy and co-starred with her in the sitcom *Moesha*. In the media coverage, he was being left far behind, even though he was rumoured to be in a relationship with Whitney Houston. The article was a useful barometer for judging where Kim stood in terms of public recognition at the time.

The piece also mentioned Damon Thomas and said Kim had been linked to Nick Lachey, the rapper known as The Game (Jayceon Terrell Taylor) and Nick Cannon, the actor, rapper and TV presenter who went on to marry Mariah Carey. Cannon dated Kim between September 2006 and January 2007.

He described their breakup on *The Howard Stern Show*. He recalled that the sex tape was to blame: 'This was my issue. We talked about this tape ... and she told me there was no tape. If she had been honest with me, I might have tried to hold her down and be like, "That was before me", because she is a great girl.

'She's actually one of the nicest people you'll ever meet. But the fact that she lied ...'

That had been Kim's knee-jerk reaction when she first heard the rumours about her tape. If she denied it, the whole nightmare might go away. Now she was taking action. She filed a right to privacy lawsuit to try to stop the release of the DVD. Her complaint accused Vivid of 'egregious commercial exploitation and violation of Plaintiff's most personal and intimate sexual relations with her former boyfriend of three years.' She described the tape as being 'extremely hurtful not only to me, but to my family as well.'

Ray J seemed strangely on the sidelines while all this was going on, but he and Kim remained on good terms. She said she didn't suspect him of handing the tape over to the 'porn pedlars'.

Kim realized that she needed to talk to Vivid if she wanted to have any kind of control of the situation. This was common practice and made good sense for both sides, then at least there would be a fixed outcome and it would call a halt to paying expensive legal fees. Kim's lawyers must have told her that there was no guarantee of success when pursuing a legal claim, and, what's more, even if she were successful, a sex tape might take on a life of its own once it was leaked and couldn't be removed from the Internet. An agreement needed to be reached.

Kim was a novice in such matters, as was her mother, despite her astute handling of Bruce's affairs. The larger-than-life character Joe Francis, so claims a source, had a hand in helping Kim. He was the boss of the mild soft porn franchise Girls Gone Wild and a great friend of the Kardashian family. He had launched the brand in 1997 and it soon became a byword for young, attractive women, often tipsy, flashing their breasts and bottoms for the camera and generally whooping and hollering as they did so. It was a brilliant concept from a smart and savvy 24-year-old entrepreneur. His cameramen would go to all parts of the country, trawling bars and college parties for girls willing to participate. There was never a shortage of volunteers. The girls might well be taking their tops off at the end of a fun night in any case, so he was just tapping into what was already happening and giving it a nudge. The favourite hunting ground was the Easter vacation time in the US known as spring break, which is traditionally a chance for college students to let their hair down.

The franchise produced a variety of videos, all with *Gone Wild* in the title. One of the most popular was *Girls Gone Wild: Doggy Style*, hosted by none other than Ray's first cousin, Snoop Dogg. The brand was incredibly popular, because it was perceived as inoffensive high spirits and not pornography. There were no penises in *Girls Gone Wild*.

Joe was very much part of the Paris Hilton set that included Kim and would descend on the clubs of Hollywood for a good time in the evening. Invariably, Joe would be accompanied by a number of beautiful blondes. His parties at his Bel Air mansion were legendary and rivalled the *Playboy* ones for popularity. He was said to be earning $29 million a year from his business and had two private planes, which he was happy to lend to his friends.

Back in 2003, it was widely reported that he'd had a fling with Paris herself. He was, however, prone to be indiscreet. He was once asked on *The Howard Stern Show* who gave the best oral sex among his many celebrity conquests. He didn't hesitate: 'Paris is the best … Paris is amazing in bed … better than anyone.'

He also reportedly dated Kourtney, and did introduce her to the father of her three children, Scott Disick, in 2005. He was good friends with Kris Jenner, who found him entertaining and great company. He often flew the Kardashians around – to Las Vegas or Mexico.

He was involved in a long, drawn-out legal saga of his own that had begun in 2003 in Panama City, Florida. He had fallen foul of the authorities there, who took exception to him using the town as a venue for a spring break pay-per-view filming for Girls Gone Wild. Both his Ferrari and his Gulfstream jet were confiscated. The chain of events would end up costing him many millions, as well as his liberty. From March 2007, he would spend nearly a year in jail.

Before he was jailed, however, he was able to help and reassure Kim. Joe was already a friend of Steve Hirsch and would be able to bring all the parties to the table. A meeting was arranged at the Girls Gone Wild offices between Steve, Kim and Ray J to discuss a way forward.

Vivid is a much more hardcore company than Girls Gone Wild and there was certainly no shortage of penises in their productions. Steve is a very different character to the larger-than-life Joe, despite their friendship. A separate source who worked for Vivid observed, 'He was the antithesis of Joe Francis. He was very clean and sober. Steve was a businessman who understood financial opportunity. He was calculating and very smart.'

Girls Gone Wild already had a connection to Vivid through its website. They had a marketing agreement that if you were buying or browsing for something on the former's site, there was a link to buy something more hardcore from the latter. In the trade, it was known as an up-sale.

The source at Vivid explained, 'We used to describe the pornographic world in terms of narcotics. *Girls Gone Wild* and *Playboy* were cigarettes. Pretty soon, though, you would want a glass of whisky to go with that and that's when you came to Vivid. Pretty soon after that, you want to move on from whisky to marijuana and that's when you started getting into crazy Evil Angel hardcore and then, finally, you end up on heroin – watching the most disgusting things you can find.'

Kim's sex tape was definitely whisky, maybe taken with a little water, and much more suitable for distribution by a company like Vivid rather than Girls Gone Wild. Steve could see great possibilities for his company and was hugely keen to agree terms. According to a source at Girls Gone Wild who had sight of the agreement, Kim and Ray J received $300,000 each in respect of the tape. They would also receive a residual on videos sold or downloaded.

The lawsuit was duly dropped. Steve Hirsch said, 'We are pleased that Kim has dropped her legal action against us. We met with her several times and reached a financial arrangement that we both feel is fair … we've always wanted to work something out with Kim so she could share the profits.' Reports that she was paid $5 million to give up the suit were wildly inaccurate, although once again such inflated figures increased the value of the product in the public's mind. The source from Girls Gone Wild claimed, 'That was all a nonsense figure.'

Ironically, the media interest in the sex tape created by Kim's legal action was just the sort of publicity that would guarantee its success. The source said, 'The appeal has to be that you are watching some footage that was supposed to have been shot in the privacy of somebody's bedroom that's never been seen before. That is the whole allure – you are seeing something that you are not supposed to see.

'Filing a lawsuit created sensationalism and media frenzy. That's the only reason why anybody cared about this tape, quite frankly – because it was forbidden fruit. You know back then if Kim Kardashian had been hired by a pornographic company to do a video, nobody would have given it a second thought.

'The implication in the legal action was that the sex tape was so scandalous and risqué that she would go to any length to prevent you from seeing it. Unintentionally, it was really brilliant marketing.'

Vivid needed to prepare quickly for the release of the tape. A series of top-level meetings was held at the offices on Cahuenga Boulevard in Studio City. The company started buying up every single domain name that its staff could think of involving Kim K, Kim Kardashian sex tape and so on. This was essential so that any related online searches would be directed back to Vivid and the sale of the tape. It was a laborious, if inexpensive, exercise, but it still needed to be done for a successful launch. When you have a property like this particular sex tape, you don't just register one site and you have to include all the possible misspellings. They made sure they registered Kim Kardashian Superstar, which would be the eventual title of the tape. One did slip through the net, however. They failed to claim Kim K Sex Tape and this one had to be bought separately; it cost as much to capture and re-register as all the other 200 or so put together. Even then, it was more about time spent than the cost, which was no more than $2,500.

Meanwhile, one editor, working alone, started assembling the footage that Ray J had shot into a marketable form. This was somewhat problematic, as the tape was an old-style pre-digital VHS one; the images they put on the website the company had created for the tape were basically poor-quality screen grabs.

Steve Hirsch, a greatly admired figure in the world of pornography, had a knack for spotting something that might be big. When he got a sense of who Kim Kardashian was, he decided this was something the company should get behind with all its resources. Ostensibly, Ray J was still a bigger name, but it's always better from the marketing point of view to concentrate on the woman involved, the more vulnerable victim of circumstance. The interracial aspect of the film would add a certain frisson for the tape's buyers.

Steve's staff initially thought they were dealing with a hip-hop artist having sex with one of his dancers. It only dawned on them during the marketing process that Kim Kardashian was actually the star and not Ray J. He was able to keep a low profile, although he was spotted driving a swanky new Lamborghini around Hollywood, thanks to his windfall.

One of the benefits to Vivid of having secured an agreement with Kim was that it would have made it easy to deal with the legal requirements of Statute 2257. It's basically a law based around the minimum age requirement for participation in porn. Kim's age at the time of making the tape wasn't a problem – nor was there now any question of privacy violation. They had set up an agreement for adult programming with CinemaNow, an online movie site that allows filmmakers to distribute their films through streaming and downloads. They had the right to pre-sell the tape online so people could buy a digital copy in advance.

Everything went smoothly. A company source observed, 'It was one of the easiest, most successful roll-outs that Vivid ever did. It was one of those things where you always expect about four or five things to go wrong and almost nothing did.'

'It just caught fire,' observed the source at Girls Gone Wild. It was a money-printing machine. From the very beginning, Vivid was making $1.2 million a month from *Kim Kardashian Superstar* in online sales alone. Thanks to her royalty arrangement, Kim was on her way to becoming a very rich woman – a millionaire in her own right.

The media stories suggested that as part of the agreement with Kim, Vivid was going to stop distributing the tape at the end of May, which naturally signalled to potential buyers that they had better order it soon or miss out altogether. Eight years later, it is still the star attraction of the Vivid catalogue.

The tag line on the video case read '*Kim Kardashian Superstar* … she's 9½" from stardom'. It became clear within a couple of minutes that the number referred to Ray J's impressive credentials.

The film itself was a curious combination of pornography and inoffensive holiday footage. It began on the night before they set off for LAX to fly to Cabo San Lucas for her birthday. There are about five minutes of very energetic sex, with some bizarre dialogue that seems to come from a very bad porno film. Kim, face down on the pillow, comes out with such gems as: 'Baby, you are fucking me so good' and 'I want you to cum all over my face.' It's not the least romantic or loving.

Both Ray J and Kim spend the whole movie talking to the camera, which is evidently set up on a tripod. At the airport, Ray asks, 'Anything you want to tell your fans, Kim?' It's as if he is shooting a showreel of Kim, which might even have been the original point.

On the plane, he is in boisterous mood, speaking to the lens: 'Check it out. We are about to do *Girls Gone Wild in Cabo*, *Kimberly Gone Wild in Cabo*.'

Kim is unimpressed. 'Don't talk about *Girls Gone Wild in Cabo*.'

Ray J continues to lark about and taunt Kim: 'I'm saying that is what you said; you wanted to do *Girls Gone Wild* ... Oh, I'm bad, we record. I'm sorry.'

Kim tells him to shut up.

During the interminable middle section in Cabo, she does her make-up, wears a bikini, sips a piña colada, swims in an infinity pool, in which she and Ray J embrace, worries that she is looking chunky in her swimsuit, goes to a fun restaurant and hangs out in a club. It's all absolutely harmless.

All the time, Ray J provides a running commentary in quite a likeable fashion, and Kim looks stunning. He specifically says that it's a 'personal private video for only our eyes to see'. The film ends a year later with some graphic sex scenes in a hotel bedroom in Santa Barbara. She complains that her boobs are saggy, but she 'puts them up real nice'. They give each other plenty of oral sex, with Kim literally having to grab Ray J with both hands. There is one priceless moment when Ray J tries to film between Kim's legs. She hides her private parts with her hand and says, 'I'm shy.'

All in all, Kim earned a great deal of money for 15 minutes of sex on film. In any case, Ray J did all the work. The Kardashians have had to face many allegations over the years that they were complicit in the sale of the tape, but they have never wavered from their version of events. Despite issuing legal proceedings against Vivid, Kim had to deny the rumours she was actively involved. She told the *New York Daily News*, 'I'm not poor; I'm not desperate. I would never attempt to sell a tape. It would humiliate me and ruin my family. I have two successful businesses, and I don't need the money.'

Some have suggested that she was just copying Paris Hilton or even that Paris herself encouraged her. Kim's former boyfriend Nick Cannon told Howard Stern that he suspected Kim of having something to do with the release of the tape, 'I still think she might have even had a part to play ...' He wasn't alone in thinking that.

Kim continues to be asked about the sex tape, year after year. She admitted to Oprah Winfrey that *Kim Kardashian Superstar* introduced her to the world, but she regretted it was in a 'negative way'.

The public interest will never go away, but the circumstances of its release into the world revealed that behind her obvious beauty and physical attributes, Kim was a powerful and strong-willed woman capable of taking control of her destiny. She spoke of it yet again in *Rolling Stone* magazine in July 2015: 'I thought about it for a long time. But when I get over something, I get over it.'

12

KEEPING UP WITH KIM

Kim was not the first Kardashian to follow in the footsteps of Paris Hilton. Her elder sister Kourtney was one of the stars of the 2005 E! reality show *Filthy Rich: Cattle Drive*, which was a blatant rip-off of *The Simple Life*, with a large helping of the hit film *City Slickers* thrown in. Intriguingly, it was Kim who appeared in the original trailer for the show, worried about what she was going to do without a hairdryer in the rugged Colorado landscape. In the short clip, she also asks, 'Are there showers there?'

In the end, though, Kim didn't do the show and it was Kourtney who set off with nine other offspring of wealthy parents to sample the delights of Steamboat Springs. At least she had a familiar face with her. Her best friend from school, Courtenay Semel, was also making her TV debut. She was the daughter of Terry and Jane Semel, who had hosted Kris and Bruce's marriage in 1991. She was very keen for the eldest Kardashian to join her when she was cast in the show.

One of the other young women was Brittny Gastineau, the daughter of the New York Jets footballer Mark Gastineau, whom she hadn't seen for many years. Brittny had already starred in another short-lived reality show for E! called *The Gastineau Girls*. Kourtney thought that Brittny would get on well with Kim and introduced them after the show had finished. She was right, because they became best friends.

During the eight-week series, the five boys and five girls were divided into two teams and made to compete against each other for rewards. The losers got nothing – a basic reality show tactic. Among the more interesting tasks was munching on bull's testicles and giving a cow a rectal examination, which basically meant sticking your entire arm up a cow's backside – perhaps that's what put Kim off.

The show ran from August until October 2005, but wasn't picked up for another season. That may well have been because E! had acquired *The Simple Life* after it had been dropped by Fox. There seemed little point in continuing both shows: they were too similar and Paris Hilton was a better prospect. None of the show's cast did particular well afterwards. Brittny became best known for her friendship with Kim, while Courtenay ended up in rehab and was a target for Hollywood gossips because of her many alleged gay affairs. She said stories of flings with both her friend Lindsay Lohan and Paris were false. In an interview with *Curve*, the bestselling US lesbian magazine, however, she said, 'I'd like to say that I'm kind of the Don Juan of the lesbian world.'

Kourtney hadn't seemed the most natural performer in front of the cameras, but the relative failure of *Filthy Rich: Cattle Drive* didn't put off the rest of the clan. Bruce Jenner was often on television as himself, popping up in an Olympians edition of *Weakest Link* and as a judge on *Pet Star*, the search for America's most talented pet. Most notably, he was a contestant in the US version of *I'm a Celebrity … Get Me Out of Here!* In the 2003 season, set in New South Wales, Bruce just missed being in the final three and was the seventh celebrity to be voted out of the jungle. The winner was Cris Judd, who would inadvertently cause some difficulties for Kim in her marriage that year. *I'm a Celeb* didn't fare well in the US, not helped by problems with the live link, caused by the time difference with Australia.

Brody and Brandon Jenner, the sons from Bruce's marriage to Linda Thompson, had starred in their own reality show on Fox called *The Princes of Malibu* in 2005. It wasn't a success, although the premise was quite fun. Their mother spoiled them and thought they could do no wrong, while their stepfather, David Foster, wanted them to get proper jobs and behave responsibly.

Fox cancelled the show after screening only two of the six episodes that had been filmed. Linda had filed for divorce from Foster the day after the show premiered, which wasn't the best timing. Brody moved on to a coming-of-age reality series called *The Hills*. It was a follow-up to the popular *Laguna Beach: the Real Orange County* and followed a group of rich young people making their way in Los Angeles. *The Hills* did well, although it received some criticism for appearing too scripted. Perhaps what was needed in the overcrowded reality marketplace was a combination of the two shows – the drama of a family and the chaos of young (rich) lives.

E! was just one of the networks desperate to find a winning formula. They didn't realise that exactly what they were looking for was on their doorstep – well, almost – in Hidden Hills,

Calabasas. Kris Jenner has always credited the casting director Deena Katz for realising that the mad family life of the Kardashians would make great TV after she was at the house for dinner one night. Deena had worked on *Big Brother* and *Pet Star*. She arranged a professional introduction to Ryan Seacrest, the host of *American Idol*, and the president of his production company, Eliot Goldberg. They successfully pitched the idea to E! Importantly, the company brought in to oversee everything and handle the daily production of the programme was Bunim/Murray, which was responsible for two of the biggest reality successes, *The Real World* and *The Simple Life*.

One of the recurring illusions surrounding the Kardashian family is the way they never seem to have to go to the lengths most wannabes have to in order to succeed. The endless phone calls, being placed on hold, waiting in reception and rejection emails seem to pass them by.

Conspiracy theorists believe that E! commissioned the show based on Kim's new sex tape fame. The timing is very tight in terms of which came first – a true chicken or egg situation. Television experts believe that E! wouldn't have placed a bet on an untried television programme when nobody knew what the public reaction to the tape might be. What E! did successfully was harness the media interest in Kim and use it to their advantage.

Filming for the first episode began with Kris and Bruce's sixteenth wedding anniversary on 21 April 2007. The news that she was dropping legal proceedings against Vivid Entertainment was reported nine days later, on 30 April. By then, the sex tape was already a huge success. A few weeks later, television media started reporting that the star of the graphic sex tape was to feature in a new reality show.

The sex tape alone wasn't enough of a hook to promote Kim and she was still referred to as Paris Hilton's best pal and Bruce's stepdaughter. However, the press material did say that the new series would focus on her family life and pointed out that she had nine brothers and sisters in total.

This didn't give entirely the right impression, as the older Jenner children had very little to do with their father during his marriage to Kris. His eldest son, Burt, for instance, told *Vanity Fair* that he didn't remember seeing his father more than twice a year for roughly a decade. Brandon went through periods of two or three years of not hearing from his dad. When the Northridge earthquake hit the Los Angeles area in January 1994, Brandon, then 12, told his mother that Bruce had called to check they were all right. She was delighted that he had rung, until Brandon confessed, 'Mom, I'm just kidding.' While he was undoubtedly a caring father to Kendall and Kylie, he didn't attend the high school graduations of his older children. He said he wasn't invited, while they maintain that he was.

There was a chasm in the family no matter whose recollection is correct. A reality show about all things Kardashian was hardly likely to improve that. The split between the two branches of Bruce's family wouldn't sit well in a show that was all about 'family' and the bond that existed between them whatever was going on in their crazy world.

The family theme would develop as the series progressed. For the moment, they needed Kim's new-found notoriety to perk up interest in the show. In the months leading up to the autumn premiere, it was important to keep Kim in the public eye. She made it onto a list of the top ten bottoms in Hollywood, but at position number eight was well behind the winner, Jennifer Lopez, and the runner-up, Beyoncé.

She also had to refute a rumour that among the out-takes of her tape with Ray J was one in which she received what is known in the sex trade as a golden shower. 'I'm not knocking anyone else,' she said, 'but I've never personally participated in that. I think it's degrading.'

The publicity leading up to the launch seemed to involve either sex or Kim's bottom. She had to counter allegations that hers had been surgically enhanced since the sex tape days. Finally, if you had missed the sex tape and the bountiful back-side, there was still time for it to be announced that Kim was going to be on the cover of the December issue of *Playboy* in a 12-page picture spread personally chosen by Hugh Hefner.

Unsurprisingly, the first-ever episode of *Keeping Up with the Kardashians*, which was broadcast on 14 October 2007, focused heavily on Kim and her rear in particular. The opening scene is a picture of her from behind, leaning over to get something out of the fridge. Her ass looks enormous, certainly several sizes bigger than when she was filmed with Ray J.

Kris says in an aside to the family, 'I think she has a little junk in the trunk.' That gives rise to some banter and a half-hearted 'I hate you all' from Kim. It is Kim who addresses the audience, 'Welcome to my family. I am Kim Kardashian ...' Kris introduces herself as Kim's manager, not everyone's.

For the opening credits, Kim is late for the family shot and then arrives wearing a knockout red dress that completely overshadows the others. In the episode, Kim has been asked to appear on *The Tyra Banks Show* in New York and her mother tells her she will be asked about the sex tape. Kris, speaking directly to the camera, says, 'As her mother I wanted to kill her, but as her manager I knew I had a job to do and I really wanted her to move past it.'

Kim explains, 'That was with my boyfriend of three years and whatever we did in our private time was our private time and never once did we think it was going to get out.'

In an amusing scene, Kourtney pretends to be Tyra and asks her why she did it. Kim replies, 'Because I was horny and I felt like it.' She goes off to record the show in New York, taking her friend Brittny Gastineau along for moral support. Disappointingly, we never see any footage of Kim's first TV interview.

We are introduced to the other members of the family, although only fleetingly to the son, Robert. Much more airtime is given to Kourtney's handsome and tanned boyfriend, Scott Disick, whom Kris doesn't trust.

The critical response to the show tended to be more negative than positive. The reviewer in the *New York Times* said, '*Keeping Up with the Kardashians* is, as the title suggests, a window into a family – a family that seems to understand itself only in terms of its collective opportunism.' She added that the show was about 'some desperate women climbing to the margins of fame.' *Daily Variety* online observed, 'Once you get past Kim's prominently displayed assets, there's not much of a show here, and no discernible premise.'

The rest of the series relied heavily on the physical attributes of the female cast. In the second episode, Kris hires a nanny to help at the house and look after Kendall, 11, and

Kylie, aged 10. She turns out to be a stunning blonde and completely inappropriate. The gag of the episode is that Kris hasn't met her and doesn't know how unsuitable she is. Bruce, settling into his role as the long-suffering dad, quickly realises that when he sees her sunbathing topless. When Kris does finally meet her, she quickly shows her the door in a plot involving some stolen jewellery. The nanny was quite obviously an actress hired for the occasion and not, as Kris said in the show, hired from a 'reputable agency'.

She was, in fact, Bree Olson, then an up-and-coming porn star, who would later become one of the best known and most applauded in the business. In 2006 alone, she had made 16 films, including *Young As They Cum 21* and *Cock Craving Cuties*. In 2007, she made 75, and *Keeping Up with the Kardashians*.

Casting directors often turn to actresses in the porn world when they want to find someone to play a super-sexy vixen completely at ease with taking off her clothes. In this episode, Bree, more a cute blonde than a siren figure, unselfconsciously removes her top at the pool.

Bree was hired for one day and spent 15 hours being filmed at the house. In the end, her footage amounted to little more than five minutes. This is the reality of the reality. The cameras are on the Kardashians all the time to see how they react to a situation that is often manufactured. Khloé was particularly outspoken in this instance, declaring on the phone to Kris, 'Mom, there is a whore watching your children.'

Bree, who is an intelligent and articulate young woman, didn't mind. She laughed, 'I'm surprised it wasn't worse.' It was the reaction she was hired to generate. The producers told

Bree exactly what to do, but the family was unscripted and allowed to roam free. She was instructed to help the youngsters with their homework, but to do a really bad job at it. She was also told to go into Kris's closet and try on her jewellery.

The youngest members of the cast, Kendall and Kylie, seemed the most unaffected by what was going on around them and shrugged off the cameras. When filming stopped, they went on their computer to show Bree a puppy they were excited about getting. When the producers sent Bree down to the pool to sunbathe, the girls followed and made her play poolball for an hour.

Bree enjoyed her day and was happy to be part of it. Each of the cast gave her a hug goodbye. 'They were super nice,' she said. In 2011, Bree, who has given up the porn business, achieved headlines as one of actor Charlie Sheen's girlfriends, or 'goddesses' as he liked to call them.

The third episode indirectly involved more porn, when the girls were hired for a photo shoot to model a new swimsuit range for Girls Gone Wild – not traditionally what the franchise was known for. Joe Francis had apparently phoned Kris to hire the girls and fly them down to his luxurious private estate, Casa Aramita, in Punta Mita, Mexico. He couldn't appear himself, because he was in jail in Florida. A company insider recalled, 'We decided it would be great publicity for both sides if the Kardashians were involved. We were going to fly a designer, Ashley Paige, to Mexico and the girls were going to try on the bathing suits and contribute, as if they had helped create them, and the E! cameras would follow along. It would all culminate with a billboard on Sunset Boulevard of the Kardashians in bathing suits. It was completely contrived.'

The billboard did appear, but the swimwear line was very short-lived. Buyers began to cancel orders when it became common knowledge that Joe was in jail. It did provide some lovely television moments, as Bruce had to pretend to be outraged and follow them to the location. Again, the plot line was an excuse to put Kim and her sisters in skimpy clothing. Kris and her daughters all agreed that it was 'classy'.

In the fourth episode, *Playboy* rang up to ask Kim to appear on the cover. The sex tape was forgotten as Kim hesitated about whether to do it or not, although there wouldn't have been much of a plot if she hadn't. Again, it was deemed 'classy'. Kim explained, 'It was something that I felt really nervous about doing at first … It's not a nude photo shoot by any stretch. It is not as revealing as some people might want. I keep it classy and covered up. I do bare my whole butt. And a little bit of my chest. But that's it.'

Kim looked sensational for the shoot. Her modesty was protected by a strategically placed large string of beads. When the issue came out, she was wearing a lovely red swimsuit on the cover. The headline wasn't at all subtle, though, and declared: 'Hollywood's New Sex Star Kim Kardashian Takes It All Off'.

The strategy of promoting Kim in these first few episodes worked. E! said the programme had already reached 13 million viewers. Young women, aged 18 to 34, were hooked on the show. The vice-president of the television company who was in charge of series development, Lisa Berger, enthused, 'The buzz around the series is huge.' After just a month on air, *Keeping Up with the Kardashians* was renewed for a second season.

Kim did well in another poll in 2007. In December, the *New York Daily News* published a list of the 'Top 50 Dumbest People in Hollywood'. Lindsay Lohan placed first and Kim was second. She would soon be proving everybody completely wrong.

13

DANCING PRINCESS

For a man who could sprint 50 metres up a football field in little more than 5 seconds, Reggie Bush was slow out of the blocks with Kim. She couldn't believe that the star running back with the New Orleans Saints didn't ask for her number when they met at the 2006 ESPY sports awards.

In July, she accompanied Bruce Jenner for the evening at the Kodak Theatre in Hollywood. She was definitely interested when she saw the handsome, well-muscled young man sitting with Matt Leinart. Kim knew Matt well, because he was dating Paris Hilton, and he was happy to introduce her to Reggie, who had been his college teammate at her father's old alma mater, USC. Kim recalled that first meeting: 'My first impression of Reggie was "This guy is so quiet. Why is he not taking my number?" Matt tried to set us up, but it took a while.'

It took months. Reggie was only 21, whereas Kim was a 25-year-old divorcee. Despite already being a millionaire, he might have been overawed by her. Eventually they agreed to a date, but it wasn't the romantic experience she was hoping for. They arranged to meet at a car wash, before heading off for a meal at Chipotle Mexican Grill on Wilshire Boulevard.

After their relationship eventually went public in the spring of 2007, they quickly became one of the top celebrity couples in Los Angeles. Reggie maintained a bachelor apartment in Beverly Hills, where Kim was now living. She had bought a condo in South Clark Drive. So when *Keeping Up with the Kardashians* began, Kim was no longer in Calabasas, preferring to be nearer her friends, even though it meant a dull drive along the freeway to get to work.

Reggie had had a modest upbringing in the San Diego area. His mother was a deputy sheriff at a correctional centre and his stepfather was a security guard at a local high school. His biological father, Reginald Alfred Bush, Sr, had split from his mother before Reggie was born and had very little to do with him growing up.

Reggie was arguably the USC Trojans' best-known player since O. J. Simpson. In 2005, he too won the Heisman Trophy and a host of other awards, but became a controversial figure following allegations that he and his family received improper benefits while he was an amateur player at the university. He returned the Heisman voluntarily in 2012 and sanctions were imposed on USC by the NCAA, the National Collegiate Athletic Association. Robert Kardashian would have been horrified.

Those off-field problems didn't stop Reggie from becoming one of the richest young sportsmen in the country after he signed with the New Orleans Saints as a top NFL draft pick. He was a good role model for Kim in that he signed endorsement deals with Pepsi, Adidas, Pizza Hut, Subway and

General Motors – making an estimated $5 million. In a three-year period with the Saints, 2007–2010, he earned a reported $27.5 million for starting 27 games. That was close to $1 million every time he put his helmet on. *Forbes* magazine didn't consider him value for money and included him in their list of the NFL's biggest salary flops.

The problem for Kim and Reggie as their relationship developed was the most common one faced by celebrity couples: how to survive long absences brought about by conflicting schedules. Kim was tied to *Keeping Up with the Kardashians* and he was living in New Orleans for six months of the year.

She did her best to fly in regularly, and particularly enjoyed their domestic time together, when they played board games or lay in bed watching television. Kim isn't a woman who wants to dress up and look fabulous all the time. She was content just to relax with her boyfriend. She would have been quite happy to have stayed at home and raised a family with her first husband and that remained an aspiration.

Kim, it seemed, has a nurturing spirit. Even with Ray J, when they weren't having sex, she kept a clean and tidy house and made sure his clothes were immaculate. She was impressed with Reggie's fashion sense, but that didn't stop her from taking him shopping and picking out what he should wear. Being a stylist was what she did best.

Kim once made the plaintive observation that she had too often been cheated on and had her heart broken. She wasn't including Reggie in that list and was looking forward to settling down with him. When Tyra Banks asked her, in a 2008 interview, if she would marry Reggie if he asked her tomorrow, she replied without hesitation, 'Of course I would ... We have such a good relationship. He gets along with everyone in my family.' She was in love.

She did her best to be the dutiful WAG to her high-profile boyfriend, but admitted, 'I'm not really a sports girl. But I sit with all the wives and they know everything and I don't, so they are teaching me ... I don't really watch if he's not playing. I'm not that big of a football fan yet.'

The trade-off for Kim taking an interest in football was that Reggie had to appear in her reality show. He wasn't especially keen on having the cameras follow him around, but he did it because it was important to Kim. He had been on television before, playing himself in the series *The Reggie Bush Project*, in which his biggest fan sets off on a mission to meet his idol.

Inevitably, Reggie was asked about the sex tape. He was philosophical: 'We don't talk about it, and we don't think about it. With Kim, and with anybody in life, it's not my place to judge, no matter what they've done – good, bad or indifferent.'

The couple seemed like the perfect fit when they were out together, usually smiling and holding hands. The media decided that only the Beckhams generated more star power as a sporting/celebrity couple. This interest meant that Kim had to counter the usual pregnancy and wedding rumours: 'I am not pregnant. I am definitely going to wait until I am married before I get pregnant. Marriage is soon, but I would say five years away. I have to get engaged first. I would say in about a year. You know, we are taking our time and he's young and I don't want to rush into anything.'

* * *

Kim was keen to embrace every new opportunity that came about because of her television exposure. It is a tried and trusted route for reality stars – one season they are on *The X Factor* and the next on *I'm a Celebrity*; they appear in *Celebrity Big Brother* and then try *Celebrity MasterChef*; a good run in *Strictly Come Dancing* leads to a part in a West End musical. One opportunity provides a window for another.

Kim, encouraged by her mother, was determined to exploit her status as the star of *Keeping Up with the Kardashians*. The first thing she wanted to try was acting. As she made clear, it wasn't a prospect she relished: 'I promised myself that this year I would do things that are kind of outside of my comfort zone.'

She was true to her word when she appeared in a bizarre video for the Fall Out Boy single 'Thnks fr th Mmrs', taken from their number one US album *Infinity on High*. Understandably, after the sex tape, she had received plenty of offers to play the hot girl riding in a car with a cool singer. She turned them all down, but her interest was piqued by the rock band's storyline: it was about the making of a video in which every character other than Kim and the band was played by a chimpanzee.

She was very nervous about performing her scenes. The closest she had got to an ape previously was at Neverland and now she had to act with a whole gang of them. It didn't help when their trainer told her not to look them in the eye or call them by name. She sat alongside them and was told not to move, which was 'basically freaking her out'. 'It was really scary because they are so strong and you don't know what they are going to do.'

In the video, Kim was the love interest of the band's resident heart-throb, bassist and songwriter, Pete Wentz. She already knew Pete, which made filming a little easier, but she had never met the chimpanzee who was playing the director. She explained, 'We had to have a make-out scene and the director, played by the chimp, kept on saying that Pete was doing it wrong. He tried to step in and show him how to kiss me. He touches me and Pete gets angry and runs off.' Kim, looking ravishing in a Marilyn Monroe-style frock, follows him to the dressing room, where they have a proper kiss, which she found almost as nerve-racking as the chimp's.

The video was different and refreshing, though it was hardly likely to further her ambition of starring in a James Bond movie. Kim wanted to film a love scene with Daniel Craig. As she pictured it: 'I would be drowning, wearing a bikini with a gun in a sachet, and he would dive in and get me.' She evidently saw herself as a mixture of Ursula Andress and Halle Berry.

Kim didn't get Bond, but she did make her first film, which, with supreme irony, was called *Disaster Movie*. It came fourteenth in an *Empire* online poll of the 50 worst films ever. Kim auditioned and was cast as Lisa Taylor, one of the main female roles, by the writer/director partnership of Jason Friedberg and Aaron Seltzer, who were responsible for other parodies, including *Date Movie* and *Meet the Spartans*.

The basic plot was that a number of reality television stars, including Kim, play characters who, while trying to deal with an end-of-the-world meteor strike, keep bumping into characters from other films, as in 'Look, it's Indiana Jones'. The highlight for male Kim fans was a spurious wrestling match with Carmen Electra, the former star of *Baywatch*, who was also a cover girl for *Playboy*. Kim's character survived the busty bout, but is subsequently killed when she is hit by an asteroid, which looked suspiciously like an enormous cheese boulder, falling unexpectedly out of the sky. The scene is actually very funny.

The reviews were poor. Nobody seemed to get the joke. The *Observer* reviewer said: 'it would be the Worst Movie Ever Made were it actually a movie at all.' He thought there wasn't a single laugh in it. The *Independent* commented, '*Disaster Movie* isn't so much a film as an insult to moviegoers everywhere.' The *New York Times* said the film had a shelf-life of five minutes, 'which may be longer than it took with most of its gags.' The film, which cost $20 million to make, grossed an estimated $31.7 million worldwide, so it wasn't a complete box-office flop, though obviously a disappointment.

Kim received her first award nomination – not for an Oscar but a Razzie for Worst Supporting Actress in 2008. She took it with good humour: 'There is steep competition in my "worst supporting actress" category, I have to admit, including my fantastic co-star Carmen Electra (you go, girl!).' In the end, the award went to Paris Hilton for *Repo! The Genetic Opera*.

Undaunted by the failure of her acting debut, Kim moved on to dancing. Family friend Deena Katz was now the senior talent producer on *Dancing with the Stars* and she picked Kim for the new series. Initially she wasn't too keen, but it seemed a great opportunity to be showcased on one of the big networks. At the time, the ABC blockbuster was the top-rated show on American television, pulling in more than 15 million viewers. *Keeping Up with the Kardashians* was the most popular on E! with just 1.6 million.

Kim and her reality series were set to receive many weeks of extra publicity. The challenge confronting her was that she had never really danced before and wasn't a natural. She wasn't one of those stage school graduates who found remembering their dance steps easy. Kim had never had lessons and had to practise day and night so she wouldn't embarrass herself. On the very first show, she revealed her problem was that she had terrible balance. It couldn't have helped wearing such high heels. She observed, 'Elegance and clumsiness don't mix. It isn't easy for me.'

She did gain some advantage, however, by being paired with the reigning professional champion, Mark Ballas. Their opening dance was a foxtrot to the *Pink Panther* theme. It was perhaps not the best choice of number, as it is normally associated with the bumbling Inspector Clouseau rather than anything smooth and sexy. She looked surprisingly slim in an elegant purple dress, with her hair in a 1920s Coco Chanel bob. She had worn it in a similar style at her eighth-grade graduation, when she was 13. The leading fashion commentator Alison Jane Reid said, 'I really like Kim in retro mode. Her hair in a bob accentuates her cheekbones and amazing doe eyes. The dress is classic showgirl – very elegant, with a liberal sprinkling of sequins and side splits, so she can show off her fabulous pins.'

To Kim's relief, she kept her feet and made few errors. The audience was cheering afterwards, especially Bruce and Kris. The judges were not so enthusiastic. Len Goodman thought the dance cold and said there was no chemistry between her and Mark. Bruno Tonioli told her, 'You have to make it more available', and that she needed to bring the audience with her. The more charitable Carrie Ann Inaba said she needed to move her neck more, because keeping it so still was preventing eye contact. She scored 19 points out of 30, which was enough to keep her in for another night.

The next evening, she and Mark were the last couple to dance the mambo. She admitted that everyone was going to expect her to be sexy, but that wasn't really her, particularly where her shapely rear was concerned. 'Everyone thinks I know how to shake my butt and I really don't!' Kim looked to be concentrating so hard that she forgot to feel the music. She found it difficult to find a rhythm to 'Baby Got Back' by Sir Mix-a-Lot. Mark danced frenetically to compensate for Kim's uneasiness, but the judges liked it even less than the foxtrot.

She needed to improve the following week for the rumba. Her friend Robin Antin, the choreographer of Pussycat Dolls, was brought in to try and cajole her to move more sexily. Once more, she looked fabulous in a white dress that highlighted her curves, but the judges were unimpressed. Bruno unkindly said she was colder and more distant than Siberia. Both *Dancing with the Stars* and the UK equivalent, *Strictly Come Dancing*, are more about forging a connection with the audience than the ability to look sensational in a frock. It's not just about trying hard, but showing improvement. Kim wasn't doing that, and the viewers voted her out.

She was the third contestant to be eliminated, but in real terms had lasted only one week on the show – a huge disappointment. It was still a surprise, because she came across as genuinely nice and modest. She had the natural charm of a girl enjoying her prom night. The producers must have been seething, because she brought so much glamour and interest to the show. Afterwards, she was gracious: 'Every dance was a huge accomplishment for me, and I did the best I could.'

One of the show's hosts, Samantha Harris, said, 'Everyone told me that getting to know her outside of the tabloids and the reality show has been so refreshing, since Kim is such a sweetheart. I feel the same way.' Mark also said she was a great girl, while observing that 'dancing was not her thing'. Her family obviously rallied round, but the best comment came from Bruce: 'She had a lot of guts to say yes to do this show with no dance background at all. Success is not measured by heights attained, but by obstacles overcome.'

After her disappointing debuts as an actor and a dancer, it seemed inevitable that Kim would try her hand at singing. Her first husband, Damon Thomas, had frequently told his beautiful wife that she should give it a go, and he wasn't the only record producer keen for her to make a disc. She didn't rush into anything, but waited for what she hoped would be the right project.

One way for the Kardashians to release information is for certain websites to carry a rumour. In this case, TMZ, one of the preferred outlets, started the whisper in the autumn of 2010 that she was in the studio working with the superstar producer known as The-Dream (Terius Youngdell Nash). He had co-written two of the biggest hits of recent years, 'Umbrella' by Rihanna and the Grammy-winning Beyoncé track 'Single Ladies (Put a Ring on It)'. An anonymous insider helpfully said that Kim had a really good voice.

At first, the stories suggested that she was recording an album. They gained credibility when Kanye West was seen entering the building in Culver City, where they were shooting the video for the first single. Nobody knew the title yet, but apparently it was written by The-Dream. The acclaimed director Hype Williams was brought in to oversee the filming.

Hype had worked closely with Kim before. He had shot the photograph for her 2007 *Playboy* cover and had made her look sensational. He also worked closely with Kanye West, winning a BET (Black Entertainment Television) Video Director of the Year Award for 'Gold Digger'. He made so many of the rap artist's videos, they were practically a team. He was also responsible for the videos of a who's who of modern pop culture, including Jay Z, Babyface, Nicki Minaj, Beyoncé and John Legend.

Kim couldn't have had three bigger hitters on her team than The-Dream, Kanye West and Hype Williams. As a bonus, the recording adventure was filmed for her spin-off reality series *Kourtney and Kim Take New York*. Kim had trouble with her vocals and at one point had to leave the studio to compose herself. The resulting single 'Jam (Turn It Up)' was played on the radio for the first time during Ryan Seacrest's morning show on KIIS FM, which was practically keeping it in the family.

The reviews were uninspiring. The *Liverpool Echo* critic wrote, 'I'm her biggest fan, but her new song is so cheesy! I think she should stick to what she knows best.' The *New York Daily News* was the most unpleasant, saying that Kim was the worst singer ever to come out of a reality series. The reviewer called 'Jam (Turn It Up)' a 'dead-brained piece of generic dance music, without a single distinguishing feature.' He wasn't any kinder about her singing, which he thought 'a bit of breathing that's been auto-tuned into something vaguely approximating a vocal.'

The track was nothing like as bad as that. The overall sound came across as retro, harking back to the catchy Scandinavian sounds of the late nineties chart band Aqua. Sales weren't strong enough for the song to reach even the lower echelons of the charts in the US, with only 14,000 downloads in its first week on iTunes.

For some reason, the video was never released. Kim posted some stills. Six months later, some footage did show up of Kim in a white top and hot pink shorts, writhing around suggestively. The implication was that the video was completed with a view to being released only if the song performed well.

Kim quickly distanced herself from the project, maintaining that there was no record deal and there would be no album. Both Kourtney and Khloé said the video was for their sister's eyes only, which made it sound like it was a sex tape. The celebrity gossip columnist Perez Hilton pointed out sarcastically that she had hired Hype Williams, practically the biggest name in the business, to produce a video just for private use.

For once, Kim's sense of humour failed her. Several years later, in 2014, she called the song a fun experience, but something she shouldn't have done. She confessed, 'What gave me the right to think I could be a singer? Like, I don't have a good voice.'

Despite her hopes for the future, her relationship with Reggie Bush had foundered. She had been so positive about it. They first admitted to problems in the summer of 2009, and put them down to spending too much time apart. Kim couldn't give up her life and career in Los Angeles, where *Keeping Up with the Kardashians* was filmed: 'It's not going to be much of a show if I'm in New Orleans separated from my family.' For his part, Reggie seemed unable to make the commitment to the future that Kim was looking for.

They managed to rekindle the romance later that year, and Kim was thrilled when the Saints won the Super Bowl in February 2010. The E! cameras filmed her running on to the pitch to give her man a kiss of congratulations. That made it seem a little staged, especially as her mother was in attendance.

By the end of March, it was all over for the second time. She had been genuinely fond of Reggie, but he was no longer a priority in her life. She was determined to work even harder and make the most of her chance of lasting fame.

14

DATING HER WORK

────────

Kim was getting a reputation for being a workaholic. She was completely driven to make her business a success. She observed, 'You have to stay committed. Some people start and stop, or get a bit lazy. Every year my mom and I write out a goal sheet.' Her elder sister Kourtney commented, 'She's dating her work.'

When *Keeping Up with the Kardashians* began, only Kris took it as seriously as Kim did. Kim was desperate for it to do well, while her sisters viewed themselves as store owners dabbling in television. They would fool around when the 'boss', as they called Kim, wasn't in the room. They would be jumping on the sofas and pushing each other about like a pair of playful puppies.

Kim and her mother were busy forging a formidable partnership. They were both proving to be smart businesswomen. It would have been lovely for Kim to have been nominated for an Oscar instead of a Golden Raspberry, or to have won *Dancing with the Stars*, but neither was meant to be. The consolation was that she was keeping herself in the conversation.

She was being talked about at water coolers, even when she failed at something.

It was as if Kim stood in front of a mirror and decided how best to utilise every bit of herself from top to bottom and head to toe. She would take every opportunity that came her way and make sure she was personally involved and not just a celebrity robot. An endorsement for ShoeDazzle, another for Famous Cupcakes and a fitness DVD were just the start of her empire building.

As her fame grew, so did her confidence and, more and more, she became her own woman. She embraced social media and was rumoured to be paid as much as $10,000 for announcing on Twitter that she liked a particular salad. She told her then 2.7 million followers at the start of 2010: 'The Carl's Jr. grilled chicken salads came out yesterday! I'm on my way to Carl's Jr. for lunch now … Have you tried them yet?'

The parent company behind the campaign, CKE Restaurants, said, 'Kim is an absolute Internet sensation and she has a vast audience that is already following her online. Her site is heavily trafficked as well.' They wanted to target 'young, hungry guys and gals' – exactly the people who followed her online and on the show. She even hosted 'The Ultimate Salad Lunch Date', in which she interacted with fans, while nibbling on a cranberry, apple and walnut grilled chicken salad in 2009.

This was one minor example of Kim's thoroughness. This was treating business responsibly – a lesson first learned from her father and then from her energetic, driven mother. It wasn't rocket science, but it worked. Kim's campaign was deemed more successful than all the company's previous celebrity campaigns put together, including 1.8 million views for a 30-second commercial on YouTube and a further 2.1 million views for all the other Kim-related salad videos. The number following her on Twitter almost doubled that year to more than 5 million – a magnet for endorsement deals.

Brad Haley, an executive vice-president with Carl's Jr, was impressed: 'Kim Kardashian has been an absolute joy to work with and her genuine charm, charisma, beauty and brains have endeared her to a huge base of fans.' The food chain initially wanted her to front a campaign for a burger, but found that she really wasn't good at eating burgers. She was, in any case, on a low-carb diet. It was lucky that they had a new salad option on the menu at the right time.

While the ink was drying on one contract, another was being prepared for signature. Kim became the face of FusionBeauty, the international skincare brand. All three sisters signed a retail deal for their own fashion line with the bebe chain. They did the same for a range of outfits for Beach Bunny Swimwear and began a beauty line with a self-tanning gel called Glamour Tan.

In February 2010, Kim brought out her own perfume called Kim Kardashian, the 'voluptuous new fragrance'. It had always been an ambition to have her name on a fragrance. Her dad would always bring her a bottle of perfume when he returned from a trip away. He gave her the first-ever scent she used, Tribu by Benetton, after a visit to New York. They don't make it any more, but she kept the distinctive yellow bottle, with the garish red top, safe in her dressing room because it reminded her of him.

She moved on from Tribu to Angel by Thierry Mugler. The only problem with that was her father would invariably buy a bottle for whichever girlfriend he had at the time. When he broke up with any of them, Kim, being loyal to her dad, would hate the women and the scent would remind her of them. She had to give up wearing it. Her own fragrance had a hint of gardenia in it, her father's favourite smell. No sooner had the first Kim Kardashian fragrance hit the shops than she was working with her team to produce a second, called Gold.

In August, she teamed up with Loren Ridinger to design a luxury range of earrings for a new jewellery line, the Kim Kollection. Then she released a line of signature watches. It was relentless. She was paid huge sums just for turning up at a club – a $20,000 fee soon grew to $100,000, a reflection of the power of television and her growing popularity.

The branding philosophy of the Kardashians was simple: first, extend your brand as far as you can and always react to situations – if you put on weight, land a deal to promote diet supplement pills; secondly, be as visible and share as much as possible – the public are as interested in the bad times as the good; thirdly, use Facebook, Twitter, Instagram and any other online method you can think of to connect with the public.

In 2010, there were more online searches for Kim Kardashian than for Barack Obama or Justin Bieber. At the end of the year, she topped a list of the highest-earning reality TV stars, with an estimated $6 million. Khloé and Kourtney were seventh and eighth with $2.5 million. Kris Jenner didn't make the list but, if her 20 per cent fee for being their manager were taken into account, it would have earned her nearly $3.7 million.

Kim's earnings had grown so fast that it was time to look for a new home. She wanted to stay in Beverly Hills to be close to her friends and favourite haunts. She found a Tuscan-style villa for $4.8 million in a quiet cul de sac off Mulholland Drive. Her new mansion had five bedrooms, four bathrooms, a Regal pool and Jacuzzi, media room and fireplaces outside for cool winter evenings. The garden boasted an immaculate lawn and a waterfall.

The original idea was that she would move into it with Reggie, but that didn't work out, so she was a single girl in a luxurious mansion. It was more private than her lovely condominium in South Clark Drive, which she put on the market for a little over $1 million. She liked the high walls and security gates that kept the paparazzi at bay until she was ready to greet them with a smile and pose for a picture.

She was working so hard, there seemed to be little time for her to enjoy her new home. Certainly, since *Keeping Up with the Kardashians* began, she appeared to have the least exciting private life of the four Kardashian siblings.

She wasn't the first to have a child. That honour belonged to her elder sister Kourtney. At 5ft 0in, Kourtney is the smallest Kardashian and, by reputation, the most intelligent – at least academically. In the first episode of *Keeping Up with the Kardashians*, we were introduced to the relationship between her and boyfriend Scott Disick, which has been a constant in the programme ever since.

Scott, who is three years younger than Kourtney, proved to be an asset to the show, because he was always antagonising Kris or Khloé and seemed to be on the verge of splitting with Kourtney or marrying her. He is a man of mystery in that nobody seems to know what he actually does for a living.

He didn't grow up as one of the Beverly Hills set, although his parents, Jeff and Bonnie, were well-off residents of Eastport, Long Island. The family money came from the real estate business of attorney David Disick, who was Jeff's father. Scott's only claim to fame as a teenager was as a young male model for the covers of a series of adolescent romance novels. He is pictured as a handsome young man gazing meaningfully into the distance in poses designed to make teen girls swoon. The grown-up Scott was a bit of a bad boy – perfect for a show dominated by women.

The relationship between Kourtney and Scott, who has a reputation as a man who enjoys a party, has never been one of cosy, happy families. They split up for the first time in 2009, during which time he allegedly saw other people, but they got back together when she discovered she was pregnant.

Scott and Kourtney had their first child, Mason Dash Disick, on 14 December 2009. His arrival at the Cedars-Sinai Medical Center on Beverly Boulevard – hospital to the stars – was shown on an episode of *Keeping Up with the Kardashians*. At the end of the delivery, Kourtney leaned forward, carefully pulled the baby out and laid him on her stomach. The birth was actually filmed by Scott, using a video camera, and the footage was handed over to the technicians at E! to make it suitable for broadcast.

Scott appeared to have anger issues during the filming of one of the show's spin-offs, *Kourtney and Khloé Take Miami*, in which he punched a wall mirror during a drunken argument. Once more, they split amid rumours that Scott had an alcohol problem. He attended therapy, and they were reunited. He told Ryan Seacrest in an interview, 'I had to take a look at where my life is going – or where it was going to go if I kept acting the way I was.'

Kourtney turned out to be a natural mother, which surprised her family, who had always cast Kim in that role. Kourtney had seemed the sister least bothered about having children. Instead, she doted on her son, who was soon crawling around happily while the cameras kept running in the reality house. She became very protective of her boy, politely but firmly refusing all requests from fans who wanted to take a selfie with the newest member of the Kardashian clan.

She returned to work, helping to run DASH, which had now expanded with branches in Miami and New York. It gave the producers at E! the excuse to devise the spin-off series featuring Kourtney.

Kim also wasn't the first of the sisters to say 'I do' on the show. Khloé married NBA basketball player Lamar Odom, after knowing him for just a month.

Khloé had always seemed the most volatile and unpredictable of the three sisters. She had gone her own way as a teenager; she was home schooled and never had a steady boyfriend. Disappointed to receive a used car for her sixteenth birthday, she decided her mother wouldn't miss her Range Rover if she took it for a joyride with some friends. She dropped it off at a valet stand while she went to a party and returned to find it in flames: 'My friends and I saw this car on fire and we were like, "Whoa, that person is screwed!" And then I was like, "Fuck, that's my car!"'

Khloé was hurt in a serious car accident when she was 16. Apparently, she was thrown through the windscreen. As a result of her injuries, she suffers from short-term memory loss. She was knocked unconscious and suffered damage to her knees that required three operations to correct.

She was unimpressed when she met 6ft 10in Lamar, a star player with the LA Lakers, at a welcoming party for the team's new signing, Ron Artest, one of the most famous players of the era. Khloé was there with her younger brother Rob and was irritated by a man she didn't know staring at her.

In a loud voice, she declared, 'You're so rude. You're staring at me.'

Rob tried to keep her quiet. 'Please be nice,' he said. 'That's Lamar Odom. He's like the best basketball player.'

She recalled, 'I did not like Lamar. I hated him.' She thought him a typical and annoying basketball player.

A week later, she had clearly changed her mind. The pair were spotted laughing and joking over dinner at STK Los Angeles. Khloé invited him to meet Kris and Bruce at their home in Calabasas. They became engaged 26 days after they met.

Lamar's upbringing couldn't have been more different than the Kardashian children's. His father, Joe Odom, was a heroin addict. His mother, Cathy Mercer, a prison officer at the Rikers Island Correctional Facility, was left to bring him up as a single parent. They lived in the notorious South Jamaica area of Queens, New York. The neighbourhood, which was also home to the rapper 50 Cent, was wrecked by the crack cocaine epidemic of the 1980s and 1990s when Lamar was a boy. He observed, 'Any time you see these inner city kids in the NBA [National Basketball Association] ... you've got to understand their background wasn't all peaches and cream.'

Lamar was left devastated when his mother died from colon cancer when he was 12. He recalled, 'She got sick in January and by July she was gone. It was tough to see somebody you love so much hurting like that.'

Instead of disappearing into an uncompromising urban world, Lamar was taken in by his grandmother, Mildred Mercer, and, because of his height, made rapid progress in high school basketball. He was so good, *Parade* magazine named him Player of the Year in 1997, when he was 18.

He joined the Los Angeles Clippers at the age of 20. He moved from there to Miami Heat on a six-year contract worth a reported $65 million. He was selected for the US team for the 2004 Olympic Games in Athens; they won the bronze medal.

He stayed in Miami for only a year, however, before going back to LA – this time with the Lakers. He said, 'This is a dream come true. This is the Yankees of basketball. The big stage.' His team, which also included Kobe Bryant, won back-to-back NBA championships in 2009 and 2010.

Lamar was by now one of the richest young sportsmen in the country, and he had a steady girlfriend. Liza Morales was his high school sweetheart and the mother of his three children. He was 18 when they had their first child, a daughter called Destiny. Two sons followed: Lamar Jr in 2005 and Jayden in 2006. Tragically, their youngest son died from Sudden Infant Death Syndrome (cot death) before he was seven months old.

Lamar and Liza eventually separated and he met Khloé not long afterwards. Liza couldn't believe it when she suddenly got a text saying he was getting married. She admitted, 'There aren't words to explain how I felt that day.'

Kris Jenner had just nine days to organise the wedding. Fortunately, a wedding planner was called in to help. The E! cameras followed the whirlwind arrangements: registering for gifts, fittings for the Vera Wang wedding dress, bachelorette party, rehearsal dinner and, of course, the wedding itself.

The ceremony was held in the garden of the Beverly Hills mansion belonging to the Kardashians' best friends, Irving and Shelli Azoff. Kim and Kourtney were bridesmaids, also dressed in Vera Wang, and Bruce walked his stepdaughter down an aisle decorated with white roses. A 10-piece orchestra played during the ceremony and later Babyface sang at the reception in a marquee in another part of the property.

A film crew captured the whole day for *Keeping Up with the Kardashians* and the episode was the most watched in the history of the programme with 3.2 million viewers. During the festivities, Ryan Seacrest was overheard saying they were thinking of yet another spin-off, involving Khloé and Lamar.

Among the guests was the singer and actress Adrienne Bailon, who was Rob's girlfriend for two years and had been a regular on the show during that time. They had split unexpectedly, and Rob later admitted that he had strayed during their time together. She said, 'He strategically planned things out so that he could cheat on me, and that to me was disloyal.' She had a new boyfriend called Lenny Santiago, an executive with Roc Nation, by the time of the wedding, so there was little chance of them getting back together.

Rob lived with Kim in her condo for a while, before moving in with Khloé and Lamar. They had bought a

$4 million-dollar home together in Tarzana, an affluent neigh-bourhood not far from Hidden Hills. The house featured regularly on the show.

The beauty of *Keeping Up with the Kardashians* was that there were so many of them. Kim may have been the marquee draw, but her mother proved to be savvy when it came to pushing forward the rest of the family so they were all increasing the market value of the brand. There was money to be made individually and collectively.

Regardless of her sisters apparently enjoying the life she wanted for herself, Kim continued to work tirelessly. The poor reception of *Disaster Movie* didn't put her off acting altogether. She made her debut in a dramatic role on the small screen in *CSI: NY*. The prime-time CBS show, starring Gary Sinise, regularly attracted close to 13 million viewers, so once again it was excellent exposure for Kim.

She played a character called Debbie Fallon in an episode broadcast in December 2009, and looked the part of the femme fatale as she sashayed through the precinct in a fetching off-the-shoulder number and sporting an immaculate tan. This didn't seem very likely at Christmastime in New York, giving the game away that the series was filmed in Los Angeles.

Debbie Fallon turned out to be a cold and calculating murderess. In the episode, her partner in crime was played by the former beauty queen and MTV host Vanessa Minnillo, who was another survivor of *Disaster Movie*. In the very small world that Kim inhabited, Vanessa became the wife of Nick Lachey and the mother of his two children. The reviews for *CSI* were a little kinder than they'd been for her movie debut, although one criticised Kim's 'vampy smugness'. She has the problem facing many famous women who take on acting roles: you can never forget that it's her.

She tried a frothier role in *Beyond the Break*, a soap that followed the fortunes of four female surfers. Kim featured in four episodes playing Elle, the new girlfriend of one of the regular characters. Her character was mean-spirited – not something that came easily. Kim was subsequently linked to co-star Michael Copon. It was another one of her occasional insignificant dates, when nothing was going on, but it garnered some publicity – this time for the spin-off *Kourtney and Kim Take New York*.

Another one of these non-dates was with the Real Madrid soccer star Cristiano Ronaldo, which momentarily had the UK tabloids flickering with interest. Some gossip regarding the Chelsea player Wayne Bridge seemed nothing more than another photo opportunity. More genuinely, she started dating a black American footballer, Miles Austin, a wide receiver with the Dallas Cowboys.

They went together to an ESPY party in honour of Kim's friend Serena Williams in July 2010. She watched him play at the Alamodome in San Antonio, and confirmed they were dating. Any romance was short-lived, and lasted barely six weeks. She was finding it impossible to conduct a relationship while she was filming *Keeping Up with the Kardashians* for 12 to 16 hours a day. Perhaps she would have better luck in New York.

15

72 DAYS

———

You wouldn't have expected Kris Humphries' name to feature in a list of the 100 people most likely to date Kim Kardashian. He and Kim, superficially at least, appeared to have absolutely nothing in common. Reggie Bush, with whom she had evidently been very much in love at one time, was brought up in California, went to USC and lived in a bachelor apartment in Beverly Hills. He was a catch, a celebrity and seemed perfect for Kim.

Kris, though handsome, was born and brought up in Minneapolis, where his family still live. His father, William, is African-American. He has two elder sisters called Krystal and Kaela and so, like the Kardashians, they all had first names beginning with K. He wasn't known for enjoying the high life in New York, where he was living when he met Kim.

As a boy, he was a brilliant swimmer and, for 18 years, held the national record for the 50-metre freestyle in the boys' 10 and under age group. Only the legendary Olympian Michael

Phelps, who is the same age, was considered to be a better prospect.

At 12, he gave up swimming in favour of basketball. He was obviously going to be very tall, so he chose a sport in which he was likely to have a bright future and the chance to earn a fortune. Michael Jordan, the most famous player in the country, was regarded as the richest man in sport and a role model for youngsters everywhere.

Kris was a junior international, before a promising college career led to him being drafted by the Utah Jazz team at the age of 19. He then moved to the Toronto Raptors in 2006, to the Dallas Mavericks three years later and to the New Jersey Nets the following season.

When he stopped growing, Kris was 6ft 9in tall, which meant he was a full 1.5 feet (18 inches) nearer the clouds than Kim Kardashian. She is only just 5ft 3in – or even a tad smaller – and many people are taken aback by how petite she is when they meet her for the first time. 'She is *tiny*,' stressed the acclaimed writer Lynn Barber.

The height difference between Kris and Kim was probably the biggest in show business, although there were some well-known couples in the foot-high club, including her younger sister Khloé, who is 13 inches shorter than Lamar Odom, Will Smith and Jada Pinkett, and Sacha Baron Cohen and Isla Fisher.

Kim had been filming the spin-off series *Kourtney and Kim Take New York* when she was first introduced to Kris in the late autumn of 2010. The Nets' point guard Jordan Farmar, who is from Los Angeles and already knew Kim, invited them both out to dinner. She found Kris attractive, but was a little stand-offish, because she wasn't entirely sure she wanted to become involved with anyone new at that point. That, of course, made Kris very interested in her.

Kim seemed no more enthusiastic about basketball than she had been about football. She is surprisingly daring and is happy to try skydiving and snowboarding, but isn't so keen on watching dutifully from the sidelines. She was prepared to do that, however, if there was a new man in her life.

She flew in to Minneapolis after spending New Year in Las Vegas and watched the first half of the game between the Nets and the local Timberwolves from a courtside seat. She met Kris's family for the opening half and joined them for dinner at the city's elegant Grand Hotel on 2nd Avenue. The head chef had already gone home for the evening, but was promptly called back to cook for Kim and her party.

Life was about to change completely for Kris, who had been little known outside the sports pages. He literally came out of nowhere into the full glare of the *Keeping Up with the Kardashians* spotlight.

He never watched the show, which was a bad start. His girlfriend immediately before Kim, Bianka Kamber, a very exotic and attractive brunette, was a palliative care nurse in Toronto. She revealed that he had no interest in the show and would disappear to play a war game on his Xbox if she were enjoying an episode. 'He would say, "When you're ready to watch something that's a lot more educational and not a load of garbage, I'm in the other room."'

Their relationship suffered when he was transferred from Toronto to Dallas and finished just before he met Kim. Bianka praised her former boyfriend for being amusing, spontaneous and charming, but wondered how he had managed to attract the attention of Kim Kardashian, because he had 'no flirting skills whatsoever'. She added, 'Flirting to him was like burping and blowing it in your face or farting and then throwing the covers over your head.'

Such habits didn't seem to bother Kim, who was happy to talk publicly about her new boyfriend. Without a trace of irony, she said in January, 'He's a really good guy and I think that for once I've really taken my time. I've known him for months and have definitely tried to keep it low key.' They were married eight months later. Everything began to unfold in a similar fashion to Khloé and Lamar's relationship, even if it was just coincidence that both men were well-known basketball players.

In May, they went on the obligatory holiday to the Joe Francis villa in Mexico, where they were photographed. Apparently, Kris was happy to get some 'alone time', although the paparazzi were on hand to record the holiday and feature Kim in a breathtaking array of bikinis.

The courtship progressed in time-honoured media fashion, with rumours of ring shopping followed by a romantic proposal that would be shared with the television audience. By this time, Kris had overcome his aversion to *Keeping Up with the Kardashians*, at least temporarily, and allowed the television cameras to follow his every move.

Kim introduced him as her new boyfriend in the opening episode of series six. They were having a conversation in a New York restaurant, which appeared to have been cleared of all the other customers. He came across as normal and funny, although he did let out an enormous burp, which Kim tried but failed to match.

By episode 13, he was preparing to ask her to marry him. Kris Jenner opened the instalment with a classic remark to Kim, 'You actually got a keeper.' After asking Bruce for permission to ask her to marry him, her prospective son-in-law was supposed to propose at a family dinner. That didn't happen after he and Kim argued on the way there. It was already confusing and a little silly that mother and future husband were both called Kris.

Kim returned to her Beverly Hills home one afternoon later that month to discover Kris on bended knee in the bedroom. On the white carpet, he had written in rose petals: 'Will you marry me?' The room was bathed in candlelight and was very romantic, if appearing rather staged for maximum TV effect. Some have speculated that this was the work of a member of the production team.

Kris produced an enormous, dazzling diamond engagement ring that you might have expected to see on the finger of Liberace or Elizabeth Taylor. It was completely ostentatious and Kim clearly loved it at first sight. The 20.5-carat ensemble by Lorraine Schwartz was valued at a reported $2 million, it was the ring of a girl's dreams. The cost to Kris Humphries was almost certainly considerably less, especially taking into account the publicity the designer received. Kim had no hesitation in accepting his proposal.

The show's editors could manipulate the footage in any way they wanted to reveal tension between the groom and other members of the family. Even so, there remained a nagging doubt about their compatibility. Kim and Kris seemed closest during bouts of rough and tumble, in which he would lift her up and bundle her on to the bed. She was disgusted when he put one of his two small dogs on the kitchen counter. He remarked that she never cooked anyway, and she pointed out that she was a neat freak. This was absolutely true. She would only take a shower if the bathroom was absolutely spotless, so finding a dog sleeping at the bottom of her bed or pooping in her garden wasn't something she was ever going to enjoy.

Still, they pressed on with the wedding arrangements. They settled on a venue in the desirable and charming enclave of Montecito in Santa Barbara County, perfectly placed for guests to travel from Los Angeles or San Francisco. Described by local writer Richard Mineards as an 'Eden by the Sea', celebrities have long chosen to escape here from the faster-paced Hollywood. The place oozes charm, and residents like Oprah Winfrey, Jeff Bridges and Drew Barrymore can dine in the cosy restaurants untroubled by selfie-seeking fans.

The Kardashians hired, at a cost of $140,000, the scenic 10-acre estate Sotto Il Monte, owned by Frank Caufield, a venture capitalist. The venue was perfect for Kim's wedding, because she was very nearly following in the footsteps of Jennifer Lopez. When J.Lo and Ben Affleck were planning their wedding in 2003, they had selected the property as the perfect setting for the occasion. Kim needed no finer recommendation.

On her big day, everyone was asked to come in either white or black. Kim wore a classic Vera Wang ivory wedding dress that suited her hourglass figure. The gown had a tulle skirt, basque waist and Chantilly lace, and was matched with a pair of Giuseppe Zanotti shoes. The fashion writer Alison Jane Reid was unimpressed: 'It was a typical meringue and revealed far too much cleavage. It just looked fussy, over the top and unflattering.'

A smiling Bruce Jenner walked Kim down the aisle, which in this case was a long, white carpet. The ceremony was conducted by a minister from Minnesota, who read out their declarations of love for each other before declaring them Mr and Mrs Kris Humphries. It was perfect and nobody describing the dream wedding remembered that Kim had been married before. The bride didn't seem as relaxed as normal, however, suggesting she may have had misgivings.

Many of the celebrities connected with the Kardashians smiled appreciatively during the ceremony, before mingling at the reception. Babyface, Sugar Ray Leonard, Mario Lopez, Ciara, The-Dream, Kathie Lee Gifford, Eva Longoria, Serena Williams, Brittny Gastineau and Joe Francis were just some of the famous names who watched the couple take to the floor for their first dance – 'Angels' sung live by Robin Thicke.

The guest of honour was her 95-year-old grandfather, Art, the father of Robert Kardashian. He was in a wheelchair, but looked happy for her. She called him Poppi. His wife, Helen, had died three years before; he would pass away in December 2012.

Afterwards, Kim said, 'My one regret is that I wish I had more time to really enjoy the wedding, because there's so much going on that you're running around and now that I look, I'm like, "That day happened so fast".'

The residents of Montecito were, according to Richard Mineards, 'totally underwhelmed by the whole proceedings'. He recalled, 'I was constantly asked what the Kardashians were famous for.' The weekend upheaval, with helicopters from entertainment TV news shows clattering endlessly overhead, led to changes in local by-laws about people renting out their sprawling multimillion-dollar estates. Future would-be renters would have to go through a thorough legal process to get the necessary permission – if they got it at all. Montecito, the fifth richest postcode in the US (93108), didn't want a repeat of the Kardashian brouhaha any time soon.

The newlyweds were oblivious to that as they flew across the Atlantic for a honeymoon at the $3,300-a-night Hotel Santa Caterina on Italy's Amalfi Coast. The trip was a last-minute surprise gift from Kris, although there was time to ensure a photographer from the Splash agency was there to take pictures of Kim, in a revealing bikini, cuddling up to her new husband. She had been planning to go straight to New York after the wedding to start preparing for the new series of *Kourtney and Kim Take New York*, so she was genuinely taken by surprise.

Within weeks of their return, rumours began to surface that all was not well with the fledgling marriage. A clue to their differing outlook on marriage was provided by an episode of the reality spin-off. Kim is concerned when Kris suggests they move back to his home town.

She asks, 'How am I going to have my career and live in Minnesota?'

He replies, 'By the time you have kids and they're in school, nobody will probably care about you.'

Kim didn't reply, but you can imagine what she was thinking. The couple had moved into the luxury Gansevoort hotel in the Meatpacking District of New York, but Kris was seen apparently moving his things out of their suite just before her thirty-first birthday. After 72 days, she filed for divorce.

Kim issued a statement: 'After careful consideration I have decided to end my marriage. I hope everyone understands this was not an easy decision. I had hoped this marriage was forever, but sometimes things don't work out as planned. We remain friends and wish each other the best!'

It turned out they weren't exactly friends, as an acrimonious divorce dragged on for 20 months – far longer than they had been together as man and wife. It would later be revealed in the divorce papers that she never wanted to go on honeymoon.

Kim had the foresight to sign a prenuptial agreement. After her first marriage, she wanted just a few items back, including her Bible. On this occasion, she wanted to ensure she kept her fortune, then estimated at $22 million, although such figures do tend to be inflated in the press.

Speculation began immediately that the whole relationship, from start to finish, had been a stunt for her reality show. The media revealed that the couple had made a fortune from the fiasco, which reinforced the view that it had all been faked. Kim was reported to have earned $2 million from her nuptials, including more than $1 million in an exclusive picture deal with a magazine. She was also said to have been paid $90,000 for holding her hen party in Las Vegas at TAO, one of her regular haunts.

Kim defended herself vigorously in a blog that was posted on her website. It was a sad reflection of how she is perceived as a young woman who would do anything for fame. She wrote: 'First and foremost, I married for love. I can't believe I even have to defend this. I would not have spent so much time on something just for a TV show!'

She repeated an opinion of herself that others have voiced about her since she was a teenage girl: 'Everyone that knows me knows that I'm a hopeless romantic! I love with all my heart and soul. I want a family and babies and a real life so badly that maybe I rushed into something too soon … I felt like I was on a fast roller-coaster and couldn't get off when I know I probably should have.'

Kim realised that adverse public opinion could become a runaway train if left unchecked. Fans were fickle and could easily turn against you. Kris Humphries was jeered when he resumed playing basketball. Kim's emotional defence of her good intentions was intelligent and believable, but it wasn't enough to draw a line under her marriage.

Kris filed his legal response on 1 December. Surprisingly, he requested an annulment on the grounds of fraud. He didn't reveal the reason for pursuing this course.

Kim and Kris were simply a poor match. In a rather sad postscript, that amazing engagement ring was sold at auction by Christie's in New York in October 2013 for $749,000. Kim had returned it to Kris, and he had waited until their divorce was finalised before selling it. In an ironic twist of fate, that was also the month she became engaged again.

ABOVE: Kim's lifelong best friend Allison Azoff, pictured on her left, is not often photographed and ignores the celebrity world. She made a rare outing to support Kim at her bachelorette dinner at TAO in Las Vegas.

RIGHT: Kim turned out to be badly matched with second husband Kris Humphries, who had a height advantage of 18 inches. Even with six-inch heels she still had another foot to go.

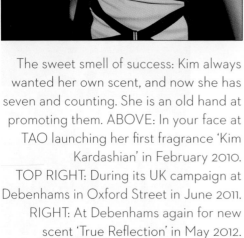

The sweet smell of success: Kim always wanted her own scent, and now she has seven and counting. She is an old hand at promoting them. ABOVE: In your face at TAO launching her first fragrance 'Kim Kardashian' in February 2010. TOP RIGHT: During its UK campaign at Debenhams in Oxford Street in June 2011. RIGHT: At Debenhams again for new scent 'True Reflection' in May 2012.

Most of the cast of *Keeping Up with the Kardashians* were on hand to launch the suitably named Kardashian Khaos at the Mirage Hotel in Las Vegas in 2011. The boutique was not a success and closed after three years.

Keeping up with the Jenners: A pregnant Kim joins her other family – Brandon, Brody, Bruce and Brandon's wife Leah – at the 2013 release party for *Cronies*, the first EP from indie group Brandon & Leah.

TOP LEFT: Kanye West is a huge influence on Kim's fashion choices. Her dress for the Met Ball in 2013 was described as a 'pair of curtains'.

TOP RIGHT: Kim and Kanye reworked her designer outfit at home for the GQ Men of the Year Awards. Kanye suggested the latex top.

LEFT: The monochrome look they both love was a dazzling success when Kim wore gold, including a new hair colour, to the *Hollywood Reporter* Women in Entertainment breakfast.

Sometimes being a celebrity can be great: Laughing in the front row at the BET Awards in Los Angeles with Kanye, Jay Z and his wife Beyoncé (although she doesn't seem to be in on the joke).

But sometimes it can be horrid: Surrounded and almost crushed by the paparazzi, selfie-seekers with their smartphones, security personnel or just people who want to gawp at the star in Paris.

LEFT: Kanye called Kim a natural mother. Here she shares a tender moment with baby daughter North at the Givenchy Show, Paris, in September 2014.

BELOW: In a relaxed mood after leaving the Valentino Haute Couture Show at the Hôtel Salomon de Rothschild in July 2012.

Kim and Kanye love Paris and, in particular, the Fashion Weeks, which they always attend if they can. Here, unselfconsciously, they share a private moment at the Balmain Show in March 2015.

Caitlyn Jenner said Kim had been 'by far the most accepting' about his gender transition. They take a walk in October 2014 before her stepfather told the world.

ARTHUR ASHE AWARD FOR COURAGE

Kim was in the audience when Caitlyn made an inspirational speech as she accepted the Arthur Ashe Award for Courage at the ESPY Awards in Los Angeles in July 2015.

Kim showed her serious side when she paid her first visit to Armenia in April 2015 and laid red tulips at the Genocide Memorial in the capital, Yerevan.

The following month, more frivolously, she turned heads at the 2015 Met Ball in New York in a Roberto Cavalli gown – truly, a bird of paradise.

PART THREE

KIM KARDASHIAN WEST

16

THE COLLEGE DROPOUT

Kanye West was different. He was a sensitive, artistic and driven young man, brought up in a Chicago household by a mother who gave him the gift of self-expression. When Kim first met him, he was producing a track he had written for Brandy called 'Talk About Our Love' and they were recording at the Record Plant studio in Hollywood. Kim was working for Brandy at the time, and legend has it that she made everyone, including Kanye, a mug of tea.

He was already recognised as one of the most talented new names in contemporary music, but he had yet to become the enigmatic and controversial figure he is today. He wasn't from the street or from any sort of deprived inner city back-ground. He hadn't subsidised his teenage years selling drugs on street corners; he had worked for Gap and in telephone marketing.

When he first met Jay Z, he was wearing a pink shirt, a smart sports jacket, tailored trousers and Gucci shoes. He looked more like a preppy East Coast college man than an up-and-coming rapper. He recalled, 'It was a strike against me that I didn't wear baggy jeans and jerseys and that I never hustled, never sold drugs.'

Kanye Omari West was born on 8 June 1977, in Atlanta, Georgia. The name Kanye, pronounced Kahn-yay, didn't have any special significance for his parents, Ray and Donda West. It simply means 'the only one' in Swahili, and Kanye would be an only child. His middle name means 'wise man'. His parents liked the fact that their son had the initials KO. For the first three years of marriage, they were determined to concentrate on their careers and not have children. Donda changed her mind, however, and persuaded her husband that they should try for a baby.

Both of his parents were highly educated. Ray West was from a military family, had lived overseas and had been brought up in mainly white neighbourhoods. At the then predominantly white University of Delaware, he had become involved in politics and was elected president of the Black Student Union. Donda recalled that he was 'militant, fiery, passionate and, above all, very, very smart.' He spoke at rallies for the controversial Black Panther Party. Kanye observed, 'He was a military brat who grew up in Germany as a black kid among white folks. So he was looking for a place to fit in, to be part of a movement, a struggle. And they accepted him.'

After college, Ray followed his first love of photography, winning awards and setting up his own business in his home town of Atlanta. One of his regular contracts was shooting pictures for Spelman College, the liberal arts women's university. He met Donda when she worked in the public relations department of the historically black institution. She was subsidising her studies for a master's degree at Atlanta University.

They married three months after their first date. At first, they both took teaching jobs. Ray taught photography and media production at one college, while she taught English and speech at another. They both decided to pursue further education and lived in married quarters at Auburn University in Alabama, where he obtained a master's in audiovisual studies and media, while she studied for a doctorate in English.

Their marriage faltered after Kanye was born, with Ray apparently devoting too much time to photography and not enough to family life. When their son was 11 months old, they separated amicably. Ray would remain in Kanye's life, but his mother basically raised him as a single parent and was by far the most significant and influential person in his development.

Donda and Ray's son would grow up to be imaginative visually and verbally – an impressive combination of their talents. On 'Talk About Love', for instance, he wrote and performed the middle rap, produced the track and devised the concept for the video, in which he appeared in a cameo role alongside Ray J, with whom Kim had just made the sex tape.

When Kanye was three, his mother decided their life needed a complete change. Encouraged by a boyfriend, she secured a job at Chicago State University and moved to Illinois. Kanye was a precociously talented child with a mother thoughtful and intelligent enough to encourage her son in the way that she thought would best prepare him for the world. She wanted to ensure that he had high self-esteem and believed in himself. She wrote, 'I began teaching him to love himself. It's something I felt I must consciously do ... As a black man and as a man period, he would need to be strong.'

Many of the values that Donda tried to instil in her son were the same ones that Kim's parents advocated for her: honesty, integrity and a strong work ethic. They attended church every Sunday at the Christ Universal Temple on South Ashland Avenue. She ensured he still saw Ray, spending summer holidays with his father and grandparents. Ray had become more religious-minded over the years and church was a compulsory event for his son whenever he visited. Sometimes they would speak on the telephone and say a prayer or two together before ending their conversation. Ray eventually gave up his job as a photographer and moved to Maryland to work as a Christian counsellor.

Donda's desire to build her son's confidence probably lay the foundation for what many perceive to be arrogance in the adult Kanye. His inner certainty allowed him to express his creative ideas from an early age. Even at three, he was thinking outside the box. His mother would tell him a banana was yellow, but he would draw one with his crayons and then colour it purple, because that's how he wanted it to look.

Kanye's self-confidence was evident when he sat an exam for elementary school. He was asked to draw a man, a task he found too dull and easy, so he told the examiners he would draw a man and put him in a football uniform. He passed the test easily and was accepted at the Vanderpoel Elementary Magnet School on South Prospect Avenue, which had a solid reputation for encouraging artistic children.

While there, Kanye began to take an interest in fashion and would sketch designs for the outfits he was going to produce when he had his own fashion label. Up until then, he had been quite happy to let his mother choose his clothes, usually from budget stores – on her salary, she had to be careful not to overindulge her child. She ignited his interest in the way he looked, however, by buying him his first pair of Air Jordans when he was 10. They cost $65, so it was an extravagant gift.

Donda broadened his education by taking him on trips around the US. They went to Washington, DC – not just to see the White House, but to tour the Smithsonian Institution as well. When they went to St Louis, they visited the zoo to have fun, but she wanted her son to appreciate the Gateway Arch, the awe-inspiring monument that had become the internationally recognisable symbol of the city. As a professor of English, she travelled abroad, but couldn't take Kanye with her. In 1987, she was offered a year teaching in China as part of an exchange between Nanjing University and Chicago State. She was going to turn down the opportunity before she was assured her son could go with her too.

China was an incredible experience for a young boy. Kanye would cycle eight blocks to school, where he was the centre of attention as the only black student. The others would come up and rub his face to see if his colour would come off on their hands. Stereotypically, because he was black, they wanted him to breakdance – fortunately, it was something at which he excelled. He was happy to oblige, but only in return for a lamb kebab. Even at the age of 10, he understood when he had something of value. He possessed an entrepreneurial spirit.

The one drawback during an adventurous year, in which he also travelled to Hong Kong and Thailand, was that his lack of fluency in the language held him back in class. He stayed in a lower grade until Donda decided to home school him. On his return to the US, he had to sit some exams to find his correct level of re-entry and performed so well that the school didn't believe the results and thought his mother must have helped him. He had to take the exams again with an invigilator standing over him. Once again, he excelled.

While he never got into serious trouble at school, he did embarrass his mother when he took a pornographic magazine in one day and got caught passing it around among his friends. When a teacher demanded to know where he had obtained the porn, he said he had found it in his mum's closet. She wanted the floor to open up and swallow her after she was summoned to the school and told what had happened. Kanye has admitted a healthy interest in sex from a young age, which included watching a hard porn movie on his VCR when he was 14. His unimpressed mother made him write an essay entitled 'The Impact of Watching X-Rated Movies on a Teenage Boy'. The project didn't dampen his enthusiasm for the opposite sex, but did teach him the benefits of proper research and preparation.

By the age of 12, he had become totally preoccupied with the way he looked. His mother, tongue in cheek, said he became Mr Style Guru. As a schoolboy, he even did his own washing and ironing to ensure he looked immaculate at all times. Once, when she gave him $200 to stock up on clothes for the new school term, he came home with just two shirts and one pair of jeans. Even then, his tastes were expensive.

He was also becoming obsessed with styling. Donda recalled, 'It was like a light went on inside of him and he poured the same kind of energy that he put into his art and music into putting outfits together and dressing well. It came without effort.' At 15, he even took over his mother's styling: 'He'd critique whatever I was wearing, whenever I had some place to go. Sometimes he'd be kind. Other times, cruel.'

At school, he formed a group called Quadro Posse with three friends. Kanye was responsible for the styling. He preferred everything to be coordinated. When they entered a school talent competition, which they won, he had decided that they all should dress completely in black. He was careful to make sure his shoes were exactly right, telling his mother, 'You can mess up a dope outfit with shoes.'

It's so easy to see that he and Kim are absolutely soulmates. If they had joined a dating agency, they would have been matched immediately and told to get married.

Kanye had moved on from Vanderpoel to Polaris High School in the affluent south-western Chicago suburb of Oak Lawn. It was demanding academically, but Kanye coped relatively easily. His teachers recall that he was prone to speaking first without thinking of the consequences of what he said. One of his teachers, Dr Carol Baker, recalled that he was easily distracted, often doodling, drawing or writing rather than paying attention: 'Back then I would have called it poetry, but it was really rap.'

His mother was determined that he receive the education he needed to be successful. 'She was the kind of mum who would pull him by the ear and drag him down the hallway if necessary,' said Dr Baker. 'I never saw her do that, but she was that kind of mum.'

One pursuit Donda was happy to encourage was Kanye's love of music. He was fiercely ambitious at a young age. His PE teacher Marilyn Gannon remembered him as a 'small kid with big dreams', who used to tell her almost daily that he was going to be the best rapper in the world. She invariably replied, 'OK, Kanye, you can get in line now.'

The characteristic that set Kanye apart from his contemporaries is an appreciation of all kinds of music. He used to impersonate Stevie Wonder at talent contests when he was a boy and often did well. He listened to proper singer-songwriters, like George Michael, Phil Collins and Michael Jackson. His favourite group was Red Hot Chili Peppers. Later, he became known for bringing many diverse elements into his music.

He wrote his first proper rap song at the age of 13. He was inspired by a favourite Dr Seuss book to compose 'Green Eggs and Ham'. He persuaded his mother to pay $25 an hour to give him enough time to record the song in a small basement studio, which was hardly high tech – the microphone was suspended from the ceiling by a wire coat hanger. Nothing from that version has ever been made public, but it was a start.

At 14, he bought his first keyboard with his own savings of $500 and the $1,000 his indulgent mother had given him as a Christmas present. From then on, he lived for his keyboard and the beats he could create on it. In mainstream pop music, a beat would be the instrumental track upon which the vocal would sit. In hip-hop, it would be the track, often using samples from other songs, on which the rap would be laid down. Kanye associated with a leading young hip-hop producer called No I.D., who took him under his wing after an introduction engineered by their mums, who both worked at Chicago State.

Like Kim Kardashian in Los Angeles, Kanye took on work as a teenager to afford the clothes he wanted, to run his battered Nissan car and to chase girls. He sold knives door to door and worked as a greeter outside a Gap store to try and encourage young black people to go inside. He made up raps to entertain passers-by: 'Welcome to the Gap. We got jeans in the back ...'

On leaving high school, he won a scholarship to study at the American Academy of Art, but was more interested in his music. He changed to English literature at Chicago State, where his mum was now head of the department, but didn't enjoy that either. He dropped out of college, which was obviously a huge disappointment to his mother. Her concern was eased when he sold a set of beats to the well-known Chicago rapper Gravity for $8,800.

Donda took early retirement from her job to move with her son to New York, where there were greater opportunities, and took on the role of Kanye's manager. She was, in fact, a 'momager' before Kris Jenner took on that role for her children. He attracted the interest of Jay Z and made his breakthrough to the major league when he produced five tracks on the master rapper's 2001 million-seller *The Blueprint*. Practically overnight Kanye was one of the biggest producers in the US, but he was frustrated at being unable to perform his own material. Dapper and short of stature, he lacked the menace of the gangsta rappers who dominated the hip-hop scene at the time.

He continued to write, composing two of the tracks that would become Kanye classics, 'Jesus Walks' and 'Hey Mama'. The latter was a tribute to his mother, who had always given her son's well-being and happiness priority over her own personal relationships. Eventually Roc-A-Fella's co-founder,

Damon Dash, signed him as a recording artist and he flew to Los Angeles to make an album.

He nearly didn't finish it. After a late night at the studio, he fell asleep at the wheel of his rented Lexus and was fortunate to escape with his life. His airbag failed to open and his face smashed into the steering wheel, causing horrendous fractures to his jaw and nose. His girlfriend, Sumeke Rainey, and his mother were on the first flight from Newark to be at his bedside in Cedars-Sinai.

His relationship with Sumeke is the quiet one he seldom speaks of, but they dated for seven years and she hasn't used that fact to gain any fame since. She sang lyrics on an occasional song, but, more importantly, her father gave Kanye a box of old soul singles that he went through carefully and methodically, and used for sampling on his early recordings. He is also said to have told her dying father that he would marry Sumeke some day – something that didn't happen.

The number of people in Kim's story affected by bad road accidents is almost beyond belief. Khloé had her bad teenage smash; Kris Jenner's natural father was killed in one; Bruce's brother was another fatality; Lamar Odom's chauffeur-driven car was involved in a fatal accident in New York in 2011; Bruce himself would be involved in a crash in 2014, in which his Cadillac hit the back of another car, resulting in the death of its occupant. And then there was Kanye, who was lucky to be alive.

He was in hospital for two weeks, only able to take sustenance through a straw, as his shattered jaw had to be wired together. It could have been much worse. His escape was a life-changing moment, as his songs became more self-aware and honest. Up until that time, he had been trying to be unrealistically tough in both his lyrics and his music, because that was the fashion. He wrote and recorded a breakthrough song called 'Through the Wire', which he sang literally through gritted teeth.

He wrote it in the hospital and, as he usually did with his songs, simply remembered it. He didn't need to write the lyric down. He rapped about half his jaw being in the back of his mouth. He speeded up a sample of a 1984 big ballad by Chaka Khan called 'Through the Fire', which had originally been produced by David Foster. Kanye recorded it at the Record Plant studio with the wire still in his jaw. When Chaka agreed for her vocal to be used, she had no idea that he was going to speed it up and 'make me sound like a chipmunk'.

When the song was eventually released in September 2003, it was a top 20 hit in both the US and the UK. More importantly, it revealed that Kanye was the exception to the rule that producers don't make good rappers. The video, which he financed himself, won Video of the Year at the 2004 *Source* Hip-Hop Awards.

The track was the cornerstone of his debut album, *The College Dropout*, which sold 3.4 million copies in the US and gained him a reputation as one of the leading rap artists of his generation. It won Best Rap Album at the Grammy Awards, the first of 21 he has won, making him the most successful modern artist at the prestigious annual ceremony. The second single, 'Slow Jamz' with Twista and Jamie Foxx, provided Kanye with his first number one. The *New York Times* described *The College Dropout* as a 'concept album about quitting school, a playful collection of party songs and a 76-minute orgy of nose-thumbing.'

Kanye made the jump to the front pages of the newspapers in September 2005, during a telethon raising funds for the victims of Hurricane Katrina in New Orleans. He began with some home truths about the victims. He said that a white family would be portrayed in the media as looking for food, whereas a black family would be described as looting. He ended with a simple observation that was heard throughout the world: 'George Bush doesn't care about black people.' He hadn't planned to say it, but let an impulse rule his head. It would be the first of many controversial moments.

Donda West was proud of her son's outspoken honesty. Mindful of the battle against racial prejudice that she had witnessed all her life, she believed he had spoken the truth. She moved from the East Coast to the West to be with her son. First, she had been there to help him convalesce follow-ing his near-fatal accident; then she stayed on to look after his affairs. She was chief executive of West Brands, LLC, the parent company of Kanye's business concerns. She chaired the Kanye West Foundation, an educational non-profit organisation, which sought to decrease dropout rates and improve literacy. She was also the person whose opinion mattered most to him.

She died suddenly and unexpectedly in Beverly Hills in November 2007, the day after she had undergone cosmetic surgery, which included breast reduction and liposuction. She was 58. The coroner said that the final manner of death could not be determined, but stated that 'multiple post-operative factors could have played a role in the death'. His opinion, though, was that she died from some pre-existing coronary artery disease.

Kanye was devastated. Before she died, she had written a book entitled *Raising Kanye: Life Lessons from the Mother of a Hip-Hop Superstar*, in which she described her love and admiration for her son. The affection was mutual. He was devastated by her death.

He was in the middle of a tour in Europe and cancelled some dates, but a week later, in Paris, had to be helped off stage when he was about to sing 'Hey Mama'. He took time away to grieve, but returned at the Grammys in February 2008. This time he sang an emotional version of the song, and had the word MAMA shaved into his head.

Kim's father, Robert Kardashian, was a year older than Donda when he died. That sense of loss would be a common bond between Kanye and Kim. She said simply, 'I can really relate to his mother's passing. He can really relate to my father's passing.' Surely it was only a matter of time before they realised they were made for each other.

17

FANCY SEEING
YOU HERE

The story of Kim and Kanye's love affair should be made into
a Hollywood rom-com. The audience would be secure in the
knowledge that they would eventually end up together,
despite a series of relationships with other people that kept
them apart for years. Her sister Khloé was always telling Kim
that he should be her husband.

When they first met, she was involved with Ray J and technically married to Damon Thomas. Kanye, too, was attached
– he was still with Sumeke. Their long relationship fizzled out
when he moved to Los Angeles. She is acknowledged as a
vocalist on two tracks from *The College Dropout*, but doesn't
feature on the follow-up, *Late Registration*, a year later.

That album was number one in the *Billboard* charts and
included one of his best-known songs, 'Gold Digger'. It sold
more than 3 million copies in the US alone and was one of
the 10 biggest-selling songs of the decade. In the UK, he
performed for the first time at the Brits in 2006, using 77
female dancers wearing little more than gold paint and skimpy
bikinis.

At the time of *Late Registration*, he was dating Brooke Crittendon, a production assistant at MTV. She seemed a refreshingly normal girl, who found it difficult dating a superstar: 'There was a lot of attention from other women. Kanye was very open and honest, but it ended up with me knowing too much. I don't want to be silly and say it wasn't cheating because I knew about it. But he wanted and needed me to be OK with certain things I wasn't OK with.'

Brooke revealed that Kanye wasn't the macho man he had set out to be in his music. Instead, he was a sensitive performer who liked to know she was standing by the side of the stage whenever he performed. Their liaison ended after one of an increasing number of rows, and Kanye went back to Alexis Phifer, a very pretty young designer he had dated briefly after Sumeke. She had been married for three years to American footballer Roman Phifer and had a young son called Jordan.

She and Kanye were together for three years and became engaged. He gave her a beautiful, large, square diamond ring by the New York-based Lorraine Schwartz. (She would also design the engagement ring Kris Humphries gave Kim.) They shared a passion for fashion – something clearly very important to Kanye in his search for a partner. Alexis moved into his home at the foot of the Hollywood Hills with views overlooking Hollywood Boulevard, but kept her design studio in downtown LA and went off to work every day. She was setting up her own label called Ghita, which she described as styles for 'the confident woman who doesn't mind showing a little of her sexuality'. Kanye never seemed to need the status of having a famous girlfriend, preferring to date unknown women most of the time.

He likes opulence and clothing. His dining-room ceiling paid homage to the Sistine Chapel, except it depicted Kanye flying among angels. His closets alone took up close to an entire floor. He clearly appreciated his fiancée's dress sense, crediting her with being the first person he would allow to style him. He said, 'Alexis was my original stylist. She helped me get fresh.' During their time together, Kanye began developing his own fashion label, called Pastelle. He spent three years on the project, but it never reached stores.

His mother Donda acknowledged Alexis as one of the family in her 2007 book and all seemed set fair for a wedding. Kanye still appreciated the curvaceous charms of Kim Kardashian, however. They were no more than friends, but he later admitted that seeing a photograph of Kim with Paris Hilton in Australia in 2006 reminded him that she had a great pair of pins.

In September 2007, a photographer caught them together at the grand opening of the Intermix boutique in West Hollywood. Kanye was with Alexis and Kim arrived with her younger brother Rob. Kanye is in the middle of a picture taken that night with Alexis on his right arm and Kim on his left. Intriguingly, in 2014 Kanye told the audience at one of his concerts that seven years earlier he had told Kim he was going to marry her one day.

She admitted, 'There was definitely a spark.' That spark was in evidence again in 2008, when they made the pilot of a hip-hop puppet show called *Alligator Boots*. This was like an X-rated *Spitting Image* and very funny if you liked that sort of humour. In the opening scene, Kanye and Kim share a stage with a deep-voiced randy bear puppet called Beary White, who serenades her with a romantic ode: 'Let me lay you down on my silky sheets and then come in close behind ya and then I'll show you my desire and put my penis inside your vagina.' Kim pretends to be outraged. 'Excuse Me!' she exclaims. Kanye was one of the executive producers, along with the television host Jimmy Kimmel. For some reason, Comedy Central decided not to commission it.

Throughout the show, Kim is a good sport, dressed as an outstandingly sexy Princess Leia, a dream costume for any *Star Wars* devotee with an interest in porn. For those with longer memories, Kanye was indulging in the same fantasy that Ross had in *Friends*, when he persuades Rachel to dress as the character. Kanye observed in the show, 'And I want to have, like, Kim Kardashian play Princess Leia, because you know Kim Kardashian's ass is so perfect.'

It may be with the benefit of 20/20 hindsight, but the pair do seem very relaxed in each other's company. The timing was always a little awry where Kim and Kanye were concerned. She said, 'We were both in other relationships and we kept our distance and that was really that.'

All was not well between Kanye and Alexis. He had struggled in their relationship after the death of his mother. Alexis was pictured arriving on the red carpet for a fashion event in New York without her engagement ring. A story in *In Touch* claimed the pair had argued when she discovered a naked picture of Kim on his mobile phone. Any thoughts of marriage were soon put to one side.

Kim was involved with Reggie Bush then, so she wasn't free. The next time they were seen at the same event was later that year, at the tenth anniversary party for *Flaunt* magazine in

Los Angeles. Kanye was now dating a shapely former stripper from Philadelphia called Amber Rose. He had seen her dancing seductively in the video for the Ludacris song 'What Them Girls Like' and decided he wanted to find out more. She was very distinctive, with buzz-cut blonde hair and a voluptuous figure, and stood out among the young women who generally inhabit hip-hop videos. Oddly, she shares the same birthday as Kim, 21 October, although she is three years younger.

She was at home in the Bronx, where her family lived in the projects, when she had a call on her mobile phone. 'Hi, it's Kanye,' he said. Amber, whose real name is Amber Levonchuck, had never met the rapper, so she hung up because she thought it was a prank call. He persisted, calling back until he persuaded her that he was genuine and wanted to fly her to Los Angeles to appear in the video for a song called 'Robocop'.

The video was never released, but Kanye invited Amber to the Grammys and bought her a Chanel bodysuit to wear. She explained why she fell in love with him: 'When I told him I was an exotic dancer, he was like "I don't care if you're a crackhead. I don't care if you're a prostitute. I just want to be with you."'

Amber moved to Los Angeles, where she and Kanye became one of the most striking couples in the music business. She signed with the Ford Models agency and said goodbye to her work as a pole dancer forever. She was with Kanye during his most controversial episode to date. At the 2009 MTV Video Music Awards, he charged on stage during Taylor Swift's acceptance speech for Best Female Video and took the microphone from her. 'Yo Taylor, I'm really happy for you and I'mma let you finish, but Beyoncé had one of the best videos

of all time. One of the best videos of all time!' He was refer-
ring to 'Single Ladies (Put a Ring on It)'.

It was a priceless moment. The audience at the Radio City
Music Hall in New York was dumbstruck to begin with and
then roundly booed him. His intervention will always feature
in the most shocking moments in music. Even President
Obama made an off-the-cuff remark about it, 'The young lady
seems like a nice person, she's getting her award and what's he
doing up there? He's a jackass.'

One can only speculate about whether Kim would have
prevented him from getting out of his seat in the first place.
Kim and Kanye have never admitted the extent of their feelings for one another in these early years, but the conspiracy
theorists enjoyed Kanye's contribution to 'Knock You Down',
a song by Keri Hilson. In his guest verse, he raps, 'You was
always the cheerleader of my dreams, To seem to only date the
head of football teams, And I was the class clown that always
kept you laughin', We were never meant to be, baby, we just
happened.' Obviously, the gossips assumed Kim was the cheerleader and Reggie was the head of the football team.

In February 2009, Kim and Reggie went to the Y-3 fashion
show in New York only to find Kanye there, practically beside
them in the front row. The actress Milla Jovovich sat between
Kanye, who looked slightly ill at ease, and Kim, who had her
arm locked around Reggie's.

The following year, Kanye and Amber Rose split up. He
was pleasant about it: 'It was an amazing time and it came to
an end.' She took a different view, later accusing Kim of
being a 'homewrecker' and her ex-boyfriend of unfaithful-
ness. She told the *New York Post*, 'He can't be faithful, and it's

not just with one person. He's just unfaithful with a lot of different women. I got to the point where I thought, my heart can't take it any more. I don't deserve this.' Amber was echoing the view of another of his former girlfriends, Brooke Crittendon.

According to Amber, Kim used to send Kanye salacious messages and photos. She claimed: 'They were both cheating on me and Reggie with each other … She was sending pictures and I was like, "Kim, just stop. Don't be that person."' Kanye subsequently denied this – when asked if Kim had sent him nude pictures while he was with Amber, he replied, 'I wish.'

When Kanye walked into the new DASH boutique in the SoHo district of New York in October 2010, neither he nor Kim was attached. She had temporarily relocated to the city to open the store and film the experience with her sister Kourtney for their spin-off show. Kanye didn't seem to mind the cameras when he flirted with Kim and gave them some advice about the shop. He also accepted an invitation to her thirtieth birthday party at TAO in Las Vegas. That was the glitzy, public celebration, but he also attended the private family party a few days later.

The great mystery about Kim and Kanye's love affair was why, after being thwarted for so many years, they didn't take this opportunity to begin a proper relationship. Perhaps they were each waiting for the other to make the first move, or maybe it was just a case of not having the time to devote to anything more than a casual friendship. Kim's work schedule for the first series of *Kim and Kourtney Take New York* was very demanding and that may have been a factor. In the best romantic-comedy tradition, they may simply not have realised what their true feelings were then.

One of the storylines for the series involved seeing if Kim could find a new man. Surprisingly, considering the rumours at the time, he turned out not to be Kanye but Kris Humphries. Kanye did help Kim with her ill-fated singing attempt, 'Jam (Turn It Up)', and appeared in the unreleased video in some steamy scenes.

Despite their obvious and natural chemistry, Kanye again took a back seat during her whirlwind romance and ill-fated marriage to Kris Humphries. He wasn't happy about it. Kim later revealed that he had expressed his interest, but she hadn't followed up, as she was being swept away on the roller-coaster that led to her wedding in Montecito. Kanye wasn't invited to the wedding, despite being continually described in Kardashian circles as a family friend.

Kanye dated a succession of attractive young women and there were even rumours that he had made a sex tape with one who bore some likeness to Kim.

At long last, Kim and Kanye's time had come. Kim made the first move to start an exclusive romance with Kanye simply by calling him. She finally admitted the obvious truth: 'I was always attracted to him.' She realised how hurt he had been when she went off and married Kris Humphries. 'I thought he was going to call me, since he knew that I was single again and he didn't. I knew what he was thinking. And so I called him and I said, "Hello. I thought you were at least going to call me or something."'

Just six weeks after she announced her split from Kris, Kim was seen in public with Kanye at an after-show party in Los

Angeles. He had been performing at the Staples Center with Jay Z, as part of their *Watch the Throne* tour, which saw the two superstars join together for a series of 57 dates that grossed $75 million. Kim attended the concert with Khloé, Scott Disick and her mother. They had seats right next to the stage, so Kanye was able to interact with them during the concert.

The party afterwards was held at the Beverly Hills estate of billionaire Ron Burkle. Kanye and Kim chatted with a very pregnant Beyoncé, who is married to Jay Z, but spent most of the night deep in conversation with each other. For once, stories that they had eyes only for each other were completely true. One eyewitness declared, 'Kanye was eating Kim up like she was a piece of cake. I think he was dying to kiss her, but there were too many people in the room.'

She continued to deny rumours that they were going out, which was hardly surprising, as her divorce was proceeding at a snail's pace. Before they were officially an item, Kanye's ex, Amber Rose, had become engaged to another rapper, Wiz Khalifa. Reggie Bush, too, had moved on to a new relationship and had settled down in Miami with a beautiful dancer called Lilit Avagyan, who bore a striking resemblance to Kim and, by coincidence, was Armenian.

In March 2012, Kanye invited Kim to join him for his Paris fashion week show. His fame had allowed him to pursue his interest for the past few years. He teamed up with Nike to release his own line of designer trainers, called Air Yeezys, a bow to the famous Air Jordan shoes he had loved so much as a child combined with his own preferred nickname, Yeezy. He designed a new shoe line for Louis Vuitton, as well as footwear for BAPE and Giuseppe Zanotti.

Since his Taylor Swift debacle, Kanye had spent much more time immersed in the world of fashion, especially after he cancelled a co-headlining tour with Lady Gaga in late 2009. Instead, he went to live in Japan to get away from the fallout. In Rome, he interned for four months at the Fendi fashion house, where he tried to interest them unsuccessfully in his design for a leather jogging pant. He also lived in Paris, which he loved and where he held two shows in 2011 and 2012.

In the romantic French capital, any reluctance Kanye had to begin a serious relationship with Kim vanished. She confessed, 'The magic happened.' Kim realised that the man she loved had been in front of her all along. She assured him that she was ready to make a commitment.

The show itself contained a lot of fur and very high, futuristic shoes. Kim wore a pair of Kanye West for Giuseppe Zanotti heels, made of calf leather and embroidered with pearls, which would cost $6,000 to buy and weren't exactly rainproof. She topped off her outfit with a striking white fur stole.

Both Kim and Kanye have become the number one celebrity target for PETA, the animal rights organisation, because of their love of wearing fur. Two weeks after Paris, Kim was flour-bombed at the launch of her new perfume, True Reflection, as she posed on the red carpet at the London West Hollywood hotel.

She had arrived looking flawless in a black blazer, blue blouse and leather trousers. A few minutes later, she looked as if she had been caught in an unseasonal snowstorm. Apparently, the female assailant shouted, 'Fur hag!' before taking aim. The fire department was called to determine what the white powder was and concluded that it was plain flour. After she had spruced herself up, Kim said, 'That probably is the craziest, unexpected, weird thing that ever happened to me. Like I said to my make-up artist, I wanted more powder …'

Kim remains a target, although that was the most obvious physical attack she has received. At the start of her promotional tour for her book of selfies, *Selfish*, in May 2015, anti-fur protesters queued for seven hours to confront her. They held up posters and spoke to her in person.

Kanye, who probably wears just as much fur as Kim, went back to songwriting after the fashion show. He couldn't resist a dig at PETA in 'Theraflu': 'Tell PETA my mink is dragging on the floor.' The main focus of the track, which he retitled 'Cold', was that he mentioned Kim by name for the first time. 'And I'll admit, I had fell in love with Kim … Around the same time she had fell in love with him'. Many took that to be about Kris Humphries, but it could just as easily be a reference to Wiz Khalifa, whom he also names in the song, if the 'she' is Amber Rose – it works just as well for both.

Kim and Kanye officially went public with their love affair in late April 2012, when they arrived hand in hand and posed for pictures at the annual artists' dinner at the Tribeca Film Festival in New York. She had already been spotted leaving his apartment one morning in the same clothes she had on the night before.

Privately, they were already talking of moving in together and starting a family. Two things needed to happen to make that possible. First, they needed to decide whose lovely house they were going to live in. Secondly, Kim needed to come off the pill, which she had been taking for 18 years. She told

Oprah, 'I want babies; I want my forever; I want my fairy tale. And I believe you can have what you want.'

The solution to the living arrangements was simple: they would both sell their homes and start afresh with something fabulous. Kim was happy to let hers go for $5 million – no more than she had paid for it, when taking into account the furniture she was including in the sale. Kanye's was a little smaller and worth a million or so less, but was probably more opulent. His house was fitted with a Crestron system, which allowed him to control the climate, lighting and music from any computer in the world.

In June, she splashed out on a black Lamborghini, costing $400,000, as a gift for his thirty-fifth birthday. Over the years, the men in her life, including Damon Thomas and Ray J, had all enjoyed driving the prestigious sports cars around the boulevards of Los Angeles. She could afford it. *Keeping Up with the Kardashians* had been recommissioned for three years by E! for a reported $40 million.

Kanye wasn't shy about publicity, but he had to get used to the media demanding a daily diet of Kim stories. She would post something on Twitter or Instagram to her millions of followers and the media would report what she said or did, thereby increasing the exposure. Her use of social media was masterful.

He had the last laugh, however. He surprised her by announcing that she was pregnant in front of a crowd of 5,000 fans at one of his concerts in Atlantic City on 30 December 2012. Kim, who was in the audience, had expected them to wait until she was showing, but Kanye always acts on impulse. He shouted into the mic, 'Stop the music!' and then pointed to Kim in the audience and said, 'Can we make some noise, please, for my baby mama right here?!'

The next day she confirmed the news on her website. 'Kanye and I are expecting a baby. We feel so blessed and lucky and wish that in addition to both of our families, his mom and my dad could be here to celebrate this special time with us.'

18

BODY CONFIDENCE

———

One of the first tasks Kanye set himself when he and Kim finally got together was to sort out her closet. Ironically, he decided to do for her what she used to earn a living accomplishing for others. Generally, he doesn't like being filmed for television, but on this occasion he was happy to let the cameras show him piling up the clothes he thought should go.

He wanted Kim to be more daring in her choices and not fall into the stereotypical look of a well-dressed Beverly Hills socialite. By the time he had finished, she literally had no clothes left; he had discarded so many of her favourite outfits. Though naturally a little upset, she trusted his judgement. She was in awe of his combination of creativity and certainty. Outside her room, dozens of pairs of barely worn shoes were dumped, ready for eBay.

She promised that everything would be prepared for online auction within the month and that some of the proceeds would go to the new church the family had founded, called the California Community Church. The pastor, Brad Johnson, had been given a fresh start by Kris Jenner after he had to leave his previous ministry following an adultery scandal. She discovered him working in Starbucks and asked him to lead the new church. They began holding weekend meetings in the ballroom of the Sheraton Agoura Hills Hotel, just a few miles from Calabasas. Church members donate either $1,000 a month or 10 per cent of their incomes. Kim chose to do the latter. Thanks to the financial support of the Kardashians and the congregation, a new purpose-built church is being constructed close by.

Kanye provided Kim with a whole new wardrobe, including some of the pieces from his Paris fashion shows, as well as other top-drawer designers. He pointed out, 'Look how dope this shit is.' Kim agreed it was the 'dopest stuff'. She tried on a long green dress with a generously plunging neckline, which met with his instant approval: 'It's like "I'm getting on best-dressed lists now, I'm stepping all into this territory".' When she tried on a busty black dress, he stroked her hips and told her, 'You look amazing.' He was obviously impressed with his girlfriend's body.

Kim is the perfect subject for a designer. She is and always has been stunning. As Alison Jane Reid points out, 'There is no denying Kim was born beautiful. At 13, for her eighth-grade graduation, she looks as if she has just stepped out of a Scott Fitzgerald novel, with her cute twenties bob, black eyes and full, rosebud lips. When she is with T. J. Jackson at her high school graduation, she has her hair up, which sculpts her face and shows off those cheekbones and sparkling, confident, look-at-me eyes to perfection. She is film star beautiful. Hers is a kind of old Hollywood beauty, like a young Elizabeth Taylor. Her features, a gift from the Armenian side of her family, give her enviable blue-black hair, peach-coloured skin and almond eyes. She has that kind of luminous, intense beauty that's impossible to ignore.'

Kim's body shape has changed so much over the years. As a young woman, she was petite and relatively slender, albeit with her much admired assets obviously on display. She has had to contend with many rumours that she has had her breasts or bottom enhanced by artificial implants. Her sister Kourtney happily admits that she first had a boob job in college and then some further work in 2009. At 5 feet tall, she was a slip of a girl growing up, whereas Kim always had curves. Her mother, Kris Jenner, is also not shy about the amount of cosmetic surgery she has undergone, including two breast ops and a facelift that she had prior to Kim's wedding to Kris Humphries.

Kim only admits to Botox. She has often commented that her breasts are completely real and quite saggy – something she first pointed out in her notorious sex tape. She has described her bottom as perfectly natural for a woman with an Armenian heritage. Many will never believe it is completely natural, however, and there will always be questions. She once tried to silence the rumours on *Keeping Up with the Kardashians* by having her bottom X-rayed, which proved there was definitely nothing foreign in there, but didn't disprove theories that she had her own fat inserted.

The problem for Kim is that her bootylicious derrière has become an essential part of her image and, consequently, her brand. Whatever she wears, we want to see how it shows off her behind. She is happy to fuel this interest. When she posted a picture of her rear squeezed into a tight pair of jeans, she added the comment, 'I think my butt looks too big in these jeans.'

It could be argued that Kim's greatest asset as a fashion role model for young women is not her boobs or backside, but her complete physical self-assurance. Alison Jane Reid observes, 'She has always had a great décolleté and has been flaunting it since her teenage years. It's a sign of her extraordinary body confidence. Her bottom definitely seems to have changed shape to the point of being quite out of balance and proportion to her tiny frame. There is a popular craze in LA to have this exaggerated, pert bottom and Kim seems to have been seduced by this. There are trainers and exercises that promise to help you achieve this look all over the Internet.'

Since Kim emerged into the limelight in 2007, she has been at the forefront of a style that has brought the overtly sexual into the mainstream. Years ago it is a look that would have been considered vulgar, but now it is socially acceptable and aspirational for young women and girls.

'The problem for Kim is that she is inconsistent,' commented Alison Jane. 'One moment, she looks like an icon and a female business entrepreneur. The next, she wears a pair of curtains to the Met Ball or a slutty latex dress that makes her look like Jessica Rabbit. When she nails it, she looks like a goddess, as she did in the sublime wine red dress she wore to the 2011 *Huffington Post* Game Changers Awards in New York. I love the fact that she isn't afraid to celebrate her voluptuous body, but then she often takes it too far.'

Being pregnant is always a challenge for a celebrity used to facing the cameras every day they step outside. Their choice of expectant wear is a target for fashion commentators. The 'pair of curtains' was, in fact, a specially designed Givenchy gown by Riccardo Tisci, a close friend of Kanye. Kim had modified it considerably to take into account her larger body shape. The jersey dress, with silver grommet detailing, was attached to long sleeves and a high neck. She wasn't completely covered, however. The dress split high at the sides to reveal her shapely legs.

The Met Ball, also known as the Met Gala, is generally regarded as the number one fashion event of the year. The official purpose of the night is to raise funds for the Metropolitan Museum of Art's Costume Institute, but in reality it is the night when a galaxy of celebrities try to outshine one another. The long-standing chair of the event is Anna Wintour, the legendary editor-in-chief of *Vogue*.

The theme of the night in 2013 was punk, but critics poked fun at Kim's dress, noting the matching accessories and describing it as a Mrs Doubtfire dress. The floral fabric seemed very old fashioned. Alison Jane observed, 'This would have been great on a supermodel, like her stepsister Kendall Jenner, but it wasn't a good pregnancy look. It really seemed as if she had just bagged the loose cover from her couch. Memo – never cover yourself in chintz when heavily pregnant.'

Tisci, the creative director at Givenchy, defended the dress: 'To me pregnancy is the most beautiful thing in the world, and when you celebrate something, you give people flowers. I think she looked amazing. She was the most beautiful pregnant woman I have dressed in my career.'

Kim also backed her choice. 'I thought it was so cool and it got a lot of criticism and I didn't care because I really loved it.' While her dress wasn't well received, it did garner by far the most publicity on the night. Kim's attitude has always been that it's better to be noticed than ignored. She and Kanye had taken to wearing matching outfits, but on this occasion he sported an elegant black Givenchy suit and crisp white shirt, matched with shiny black shoes – a sharp contrast to Kim's fussy ensemble.

The Met Ball was her last big public outing before she was due to give birth. She was fortunate to have avoided morning sickness, but did admit that being pregnant was a 'little painful'. Her sister Khloé was more direct: 'Her back hurts, her breasts hurt, her stomach hurts, her feet hurt, her head hurts, her eyes hurt, her nails hurt. And she cries all the time.' In fact, Kim was quite poorly during the pregnancy. On one occasion, she was taken ill on a plane and was told by doctors that she needed to throttle back on her work commitments.

Kimye, as the media had named the couple, prepared for the arrival by buying a new family home, although palace would be a better description of the 10,000 square-foot property in a gated Bel Air community, where their neighbours included Jennifer Aniston and Joe Francis. Set in three-quarters of an acre, the house was so large, it had an elevator to access the five bedrooms and seven bathrooms. It was built in the Tuscan style that Kim liked, but Kanye was intent on remodelling and began a huge redevelopment that practically meant pulling down the house and starting again. There was little chance it would be ready by the time their first child was born.

Kim decided that she wasn't going to be filmed giving birth on *Keeping Up with the Kardashians*. Kourtney, who now had two children, had already done that successfully and apparently easily, and Kim didn't want millions of viewers watching her push her daughter into the world. She hinted that she intended to be a touch more private in the future. She did, however, share early on in her pregnancy that she was expecting a girl.

Kanye spent much of Kim's pregnancy away from home, recording a new album in Paris, where he always felt so inspired, and returning by private jet when he was required for doctor's appointments. The cast of the reality show never saw him. Bruce Jenner confided that he had met him only once, while his son Brody, who had joined the cast for the ninth series, had never met him. Kim likes Paris, so she would travel over to stay at his loft apartment above a hotel while he concentrated on recording. The result was the critically acclaimed album *Yeezus*.

He made it back to Los Angeles for the baby shower, but arrived, hidden underneath a hoodie, when it was nearly all over. This wasn't a cosy gathering of a handful of guests in the lounge, but a full-blown occasion, bigger than most weddings. The white-themed party was another Kardashian event held in the gardens of the Azoff home in Beverly Hills. A series of marquees was erected, so that guests could dine alfresco while keeping out of the sun. Kim wore a voluminous, flowing white gown and kept cool, thanks to a security guard walking beside her with an open parasol shielding her from the brunchtime sun.

Thousands of dollars of white bouquets and table arrangements were shipped in as more than 50 guests, including Mel B, Kelly Osbourne, Nicole Richie and Kimberly Stewart mingled and waited their turn to wish the mum-to-be the best of luck. All the women wore white garlands in their hair

211

to match the dress code. Kendall Jenner, who had grown up before the eyes of a television audience, stood out, as any top model should, by wearing all turquoise.

Very few men braved the day. Lamar Odom and Scott Disick dutifully arrived together. Kim's nephew, Mason, wore white and looked the image of his father. Kanye clearly didn't want the photographers to take his picture on this particular day, although his reluctance to show his face may also have had something to do with him ending his association with Irving Azoff. The Live Nation company had promoted his *Watch the Throne* tour with Jay Z, but apparently Irving and Kanye didn't agree about how his career should progress.

Inevitably, Kanye's prolonged absence in Paris led to whispers that all was not well with the relationship. On top of that, Kim had to deal with a kiss-and-tell story in which a Canadian model claimed to have slept with Kanye after a concert in Atlantic City the previous summer. She also alleged a meeting took place in October in New York, where he kept an apartment. Considering the high profile of the Kardashians, there have been relatively few exposés over the years. The most graphic, as far as Kim personally is concerned, was when a porn star called Julian St Jox alleged he had a threesome with Kim and another woman – a porn actress – at a swingers' party in Culver City when Kim was 20.

The rumours were well wide of the mark, as Kanye prepared to be based full time in California by quietly listing his Manhattan bachelor apartment for $4.5 million. He intended to take family life seriously when his daughter was born. He instructed removal men to ship his most precious possessions to Los Angeles.

His move coincided with the news, a week after the baby shower, that after many months Kim was finally divorced. Apparently, the lawyers reached a settlement in April that put an end to nearly two years of legal jousting. Kim and Kris had both signed a prenup, but the prolonged proceedings were due to Kris demanding an annulment rather than a straightforward divorce. In the end, agreement was reached before she was due to give birth, which was a huge relief to her. In any self-respecting rom-com, the heroine takes a wrong turn before realising where true love lies and, unfortunately for all concerned, the marriage to Kris was Kim's.

She was supposed to have six weeks before the delivery date, but that didn't happen. Instead, 12 days after becoming a free woman again, she was rushed to her birthing suite at the Cedars-Sinai Medical Center, complaining that all was not well. She needed to go into emergency labour, because she was suffering from pre-eclampsia, a condition that can affect women in the latter stages of pregnancy and result in soaringly high blood pressure. The only way to cure it is to deliver the baby, so Kim gave birth five weeks early, on 15 June 2013, to a girl weighing 4lb 15oz. Kanye made it to the hospital in time, although he waited outside during the emergency delivery. Sweetly, he couldn't contain his excitement: 'When I walked in to see her, Kim was holding the baby. I said, "Oh my God, you're a natural." Kim said, "I know, it's so weird."'

The expectation was that they would name the child something beginning with K, and Kaidance was an early favourite. Speculation ended when news was leaked that she was going to be called North, which led to much guffawing in the

213

media. One humorist suggested the child was going to go straight to the top … and a little to the left. According to Kris Jenner, the choice had nothing to do with points of the compass. Instead, Kim explained to her that the significance of North was that to them it meant highest power, and her birth was the highest point of their life to date. Kris said, 'I thought that was really sweet.' Mostly, Kim and Kanye called their new daughter Nori, a neat combination of their middle names – Noel and Omari.

Their new home wasn't ready. They were still choosing the furnishings, including gold fittings for the four luxury toilets, a Swarovski-encrusted fridge-freezer and six special edition beds similar to the ones in the best suites at the Savoy Hotel in London. The new family moved into Kris Jenner's house in Hidden Hills. She and Bruce spent most of their time at a property they still owned in Malibu, which gave Kim and Kanye some privacy – although they employed a nurse to make sure their premature baby suffered no problems in her early weeks.

Three days after North was born, the album *Yeezus* was released and went to number one in both the UK and the US, as well as another 29 countries worldwide. June was turning out to be a very good month. They decided against negotiating a fee for the first pictures of their baby. They didn't need the money, as *Forbes* placed them fifth among the highest-earning celebrity couples, with $30 million – still some way behind top-ranked Jay Z and Beyoncé, who had collected $95 million the previous year.

Instead, Kanye was a guest on the season finale of Kris Jenner's new talk show and proudly showed a picture of his child on screen. He spoke movingly of his love for Kim and North: 'Now I have two really special people to live for, a whole family to live for; a whole world to live for.' Disappointingly for Kris, who up until this point seemed to have a Midas touch on TV, the show was cancelled by Fox after six episodes – even a rare interview with Kanye couldn't save it.

Now that the baby was thriving, her parents could think about marriage. Kanye didn't disappoint. He met Kris and told her confidentially that he was going to propose. She loved his grandiose plan, and persuaded him to allow them to film the moment for *Keeping Up with the Kardashians*. He agreed on the basis that nothing would be shown immediately. He intended to make his move on Kim's thirty-third birthday. Only Kris knew what was really going on. Everyone else in the family was told that he had a big surprise planned for Kim's birthday and they needed to be at the AT&T Park, home of the San Francisco Giants, on 21 October.

On the night, Kanye led a blindfolded Kim out into the centre of the ballpark. Fireworks lit up the sky and a 50-piece orchestra serenaded her with her favourite Lana Del Rey song, 'Young and Beautiful'. When he told her to remove the blindfold, he was down on one knee, with the widest smile on his face and his arm outstretched with an engagement ring in his hand. Above, fireworks spelled out 'Pleeease Marry Meee!'. Kim, who thought it was going to be an extravagant birthday party and genuinely didn't know what was going to happen, couldn't conceal her delight, as she shouted yes and took her new fiancé in her arms for a loving kiss. In the rom-com film of their lives, *When Yeezy Met Kimmy*, this was the perfect ending, without a dry eye in the cinema.

Two people were conspicuously absent from the big night: Lamar Odom and Bruce Jenner. When asked, Lamar would only say that he had something to do. Bruce, however, had quietly split up with Kris and it seemed inappropriate for him to join the celebration.

After becoming a mum, Kim worked hard to lose the 50 pounds she had gained during pregnancy. It paid off, because in December she looked back to her fashionable best at the *Hollywood Reporter* Women in Entertainment breakfast in a mustard silk dress and coat that matched her newly dyed blonde hairdo. Kanye had always been an advocate of mono-chrome outfits, using all one colour to create a striking effect.

Now that she was seeing more of him, they were able to confer every day on her outfits. She stopped using a stylist all the time, preferring to share the task with him. If she was going to a shoot, then he would often show up to give his opinion and input some ideas. She said simply, 'He is my best stylist.'

As a preface to their actual wedding, Kim fulfilled a long-term ambition when she appeared on the front cover of *Vogue* for the first time at the beginning of May. She said it was a 'dream come true'. For the shoot, she wore a Lanvin wedding gown, with her engagement ring, another creation by Lorraine Schwartz, prominently displayed. Kanye stood behind her and held her in his arms. Annie Leibovitz, one of the finest and most prestigious photographers in the world, had taken the sort of understated shot that always seems to work best for Kim.

She looked beautiful. Would her own wedding dress look as good later in the month when they married in Florence? Kanye has a great affinity with Europe and he wanted his wedding to be across the Atlantic. He might well have settled in Paris permanently if he had chosen to pursue a career exclusively in fashion.

Their wedding celebrations began on a Wednesday in Paris, at Givenchy, where presumably Kim was having a final fitting for her wedding dress. The next day, she chose a pearl-covered outfit from Balmain couture to pose with her girlfriends in front of the Eiffel Tower and the Louvre Museum. In the evening, her closest female friends joined her for a special dinner. Her mother's best friend, Shelli Azoff, proposed a toast that gave an emotional insight into the kind of woman Kim is behind the glamour of her celebrity image. Shelli said, 'I am incredibly proud, and always have been, of who you are as a human being, as a person. I am incredibly proud of how smart you are. I am incredibly proud of how kind you are. I am incredibly proud of where you are today and I love you very much.' Kim beamed.

On Friday, Kim and Kanye joined their guests for a brunch hosted by the legendary designer Valentino in the gardens of his seventeenth-century Chateau de Wideville, just west of the capital. In the evening, there was a private tour of the Palace of Versailles.

On Saturday, 24 May 2014, they were married in Florence at the sixteenth-century Forte di Belvedere, next to the Boboli Gardens, with views across one of the most beautiful settings in the world. It was perfect. One hundred white doves were released into the sky as they exchanged their vows. As Kim walked down the aisle on the arm of her stepfather, she heard the sound of one of her favourite singers, Andrea Bocelli, singing 'Ave Maria'. She looked up and, amazingly, he was actually there in person, performing for her at her wedding. He continued with 'Con te partirò' during the service. Later, at the reception, John Legend, a good friend of Kanye, sang his soulful ballad 'All of Me'. Rumours that Beyoncé was going to perform proved to be untrue, as neither she nor Jay Z attended.

Kim couldn't have looked lovelier. She had three wedding dresses ready, but on the day chose a sublime couture gown by Kanye's friend Riccardo Tisci for Givenchy. Alison Jane Reid enthused, 'It was a demure lace and pearl embellished work of art that fitted and flattered her body like a second skin. Most importantly, the dress is flattering from all angles.

'The dazzling white of the gown gave her a look of extraordinary radiance and contrasted brilliantly with her dark hair and black eyes. For once, Kim didn't flaunt an ounce of flesh and she looked luminous, elegant, timeless and as regal as a royal bride.' For many, Kim's dress outshone Kate Middleton's Alexander McQueen gown when she married Prince William, simply because it wasn't as safe and successfully walked the fine line between demure and sexy. Alison Jane explained, 'The Givenchy gown works because it shows the line of her body, while the flesh stays covered. This is a great fashion conceit – to give tantalising hints at what lies beneath.'

This time the wedding wasn't filmed for *Keeping Up with the Kardashians*, although the reality show was there for all the build-up. E! no doubt helped with the bill. Both Bruce and Kris Jenner gave speeches at the dinner afterwards. Bruce wasn't the centre of attention on this day, but he soon would be.

19

CAITLYN

Kim kept the biggest Kardashian family secret for more than a decade. She had arrived home unexpectedly and found her stepfather wearing a dress. Apparently, she was so taken aback that she ignored his efforts to explain, ran straight out of the house and never mentioned what she had witnessed to anyone. She said later that she thought it was something she wasn't supposed to talk about.

Nobody spoke about Bruce's gender or cross-dressing issues in the Kardashian or Jenner households. He insisted that when he met Kris he was 'a good solid B cup' because of his hormone treatment. She doesn't agree with his version of events, maintaining that there was nothing obvious, just a hint of man-boob.

The first time the public had an inkling was when Robert Kardashian's widow, Ellen, revealed that Bruce was a secret cross-dresser in an interview with a tabloid magazine in January 2012. She claimed then that his first wife had confided in her at a drinks party.

Ellen said that Chrystie Crownover, who had remarried and was now called Chrystie Scott, had told her that she discovered what was going on when she returned from a trip and realised he had gone through her clothes. He had even clipped an elastic band to one of her bras, so he could fit into it.

Surprisingly, the revelation didn't lead to a public clamouring for more information. Perhaps they didn't believe that the Olympic hero liked to wear female clothing around the house. It seemed so far-fetched, especially as it hadn't featured in any episode of *Keeping Up with the Kardashians*.

The story said that Kris Jenner had always known about it. The suggestion in the ground-breaking *Vanity Fair* interview was that she had set some rules, which meant he could only indulge in cross-dressing when he was away from home. She denied this.

A man dressing as woman is largely a subject of comedy in modern culture, with films such as *Tootsie* and *Mrs Doubtfire* becoming box office success stories. In the UK, there is a long tradition of hugely popular entertainers, including Dick Emery, Les Dawson and Paul O'Grady (Lily Savage), relying on cross-dressing to get a laugh. The implication as far as Bruce Jenner was concerned was that, even if it were true, it was just a bit of eccentric fun.

The Jenners' marriage had been going downhill, practically ever since the cameras invaded their lives. Bruce felt he was being sidelined in his own home, as Kris seized the opportunity to build an empire that left him on the fringes. They argued all the time, seemingly wanting different things from their lives.

Bruce hated the way he had become unimportant. He told *Vanity Fair* that gender issues weren't the principal reason for the breakdown of his marriage: 'Twenty per cent was gender and 80 per cent was the way I was treated.' Her opinion was that he never fully explained his gender dysphoria until after they were divorced.

The rumours that all was not well had been in circulation for months before the Jenners finally split in June 2013. Bruce stayed in Malibu, where he had always preferred to live. Kris moved back permanently to Hidden Hills and shared the house with Kim, Kanye and baby North.

Bruce and Kris issued a joint statement: 'We are living separately and are much happier this way. But we will always have much love and respect for each other. Even though we are separated, we will always remain best friends, and, as always, our family will remain our number one priority.' The statement, which yet again emphasised the importance of family, had the air of something dictated by Kris.

Bruce decided that now was the time to move forward with his gender transformation, although he had no plans to go public with his decision before the divorce had been granted. It's easy to forget that Bruce and Kris had been married for more than 20 years. In her autobiography, published two years before, in 2011, she had acknowledged Bruce for 'twenty years of unwavering love, happiness and support'.

While Kris was announcing to the world that they had a 'pretty fabulous' relationship after their separation, he was intent on embracing his female identity fully. He made an appointment for a tracheal shave, a common process for transgender women, which reduces the size of the Adam's apple. A surgeon makes an incision in the throat and slices off part of the cartilage to achieve a more feminine appearance.

Unfortunately, in December 2014, he was seen leaving a consultation in Beverly Hills, and a story appeared online that he was planning the procedure, which is often one of the first steps towards gender reassignment surgery. It was nearly the final straw for Bruce, who had lived a lifetime of agony. He contemplated suicide, using a gun he kept in the house: 'I've been in some dark places.'

A week before Christmas, his divorce from Kris was finalised. There had never been a prenup agreement, so, basically, they each kept their own assets and existing contracts. Both had become extremely rich over the years, although Kris was by far the wealthier of the two, thanks to her business acumen.

She kept the family home in Hidden Hills and agreed to pay Bruce $2.5 million, but no spousal support was involved. Bruce had by now bought a new $3.5 million home in Malibu. They divided up the vehicles. She had the Bentley, a Rolls-Royce Ghost and a Range Rover, while he kept a Porsche Coupe, a Cadillac Escalade and the Harley-Davidson motorcycle that he had always loved.

The appearance of the story about his tracheal shave meant he needed to tell his children his plans as a priority. He was no longer in control of the time frame. He discovered that his four elder children already knew of his struggle with his gender identity. Chrystie had told Burt and Casey 20 years before and they had kept his secret, as so many had in this story, because of their love and regard for him.

Linda didn't tell Brandon and Brody until after the first stories started to appear about the cross-dressing, but it gave them an insight into their father and to some extent explained why he had found it difficult to maintain a connection with them. That was about to change for his four eldest children. For the first time in many years, they would feel they were genuinely part of their father's life, as he became the person he had always wanted to be – a woman of poise and grace called Caitlyn Jenner.

The Jenner side of the family readily accepted his frank admission about how he wanted to live his life in the future. His daughter Cassandra, in particular, bonded with her father during a girls' night at the house in Malibu, when he was finding his feet with female company in a social setting. When he first told her, she asked him what she should call him. He replied, 'I'm Dad. You can call me Dad.'

After he had told all his children individually, he underwent an exceptionally painful 10-hour procedure called facial feminisation surgery, which involved reconstructing the contours of his face to give him more recognisably female features. He also had breast augmentation.

Bruce decided it would be best to move out from under Kris's management umbrella, and hired a new team to mastermind his public revelations. A masterful campaign took shape under the watchful guidance of Alan Nierob, a long-standing executive at Rogers & Cowan, who had helped to suppress a story about Bruce's cross-dressing as far back as the 1980s.

Nierob decided the journalist Buzz Bissinger could have three months' access for a *Vanity Fair* article, in which he would reveal Bruce's new identity for the first time. The accompanying pictures would be taken by Annie Leibovitz.

The world became aware of what was happening to Bruce for the first time in April 2015, during a two-hour *20/20* special with Diane Sawyer, *Bruce Jenner: The Interview*. It was filmed at his Malibu home and watched by 16.9 million viewers. He told the distinguished broadcaster, 'To all intents and purposes, I am a woman.' He also told her that this would be the last interview he would ever give as Bruce Jenner.

The programme was universally praised for handling a difficult issue with humanity and frankness. Diane didn't avoid asking the questions that needed to be answered for the public to understand what Caitlyn was going through. That included clarifying the issue of his sexuality. He told Diane that he was heterosexual, had never been with a man and wasn't gay. This was an issue of gender, not sexuality. He understood that it was confusing for some people to understand that sexual orientation and gender identity aren't the same thing. He said of his own sexuality: 'Let's go with asexual for now. I'm going to learn a lot in the next year.'

Bruce also admitted that he had downplayed the extent of his true nature to Kris, and was generous in his appreciation of his third ex-wife: 'I loved Kris. I had a wonderful life with her. I learned a lot from her.'

The Kardashian side of the family didn't appear in the broadcast. Their involvement would come later in episodes of their reality show. Bruce did reveal, however, that Kim had been by far 'the most accepting and easiest to talk to about it'. She had said to him, 'Girl, you gotta rock it, baby. You gotta look good.'

Up to that point, Bruce hadn't got on particularly well with Kanye West. They weren't close. It was the superstar, however, who held the most enlightened view in the Kardashian camp. He had an enormous influence on Kim's ability to accept what was happening and persuade the rest of her family to do the same.

During the Diane Sawyer interview, Bruce spoke about the role Kanye had played. 'He said to Kim, "Look, I can be married to the most beautiful woman in the world and I am. I can have the most beautiful little daughter in the world and I have that ... But I'm nothing if I can't be me. If I can't be true to myself, they don't mean anything."'

Khloé found it most difficult to process the news. Bruce said she had taken it hardest. She had been most obviously affected by the death of her father and seemed the most sensitive of the children.

At times, Bruce was emotional and a little tearful as he explained that his brain was much more female than male. That was where his soul was, and what he had tried to explain to his children. He told Diane, 'I'm saying goodbye to people's perception of me and who I am. I'm not saying goodbye to me. Because this has always been me.'

The response to the broadcast, particularly among celebrities, was supportive and positive. Elton John said, 'It's an incredibly brave thing to do, especially when you're older.' Lena Dunham observed, 'I think it's an incredibly powerful and brave move to disclose anything about your gender identity or sexuality in such a judgemental society. The interview is going to mean a lot to a lot of young people.'

His family tweeted their love and support. Kim used the hashtag 'ProudDaughter' and wrote in Kanye-like terms: 'Love is the courage to live the truest, best version of yourself. Bruce is love. I love you, Bruce.' Kris Jenner said, 'Not only was I able to call him my husband for 25 years and father of my children, I am now able to call him my hero.' The most touching reaction came from Rob Kardashian: 'You have always been a role model to me and now more than ever, I look up to you. LOVE YOU!!!!'

The one voice that jarred with the prevailing mood belonged to Kris Humphries, who tweeted, 'Man, I'm glad I got out when I did.' After a night's sleep, Kris hastily apologised for his ill-considered remark, which proved an interesting contrast with the attitude of Kanye, the man who replaced him.

Another two months would pass before the *Vanity Fair* issues hit the news-stands, revealing that Bruce was no more. 'Call me Caitlyn' proclaimed the cover, which featured her wearing a one-piece white swimsuit. The picture, a throwback to old-style Hollywood glamour, is already an iconic image. Caitlyn looked astonishing for a woman of 65, an age when you normally collect your pension and a free bus pass.

It hadn't been easy for Caitlyn to choose her new name. She considered both Heather and Cathy, before settling on a name she had felt an affinity with since childhood. It would have been unbearably twee to have spelt it with a K and, in any case, the choice was made more complicated by the fact that her son Brody's girlfriend was the blogger Kaitlynn Carter.

The most seized-upon revelation in *Vanity Fair* was Caitlyn's claim that she hadn't been treated well by her former wife. She said Kris had become less tolerant, controlled the money and had mistreated Bruce. It was strong stuff. Caitlyn said, 'A lot of times she wasn't very nice.' Kris was, by all accounts, 'beyond distraught' after these remarks.

Inside the magazine, the photographs were as glamorous as the cover. Caitlyn reclined on a sofa in a black Hervé Leger top and skirt. She sat in her dressing room in an Agent Provocateur corset. She posed confidently behind the wheel of her Porsche, a $180,000 gift from Kris, in a scarlet dress by DKNY. She compared the shoot with winning Olympic Gold in 1976: 'That was a good day. But the last couple of days were better.'

The *Vanity Fair* exclusive was empowering for the transgender community. One of the most powerful effects was when 18 transgender people posted their own '*Vanity Fair*' covers, introducing themselves to the world, proclaiming 'Call me' followed by their new name. Some commentators pointed out that not everyone had the money to afford the treatment and surgery that Caitlyn had undergone. They also might not be able to afford high-end designer dresses to look as good as she did.

Kim met Caitlyn for the first time when she was invited to attend the Leibovitz photographic sessions. She observed, 'She's beautiful and I'm so proud that she can just be her authentic self. I guess that's what life is all about.' Under Kanye's influence, Kim has been able to approach important issues in a sensitive and intelligent manner. She drew attention to the plight of the many transgender men and women who didn't have the family support Caitlyn enjoyed: 'There's such a high suicide rate in the transgender community, which is heartbreaking.'

Kim had touched on an issue that would become Caitlyn's cause in the coming months – the treatment of transgender men and women, particularly the young and vulnerable, in society. Caitlyn began a series of blogs to highlight the ordeals of people fighting for survival in the world. She wrote, 'Many trans teens are bullied and abused in high school. It's just horrendous.' In a second blog, she told the heartbreaking story of a 14-year-old trans boy in San Diego, who had been unable to cope with the pressures and had committed suicide.

Caitlyn drew further attention to the plight of the transgender community when she received the Arthur Ashe Courage Award at the 2015 ESPYs in Los Angeles. She received a standing ovation and delivered a powerful speech, which harked back to the hundreds of motivational speeches she had given as Bruce Jenner.

She said, 'All across this country right now, all across the world, at this very moment, there are young people coming to terms with being transgender … They're getting bullied, they're getting beaten up, they're getting murdered, and they're committing suicide … Trans people deserve something vital. They deserve your respect. And from that respect comes a more compassionate community, a more empathetic society and a better world for us all.'

The stirring speech pointed to a future role for Caitlyn. It seemed incredible that this was the put-upon dad figure from *Keeping Up with the Kardashians*. She had managed to hide his true self for more than 400 episodes.

Her own television series, *I Am Cait*, premiered 10 days later on E!. It was another Bunim/Murray production and apparently the Jenner children decided not to take part in what they feared was just another entertainment show. His 95-year-old mother Esther featured, however, and poignantly referred to Caitlyn as Bruce throughout: 'It's overwhelming. I knew he was going to be dressed as a woman. I think he is a very good-looking woman, but he is still Bruce to me.'

Kim and Kanye were also involved. Kim bonded with Caitlyn over her wardrobe. They went off together to investigate her clothes and Kim told her which outfits looked chic and which had to go – presumably on eBay. The Queen of the Closet Scene hadn't lost her magic touch when it came to styling.

The rapper told Caitlyn that her transition was 'one of the strongest things that has happened in our existence as human beings who are controlled by perception.' Kanye, who seldom features in his wife's reality show, praised the way Caitlyn had overcome so many hurdles: 'You couldn't have been up against more. Like, your daughter [Kendall] is a supermodel, you're a celebrity, you have every type of thing, and it was still like, "Fuck everybody, this is who I am."'

20

DOUBLE THE POWER

Kim works just as hard today for *Keeping Up with the Kardashians* as she did when it started 10 seasons ago. She has been up for six hours by the time filming begins at noon. She wakes at 6a.m., checks North's baby monitor by the side of the bed and then her emails on her phone. She gets tired, but is never hungover, so she hasn't lost the knack of springing out of bed to face the day.

After popping into her daughter's bedroom to say good morning, she is straight into her jogging gear for a run along one of the many trails that twist around Hidden Hills. It's scenic and safe, although many of the residents do like to ride their horses first thing in the morning. If she doesn't fancy leaving the house, she can make do with an hour in the home gym.

They never moved into the mansion in Bel Air, which they have been renovating since they bought it at the beginning of 2013. It seems likely they will sell it quietly when a potential buyer comes along who will ensure a tidy profit. Instead, they both seem to have settled on Hidden Hills as a better place to raise their family. Living at her mother's house reminded Kim how much she enjoyed the quiet of the gated and guarded community.

Kanye often preferred to keep away from the madness of *Keeping Up with the Kardashians* and stay at his old bachelor home at the foot of the Hollywood Hills, which has been on the market for five years. That unsatisfactory arrangement changed when they finally bought a family property to move into in August 2014.

The fully landscaped three-acre estate was previously owned by Lisa Marie Presley, and reportedly cost them just under $20 million. It boasts eight bedrooms, 10 bathrooms, eight fire-places, two swimming pools, two spas, tennis courts and a vineyard, a rose garden, an acre of lawn and a gated motor court. For good measure, there's an entertainment pavilion and a separate, secluded guest house – and they bought the house next door for a miserly $2.9 million to guarantee their privacy. The main, stone-fronted manor house is actually a new-build in the French country style. This may be what the snobs of Beverly Hills and Bel Air call the suburbs, but it's undeniably grand even for someone brought up in Tower Lane.

They can easily afford this luxury. Kim could write the cheque from her own earnings alone. Rich list figures often seem to be plucked from thin air, but *Forbes* suggests that from 2014 to 2015 her income has risen from $28 million to $53 million. Much of that increase is due to the success of her iPhone and tablet game, *Kim Kardashian: Hollywood*, which launched in June 2014. It's a brilliant concept. You create your own Kim Kardashian-like character and see yourself rise to fame and fortune. Within nine months, it had become a huge hit, with an estimated 28 million downloads and 11 billion minutes of play.

The concept of being able to update the game in real time came about by accident. Kim put a picture of herself in a bikini on Instagram the day of the launch, when she was on holiday at Joe Francis's Mexican estate. Fans immediately thought it was part of the game and started to update their app with the swimsuit she was wearing.

The characteristics of the game mirror Kim's own lifestyle and progress. You can customise your look from literally hundreds of style options, just as Kim does when her make-up and hair team descend on the house every day at 10 a.m. to prepare her for filming. It normally takes about an hour and a half. If she has an early meeting in Los Angeles, then she will forgo her morning run and be in the 'glam room', as she calls her dressing room, at dawn to be fashioned into Kim Kardashian. Her make-up artist will have hundreds of brushes and blushes ready to contour her face into her now iconic look. The result is somewhat futuristic, and one that suppresses individual beauty in favour of a flawless mask, but it is very much of the moment.

Kim has a lot of meetings because her projects are on a conveyor belt, whizzing by like the prizes at the end of a game show. They either generate publicity and greater fame or cash in on it. The inspired 'Break the Internet' campaign was part of the former, based around a nude photo shoot for *Paper* magazine, in which she posed with a champagne glass balanced on her butt. Other front and rear shots were great fun and cheeky. They seemed much more brazen than the more innocent days of *Playboy*. It was just the image boost she needed before she starred in the 30-second commercial for T-Mobile's Data Stash, which premiered during the 2015 Super Bowl.

Kim is careful to build her diary around the reality show rather than try to squeeze it in between other business meetings, pet projects or family time. The Kardashians, on the other hand, made a sort of Faustian pact to live their lives as if they were the cast of *The Truman Show*, the famous 1998 comedy-drama starring Jim Carrey. The main character is unaware that his life is a carefully constructed reality television show, broadcast to millions around the world. The Kardashians are well aware that they live in a constructed reality show. Kim has even made the connection to the movie herself in trying to describe what her life is like. When they are filming, they often don't stop for lunch. One camera crew breaks and another comes in, so they never stop rolling and can capture Kim eating what her chef has prepared that day.

'They are consummate performers,' observed Kevin O'Sullivan, TV critic of the *Sunday Mirror*. 'They know what to do in front of the camera to an excruciating extent. Sure, the Kardashians play to the cameras, but there is innately something about them that makes them born reality television stars. Their lives would be car crashes with or without the prism of reality television. I firmly believe Kim would go out and marry someone for 72 days whether or not she was on telly.'

The success of the show was never better illustrated than in February 2015, when the Kardashians signed a new four-year deal with E! reputed to be worth $100 million. They were

already the highest-paid stars in reality television and this reinforced their status. The figure is probably inflated, nevertheless
they do make an absolute fortune. The show will be even
more female dominated than before, with the six women
taking the limelight: Kim, Kourtney, Khloé, Kendall, Kylie and
their mother, Kris Jenner.

All the major events of the family's lives are chronicled.
Everything is shared. No storyline could ever match the journey of Caitlyn Jenner from Olympic champion to the most
famous transgender person in the world. The tenth series of
Keeping Up with the Kardashians will be her last, although
crossovers with her own show, *I Am Cait*, will almost certainly
continue. The publicity surrounding Caitlyn's transition has
understandably eclipsed everything. The emotional struggle of
Kris Jenner, whom she was married to for 23 years, was largely
forgotten, as viewers became absorbed in which swimsuit
Caitlyn would choose for her first dip in a pool as a transgender woman.

Khloé Kardashian observed that her mother was probably
the most 'jarred' by what had happened and was left wondering if her life for all those years they were together was still
validated. She was questioning, according to Khloé, whether
Caitlyn was ever truly in love with her. Whatever her private
thoughts, Kris has been very supportive of her ex-husband in
public: 'I think that someone following their dream is truly
inspirational to a lot of people ... You have to do what makes
you happy.'

At the age of 58, she embarked on a new relationship with
a music executive, Corey Gamble, whom she met in August
2014 in Ibiza at the fortieth birthday party for Riccardo Tisci,

Kanye's great friend and the designer of Kim's wedding dress. Corey, who is 24 years younger than Kris, comes from Atlanta, the same home town as Kanye.

Corey is very stylish and stands out from the crowd, with his diamond earrings and shaven head. For the first time, Kris is following the lead of her famous daughters and dating a handsome and fashionable African-American. He works for Justin Bieber's manager, Scooter Braun, and is usually part of the superstar's entourage around the world.

Kris and Corey were seen enjoying dinner dates back home in Los Angeles and he was her plus one for Kim's thirty-fourth birthday celebrations, which were held, as usual, in Las Vegas. A year later, they are still a couple, despite him being younger than Kim. Her children have found it interesting, to say the least, watching their mum date again after all these years.

On one occasion, when Kim and Khloé popped round to their mother's house, they heard the banging of the headboard coming from Kris's bedroom, a sign that vigorous sex was being enjoyed. The two sisters kept as quiet as possible, waiting for them to finish, so they could have a cup of tea and a visit. When everything went silent, they expected to see their mum walk into the kitchen. Instead, the headboard started banging again, as they went for round two. Kim and Khloé had heard more than enough and crept away.

Kris and Corey flew to Europe in June 2015 for a romantic break, but also to support Kendall Jenner, who was one of the catwalk stars of Men's Fashion Week in Paris. They sat in the front row at Riccardo's show for Givenchy and watched Kendall and Naomi Campbell vie for attention in daring outfits that seemed to have nothing to do with men's fashion.

Kendall and Kylie were youngsters when *Keeping Up with the Kardashians* was first broadcast in October 2007. Kendall was 11 and Kylie just 10 when they made their debut as refreshingly normal, sometimes sulky girls. The elder one grew up to be a stunningly attractive girl who dreamed of being a model: 'I would sit at home and have my friends take pictures of me on my little Canon camera that my mom gave me for Christmas.'

While she can't yet match Kim's following on social media, the gap is closing. When Kim broke through the barrier of 27 million followers on Instagram, Kendall had more than 20 million.

She has used her online presence to generate interest in her modelling career, which began at the age of 14, when Wilhelmina Models signed her. In the early years, her mother helped guide her career, but in 2013 she joined The Society management and moved into the runway world of high fashion. Their biggest coup to date was landing her the contract as the face of cosmetics giant Estée Lauder. The company shrewdly allowed her to make the announcement on Instagram and Twitter, thus immediately hitting millions of young women within the right age demographic. The slight irony in choosing Kendall is that, unlike Kim, she rarely looks like she's wearing any make-up.

The media, which can't bear the fact that she never seems to have a steady boyfriend, have tried to link her with Justin Bieber, Harry Styles, Lewis Hamilton and the bisexual model Cara Delevingne.

Much of her personal branding, which has been set up by her mother, consists of joint ventures with her more controversial sister Kylie. It very much follows Kim's blueprint for commercial success with her personal clothing and jewellery lines.

Kylie, meanwhile, admitted on an episode of *Keeping Up with the Kardashians* that she had lip-fillers, which was no surprise to anyone who could see how much her face had changed recently. She also had to contend with rumours that she had a boob job at 17, claims that she firmly denied online.

Most controversial is her ongoing relationship with Tyga (Michael Ray Nguyen-Stevenson), the Vietnamese-Jamaican rapper. He apparently met her for the first time when he was the guest artist at Kendall's Sweet 16 party. She was 14 and he was 21. At the time, he was with his fiancée, a hip-hop model and former stripper called Blac Chyna (Angela White), and the pair had a little boy, King. Kris and Kim, resembling an expensively dressed aunt, were both at the party, looking obviously out of place, as the latter politely thanked the shirtless Tyga for coming.

Neither Tyga nor Kylie confirmed anything more than a friendship. Kris Jenner was diplomatic when asked about it. Tyga lived in the same neighbourhood as Khloé, she said, and he and Kylie shared many mutual friends. It became slightly harder to conceal their true feelings when Kylie became 18 in August 2015 and he gave her a white Ferrari worth $320,000 as a birthday present.

He parked the car, tied with a red ribbon, outside the Bootsy Bellows nightclub in West Hollywood, where Kylie, with a new blonde hairdo, was celebrating with her friends and family, including her father, Caitlyn Jenner, who was meeting Tyga for the first time.

When Tyga and Blac Chyna were together, they were very good friends with Kim and Kanye and were pictured out with them. She even appeared in an episode of *Keeping Up with the Kardashians* during the ninth season. To make matters even more awkward, she is now best friends with Kanye's ex-lover, Amber Rose.

Both Kylie and Kendall's ongoing storylines in real life already reveal just how much more mileage there is left in the Kardashian family reality show. Kim and Kourtney are mothers in their mid-thirties, so it's important that the younger women can bring fresh material and new characters into the family's world.

Kourtney has, for some time, ensured that the show takes second place behind her three children in her list of priorities. As well as Mason, aged five, she has Penelope Scotland, who was born 8 July 2012. She gave birth to a second son, Reign Aston, on 14 December 2014 and, by an unusual twist of fate, he shares Mason's birthday. She has always been single-minded and decided early on that she was always going to be home to put her children to bed and she wasn't going to work weekends.

The roller-coaster of her relationship with Scott Disick has been one of the main threads throughout the years of the show. They always seemed a step away from getting married. He first proposed during an episode of *Kourtney and Kim Take New York* in 2005. She said no. When asked about their status at the beginning of 2015, he said, 'If it's not broke, don't fix it.'

By July, it was broke and they split up. He had struggled over the years with bouts of heavy drinking and partying. Kourtney once recalled that their fights always appeared fresh and new and kept playing on her mind, because, instead of being forgotten about, they were endlessly on repeat on the show. He had three bouts of rehab, culminating at a centre in Costa Rica, but he checked out after only a week.

The final straw came when he was pictured in Monaco at the beginning of July 2015 in the company of Chloé Bartoli, a celebrity stylist and old flame. They appeared affectionate, but you never know when that's just for the benefit of the photographers. It was enough for Kourtney, however, and she threw him out of their house in Calabasas. Fortunately, he already had another home in Beverly Hills.

Following the breakup, Scott was seen partying in Las Vegas and Calgary, while Kourtney posted pictures online of herself with her sons and daughter. She sought legal advice about custody of the children, but reports suggested she would be happy with joint custody. Scott isn't part of the new TV deal, but is already rumoured to be in talks with E! for a new reality show based loosely on the theme of *Entourage*. Nobody is still sure what he does for a living. He seems to invest in a variety of businesses but earns most from his celebrity appearances. Scott has always been one of the more interesting people in *Keeping Up with the Kardashians* – a show not blessed with strong male characters.

Kevin O'Sullivan explained that reality shows, like the most popular soaps, are based on strong female characters, usually headed by a matriarch. If Kris were in *Coronation Street* or *EastEnders*, she would be the landlady of the Rovers Return or the Queen Vic. 'These shows are about strong women and weak men revolving around them. That's why the Kardashians are like they are. Stupid men are exposed as idiots by strong women. This is the DNA of all soap operas and, leading on from that, of all reality shows, because women, mainly, watch the shows. All women in these programmes are ultimately winners, and all men are ultimately losers.'

While it would be no surprise if Scott and Kourtney rekindled their relationship in season 11, for the moment at least the men on the show are becoming thin on the ground. Robert Kardashian, makes such infrequent appearances that he gets paid by the individual episode. He seems to hate the goldfish bowl in which the other Kardashians happily go about their daily lives.

Of course, his insecurity, his growing bulk and his lack of desire to be filmed all featured on the show. He missed the Christmas celebration and couldn't face being a much-photographed guest at Kim's wedding to Kanye. Apparently, he flew to Europe before realising that he didn't want to be pictured so heavy, and caught a flight straight back home. When they discussed their worries about him on the show, Kim observed, 'He obviously has some kind of depression.'

He has always been in the shadow of his glamorous sisters, although he did far better than Kim on *Dancing with the Stars*, finishing runner-up in 2011. Kris found him enough commercial deals to become a millionaire, but he is nothing like as successful as his sisters, who have all manner of clothing shops and brands on their CV. Rob had to make do with his own sock line, called Arthur George.

He dated Rita Ora for a moment or two in 2012, but that quickly became nothing and he hasn't had a serious relationship since Adrienne Bailon, which ended in 2009. He may return to the show on a more full-time basis in the future, because it clearly needs a regular male character, but they may well build up roles for Corey and Tyga.

Kim has been surprisingly unsympathetic towards her kid brother, believing the family is being overindulgent. She acknowledged that he doesn't feel comfortable appearing on the show because of all the weight he has put on, but said: 'Do I think he smokes weed, drinks beer, hangs out and plays video games with his friends all day long? Yes.' Rob was reportedly furious that she spoke about him and was said to have blocked her from his phone. A few weeks later, however, relations appeared to have thawed again when he shared a picture of Kanye and North on Instagram and subsequently went for a hike with Kim, which she tweeted about as 'the hardest hike ever'.

Rob, now 28, still lives with Khloé in the house she bought after breaking up with Lamar Odom. She filed for divorce in early December 2013, after a turbulent year that included her husband's alleged battle with substance abuse and his arrest for driving under the influence – she herself had a DUI during the first series of the show. She also had to contend with various women coming forward to claim they've had affairs with the basketball player. Unsurprisingly, they sought marriage guidance, but that failed to provide any solutions.

Khloé is the most extrovert and emotional of the Kardashians. She is also extremely popular with people she meets every day in restaurants and stores. In the show, she plays the volatile sister, Kim is the sweet one and Kourtney is the thoughtful sibling. This represents only one aspect of their personalities, but it's the trait that has been developed to give them an individual identity on the show.

Khloé has had more than her share of the drama – not least in the question of her parentage. It's become almost a game online to speculate who her father might be, with suggestions ranging from O. J. Simpson to Lionel Richie and her mother's hairdresser, Alex Roldan. In one episode of *Keeping Up with the Kardashians*, Kris had a DNA test to prove that her daughter wasn't adopted, but it proved nothing about her father.

Both of Robert Kardashian's other wives, Jan Ashley and Ellen Kardashian, have claimed he told them he was not Khloé's dad, which wasn't very helpful to her. It's really a Prince Harry syndrome. Conspiracy theorists will always believe he is James Hewitt's son on the spurious grounds that he has red hair. Khloé has never looked like her older sisters, but in terms of biology, their comparative looks are completely irrelevant.

After her split from Lamar, Khloé became involved with rapper French Montana (Karim Kharbouch), but it turned into nothing more than a friendship. She offered him support after his best friend and fellow rapper Chinx was the victim of a drive-by shooting in New York. French, the CEO of Cocaine City Records, had himself survived being shot in the head outside a recording studio in NYC in 2003.

Khloé has since been linked to James Harden, who is a star basketball player like Lamar. He's 6ft 5in, is nicknamed 'The Beard', for obvious reasons, and plays for the Houston Rockets. He also won an Olympic gold medal with the US basketball team at the London 2012 Olympics. Khloé has been pictured supporting him courtside, but it's early days to see if anything will come of it.

Her divorce proceedings have been as drawn out as those of Kim and Kris Humphries but reports suggest they finally signed the papers in July 2015. She still talks to him as often as she can. She remains very gracious about him, telling *Complex* magazine, 'Lamar is genuinely one of the best people I've ever met and everyone says that when they meet him … He's had a really hard life.'

Since the breakup, she has concentrated on working out and looking her best for her first time on the cover of *Complex* magazine, emulating Kim from 2007. She has never looked so good. Ironically, she managed to keep her marriage problems entirely secret during the filming of *Keeping Up with the Kardashians*. Like Caitlyn's gender issues, there are some things that are too too private to share with millions of viewers.

For once, Kim's wasn't the biggest story in the Kardashian world when she announced, at the beginning of June 2015, that she was pregnant with her second child, a son. The iconic cover of *Vanity Fair*, featuring Caitlyn's first picture as a woman, overshadowed it. Kim didn't mind; she was just grateful that after some fertility worries she was able to conceive. She and Kanye had been having sex a 'thousand' times a day to ensure conception. It evidently worked.

The demands of a second child seem unlikely to slow Kim down, especially as her brand continues to flourish and now, in effect, has double the power, because she is married to such a famous man. Intriguingly, she has become an executive producer on *Keeping Up with the Kardashians* for the new season – a sign perhaps that she intends to step away from the limelight a little, despite her brand relying so much on a daily diet of exposure.

At first, Kim seemed almost too eager to please, too quick to be influenced by a very talented man. Since her wedding, however, her fashion and lifestyle choices seem inspired. Husband and wife find time every day to speak to each other – not just about their own lives, but about what's going on in the world. And they support each other.

Kim was a step behind her husband when he was the star attraction at the 2015 BRITs. He performed his single 'All Day', surrounded by what the *Guardian* described as a 'Greek chorus of 40-odd men in black tracksuits and hoodies, two of them holding giant flame-throwers.' It was a theatrical tour de force. He was upholding the Kardashian edict of making sure you are part of the conversation. In this case, he was the *only* conversation at the usually tepid awards, hosted by Ant and Dec.

Kim made sure she got in on the act by presenting the Global Success Award to Sam Smith for his number one UK single 'Stay with Me'. She shouted 'Wassup, London!' not entirely convincingly, but was dressed breathtakingly. She showcased the Kardashian Wests' now preferred monochrome in an all-black Julien Macdonald jumpsuit that barely covered her generous chest and looked as if someone had attacked it with a pair of scissors. After Sam had been ushered off stage, she had the chance to take a selfie with the grinning hosts, which was neat publicity for her book, *Selfish*.

She was also at Glastonbury at the end of June, when Kanye was a controversial choice to headline the festival. Kim looked uncertain as she arrived by helicopter in the middle of a Somerset field in unsuitably high heels. While her sister Kendall danced away with Cara Delevingne, she watched proudly from the wings as her husband performed. Some wise guy in the crowd tried to dampen the excitement by producing a banner showing a scene from her sex tape in which Ray J's penis was perilously close to her mouth, presumably to try to distract Kanye or provoke a reaction.

The *Daily Telegraph* pointed out: 'Kim Kardashian made a sex tape in 2003, and despite becoming a billionaire business woman with one of the world's strongest brands, finding love and becoming a mother, we are still somehow totally unwilling to let go of something that she did when she was 23 years old and that she presumably thought would remain private.'

Kanye took his turn to support his wife in Armenia in April and the following month, when she once again braved the red carpet at the Met Ball in New York. Kanye, she admits, has given her a new confidence in fashion, but more importantly has convinced her that it is acceptable to experiment, even if you don't always get it right. He has moved her away from treating fashion as a commercial opportunity.

This time her dress, by Peter Dundas for Roberto Cavalli, was a total success. Alison Jane Reid enthused, 'As a perfect celebration of a woman's form, and the art of the couturier, this earthly bird of paradise dress is a masterpiece. It is a glorious, trembling, unabashed homage to the glory of sensuous curves and the ability of well-placed exquisite embroideries and precision engineering to reveal and conceal at the same time. This is how you do sexy Kim Kardashian – in lace, not latex, and fluttering, shake-your-tail feathers. I think a gown like this does wonders for voluptuous women the world over.'

Kim then had to return to the day job, dressing around her pregnancy and ringing Silicon Valley every day to talk about the latest ideas for her app, now her principal money-spinner. All her businesses so far have relied on the success of *Keeping Up with the Kardashians* for their oxygen.

Reality television is now an acceptable genre. Kevin O'Sullivan observes, 'The Kardashians are artistically under-rated. This family is not just going in front of the cameras and being filmed. They are putting on a performance. There is a dazzling brilliance about the Kardashians. It may be staged and slightly ridiculous, but, by Christ, they are doing it well. They are the first and the best.'

At the heart of that brilliance is Kim, a consummate professional in all she does. She continues to be derided as devoid of talent, as if winning a television dance contest would in some way legitimise her success, huge wealth, lovely home and a family that loves her. If what she did were easy and everyone could do it, there would be a million Kim Kardashians out there, but there aren't. There is only one.

LAST THOUGHTS

The car park at the Sheraton Agoura Hills is full. I'm here, like everyone else, for the 11a.m. service of the California Community Church. When Kris Jenner founded the church in 2010, it was called the Life Change Community Church, but was rebranded three years later. It's the Kardashian personal place of worship, although you aren't going to see them in the front-row seats every Sunday. The last time they came en masse was for the Easter service. Everyone wore white, including Kim, Kanye and baby North.

Kim attends occasionally, usually with her mother, and, in particular, when it's been a bad week, as it was when she decided to split from Kris Humphries after only 72 days of marriage. After a trip to hear Pastor Brad Johnson speak, she tweeted that she 'needed that'.

I was expecting a Californian experience of Botox and gospel, but it is surprisingly cool. There's coffee and cake before we get underway and everyone is happy to welcome a new face. The Kardashians are invariably fashionably dressed when they turn up, but the regular congregation doesn't overdo it. Pastor Brad is wearing an extra-large T-shirt and has very white celebrity teeth, but he is funny, likeable and self-deprecating. He talks about his grandson, but there isn't a grey hair on his head.

There's no church organ being played by a local piano teacher here. Instead, a house band with a good sound system plays tight God-rock. Of course, the lyrics have a happy-clappy slant and flash up on a big screen: 'Sing Holy, Holy, Holy' and 'Beautiful One I Love', but it's a perfectly pleasant introduction to worship.

The idea of the church is to promote a sense of community in an area where it's hard to get to know your neighbours, because everyone values privacy and security so highly. One idea, projected on the screen, is called 'Dinner for Eight', in which one member of the congregation hosts a getting-to-know-you supper for seven others. Another initiative is for a women's weekend retreat costing $230. They won't be going to a remote part of the Nevada desert or the Rockies, however. It's in Malibu. My overall impression is that this church could be a slimming club or a Women's Institute gathering – an informal and relaxed way of getting out of the house and meeting people who share a common bond – in this case, using God to find meaning in their lives.

Kim told Piers Morgan, when he interviewed her in 2011, that she gave 10 per cent of her earnings to good causes – partly to the community church. She confirmed that she had given away millions. As well as the church, she supports a charity called Dream Foundation, a national organisation, based in Santa Barbara, which grants wishes for terminally ill adults, aged 18 or over. 'It's not just about giving away,' she said. 'It's about finding something you really connect with. So when I find something like the Dream Foundation, it makes it so much more meaningful.' She also donated the financial worth of her wedding gifts from her ill-fated second marriage to the charity.

Sometimes Kim will be moved to give to something in the news. In November 2013, she donated the profits from an eBay auction to the International Medical Corps (IMC) to aid those affected by the deadly Typhoon Yolanda, which killed thousands of people in the Philippines. She tends to change the beneficiary of her eBay auctions, depending on what has caught her eye.

She started supporting the Children's Hospital Los Angeles seven years ago and, as well as regular donations, continues to find time in her schedule to pop in unannounced to visit the sick patients. Sometimes Kanye or her sisters will go with her, but often she is quite happy to slip in by herself and sit at a bedside.

When she arrives, she has presents such as iTunes gift cards or beauty products. All the children, of course, want to have a selfie taken with Kim Kardashian and sometimes she posts them online for them. At other times, she will just chat or help a young girl to do her nails.

Her guiding light here, as in so many areas of her life, is her father, Robert Kardashian, who died from cancer: 'I remember what it was like when my dad was going through it. You see the kids that are so strong. They feel so helpless. You want to do anything to help them.'

The cynical will always believe that celebrity charity is all about tax advantages and publicity. That may be the truth where some well-known names are concerned, but not Kim Kardashian. Just because she has built her brand around a frivolous TV show doesn't mean she lacks a social conscience. When all the extravagance and opulence of her baby shower during her first pregnancy was over, she quietly arranged for all the presents to be packed up and sent to a children's hospital in Chicago, the city where Kanye grew up.

Variety reflected the improved perception of Kim by naming her in their list of five Inspiration Impact Honorees at the Power of Women lunch in New York in April 2015. She was recognised for her support of the children's hospital in LA. Perhaps her next book will be entitled *Selfless*.

While her father remains the biggest influence on Kim's character, Kanye has empowered her to be a stronger woman. Her sister Khloé acknowledges the difference he has made: 'What I love about Kanye is he wants to build her up instead of take her down ... She finally has someone who wants to elevate her and make her like this queen and beautiful princess that she is.' Kanye is firmly in the camp that believes celebrity can be used to make a difference, to project one's own ideas, and one should never be frightened of being passionate about something.

His support was clear during her first visit to Armenia in April 2015 with the mission of bringing the anniversary of her mother country's genocide to the world's attention. This was Kim Kardashian, selfie queen, meeting the prime minister of a country to talk about something that really mattered. It's part of a gradual process over the past year of making Kim more serious. The Armenian trip raised awareness of one important issue, but there have been others.

She was the initiator and executive producer on a documentary called *#RedFlag*, which aimed to heighten awareness of mental health issues. The premise of the film, which was shown on the American channel HLN (Headline News), was that social media could help people who were distressed. She was hoping to break down the taboo of mental illness. She wanted to let social media users, particularly youngsters, know that it was OK to admit to an issue with their mental health and understand that they weren't alone, there was assistance available to them. Kim explained her motivation: 'I have so many friends who have suffered from depression and other mental illnesses. And because I've never experienced it, I don't understand it. I wanted to really inform myself because it's not something you can snap out of.'

The newly serious and enlightened Kim has been able to accept and support Caitlyn Jenner and share her concern at the treatment of transgender people. Her relationship with Caitlyn has changed: 'We're definitely closer and I understand her a bit better, and her struggle.' She wasn't particularly happy with her remarks about Kris Jenner in the *Vanity Fair* article, however, and told her that she didn't need to bash the family on her way up. For the moment, there is an overwhelming public love affair with Caitlyn Jenner and her brave decision to reveal her transition, but it will be interesting to see if that changes in the future, as people become more accustomed to treating her like any other celebrity.

People who think Kim can't be taken seriously because she posts naked pictures of her famous rear online are confusing the brand with the person. Kim Kardashian, in my opinion, is a product just as much as a chocolate bar or a smartphone.

You need to be highly visible to be successful. If you are the CEO of one of these concerns, you want to get on the Tube and see people eating your snack or playing a game on your make of mobile. If you are Kim Kardashian West, you are the CEO of the Kim Kardashian brand and you want to see it everywhere – in magazines and newspapers; you want to smell the perfume on a young woman going to work and recognise that it's yours or see a piece from your jewellery collection dangling on her wrist. It's part of the job description to promote the product, which, in this case, just so happens to be herself.

A problem Kim has as a brand is: how can she be judged to be successful? If you are an actress, you can win an Oscar or an Emmy. A musician like Kanye will win applause for taking home a Grammy or a BRIT Award. As a brand, Kim's success can best be measured in financial terms. By that yardstick, she is doing fantastically well, with a current net worth estimated at $85 million, which, combined with Kanye's $130 million, gives them a family fortune of $215 million, but that figure is rising rapidly. It will greatly increase in the next year, thanks to the new E! deal and her *Kim Kardashian: Hollywood* app.

The first question she was asked, when she was interviewed at the prestigious Code/Mobile conference in Half Moon Bay, California, in the heart of Silicon Valley, was: 'Why do people not take you more seriously?' In her reply, she expressed her frustration about this, but admitted, 'I think when people hear that I might have gotten success off a reality show they take that as a negative.'

That is certainly true. If reality TV programmes were a sport, they would be in the Olympics by now, but for some reason they aren't considered an acceptable genre in which to excel. There are so many bad ones that I can't see why you can't be applauded for being good at it. 'I don't think reality TV gets the respect it deserves,' she said firmly. If there's one question she hates, it would have to be: 'What do you do?'

Kim and the entire cast continue to emphasise the importance of family at every opportunity. She loves the fact that her job involves the people she cares about most. They are a raggle-taggle bunch who can't seem to sustain proper relationships. Hopefully, Kim and Kanye will break the mould and not fail. Absolutely anything and everything happens to this family – the rest of us might have at least one thing in common with them, but the Kardashians take everything to the extreme, and that's part of their appeal.

Should I ever return to that hotel in Calabasas, I hope that I can catch up with the receptionist who wondered about the point of Kim Kardashian. I would tell her why I think she should be applauded for what she has achieved. Kim is always going to get those who will sneer at the sex tape and the role that it played in her subsequent career. She just has to live with that, but I don't suppose she loses any sleep over it.

This time next year I expect we will see Kim and Kanye walking along a Calabasas mall with their two children in their arms. Goodness knows how she will manage to fit in being a mum of two with her already ridiculous schedule. I remember reading a week in the life of Kim back in 2012: Paris one day, Los Angeles the next, then New York for the *Late Show with David Letterman*, home to Los Angeles for a day, on to the Ivory Coast in Africa for a mobile-phone launch and then Paris for Fashion Week. That's changed a little because of North, but she still works all the hours she can.

When Piers Morgan asked Kim what she put down under occupation on her passport, she said she usually made up something, like teacher. There are so many real things she could list – TV star, businesswoman, entrepreneur, model, photographer, mother. She is all these things and many more. In our modern world, there is something that she could choose that, for me, best reflects her position in society ... I think she should just put down 'fame'.

KIM'S STARS

It can be so easy to become accustomed to good fortune. Kim has the birth chart of someone destined for enormous success. Jupiter, planet of royalty and excess, stands proud at the Virgo Midheaven, the highest point of her chart, and its godly rays protect and enlarge many areas of her personality and life. Jupiter bestows confidence and optimism, allows a sense of control over one's destiny and promotes growth beyond the limits many endure in their lives. However, as a double dose of cosmic luck, a tight link between Jupiter and its starry opposite, Saturn, planet of restrictions and limitations, suggests Kim is someone who will never take things for granted. There is always fear wherever Saturn sits. In this chart, the fear is of public failure – one of the many spurs that will motivate her to give of her best.

This placement of Saturn and Jupiter in discerning, perfectionist Virgo warns us that she will not accept anything second-rate, either in those upon whom she depends, or indeed herself. Kim also knows how to read the world – she is astute, savvy, with an eye for detailed analysis of situations

257

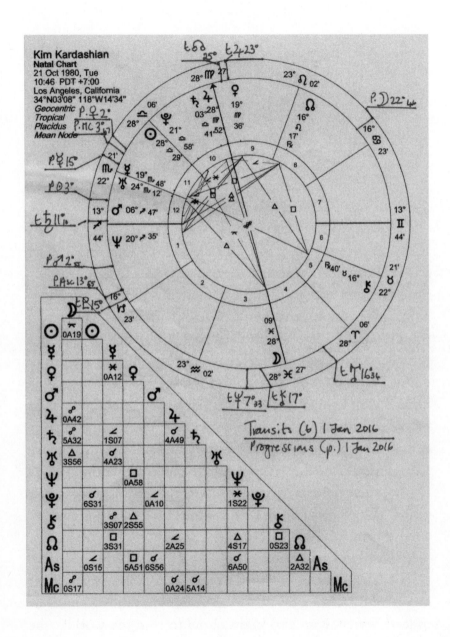

and an understanding of how organisations and people operate.

Mercury, planet of commerce, communication and mischief, rules her Midheaven, so a natural environment for Kim's success would be within the media or, indeed, big business. A tendency to overanalyse might seem like indecision, but this will be offset by an ability to think far ahead of her time. She has a gift for pulling disparate factors and people together, creating order. Such is her inherent instinct and skill for enterprise that she would be an enormous asset to any international corporate establishment.

Success is one thing, reputation another. Kim's career accomplishments will make her a commanding figure; nonetheless, there will be occasions when she may feel undermined, her power eroded. Mars, planet of assertion, in the sign of Sagittarius and awkwardly placed, suggests potential shortcomings, one of which is ever-expanding goals and a level of consequent dissatisfaction. But perhaps, more importantly, there will be occasions when she struggles to define and ask for what she wants, as opposed to what others want. Then this inability to steer her own course may result in actions that make little sense to anyone and behaviour that is emotionally explosive, even self-destructive. Things will fall into place best when Kim directs her very great gifts into fighting for a collective cause – this is when her courage will flow and her reputation will be assured.

Kim has a very strong instinct for speaking the truth. Her ideas will often be radical and her views won't be constrained by traditional values unless she wholly believes in them. Indeed, her inclination for holding nothing back will supersede any bond of loyalty, even to herself. Clearly then, this gabby gift to the gossipmongers will sometimes trip her up. Ultimately, however, as detailed later on, it is likely to be her greatest strength.

With her Sun, the planet of identity, in the harmony-loving sign of Libra, Kim will have acted as a mediator and peacemaker between her siblings and parents. She may have performed the role of emotional caretaker and will be highly sensitive to those within society who are excluded. It is likely she will have developed both humour and resignation in this role as go-between and there will have been times when she needed all of her mercurial skills to extricate herself from some hidden agendas. With Uranus, planet of sudden change, rebellion and independence, influencing the area of her chart linked to siblings, her relationships will be marked by unpredictability – periods of disconnection, followed by closeness. With the sign of Scorpio implicated, bonds will sometimes be affected by suspect motives, rivalry and manipulation, but she needs her siblings and loves them very much. As part of an extended family, Kim will be matchless at promoting genuine friendships; that is, relationships of equality, tolerance and fairness. She will work through her own wounding to give practical and kind support.

Kim's father will have had an enormous impact upon her, revealed by the dominant placement of the patriarchal planets Saturn and Jupiter. The position of this first planet will act as a spur, either by exciting a need to live up to her father's success and expectations, or by burdening Kim to achieve a failed paternal ambition. Her achievement would thus be perceived as redemption of the family reputation. Jupiter, king of the gods, is associated with ethics and integrity, so Father would have modelled these virtues and handed on to her an appreciation of the divine – a sense of religious identity or set of beliefs that will have made a huge impact on her. She will carry them with her all of her life.

Looking at any of the planets taken to signify Father – Sun, Jupiter, Saturn – it is clear they all link awkwardly to the Moon. The latter, being the planet that symbolises Mother in a chart, suggests an inherent tension between the parents. Kim's Moon in Neptune, sign of unconditional love, suggests a compassionate mother, but one who was unavailable at times, perhaps uncertainty around her own primary relationship creating emotional distance. Her importance to Kim is enormous, although there may be a blurring and confusion around the role she plays – often she will be more like a sister. It is likely, though, that Kim will place her on something of a pedestal.

The awkward link between the Sun and Moon once again, at a personal level, spells out a message. Kim's uncertainty in integrating what she needs with what she wants and defining her own agenda will cause inner discomfort. Compromising and adjusting will be the pattern activated by an overdeveloped need to please others. The main arenas in which this will play out will be those concerning her image – the face she presents to the world – and her partnerships.

Neptune, planet of glamour, illusion, victimhood and sacrifice, is placed prominently in Kim's chart at a point called the Ascendant. She is highly sensitive to others and this instinctive speed-reading of their needs allows her to respond in a way that will ensure her acceptance and popularity. With a partner, a guardian figure or even the public, Kim's compliance will ease her journey through life, but the path could be a slippery one. Kim is someone who charismatically embodies ideals of femininity, not least those defined by commercial values, so her own desire to live up to the expectations of others can undermine her. The real question is whether a certain naivety and her desire for fame have been exploited; whether those who should have protected her have occasionally let her down. Awareness is everything if patterns are not to be repeated.

Kim will look foremost for a partner who is companionable and mentally stimulating. Gemini, sign of the twins, marks the chart area associated with partnerships, suggesting an attraction to those who are adaptable, flirtatious, fun-loving and, above all, easy communicators. She will enjoy arguments, not least because they are a way of clarifying her own views and ideas and are a means of learning. Discussions could become very heated, however, if she uses her perceptive insights in a manipulative way. At an emotional level, Kim can be an instinctive strategist, able to play the victim or innocent party to great advantage – perhaps something she learned as a defence mechanism early on.

Kim's Sun, a symbol of men in her life, is linked to Pluto, shadowy planet of power. It is likely her father was a figure of potency, somebody exposed to the darker sides of human nature and society in general and able to deal with the grittier aspects of life. Perhaps through his experience Kim learned about confrontation and ways of dealing with it. Friendship in marriage will be vital for her, but there will also be a desire for magnetism and strength – the type of individual you don't ignore. Most importantly, acknowledging her own very great need for independence will help her to choose wisely; otherwise, she is likely to pick someone who will give her that freedom when she least expects it.

Looking ahead, Kim will shortly experience a number of important planetary transits. Jupiter, planet of good fortune and hope, links to Venus in November 2015. This will be a time when she will enjoy being the centre of attention and her current relationships are harmonious. Any relationship that starts now will be one in which the balance between freedom and love is easily achieved. She will want to surround herself with beauty, but should be careful not to squander resources.

This will be followed by a period of responsibilities in January 2016, as Saturn, planet of restrictions and authority, crosses the Ascendant. This really is the beginning of a new cycle for Kim, one that feels initially constraining, but will lead to greater maturity, realism and status. Kim will need to complete what needs to be finished, so that life can be simplified, cutting away excess and all distractions that are not conducive to her development over the next seven years. Relationships that aren't strong and worth fighting for may not last – she will know they no longer belong to her future.

This is an important period for her, because it presents a time when she can put up proper boundaries and take greater control of her life, possibly something that will feel very alien to her. To have Neptune on the Ascendant in the birth chart is a mixed blessing. At its best, Kim can give expression to collective feelings and images. She embodies modern femininity for countless women, who admire the way she has used her looks and brains to build a successful public presence. She is open about her sexual nature. She is powerful. All of this is of vital importance when women in many areas around the globe are subjugated, abused, even culled at birth, creating a psychic wound in the world. The openness with which she deals with the emotional realm is another important validation of the feminine. At a personal level, however, there may have been some cost, and this transit of Saturn will provide her with the chance to be discerning and more selective both in whom she chooses to trust and in the way she allows the public access to her.

Kim's ascendant sign, Sagittarius, the centaur, also hints at the way this resourceful woman may develop. The symbol is part animal, part human. Thus, early on, one may be driven by instinctual needs – greed, the need for attention or whatever – but could begin the lengthy journey towards the noble ideals and lofty vision of the philanthropist, given a supportive birth chart and a heavy Saturn transit. As mentioned earlier, perhaps Kim's greatest asset is her instinct and ability to speak the truth and one day this will be employed for the greater good. Meanwhile, Kim will continue to experience worldly success.

Later in September 2016, Jupiter reaches the very top of her chart, an augury of prosperity, and spends approximately a year highlighting her achievements. There will be some conflict between her home and public life, possibly coming to a head in July 2016, when she experiences an awkward link between Uranus, planet of rebellion, and natal Uranus in her chart, associated with her siblings. This could be a period of family tension. This transit will reccur in August 2016 and again in April 2017 and will mark out the steps of growing independence and individuation for her.

Finally, in February 2016, the planet Pluto, moving forward, will wield an influence on her personal finances and her values. Pluto is the planet of breakdown and regeneration, so she may have to deal with a period when her resources are reorganised. Perhaps more importantly, there will be a major and irrevocable change in the way she thinks of and uses her assets. Eventually, there may be a shift away from an emphasis on material acquisition in her life towards a greater endorsement of moral and spiritual imperatives. In the words of another fashionista, 'There are people who have money and people who are rich' (Coco Chanel).

Madeleine Moore
August 2015

LIFE AND TIMES

21 Oct 1980: Kimberly Noel Kardashian is born in Los Angeles, California. She has a sister, Kourtney, who is 18 months older. Her parents are businessman and former lawyer Robert Kardashian and his wife, Kristen Houghton. The family lived in a private cul-de-sac in Beverly Hills called Tower Lane.

June 1984: Younger sister Khloé is born. The children lead an idyllic and privileged existence surrounded by cats, dogs, rabbits and birds. For a time, both Madonna and Bruce Springsteen are neighbours.

March 1987: Her brother Robert, known as Rob, is born. Kim goes to the Buckley School in Sherman Oaks, where she meets Paris Hilton, Nicole Richie and Kimberly Stewart.

April 1991: Is a bridesmaid at the wedding of her mother Kris to Olympic champion Bruce Jenner four weeks after Kris's divorce is finalised.

June 1994: 'Auntie Nicole', Nicole Brown Simpson, is murdered. O. J. Simpson is subsequently charged and Robert Kardashian renews his licence to practise law to join his defence team. The trial causes much tension within the family.

Oct 1994: Celebrates her fourteenth birthday at Neverland, the famous Santa Barbara ranch of Michael Jackson. She has started dating his nephew, T. J. Jackson, who would be her boyfriend throughout her high-school years.

Oct 1996: On her sixteenth birthday, Kim is given the keys to her first car, a brand-new white BMW 318 saloon. She has to sign a contract with her father that she will be responsible for any repairs – and promptly drives into the back of another vehicle.

Nov 1995: Kendall Jenner, Kim's half-sister, is born. She is given the middle name Nicole in memory of her mother's dead friend.

Aug 1997: Kylie Jenner is born. She is the last of Kris Jenner's six children; the eldest, Kourtney, is now 18.

Jan 2000: Gets married in Las Vegas to record producer Damon Thomas without telling her family. She is 19. It proves to be an unhappy marriage.

July 2003: Her father tells the family he is suffering from oesophageal cancer. All four of his children attend when he marries Ellen Pearson at a ceremony at his house in Encino.

Sept 2003: Robert Kardashian dies, aged 59. Kim gives an address at the funeral at Inglewood Park Cemetery.

Oct 2003: Now separated from Damon, she makes a sex tape with her well-endowed boyfriend, Ray J, a hip-hop artist and actor. They fly to Mexico the next day to celebrate her twenty-third birthday.

Feb 2004: Her divorce from Damon is finalised. She receives $56,000 in the settlement and the return of an inscribed Bible, a gift from her father, which she had left behind at their house.

Jan 2006: Opens a Myspace profile under the name of Princess Kimberly. Says she is in a relationship (with Ray J), is straight, Christian and would like children some day. Acquires 856 friends.

May 2006: Goes to the movies in Calabasas with singer Nick Lachey and has her picture taken by the paparazzi. Publication of the pictures gets her noticed for the first time.

July 2006: Accompanies Bruce Jenner to the ESPY Awards at the Kodak Theatre in Hollywood and meets American football star Reggie Bush, but it takes months for him to ask her out. On their first date, they go to a car wash and Chipotle Mexican Grill.

Dec 2006: Spends the run-up to New Year in Sydney with Paris Hilton, who has flown to Australia to choose the face of a new beer. Kanye West sees a picture of the two young women on Bondi Beach and knows he wants Kim to be his girl.

Feb 2007: Announces she is suing Vivid Entertainment in a right-to-privacy lawsuit over the distribution of her sex tape.

April 2007: Settles her suit with Vivid after reaching an agreement with the company. *Kim Kardashian Superstar* reportedly becomes the biggest-selling sex tape of all time. Filming begins for the Kardashian family's reality TV show, focusing on Kris and Bruce's sixteenth wedding anniversary celebrations.

Sept 2007: Attends opening of the Intermix boutique in West Hollywood and is pictured with Kanye West and his girlfriend, Alexis Phifer. Kim later admitted 'there was definitely a spark' between them.

Oct 2007: *Keeping Up with the Kardashians* begins on E! and, including repeats, draws an audience of more than 13 million during its first four weeks. Less than a month after the premiere, the family starts shooting its second season.

Dec 2007: Appears on the front cover of *Playboy* magazine. The shoot was documented in an episode of the reality show and Hugh Hefner helped to select some nude shots for inside the magazine.

March 2008: Plays the love interest in video for 'Thnks fr th Mmrs', a song by rock band Fall Out Boy. Shares billing with a bunch of chimpanzees, who she says were 'scary'.

Aug 2008: Makes her feature-film debut in the ironically named *Disaster Movie*. The critics hate it and Kim is nominated for a Golden Raspberry Award (Razzie). Says her ambition is to be a Bond girl.

Sept 2008: Is the third contestant voted off season 7 of *Dancing with the Stars*, despite being paired with reigning champion Mark Ballas. Judge Bruno Tonioli called her rumba colder than Siberia.

Dec 2009: Guest stars in an episode of *CSI: NY*, playing a femme fatale called Debbie Fallon. She turns out to be the villain.

Feb 2010: Watches Reggie Bush and his team, the New Orleans Saints, claim the Super Bowl in Miami by defeating the Indianapolis Colts. She invades the pitch afterwards to give her man a congratulatory kiss. Launches her first perfume, Kim Kardashian, at TAO nightclub in Las Vegas.

March 2010: Splits with Reggie for a second and final time. She buys a $4.8 million Tuscan-style villa in Beverly Hills, with swimming pool, Jacuzzi, movie room and a waterfall in the garden.

July 2010: Unveils a wax statue of herself in Madame Tussauds, New York. She wears the same pink Hervé Léger dress as the figure and exclaims, 'I think she's pretty hot.'

Nov 2010: Demonstrates she never turns down an opportunity by opening a new toilet facility in Times Square, New York. She doesn't go inside to be the first to spend a penny. Poses dead in a coffin for the Digital Life Sacrifice in support of a World Aids Day campaign. Watches new boyfriend Kris Humphries play basketball for the New Jersey Nets.

Dec 2010: Is officially the top-earning reality TV star with $6 million. She launches the premier Kim Kardashian Signature Watch Collection. Distributes hundreds of toys at Children's Hospital Los Angeles on Christmas Day.

March 2011: Releases her first and only single to date, a dance song from The-Dream entitled 'Jam (Turn It Up)'. The record is not a success, despite being for charity, and Kim doesn't pursue a pop career. The video, directed by Hype Williams and co-starring Kanye West, is never released.

May 2011: Walks into the bedroom of her Beverly Hills home to discover boyfriend Kris Humphries on bended knee, holding out a 20.5-carat diamond ring, worth a reported $2 million. 'Will you marry me?' is spelled out in rose petals on the floor. She says yes.

June 2011: Kim is named Entrepreneur of the Year at the *Glamour* Women of the Year Awards in Berkeley Square Gardens, London. Has bum officially X-rayed to prove that she hasn't had butt implants.

Aug 2011: Marries Kris Humphries in a lavish ceremony in Montecito, California, which is filmed for *Keeping Up with the Kardashians.* He surprises his new bride by taking her for a quick honeymoon on the Amalfi Coast.

Oct 2011: A two-part special, *Kim's Fairytale Wedding: A Kardashian Event*, airs on E! and is a big ratings success. The first night attracts 4.4 million viewers; the second night 4 million. Kim files for divorce after 72 days of marriage, citing 'irreconcilable difficulties'.

April 2012: Kim is a guest at the White House for the Correspondents' Dinner. Arrives hand in hand with Kanye West at the Tribeca Film Festival in New York.

Nov 2012: Launches a new clothing line for curvy girls, the Kardashian Kollection, at Dorothy Perkins in London. She and her sister Kourtney are accompanied by an entourage of 47.

Dec 2012: At his concert in Atlantic City, Kanye stops his song 'Lost in the World' and points at Kim. 'Can we make some noise, please, for my baby mama right here?!'

May 2013: Fails to please everyone in her Mrs Doubtfire dress at the Met Ball. The theme of the night was punk, but critics thought her outfit from Riccardo Tisci for Givenchy resembled a pair of curtains.

June 2013 Finally divorced from Kris Humphries after divorce proceedings that lasted seven times longer than her marriage. The marriage is dissolved, not annulled, as he had asked for.

Her first baby, North West, is born a month prematurely at the Cedars-Sinai Medical Center in Los Angeles. Nori, as she is called, weighs 4lb 15oz. The *Keeping Up with the Kardashians* cameras are not invited to the birth. Kim's mother and step-father separate after 23 years together.

Oct 2013: Kanye's birthday surprise for Kim is to take her blindfolded to the AT&T Park in San Francisco and pop the question, with an orchestra playing her favourite song, 'Young and Beautiful' by Lana Del Rey. The message 'Pleeease Marry Meee!' lights up the night sky. Kris Humphries sells the engagement ring he gave her for $749,000 at Christie's in New York.

March 2014: Wins the Razzie as Worst Supporting Actress for her role in *Temptation: Confessions of a Marriage Counselor*, written and directed by Tyler Perry.

April 2014: Realises a long-held ambition to appear on the cover of *Vogue*. The picture, with Kanye, is taken by Annie Leibovitz. Kim tweets, 'This is such a dream come true!!!'

Aug 2014: She and and Kanye buy a $20-million estate in Hidden Hills, boasting 10 bathrooms, eight bedrooms and two swimming pools. They purchase a $2.9-million property next door to ensure their privacy.

May 2014: Kim and Kanye marry in the most romantic setting, Forte di Belvedere, on a hilltop overlooking Florence, Italy. The cameras aren't invited and her beautiful Tisci-designed wedding dress is kept hidden until the big day. Her brother Rob doesn't attend, nor does stepbrother Brody Jenner. Andrea Bocelli sings 'Ave Maria' as Bruce walks her down the aisle. The not-so-secret honeymoon is in Ireland.

July 2014: *Kim Kardashian: Hollywood*, a video/mobile game created by Glu Mobile, is an instant hit, with 28 million downloads and 11 billion minutes of play in the first six months.

Sept 2014: Kim is named *GQ* magazine's Woman of the Year at the Royal Opera House in London.

Nov 2014: *Paper* magazine features Kim on the front cover and inside, with nude images of her famous rear end, and the inspired marketing tag 'Break the Internet'.

Jan 2015: Premieres her 30-second commercial for T-Mobile's Data Stash during the Super Bowl. She is filmed taking selfies and says, 'It's your data. Keep it.'

Feb 2015: Joins her family in signing a deal worth a reported $100 million with E! for another four years of *Keeping Up with the Kardashians*. The show is now broadcast in 160 countries. Presents a prize to Sam Smith at the BRITs in London and introduces her husband Kanye West's performance.

April 2015: Visits Armenia for the first time with Kanye, North and Khloé. She lays flowers at the Genocide Memorial in Yerevan and meets Prime Minister Hovik Abrahamyan. They journey on to Jerusalem, where North is baptised. Named as one of *Variety*'s Power of Women Inspiration Impact Honorees for her charitable work. Both Kim and Kanye make *Time* magazine's list of the 100 Most Influential People in the World.

May 2015: Wears a show-stopping Roberto Cavalli bird-of-paradise gown to the Met Ball. Her book of selfies, *Selfish*, is published and becomes a bestseller on both sides of the Atlantic. Announces she is pregnant with her second child. Meets Caitlyn Jenner for the first time at her photo shoot for *Vanity Fair* magazine. She says, 'She's beautiful.'

June 2015: *Forbes* places her thirty-third in their Celebrity 100 list of the world's highest-paid celebrities, with annual earnings of $52.5 million. Watches Kanye perform on the main stage at Glastonbury.

Aug 2015: Has combined following on Twitter and Instagram of 77.8 million and rising. The population of the United Kingdom is 63.5 million.

ACKNOWLEDGEMENTS

Just for a change, I wanted to begin by saluting the brilliant work done by the astrologer, Madeleine Moore. She has written birth charts for all my best-known books and they have never been less than fascinating. In the case of Kim Kardashian West, however, she has excelled herself. She may be one of my dearest friends, but she never sees the manuscript or discusses the subject with me beforehand. I am always amazed and delighted if some of what she reveals reflects the story I tell. I couldn't put down the pages about Kim – a powerful woman who can make a difference.

On the subject of unsung heroes on Team Sean, thank you to Jen Westaway, who somehow manages to transcribe my interview tapes, even when it's quite clear I am chatting over a nice lunch in a very noisy restaurant. Once again, Arianne Burnette has done a marvellous job copy-editing the text. My researchers, Emily-Jane Swanson, Jo Westaway and Alison Sims have been terrific and they, like me, are in awe at just how much Kim Kardashian has achieved in her 35 years.

Special thanks to my old friend Kevin O'Sullivan, the best television critic in the country, for his insight into reality television, and *Keeping Up with the Kardashians* in particular. On that subject, Elliot Mintz, the former media consultant for Paris Hilton, was fascinating. I loved his stories of clubland with Paris and Kim. Alison Jane Reid was as incisive as ever regarding Kim's fashion. Good luck with your website: http://www.ethical-hedonist.com/

Congratulations to my agent, Gordon Wise at Curtis Brown, on deservedly being named Agent of the Year at *The Bookseller* Awards of 2015. I always knew he was the best agent in the business and now it's official. Thanks also to his assistant, Richard Pike, for dealing so expertly with far too many enquiries from me.

In Los Angeles – and Calabasas – I enjoyed meeting a number of aspiring actresses and singers working in bars, restaurants and hotels while they pursued their dream. Many people in LA preferred not to be named when they talked about Kim, because it's a very small world out there. Thank you, and I won't forget that I owe a lot of lunches. It was great to see Gill Pringle, Katie Hind and Richard Mineards while I was there. Thanks to Cliff Renfrew for putting me up and sharing an excellent meal at Carousel, the Kardashian's favourite Armenian restaurant. I can see why – the food is excellent.

There's a superb team at HarperCollins backing me up. Sincere thanks to my editor Kate Latham for her enthusiasm and expertise; Georgina Atsiaris and Mark Bolland for project editing; Anneke Sandher and Martin Topping for their breath-taking cover design; Virginia Woolstencroft for looking after publicity; and Kate Elton for overseeing the whole project. Finally, a special word for my publisher, Natalie Jerome, who first suggested that Kim would be a great subject for me. I hope you are enjoying your time with the new baby.

You can read more about my books at seansmithceleb.com or follow me on Twitter @seansmithceleb and facebook.com/seansmithcelebbiog.

SELECT BIBLIOGRAPHY

Beaumont, Mark. *Kanye West: God & Monster*, Omnibus Press, 2015

Behan, Pam with Sara Christenson. *Malibu Nanny: Adventures of the Former Kardashian Nanny*, Minnesota Girls Press, 2013

Billieon, Maxwell and Ray J. *Death of the Cheating Man: What Every Woman Must Know About Men Who Stray*, Strebor Books, 2012

Cohen, Nadia. *Kim & Kanye: The Love Story*, John Blake Publishing, 2014

Crawford, Byron. *Kanye West Superstar*, CreateSpace Independent Publishing Platform, 2014

Jenner, Bruce and Phillip Finch. *Decathlon Challenge: Bruce Jenner's Story*, Prentice-Hall, 1977

Jenner, Bruce with Mark Seal. *Finding the Champion Within: A Step-By-Step Plan for Reaching Your Full Potential*, Simon & Schuster, 1999

Jenner, Kris. *In the Kitchen with Kris: A kollection of Kardashian-Jenner family favorites*, Gallery Books/Karen Hunter Publishing, 2014

Jenner, Kris. *Kris Jenner ... and All Things Kardashian*, Simon & Schuster UK, 2012

Kardashian, Kourtney, Kim and Khloé. *Kardashian Konfidential*, St Martin's Press, 2011

Schiller, Lawrence and James Willwerth. *American Tragedy: The Uncensored Story of the Simpson Defense*, Random House, 1999

Simkin, Ryan. *Flash! Bars, Boobs, and Busted: 5 Years on the Road with Girls Gone Wild*, 4 Park Publishing, 2010

West, Donda with Karen Hunter. *Raising Kanye: Life Lessons from the Mother of a Hip-Hop Superstar*, Pocket Books, 2007

PICTURE CREDITS

Page 1: (top) Mirrorpix; (middle left) Mirrorpix; (middle right) Mirrorpix; (bottom) Ron Galella Ltd/WireImage.

Page 2: (top) Maureen Donaldson/Michael Ochs Archives/ Getty Images; (bottom) Donaldson Collection/Getty Images.

Page 3: (top) Splash News/Corbis; (middle) Lawrence Schiller/Polaris Communications/Getty Images; (bottom) Fred Brown/AFP/Getty Images.

Page 4: (top) John Shearer/WireImage; (middle left) Johnny Nunez/WireImage; (middle right) Michael Tran/ FilmMagic; (bottom) Chris Graythen/Getty Images.

Page 5: (top) PhotoNews International Inc./Getty Images; (middle) Chris Polk/FilmMagic for Bragman Nyman Cafarelli; (bottom) Splash News.

Page 6: (top) Jeff Vespa/WireImage; (bottom) Jeff Kravitz/ MTV1415/FilmMagic.

Page 7: (top left) Mark Davies/Getty Images; (top right) Rob Loud/Getty Images; (bottom) Richard Bord/ Wireimage.

Page 8: Stefanie Keenan/WireImage for PMK.

Page 9: (top left) John Shearer/WireImage; (top right) Denise Truscello/WireImage; (bottom) Startraks Photo/ Rex Shutterstock.

Page 10: (top left) Denise Truscello/WireImage; (top right) Mark Cuthbert/UK Press via Getty Images; (bottom) Neil Mockford/Getty Images.

Page 11: (top) Ethan Miller/Getty Images; (bottom) Paul Archuleta/FilmMagic.

Page 12: (top left) Jennifer Graylock/FilmMagic; (top right) Jonathan Hordle/Rex Shutterstock; (bottom) Steve Granitz/WireImage.

Page 13: (top) Christopher Polk/Getty Images for BET; (bottom) Marc Piasecki/GC Images.

Page 14: (top left) Pascal Le Segretain/Getty Images; (top right) Trago/Wireimage; (bottom) Pascal Le Segretain/ Getty Images.

Page 15: (top) Gonzalo/Bauer-Griffin/GC Images; (bottom) Kevin Winter/Getty Images.

Page 16: (top) Karen Minasyan/AFP/Getty Images; (bottom) Dimitrios Kambouris/Getty Images.

INDEX

Tony Park was born in 1964 and grew up in the western suburbs of Sydney. He has worked as a newspaper reporter, a press secretary, a PR consultant and a freelance writer. He also served 34 years in the Australian Army Reserve, including six months as a public affairs officer in Afghanistan in 2002. He and his wife, Nicola, divide their time equally between Australia and southern Africa. He is the author of nineteen other African novels.

www.tonypark.net

THE
PRIDE
TONY PARK

MACMILLAN
Pan Macmillan Australia

Pan Macmillan acknowledges the Traditional Custodians of country throughout Australia
and their connections to lands, waters and communities. We pay our respect to Elders past
and present and extend that respect to all Aboriginal and Torres Strait Islander peoples
today. We honour more than sixty thousand years of storytelling, art and culture.

First published 2022 in Macmillan by Pan Macmillan Australia Pty Ltd
1 Market Street, Sydney, New South Wales, Australia, 2000

A catalogue record for this
book is available from the
National Library of Australia

Typeset in 12/15 pt Birka by Post Pre-press Group, Brisbane
Printed by IVE
Cartographic art by Laurie Whiddon, Map Illustrations

The characters in this book are fictitious and any resemblance to
real persons, living or dead, is purely coincidental.

The author and the publisher have made every effort to contact copyright
holders for material used in this book. Any person or organisation
that may have been overlooked should contact the publisher.

The paper in this book is FSC® certified.
FSC® promotes environmentally responsible,
socially beneficial and economically viable
management of the world's forests.

For Nicola

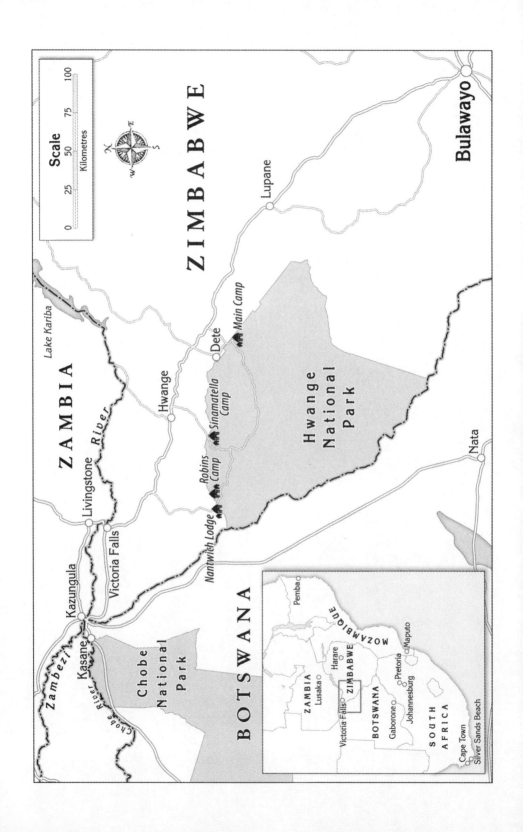

CHAPTER 1

S onja Kurtz waded onto the beach and tossed two seashells on the sand. She savoured the warmth of the sun on her skin as she slid off her dive mask and wrung the sea water from her ponytail.

The Indian Ocean was cool enough to raise goosebumps here, close to where it mixed with the Atlantic off Africa's southern tip. She bent, slowly, to retrieve her spoils and examined them. Dressed in a cream bikini, diving knife and weight belt hugging her waist, she walked across the squeaky-fine sand. And fell over.

'Mum!'

Sonja creaked her way back to her feet, brushed the sand from her legs and belly with her free hand and threw the shells at Emma with the other. 'Fucking knee.'

'You're a little old to be impersonating a Bond Girl, with the knife and all.' Emma put a hand to her mouth, not quite managing to hide her smile as she put down her book and looked over the top of her sunglasses. 'You should get that knee seen to.'

'*Ja*, and my back, and my rotator cuff, and my neck.' She flopped down on her towel, next to Emma. 'Do you at least like the shells?'

1

Emma picked one up. 'You should take these back to where you found them. People don't collect seashells any more. It's not woke.'

'What's woke?'

Emma shook her head. 'You've been in the trenches too long.'

Sonja looked up and down the beach, surveying the terrain out of habit. She'd set them up on high ground, in the dunes at the quiet end of six-hundred-plus metres of sand so white she had to put her sunglasses on to cut through the glare. The Blesberg, a steep sand hill fringed with vegetation, rose steeply to their right, protecting the flank of their commanding position.

It was early and there were not yet enough people around to make her feel uncomfortable. All the same, she registered them – the very handsome young man in white briefs, oiled and gelled; the Joburg family, red-skinned and noisy; a young woman, milk-white skin and long black hair hanging beneath a floppy sunhat – another European swallow in Cape Town for the northern winter; the silver fox, faded tattoos, who looked at Sonja, again. A gull hovered over them, squawking, looking for food. The woman in the hat looked their way for a moment and Sonja caught a glimpse of mirrored glasses. *Stop being paranoid*, Sonja told herself. Threat status, low.

Sonja glanced at Emma, who had picked up her book again. 'You used to love seashells when you were a little girl.'

'Yes, but I didn't know any better. They're part of the natural habitat and now you've gone and disturbed it.'

Sonja patted the diving knife against her thigh. 'You weren't complaining when I told you I was going to get us a nice fat *kreef* for lunch.'

'A what?'

'Crayfish.'

'Oh, well, that's OK. They're not on the green list, and just so long as you don't get a female. If you go back in the water, check it's not a female, with eggs under the tail.'

Sonja saluted. '*Jawohl!*'

'Don't pretend you're some sort of dinosaur.'

2

'I'm not quite that old, though not far off it.' Sonja put her knees together, checking for swelling on the right one. The left one bore a long, vertical scar from the reconstructive surgery; starboard side would be next.

'And stop talking about how old you are,' Emma ordered. 'You're making me feel old.'

'You started it. Stop telling me off,' Sonja said. She tried to make it sound light; she did not want to spoil this. She hadn't seen her daughter since before the pandemic and even then she hadn't been on a holiday, either alone or with Emma, for years. Less work, and more time alone while Hudson was working in Zimbabwe, fed her underlying guilt.

Leaning back on her elbows, the paperback she'd brought virginal and unopened beside her on the towel, she went back to scanning the beach, trying to think like a holiday-maker. The knife on her belt was not just about fishing; she liked South Africa and America because she could carry a weapon and not feel like she was overly crazy. On the rare occasions she did go out unarmed she caught herself time and time again reaching for her missing pistol.

Sonja's phone beeped. She picked it up and saw it was a WhatsApp message from Andrew Miles, a former military pilot she knew. *Mozambique is kicking off. I'm flying in some reinforcements for Oosthuizen next week. He wants to know if you're in?*

Below the message was a link, which Sonja clicked on. It was a News24 report.

Mercenaries are being flown by helicopter to the besieged Mozambican coastal town of Palma to evacuate civilian employees of a large liquefied natural gas plant following attacks by armed insurgents with links to the Islamic State group.

She chewed her lower lip. Her thumb hovered over the phone's screen as she debated her answer.

'Anything interesting?' Emma asked.

Sonja looked up; there was the damn guilt again. 'No, just a friend.'

'You don't have any friends.'

Sonja poked her tongue out and Emma went back to her book.

She read more. A Mozambican army base had been overrun, the lightly manned garrison taken unawares, the article said, and two hundred AK-47s and machine guns and a score of RPG-7s – rocket-propelled grenade launchers – had been stolen. Cabo Delgado province, where Palma was located, was home to palm-fringed white-sand beaches and old Indian Ocean slave trading ports which now acted as import–export hubs for heroin from Afghanistan, methamphetamine from China, and ivory, rhino horn and abalone from Africa.

There was a video embedded in the report. An ageing Alouette helicopter came in to land, and armed men jumped off even before the wheels touched ground. They ran to a group of civilians who were carrying backpacks or suitcases. Sonja thought she recognised Steve Oosthuizen, carrying an AK-47. Despite Emma's jibe Oosthuizen was, actually, a friend about her age, and happily married, last she'd heard. He was ex–32 Battalion, one of the old South African Defence Force's 'terrible ones' from the war in Angola, like Hudson Brand, her on-again, off-again long-term partner. Sonja had worked with Steve as a private military contractor in Iraq and Afghanistan.

Sonja went back to her messages. *Tell Steve thanks, but no thanks. I'm retire . . .* She deleted the last word and tapped *on holiday* instead, then hit send. *Retired* sounded too old, and she did not need to abandon her daughter in search of yet another foreign war. All the same, watching the chopper come in had given her a flutter in her belly.

If you change your mind, you know where to find me, Miles messaged back.

She returned to the news link. A second report had caught her eye; it was an article from the UK, foreshadowing a return to serious sectarian violence in Northern Ireland. When she looked up from her phone she saw that Emma was staring at something, or, rather, someone.

Two young men, late teens or early twenties, fighting age, appeared in Sonja's peripheral vision, traipsing up the path through the dunes from the car park behind them. Smooth brown skin, wetsuits rolled down low below their hips to show off washboard abs, they each carried fins, a regulator, a diving cylinder, a mask and BCD – a buoyancy control device vest. One of them elbowed the other, nodded towards Sonja and Emma and whistled.

Emma frowned and went back to her book.

'I think he likes you,' Sonja said.

'I'm getting too fat. It's the skinny Milf he likes.'

'Hah!' Sonja's phone rang. She checked the screen; it was Hudson Brand. She accepted the call. 'Howzit?'

'Fine. How you doing? I saw from Emma's Instagram that you're back at Silver Sands. Weather looks good.'

'*Ja*, fine. It's beautiful here.' Sonja had mostly picked the Airbnb at Silver Sands on Betty's Bay because it looked quiet and remote, an hour and a half's drive from Cape Town. She avoided crowds. 'I won't ask what you're doing stalking young women on social media. How's Zimbabwe?'

'Hot,' he said. 'Oh, and some of the guys from the charity that maintains the waterholes in the national park stumbled on a mobile drilling rig and some Chinese miners today.'

'Serious?'

'Yup. Shit's hitting the fan up here, and rightly so. The miners claim they have government permission to be in the park, but the Zimbabwe parks and wildlife guys know nothing about it.'

Beside her, Emma sat up straight, put her book to one side and shielded her eyes. 'The men in the water have both got bags, and look, the one on the right has a piece of metal, like a tyre iron. Big knives, as well.'

'Standby,' Sonja said into the phone. She looked at Emma. 'So?'

Emma lowered her voice. 'They're hunting abalone, I'm sure of it.'

'So?' Sonja asked again.

'So, they're *responsible* for the destruction of one of South Africa's natural treasures. They're *poachers*, Mum.'

Sonja and Emma had visited an African penguin colony the day before, at the old whaling station at the other end of Silver Sands Beach; Sonja had made a conscious effort to do something fun and touristy, but Emma had met and struck up a conversation with an older guy, an academic who lived locally and knew all about abalone poaching. Now Emma was an instant expert on endangered sea creatures, and poaching had once again intruded into Sonja's life.

It was annoyingly interesting, Sonja thought, because she had just been reading about abalone being smuggled out of Africa via Mozambique. The scale of the illegal trade in wildlife – animal products, shellfish, even plants – was depressing. Sonja had not come to the beach to think about wars or poaching, but here they were, once more, trying to drag her in.

Emma stood. 'They use scuba tanks these days because the abalone's been cleared out close to shore and they have to dive deeper for it. Bloody disgusting.'

'Emma . . .'

'What's that about poachers?' Hudson said, on the phone.

'I'll call you back,' Sonja said.

'Love you,' Hudson said.

'Same. Whatever; got to go.' She ended the call. She did love him, and was letting her defences down with Hudson more and more, but that scared her, sometimes. There were things she needed to discuss with him, secrets to share about her past that no one alive knew, and the thought terrified her. For now, she had a daughter to worry about. Emma had started walking towards the water. 'Where are you going?'

Emma looked back over her shoulder and Sonja saw her own face, twenty or more years earlier, all blue eyes, auburn hair and sneer.

'I'm going to get some pics of them and SMS them to the marine anti-poaching hotline.'

'Emma!' Sonja recalled that the guy Emma had befriended when visiting the penguins was part of a volunteer poaching monitoring organisation.

The phone rang. It was Hudson again; she hit the decline button and struggled to her feet.

'Hey!' One of the men was knee-deep in the water, suiting up, and had seen Emma holding her phone up. '*Wat doen jy?*'

'Emma, come back,' Sonja said, but as she got closer to the water where Emma stood, checking the pictures she had just taken, Sonja could make out what the men were saying to each other in Afrikaans. Emma would not have understood, but one of the men had just said: '*That cunt won't be a problem, when I get finished with her.*'

Emma held up her phone again, in video mode this time, and addressed the camera. 'These men are abalone poachers and they're obviously heading out to those rocks,' she pointed to a low, dark-coloured island, 'called the "bait bar", a place where abalone still grow.'

Sonja marched across the sand and grabbed Emma from behind, by the upper arm. 'Turn the camera off.'

'Ow. Let go, you're hurting.' Emma shrugged off her mother's grip.

Sonja released her, but kept an eye on the men. The one who had threatened Emma glared at her. 'Go back and sit down,' Sonja said quietly.

Emma cupped her hands either side of her mouth. 'I know what you're doing!' she shouted.

The foul-mouthed man shrugged off his BCD and began wading through the water towards them.

'What are you going to do, big man?' Emma said, hands on hips.

'Emma . . .' Even as she said her daughter's name once more, going through the motions of trying to calm things down, Sonja felt her pulse rate slow and the adrenaline tap open. She saw the plan unfolding in her mind as the boy approached them.

Every single pre-conceived thing this cocky young buck thought was weak about her was working to Sonja's advantage.

'You can't take my fucking picture,' he said in English.

Emma stood her ground, continuing to film as the young man left the water and closed in on her.

He was both tall and solid. He lunged for Emma, ignoring Sonja, who had positioned herself on his right, as if she were stepping back from the action. The moment the man's hand touched her daughter's, Sonja struck.

Her right fist popped, like a forty-millimetre grenade leaving its launcher, and smacked into the man's temple. He folded into the sand.

Sonja fell on him, one knee on his neck, and directed another jab into his nose for good measure. He howled, but still tried to reach his right hand down towards his leg. Sonja had long ago seen the dive knife strapped to his calf and was already on it. She slid the blade from its sheath and pricked her victim's hand with the point, making him gurgle and yelp again.

'Hey!'

Sonja and Emma looked from the squirming cockroach to the other wetsuited man who now emerged from the water. Unlike his friend, this one had his hands up.

'I'm sorry,' the man called. 'We didn't mean any trouble, ma'am.'

'You should have told this one to behave before he came at my daughter.'

'We were just going for a dive is all. I apologise if he offended you.'

Sonja held the knife up and pointed it at him. 'You or your friend come near my daughter and I'll gut you, understood?'

The man nodded. 'Denzel, come. Let him go, please, ma'am. I'll take him away.' He looked Emma in the eye. 'I'm sorry.'

Denzel was flailing at Sonja's leg so she eased the pressure off his neck.

'Need any help here?'

Sonja glanced around and saw that the Silver Fox had come over to them. Others on the beach were also staring; the woman with the floppy hat stood, hands on hips as she watched them, but came no closer.

'I think I've got the situation in hand,' Sonja said.

The grey-haired man held up a phone. 'Want me to call the police?'

Sonja looked to the standing man.

'We were just leaving,' he said.

Sonja stood. Denzel punched a fist into the sand to help himself stand and swore under his breath. His friend grabbed him by the arm and drew him away. Denzel pointed his forefinger at Sonja, pantomiming a pistol.

'*Fokof, seuntjie,*' Sonja said.

Denzel was shrugging his friend's hand off him as the two of them went to the water's edge and picked up their dive gear. Instead of leaving the beach, though, they quickly suited up and waded into the water, disappearing below the shimmering blue surface.

Sonja went back to their towels and gathered their things, stuffing them into a beach bag. She noticed that more onlookers had appeared from the beach car park, a line of them looking down at them. She felt the first prickling of panic, not as a result of the fight but because she now felt hemmed in, caged.

'Let's go,' Sonja called to Emma.

Emma held up her phone again, as if to take another video. Sonja hurried over, snatched it out of her hand and strode off.

'Give that back!'

Sonja ignored her as she trudged through the dunes.

'Those men are responsible for the destruction of precious marine life, Mum.'

'Come on.'

'But, bloody hell, I thought you were going to kill that guy, the way you were kneeling on his neck, like that poor man in America.'

Sonja stared at her daughter. The youth had come at her, full of anger and arrogance, and now she was talking about human rights? Sonja walked on, the anger boiling up inside her. She'd come on this holiday to reconnect with her daughter, but Emma talked like she was from another world. Her daughter thought poaching could be stopped by posting a video on social media; Sonja had gone into the bush hunting rhino poachers and her husband, Sam, had been killed filming a documentary about the plight of the animals. The gulf between her and Emma seemed to widen all the time.

'Mum?'

She walked on, knowing that if she spoke it would make things worse. Her phone rang again and she snatched it out of the beach bag as her feet squeaked angrily on the sand. It was Hudson. She dropped the phone back into the bag where it continued to ring and vibrate, taunting her, reminding her there was a man a few thousand kilometres away who would ask her, again, if she was all right, and tell her, again, that he loved her and wanted to be with her. If he meant it, why was he there, in Zimbabwe, when he knew that she split her time between America and South Africa?

Sonja ignored the looks from people in the car park, even the impromptu applause from a couple of young men as she transferred the beach bag to her left hand and shook out her right, trying to ease the pain in her knuckles. She pushed the button on the remote to unlock the rental car, got in, started the engine and turned the air con up to full blast. She felt like she was overheating. She craved a cigarette, even though it had been years. She had to acknowledge that for all her anger and disquiet, there had also been the rush, as she took charge and took the boy down, and as much as she hated to admit it, there had been the thrill.

Looking up into the rear-view mirror she saw crow's feet and emptiness.

'Get a grip,' she said to the woman in the reflection. 'You're on holiday.'

CHAPTER 2

Emma Kurtz lay on her bed in the house where she and Sonja were staying, golden late-afternoon sun streaming into her room. Her phone buzzed.

Hey kiddo, how's things?

The message was from Hudson Brand. Although Hudson was away working in Zimbabwe, managing a safari lodge in Hwange National Park, as far as Emma knew he and her mother were still an item.

OK.

That bad? How's Mom?

Hudson was an American – well, half; his mother had been of Portuguese and Angolan descent – so like South Africans he said 'mom' instead of 'mum', something that Emma, who had grown up in England, could never get her mouth around.

Emma chewed her lip. *Three double Klipdrift and Coke Zeros for lunch.*

What happened on the beach today?

As well as being a safari guide, Hudson was a part-time private investigator, and very little got past him. He was not her father, but Emma knew Hudson cared for her, and probably loved her like a daughter. She didn't want to alarm him.

11

No biggie, just some guys acting like jerks. Mum sorted it.

With a gun?

She laughed out loud, adding an *LOL* for effect. *Can you talk?*

Her phone rang before she had time to dial.

'You OK, really?' he asked.

'Um, yeah.'

'Once more, with feeling,' Hudson said. 'Want to tell me about it?'

Unlike with her mother, Emma felt as though she could pretty much tell Hudson anything, such as if she was having trouble with Sonja, or with boys, or even with her work as a battlefield archaeologist. He knew how to read people, possibly because of his time as an investigator. He'd also been with the CIA when he was younger. Emma explained what had happened with the two young men on the beach.

'She hit him in the *temple*?'

'Yeah.'

'The guy's lucky to be alive, the way your mom throws a roundhouse.'

'Straight jab.'

'Then doubly lucky. How's she doing otherwise?'

Emma sighed. 'Usual. Short temper, jumpy, doesn't like crowds, either moves at full speed ahead or dead slow, like now. She's sleeping. I was hoping we could just have a normal holiday, like regular people, and maybe reconnect. It was going OK – we saw penguins and a couple of days ago we drove to the V&A in Cape Town and went dress shopping.'

'Sonja? Dress shopping?'

'I know, right?' Emma tried to smile, but squeezed her fingers to her eyes. 'I just feel like now we've gone backwards again.'

'PTSD's a bitch, Emma.'

'What can I do?' Emma asked. She knew that Hudson had been to war, in Angola, when he was younger.

'Keep her active, doing stuff that's healthy and a positive distraction. The problem is that if she spends too much time

12

indoors, alone, drinking, she'll keep going over and over all the stuff in her head. And trust me, there's plenty of it.'

Emma knew Hudson's last remark wasn't meant to hurt her, but she felt it. 'I try to get her to talk, but she clams up.'

'Yeah.' Hudson paused. 'I hear you. Talking's good if it's done a safe way, but it can also trigger too many bad memories. She's trying to protect herself, and you, Emma.'

'I guess. But I'm twenty-seven now, for God's sake.'

'No one's saying you're a kid.'

No, Emma thought, but she did feel like Hudson and Sonja were part of a club that she wasn't entitled to join. It was frustrating.

'I know it's hard, believe me,' Hudson said. 'Your mom knows all about PTSD and I've heard her, seen her, talking to people she knows who are suffering. She just can't deal with it herself. Give her time, Emma.'

Emma looked out her window. Betty's Bay was dappled with golden light. There was a line of people walking along the beach. She wanted to ask, 'How long?' but knew there was no point. 'Thanks, Hudson.'

'I know it's not much help, but I'm here, any time you want to talk.'

'Thanks.'

'Bye, Emma.'

She ended the call.

Emma felt restless. She scrolled through Instagram, but when she saw a picture of her ex, Alex Bahler, who was posed on a ski slope in Canada with a blonde with big lips by his side, she slammed the phone face down on the bedside table. Jumping up, she changed out of her denim skirt and T-shirt into running clothes and laced up her trainers. She put her phone in an armband, pulled it on and then activated her wireless headphones.

Her rubber soles squeaked on the polished floorboards in the corridor. The houses at Silver Sands, nestled in the stunted but thick zone of coastal fynbos behind the beach, were a mix of old seventies holiday homes and more contemporary designs, like the grey steel and glass place Sonja had found.

Emma knocked on Sonja's bedroom door. 'Mum?'

When there was no answer, she scrawled a note on the pad fixed to the refrigerator with a magnet and left it on the kitchen counter, telling her mother she had gone for a run and would be back in half an hour. Emma figured Hudson's advice about staying fit and active applied to her as much as to Sonja.

It was cool outside; the weather here could change by the minute and grey clouds were amassing above the rocky Kogelberg mountains that rose steeply back from the narrow stretch of coastline. Emma thought she had enough time to run a couple of lengths of the beach before the rain came.

She did some quick stretches then set off. Her time in lockdown in the UK had not been good for her. Exercise had been restricted, but she hadn't made the most of the periods when it was available, and she'd drunk and eaten too much. She had not been on a dig for over a year, either, and had missed even the exercise that the hard, physical side of her life as an archaeologist demanded. She'd been productive, though, doing some post-graduate study remotely, and Sonja had covered her loss of earnings when the consultancy Emma had been working for inevitably laid her off.

A woman walking a dog smiled and nodded to her as she followed Watsonia Road, which ran parallel to the beachfront. A cute guy, also running, nodded to her and she flashed him a quick, if somewhat pained, grin. She was breathing hard already.

The salt air felt raw and clean and she told herself again how good it was to get out of Glasgow for a while. Unlike Sonja she had not been born in Africa, but she could not deny that the continent had hooked its thorny barbs into her.

Emma tried not to replay the scene on the beach that morning as she ran past the spot where they had been happily sunbathing, but the memory of the man, Denzel, coming towards her, and the touch of his hand on hers came back unbidden. She ran harder, trying to blot out the image, the feelings.

She had been full of bravado on the beach, trying to film even after the attack, but now, with time to think about it, she felt anxiety rise up in her chest like heartburn.

Emma had thought that the two boys would back down, or be scared by the threat of her catching them on camera. Instead, Denzel had come at her, his face growing larger on the screen with every pace, so that she need not have zoomed in. Emma had been in danger before in her life, but this time the young man had been armed with nothing but his bare hands and the single-minded intent to do her harm. He hadn't even bothered drawing his knife, so sure was he that he was taking on two help-less females.

Well, one.

Sonja's unleashed violence, devastatingly quick, momentarily merciless, but ultimately controlled, had scared her almost as much as Denzel had.

Emma had never romanticised her mother's calling as a soldier or, later in life, as a private military contractor – a modern-day euphemism for a mercenary. Half-remembered platitudes, such as 'Mummy protects people from baddies', didn't cut it when you were a four-year-old wetting the bed at Grandma's house, or a spotty-faced teenager being bullied at boarding school.

Emma was the first to admit she had been a handful as a teen-ager, a situation not helped by the fact that Sonja's then partner had tried to groom her for sex, but beyond the normal teen angst she knew she was suffering from the years Sonja had spent away from her. As a single mother Sonja had done well, materially, putting Emma through private school and university, and she was still comfortably off. Life, however, was about far more than bank balances.

They'd led separate lives in recent years – perhaps all their lives – but lately Emma had found herself wanting to reach out and connect with her mother, possibly because it was becoming clear to those very few people who were close to Sonja that she was not doing well.

Emma looked out to the sandhills and saw a procession of people emerging. The line of beachgoers she had seen on the sands earlier had moved on, but as she continued to jog, closing the gap, she saw that these were not retirees or holiday-makers out for a late-afternoon stroll on the beach. These people were on a mission, on their way to work.

She could see men, mostly young, but a few with grey hair, wearing wetsuits and either carrying or wearing diving cylinders. Interspersed with them were younger men and boys, and a few women and girls, all carrying backpacks or bags slung over their shoulders. Some were also carrying spare cylinders, presumably for the men who would go underwater. In all there were about thirty people and when Emma came to the car park, she saw half a dozen vehicles, mostly old and rusty. She recalled the academic telling her that this was a drop-off place for poachers, but she was surprised that the criminals were so blatant; it was as though they were walking to work and there was no one about to try to stop them. Emma knew the problem of illegal abalone harvesting was serious, but it seemed it was also too big to police.

Emma made her way through the low, hardy vegetation and then decided that instead of running on the flat beach she would try the steep sandy path up the Blesberg. She'd only gone a few metres when she saw a mound of opened shells, lying in the bush. She crouched and picked one up and, as the coastal breeze shifted, a foul stench filled her nostrils. She straightened and stepped back. Among the midden was a purple and black gelatinous goo, rotting away. She looked at the shell; it was as big as her palm, and scraped clean.

Abalone.

This was what Denzel and his friend had been after. Sickened, Emma tossed the shell back on the pile and turned away. She started violently when she found a man right behind her.

Denzel.

As Emma started to raise one hand protectively, Denzel's fist shot out, Emma's head snapped back and she fell into the sand

and the tangle of bush. He fell on her, punching her again, then put a hand over her mouth. In his other hand he held a knife.

Emma tried to scream, but he clamped her cheeks, painfully. The blade scratched her through her shirt, over her shoulder to her upper arm, where Denzel sliced through the band holding her phone. He moved the knife to her neck and terror and panic overwhelmed her. She tried to remember something – anything – Sonja had ever taught her about self-defence as Denzel put his knee between her legs and began to force them open. Emma tried to bite his hand, but she felt the knife pressing into her skin. He smiled at her.

A dog barked.

'Hey!' a man yelled from the pathway below them.

A Doberman came bounding up the steep hill, paws scrabbling for purchase in the loose sand. Denzel looked over his shoulder; he grabbed Emma's phone, got up and ran off.

*

Sonja put Emma to bed.

She stroked her daughter's hair and passed her another tissue so she could wipe her eyes. The sight of Emma's cut lip and the swelling around her cheek made Sonja clench her jaws together so tightly she thought she might shatter a tooth.

The police officers had left after taking Emma's statement and that of the man who had found her. Sonja had thanked the man profusely. The female officer had said that the description of Denzel and his name were not immediately familiar, but that many local men had joined the ranks of abalone poachers.

'I'm sorry,' Emma said once again.

Sonja laid her fingers softly against Emma's cheek. 'I told you already, four times now, you have nothing to apologise for.'

'You warned me about running at dusk.'

'Shh. It was still light. You are not at fault here, that boy, Denzel, is.'

An ambulance had also come, called by Sonja as soon as she

saw the state of Emma, even though her daughter had tried to protest that she was all right. Sonja popped one of the Valium the paramedics had left out of its foil pack. 'Take this.'

'I'm OK.'

'It will help you sleep.'

Emma sat up in bed and took the pill.

'You're sure he didn't –'

'*Mum . . .*' Emma said, 'I told you, he hit me and took my phone off my arm. It was my own stupid fault for taking that video of him.'

'No.' Sonja balled her fists. 'You are not to blame in any way for this.'

'And now I've lost my phone . . .'

'It's just a phone, Emma. We'll buy you a new one tomorrow, if you're up to it. We can go into town, play tourists, go shopping again.'

Emma gingerly touched her cheek. 'I can't go out looking like this.'

'You can.'

'Mum?'

'Yes?'

'Will you teach me to fight?'

'We'll talk about that in the morning.' Sonja sighed and rubbed her forehead. She had the makings of a hangover after her lunchtime drinking. Emma closed her eyes and Sonja left the bedroom, quietly closing the door.

She went to her own room and dragged her military-green vinyl dive bag from the closet. She hefted the bag onto her bed and unzipped it, then selected her kit and laid it out on the bed. She had matching black Lycra leggings and a long-sleeve T-shirt from her selection of workout gear, which would do fine, and a lightweight black beanie. She also took out the weighted dive belt she'd had on earlier that day; the knife was in its scabbard. She unsnapped the fastenings on a waterproof Pelican case and took out her Glock 19 and two magazines of ammunition. From elsewhere in the dive bag she retrieved a silencer and screwed it onto the end of the Glock.

Into a small, black running pack she placed cable ties and duct tape – she never travelled without either – as well as antiseptic wipes and a couple of military-issue wound dressings, just in case.

Sonja dressed, threaded a pancake holster onto the dive belt, then put it on and slid the pistol into the holster. She put on the beanie and tucked away her hair, already in a ponytail. On her feet she wore lightweight black climbing shoes. She put on a dark grey nylon windcheater, zipped it up and pulled it down low enough to cover the pistol and knife handle; that would be enough not to alarm a casual onlooker. From the kitchen she took four resealable plastic bags and put them in her running pack.

She went back to Emma's room, opened the door a crack, and confirmed her daughter was asleep. She stopped there a moment, looking down at her. Emma would never truly know just how much she meant to her, and Sonja knew she would never be able to find the words to tell her; there were some things she just could not explain and they ran deeper than a normal mother's love for a child. Sonja was not normal.

She didn't bother leaving a note. If Emma happened to wake before she returned, her daughter would be able to guess where she had gone.

Outside the cottage a chilly fog, trapped by the Kogelberg behind her, was rolling down the steep mountain wall to the ocean. Sonja pressed the home button of her phone and opened the app she had installed on her phone and Emma's. Her daughter didn't know it, but Sonja could track her. It took just a few moments for Sonja to detect the signal from Emma's phone. Interestingly, it was showing out in the blue of the Indian Ocean on the phone's map screen.

Sonja walked along Watsonia Road, past holiday homes and retirement nests towards the car park by the beach. She made her way through the dunes, among the scrubby coastal vegetation. As she moved, she picked up the sound of voices, carried on the onshore breeze.

She saw people moving, silhouetted against the night sky, and dropped down into a crouch between two dunes.

A girl in her early to mid-teens struggled uphill from the beach, a bulging net bag full of abalone shells on her back. Next came a younger boy with an old backpack, which clacked with the sound of shell on shell as he walked.

Sonja dropped to her belly and leopard-crawled to the edge of the trail, hiding herself like a snake in the low fynbos.

The next person on the well-worn trail was a man in a wetsuit, barefoot, still wearing his BCD vest and oxygen tank and carrying a pair of fins. Sonja drew the Glock from its holster. As he walked past her, oblivious to her presence, Sonja sprang up, moved silently behind him and hooked her left arm around him, hand over his mouth as she jammed the tip of the pistol's barrel up under his jaw.

'With me,' she hissed. She led him back between the dunes, deeper into the tangled coastal vegetation.

'Hey . . .' he tried to say behind her hand.

'Shut up. Unless you'd like to die?'

He shook his head.

'Take your cylinder and BCD off, and your mask.' He hesitated so she shifted the pistol to the side of his head with enough force to push his head over onto his left shoulder. He undid the tank and vest and let them fall to the ground. 'Face down, hands behind your back.'

She knelt on his back, shrugged off her hiking pack, and secured his hands behind him with a cable tie. Then she relieved him of a knife and a tyre iron, which were stuffed in his belt. She threw the lever away, assuming it was the tool he used to prise abalone off rocks and reefs.

'What's Denzel doing?'

'I don't know any −'

She smacked the side of his head with the butt of the pistol and put the barrel back to his temple. 'You mean nothing to me. I've killed better men than you.'

'He's still diving, even in the dark. He's always one of the last to leave. It's getting late, though – he'll be finished just now.'

Sonja took out the tape, tore off a strip and fastened it over the man's mouth. Next she bound his ankles and knees with several turns from the roll. Sonja hauled on the man's vest and dive cylinder, then left him lying in the bush and moved to the tallest stubby tree she could see. There, she cached her hiking pack and used a couple of the antiseptic wipes to clean the poacher's mask and the mouthpiece of his regulator. She double-bagged her phone, secured her pistol back in its holster, and picked up the man's fins.

Someone would find the diver, eventually, but Sonja planned on being long gone before then. She wound her way down through the dunes, skirting the procession of other poachers and shell bearers following the same track as the others. She assumed they were heading for the rusty *bakkies* in the car park.

Sonja checked her phone screen through the protective plastic layers. She could see the pulsating red dot that indicated Emma's iPhone and waded into the ocean towards it. Another diver exited, off to her right, but paid her no attention; with her long hair concealed he probably thought she was just another poacher going in for one last look.

Glancing at the phone and then pressing the menu button on her GPS-enabled running watch, Sonja selected the compass widget and worked out a bearing towards where Denzel was currently diving. She put on the fins, adjusted the man's mask and started finning.

Without the benefit of a wetsuit she shivered, but had long ago learned to ignore temporary discomfort. These days military people called it 'embracing the suck' – not complaining about things out of one's control, such as cold or rain or heat or dust, but accepting them, even revelling in them. As a young soldier in the British Army she had been put through a gruelling special forces selection course, run by the famed Special Air Service, to prepare male and female recruits from the British Army's Intelligence Corps to withstand the rigours of undercover surveillance operations against extremists in Northern Ireland. She had experienced near-hypothermia in the snow- and sleet-covered Welsh mountains. This was nothing.

Sonja followed the bearing on her watch, wondering how Denzel could continue stealing abalone in the dark. She had her answer when she picked up the stabbing beam of an underwater torch. She finned her way closer.

Being careful to stay behind the man with the torch, she slowed and adjusted the air in her BCD so that her buoyancy was neutral. She hung there, suspended in the chilly gloom, watching the man at work.

She picked up movement in her peripheral vision, and forced herself to hover motionless as the sleek, grey bulk of a shark cruised past. Sonja looked at the man. If he was aware of the presence of danger, he resolutely ignored it, efficiently working his tyre lever under shell after shell, prising abalone off the rocky reef and slipping each sea creature into the net bag slung around his neck.

Checking around her, Sonja finned her way close enough to confirm, by his athletic build and wavy hair billowing around him, that the diver was, in fact, Denzel. There was no sign of his offsider, the other young man who had tried but failed to calm him down on the beach.

Sonja paused to draw her knife and then closed on the unsuspecting poacher. She came up behind him, reached out and ripped his mask from his face. As his hands came up, trying to grab at whatever or whomever had attacked him, Sonja grabbed Denzel's air hose and sliced through it. She disengaged, waiting for his next move.

She underestimated him.

Instead of panicking and finning for the surface, Denzel pulled on a slip knot or buckle and let his bag full of abalone fall to the bottom of the sea. He rolled onto his back, pulled his right knee into his chest and drew his knife, which he must have retrieved or replaced. As Sonja tried to close on him again, he kicked out at her. She sliced her knife down as his fin connected with her chest. Denzel's wetsuit protected him from the worst of the cut, but she did see some blood swirling from the wound on his leg.

Pushed back by Denzel's kick, though unhurt because the water had slowed the momentum, Sonja swam out of his reach. She had the benefit of oxygen. He gave her a final glare, then headed for the surface.

Sonja headed back to shore, as fast as she could, knowing that she would have the advantage of speed unless Denzel ditched all of his now useless, heavy diving gear; she doubted he would. When she neared the beach she paused to unbuckle and jettison her stolen cylinder, BCD and fins. She emerged from the water cold and wet, but satisfied.

As she trudged through the sand back to where she had left her pack, she took her phone out of the plastic bags and called the number she had saved, that of the police officer who had interviewed Emma.

'Get down to Silver Sands Beach, now,' she said without preamble when the woman answered her phone.

'Who is this?'

'Denzel, the boy who beat the English girl and stole her phone, will soon be getting out of the water. He's bleeding, though, so maybe a shark will get him first.'

'Mrs Kurtz, is that you?'

It was 'Ms', but she said nothing and ended the call.

Sonja took up position in the sandhills and watched the granite-like surface of the water. All the other poachers had given up for the evening. Off to the west she saw a couple of people walking, perhaps the last of the bearers. She checked her phone and the app told her that Denzel, stupidly, was still carrying Emma's iPhone, stuffed somewhere in his wetsuit. She'd made no attempt to take it from him in the water – that would have been too hard without killing him, and it would be better if the police caught him with stolen goods.

She picked up the sight of splashes out in the sea; it was Denzel, laboriously swimming back to shore. She was right, his dive gear was his life. If he hadn't acted like such a bastard and hurt her daughter, she might almost have felt sorry for him. Sonja drew her Glock and sat waiting.

Here and there lights shone from houses set back from the beach, but there was no night life here, nor beachside bars or restaurants – the nearest place still open was the takeaway shop at the penguin colony, and that was out of sight. The last of the poachers and bearers were now struggling through the dunes.

Denzel was getting closer to shore. Sonja looked up at the sky. Venus was rising, the moon just a low-hanging sliver. She racked the Glock, chambering a round.

CHAPTER 3

Emma woke the next morning to the sound of knocking on the door of the holiday cottage. She checked her watch on the bedside table; her neck hurt when she turned her head. It was just after eight in the morning.

'Mum?' There was no answer. Well rested but groggy, Emma swung her legs out of the covers. 'Coming.'

She slid her lower jaw from side to side as she walked; it was still sore. She wondered if she had a black eye. She padded down the hallway, still wearing socks and pyjamas. On autopilot, she opened the front door.

A man stood there, holding a dozen roses – except that rather than being a delivery man, he was the friend of the man who had assaulted her.

'Shit!' Emma started to close the door, fear and panic rising up inside her as she remembered Denzel's hands on her.

'Wait, please wait.' He held up his empty hand, palm out, and stayed back from the door.

Emma closed it to a crack, fumbled for the security chain and latched it. She'd still been half asleep, not thinking at all about her personal security despite the rawness of her injuries. If she'd had half a brain, she told herself, she would have asked who was there. 'What do you want?'

'I came to say sorry.'

Emma watched him. The last time she'd seen him he had been in an old wetsuit, worn and torn. Now he wore jeans, perfectly white sneakers and a pressed, collared shirt. He smiled. Any other time and place she would have fancied him.

'Your friend fucking punched me.'

'Yes, I heard. That's why I brought these.' He held out the flowers, though did not take another pace closer to the door.

'How did you know where to find me?'

He looked at his shoes for a moment. 'I've seen you, out running.'

'So, you're a stalker as well as a poacher?'

He shook his head. 'No, please, no. I'm sorry.'

Emma held the front of her pyjama shirt tightly together. 'Why are you apologising?'

'I tried to stop him, on the beach, when you were filming us –'

'Not hard enough.'

'No, that other woman on the beach with you took care of that. That's what I was about to say – I'm apologising for not trying hard enough to stop Denzel from coming at you, then, and . . . later. I don't like seeing men treating women badly.'

Emma narrowed her eyes. 'You still went into the water with him, like nothing happened.'

He looked down at his shoes. 'I was wrong and I was scared, and I'm sorry for that, as well. We had it out, later, got into a fight.'

It was only when he looked up that Emma noticed that he, too, had a cut over his eye. She nodded towards it. 'He did that to you?'

'Yes. Though I hit him as well. He's my cousin.'

'Your cousin the poacher.'

He frowned, glanced down at the flowers and then held them out again.

'I'm not taking anything from a poacher.'

'I'm not a poacher. That was my first time in the water with Denzel, and I didn't take any abalone. My heart wasn't in it after all.'

'After all?'

'I'm studying at varsity and I lost my job as a waiter. I'm stacking shelves at Pick n Pay at the Waterfront, but I'm short for my fees and I needed to get some cash. I knew Denzel was poaching; he'd asked me many times to join him, but I always said no. He told me I could make fourteen hundred rand, nearly a hundred US dollars, per kilo taking abalone, and that I might be able to get eight or nine kilograms in one dive. I think poaching is terrible, but . . . Well, having no money is no excuse, but I've never broken the law in my life.'

'Yeah, right,' Emma said.

'You sound like you're from overseas,' he said, 'but not everyone in Africa is a criminal.'

Emma closed her eyes and put a hand on her forehead. She felt a pang of guilt – she had, borderline, insulted him. His words had got under her armour, and he did seem genuinely contrite. 'You want a cup of coffee?' She opened her eyes and saw, just then, how his widened.

'I just came to drop off the flowers and say sorry.'

Emma slid the security chain across and opened the door. 'Come in.'

'You sure?'

Emma glanced over her shoulder. 'My mum's in her room. She has a gun. Maybe two.'

'Noted.'

Emma stepped back as he walked in. 'What's your name?'

'Oh, sorry, it's Kelvin.'

'Come in,' Emma repeated, opening the door fully for him and taking the flowers when he offered them to her again. 'I'll get some water for these.'

Kelvin looked around as she led him along the corridor to the kitchen. 'Nice place.'

'It's an Airbnb.' Emma filled the kettle. 'Coffee?'

'Please. Where do you usually live? England?'

'Scotland. I studied there, at university, and liked it, so I got a job there and ended up staying.'

'So I was right; you're not local.'

She shook her head and took two cups out of the cupboard. 'I'm not. My mum's Namibian-German, but her mother, my gran, was English, so I grew up in England and went to school there. My mum was away, on business, a lot of the time.'

'What does she do?'

Kelvin seemed nice enough, unlike his cousin, and Sonja was only a scream away, but Emma had always felt a need to be careful about describing what her mother did for a living. She had gone through stages in her life when she'd been honest about it, but as a child this had often led to people bullying her, accusing her of lying. 'She's a personal trainer.'

Kelvin nodded. 'She certainly looked fit. Sorry, I didn't mean that to come out sounding weird.'

It was Emma's turn to laugh. She couldn't tell Kelvin that her mother kept fit training other people to kill, nor that she had shot more people than Emma could possibly have imagined during her career as a mercenary. To change the subject, she asked, 'What are you studying?'

Kelvin smiled. 'Medicine. My mom was so proud – I'm the first person in the family to go to varsity. I was stupid getting involved with Denzel. If I'd been charged by the cops it wouldn't have been good for me.'

The kettle boiled and Emma poured. 'So, you and Denzel?'

He shook his head and whistled through his teeth. 'He's been in trouble since we were kids. I can't tell you how sorry I am.'

'Tell the police.'

Kelvin looked away, out through the kitchen window at the view of the nature reserve. Emma handed him his cup and he nodded his thanks.

'I take it you didn't see him attack me in the dunes?' Emma pressed.

He looked her in the eye. 'No. If I'd been there it wouldn't have happened.'

'Yet my mum had to stop him from assaulting me on the beach.'

'Because I couldn't get to him first.'

'So, go to the police,' Emma said again, 'tell them what he's like.'

Kelvin paused. 'His father, my uncle . . .'

'What about him? You're scared of what your uncle will say about his son who beats up women and robs them?'

Kelvin looked away again. 'It's not what he'd say, it's what he'd do, especially if he knew the police were involved.'

'What does your uncle do?'

Kelvin said nothing, just stared out the window.

'Answer the question.'

Both Emma and Kelvin turned at the sound of Sonja's voice. She'd arrived from her room without a sound, thanks to her bare feet. She wore a man's blue cotton Oxford shirt, sleeves rolled up, the tail barely covering her pants. Emma knew the shirt had been Sam's. Sonja pointed her Glock at Kelvin, who set down his cup and put his hands up.

'Please . . .'

'It's all right,' Sonja said, 'I won't kill you. Not immediately. I've been listening to your bleating.'

'Ma'am, I'm sorry, I –'

'Save it. Who's your fucking uncle?'

'Ma'am –'

'After what happened to Emma the police will believe that an intruder came to the house, a relative of the accused, to silence her,' Sonja said. 'That's what you're saying your uncle would do, aren't you? Kill any witnesses if his precious boy is charged with a crime? Usual bullshit?'

'Ma'am, I came here to apologise, for what happened to . . .'

'Emma.' Sonja rolled her eyes. 'Good doggy. Now roll over and make yourself useful. Tell me about your uncle and your cousin or I'll call the cops and then a lack of money will be the least of your problems. Pretty boy like you wouldn't stay intact for long in Pollsmoor Prison.'

Kelvin grimaced. 'My uncle, he's . . . into things.'

'Such as?'

'Money-making ventures, ma'am, if you know what I mean. Big money.'

'Abalone?' Sonja asked.

Emma sipped her coffee, watching her mother at work. She could see how Kelvin had gone from being confident yet caring, to terrified. There was something about Sonja that made it very clear to anyone who came up against her that she would not hesitate to pull a trigger.

'Yes, ma'am.' Kelvin bit his lower lip.

'Go on. Your coffee's getting cold, and I'm getting bored. Emma, get my phone and be ready to call the last number, the police.'

Kelvin held up a palm. 'Yes, ma'am, my uncle is an abalone dealer.'

'Can we at least sit down and maybe put the gun away, Mum?' Emma interjected.

Sonja nodded. Emma led them through to the lounge room and they all sat on white sofas, around a coffee table inlaid with seashells under glass. Sonja kept the Glock resting on her thigh.

'Dealer?' Sonja prompted.

Kelvin sat on the edge of his seat. 'Ma'am, the trade is worth millions, billions of rand.'

'And if your uncle is a middleman, then why were you and your cousin diving?'

Kelvin shrugged. 'Denzel looks for adventure, and to prove himself in the eyes of his father. He's got money, you're right, but . . .'

'He likes the thrill.'

Emma watched her mother. The way she'd said it made it sound like she understood. Sonja's late husband, Sam, was a television star and he'd left her a small fortune and a house in Los Angeles. Yet, still, until recently her mother had regularly headed off to third-world shitholes looking for small wars to fight. Emma shook her head. Sonja ignored her.

'How does the trade work? Markets, players, the lot,' Sonja asked bluntly.

Kelvin spread his hands. 'It's no great secret. Abalone is highly prized in Asia, especially Hong Kong, where the money is, and parts of mainland China. It's a delicacy, fresh or dried. South African abalone is considered some of the best in the world, so it commands top dollar. The poachers have cleaned it out of large parts of the coastal waters – and the rarer it gets, the more it's worth.'

'So the Chinese buy from your uncle?' Emma asked.

Kelvin hesitated. 'I'm not saying that on the record, but if we can just talk about the trade in general . . . it's not like the middlemen here get paid in cash. The Chinese learned pretty early on that if they show up in a coastal town in South Africa with bags of money, someone's going to *moer* them and steal their cash. The Chinese pay with commodities now – drugs, or the chemicals needed to make Tik.'

'Tik?' Emma said.

'Methamphetamine,' Sonja said to her. 'What the Americans call "ice". It's all too common here in the Cape.'

Kelvin nodded. '*Ja*, I know too many people and families who've been ruined by that stuff.'

'And yet still you're protecting your uncle, sticking up for him,' Sonja said.

'No,' he said. 'I'm not defending him, I'm just –'

'Scared of him.'

Kelvin glared at Sonja, but he broke eye contact first.

'Where is Denzel?' Sonja asked.

'I don't know, ma'am, and that's the truth, I swear. We were supposed to catch up this morning, but he didn't show. I was going to have it out with him, tell him that what he did was wrong and that I didn't want anything to do with poaching or hurting women.'

Sonja scoffed. 'The money would have lured you back.'

'I was never "there" in the first place, ma'am. Like I told your daughter, this was going to be my first time and even then I felt sick to my stomach about it. I promise you.'

'Kelvin,' Emma said, 'can't this stuff, abalone, be farmed?'

He sat back in his chair, grateful for an easy question. 'It's been tried, but despite the government declaring marine national parks and setting quotas for big companies and even what they call "artisanal fishermen", the illegal market is much bigger than the legal market. The demand is just too high.'

'You and your cousin, you're just common poachers, out to make a quick buck and screw the environment,' Sonja said.

Kelvin sat up straighter. 'That's easy for you to say, as a white woman, ma'am, with respect. My people are descended from the Cape Malays who the Dutch brought here as slaves. We were screwed by the whites under the apartheid regime, when they kicked us out of our homes in the old part of Cape Town and got the contracts and the leases to fish for abalone, and when the ANC took over with Mandela the contracts went to fat cats of a different colour. My people could still make a living, before, selling *kreef* and abalone to local restaurants, but those days are gone. Now honest fishermen watch everyone get rich off this stuff; everyone except us, that is. Only people like . . .' he looked down at his feet, 'only people like my uncle do well from our community. We've got no work, no money, no options.'

'Yes, but you were quite happy to do your bit to destroy the last remaining abalone on this part of the coast,' Sonja said.

'I told you. I knew it was wrong, so I didn't go through with it.' Kelvin looked Sonja in the eye. 'I've got nothing, ma'am, except an apology for what happened.' He turned to Emma. 'I should go. I'm sorry, Emma.'

Kelvin stood up to leave.

'No, wait,' Emma said. She found she didn't want him to go.

She sensed he was very different from his cousin, and he'd owned up to what he'd done, or almost done. There was also something genuine about him, she thought. It couldn't have been easy to come and apologise for his cousin's actions.

Sonja got up and went to the front door, the pistol hanging loose but ready by her side. 'The boy said it's time to go, and I agree.'

'Mum . . .'

'No, it's fine, Emma,' Kelvin said.

'See you around, maybe?' Emma said.

Sonja opened the door. 'Tell your woman-beating coward of a cousin to go to the police and be a man and plead guilty, before I find him again.'

Kelvin nodded and walked past her down the path and out the front gate of the cottage. There he stopped and turned and waved to Emma, who was standing close behind Sonja.

Emma returned the wave. Kelvin nodded and walked down the street, not looking back at them.

'What did you mean by "again", Mum?'

'Nothing.'

Emma put her hand on her mother's shoulder and Sonja shrugged it off immediately, spinning around with a look in her eye that said, 'Don't ever touch me like that again'. Emma tried hard not to be intimidated. 'Did you go after him, did you do something, Mum?'

'You don't need to worry, Emma.'

Emma went back to her room and dressed in some clean activewear as fast as she could. When she had laced her running shoes, she went out of her room and brushed past Sonja, who was still in the front doorway, watching the street. She was mad at Sonja; her mother was treating her like a child, and now Emma wondered if Sonja had done something stupid or illegal.

'Where are you going?' Sonja said as Emma ran outside and down the steps.

'None of your business.'

CHAPTER 4

Sonja pulled on jeans, a T-shirt and a hoodie long enough to hide the pistol tucked into her waistband.

She went outside and, in the distance, saw Emma jogging along one of the lanes that led through the coastal vegetation towards Silver Sands Beach. In the distance she could see Kelvin, and Emma had almost caught up with him. Sonja shook her head, remembering some of the choices in men she'd made. They had not all been good.

The sky was clear and the sun was subverting the morning chill in the air. Sonja took out her phone and called Warrant Officer Desiree February.

'You?' Desiree said when Sonja greeted her and identified herself.

'Yes, me. What about it?'

'Thanks for the wild-goose chase last night.'

'What do you mean?' Sonja looked both ways and crossed the road to the beach, then walked onto the sand.

'No sign of Denzel Hendricks.'

'So, now you know his surname?' Sonja said.

There was a brief pause. 'Um, I made some enquiries. I also found a young man cable-tied face down in the sand who was shaking to death, and not just because of the cold.'

'Is that right.'

'Yes, it is. He said some "big guy" assaulted him and stole his dive gear.'

Sonja smiled to herself. Men. 'None of my business, then.'

'No, but the "big guy" had left remarkably small footprints, like about a woman's size nine.'

February had tried to quickly to change the subject when Sonja had asked her how she knew Denzel's surname. Sonja wondered if the detective had known all along – if Kelvin's uncle was a bigshot gangster, perhaps the whole family was known to the police. Had February played dumb the day before to avoid upsetting a mobster?

'Nothing on the shoreline?'

'No. We waited a while, my partner and me, and then we went up into the hills in the nature reserve – the poachers come and go that way. We picked up plenty of spoor. I suppose Denzel just got away from us that way. No sign of him at his home in Hawston, though. He's missing. His father's angry.'

'Not a man to be messed with, I hear,' Sonja said. Now, she thought, February sounded like she was telling the truth. She seemed more worried about Denzel's disappearance and the gangster's ire, than what had happened to Emma.

There was a pause. 'I'm not scared of anyone, but Vincent Hendricks is not a man I want to get offside,' February said. 'Tell me, where did you last see Denzel, after your altercation on the beach?'

'Who says I saw him after?' Sonja crossed the beach to the ocean's high-water mark and turned right, following in Emma and Kelvin's footsteps. Looking along the beach she saw that Emma had now caught up to Kelvin and they had stopped, so Sonja waited where she was.

'You called it in, let me know where and when Denzel would be on Silver Sands Beach. Come on. What's going on?'

'I don't know.' Neither did the policewoman. Sonja ended the call.

Emma and Kelvin were moving into the dunes at the end of the beach, towards Blesberg. They disappeared.

Sonja started to run, fearful of letting Emma out of her sight again.

*

Emma was glad she'd managed to catch up to Kelvin. He had looked gratifyingly pleased to see her when she'd called after him. Before she'd lost her nerve, she'd said, 'Um, I just thought, well, maybe I could get your phone number? My mum and I are still here for a while and, well, I thought it might be good to get to know a local person; maybe you could tell us some nice places to visit . . .' She'd stopped then before making even more of a goose of herself.

Kelvin broke into a grin. 'Yes, for sure. That would be *lekker* – great.'

There'd been silence for a few steps. Emma thought that maybe Kelvin was actually a little shy, even though he'd had the courage to come and confront her – and Sonja – with an apology. But Kelvin had reached into a pocket and took out a pen – he was a prepared kind of guy. He'd handed it to her and she had written his phone number on her hand.

It was then Emma had heard a strange noise from the dunes. 'What's that? Growling?'

'Dogs,' Kelvin said, leading the way.

Gulls were crying and swooping ahead of them.

'Hey!' Kelvin clapped his hands together several times.

Emma saw two dogs worrying at something. Up ahead there were the walls of what looked like an early beach cottage which had been reclaimed by the sand. The dogs were growling at each other and Emma wondered if the object they were fighting over was a dead seal. Kelvin jogged forward, clapping his hands, and the dogs ran off. He froze, raised one hand to his mouth, then put the other up in the air, signalling her to stop. 'Go back, Emma.'

'Why?'

He turned to her, mouth open in disbelief or horror. 'No.'

'What is it, Kelvin?'

Emma moved up and he came to her with his arms out. He tried to stop her, but she brushed past, then gagged.

Lying in the sand, between the dunes, was a body. It was Denzel, in his wetsuit, and there was blood on his exposed hands and face.

'My God, is he . . .?'

'Dead.'

Emma saw the blood coming from one of Denzel's eyeballs and gagged again. She turned and walked a few steps away, trying hard not to throw up.

'Emma!'

She looked up and saw her mother.

'What is it, a body?' Sonja called as she strode towards them.

Emma wiped saliva from her lips. 'How did you know?'

'I've seen those reactions enough times to know when some-one's found a corpse. It's him, Denzel, right?'

Kelvin looked away from the body, to Sonja. 'Ma'am, how could you know it was my cousin?'

Sonja waved a hand in the air and came to them, then carried on. She looked down at Denzel's body, then knelt beside it.

Emma crept closer. 'What happened to him?'

'Gunshot, back of the head, though something's been gnawing at him.'

'Dogs.' Kelvin cast a shadow over Sonja. Emma could see that he was looking down at her mother's pistol, stuck in her jeans and visible now that her white T-shirt and hoodie had ridden up.

Emma flinched as Sonja rolled Denzel's body onto its side.

'What are you doing?' Kelvin asked. 'Ma'am, this is a crime scene, right?'

Sonja didn't look up. 'Looking for evidence.'

She pulled down the zip running down the back of Denzel's wetsuit and reached her hand in. Gore oozed from Denzel's head and Emma couldn't control herself any longer; she stepped away and threw up.

'Ma'am!'

Sonja ignored them both. While the boy was fussing over Emma, with his back turned to Sonja, she located Emma's stolen phone, which was sheathed in two condoms, next to the dead poacher's heart. She slipped it into her pocket.

When Emma forced herself to look back at the terrible scene, Sonja was zipping Denzel's suit up and rolling his body back to the position it had been in. Then she stood and wiped her hands down the front of her jeans.

'Come,' she said to Emma.

'Where?'

Sonja took her aside, out of earshot of Kelvin, who was crouched next to Denzel's body.

'Back to the cottage. We're going to pack and get out of here.'

'Mum, we can't –'

Sonja grabbed her upper arm, and just as her mother had done to her, Emma shrugged her off. Two could play at that game.

'Just do as you're bloody told for once in your life, Emma.'

Emma put her hands on her hips. Sonja was treating her like a child.

Sonja looked around. Emma realised she was scanning, something she often did, as if looking for hidden gunmen or a roadside bomb. Her eyes returned to Emma's, like a laser-guided weapon locking on. 'You don't want to be caught here.'

'Caught? We have to tell the police.'

Sonja nodded to Kelvin. 'He can do that, if he wants to. His family are criminals, Emma, you heard him admit as much. Come.'

'I'm not a dog, Mum!'

Sonja stabbed a thumb at the dead man. 'No, but he treated you like one. You don't want to get involved in this.'

Kelvin left his cousin's body and strode towards them. He had his fists balled at his sides.

Sonja squared up to him. 'What do you want?'

'You . . . he was shot. You've got a gun.'

'Mum?' Emma said.

Sonja took a pace towards Kelvin. 'If I'd wanted him dead, I wouldn't have wasted a bullet on him. I would have punctured his lungs and let him sink last night.'

Kelvin's eyes widened. 'I saw an injury on his leg. Did you cut him? Was that you?'

'Come on, Emma. *Please.*' Sonja started walking away in the direction they'd come.

'Mum!'

Sonja carried on, not looking back.

Emma wanted to scream. She turned to Kelvin.

'Go,' he said, then glanced down at his dead cousin again. 'Your mother's done enough damage already.'

Emma felt bad leaving Kelvin, especially when he sniffed and wiped a tear from his eye. Denzel had been a criminal and a thug, but she felt for Kelvin, having to see his cousin shot dead and mutilated. Her eyes were drawn to the horror again. Could her mother really have done this, like Kelvin was suggesting?

Emma turned and ran after her mother, half stumbling in the soft, white sand. 'Wait.' Sonja carried on, but Emma caught up with her and grabbed her shoulder.

Sonja stopped. 'We don't have time to hang around here.'

'Just tell me one thing.' Emma was breathing hard. She was angry and exhausted. 'Did you kill Denzel for what he did to me?'

Sonja looked back to where Kelvin was again kneeling by Denzel. Emma could see Kelvin had his phone out. She looked for Sonja's eyes, but her mother refused to meet her stare.

'No,' Sonja said, then kept on walking.

Emma paused a moment, fists clenched. She honestly didn't know whether to believe her mother or not.

*

Vincent Hendricks was picturing the journalist sitting across from him, Vanessa, naked, when his phone buzzed on silent. He took it out of the inside of his sports jacket pocket, glanced at the screen and saw that it was a policeman in his employ. He let the call go through to voicemail.

Vanessa looked out the window of La Petite Colombe, the elegant restaurant set on a vineyard in the winemaking town of Franschhoek.

The phone rang again, same number, and he switched it off completely.

'Do you need to get that?' she asked, nodding at his phone and catching him looking at her.

He shook his head. 'No, I'm sure it's nothing as important as you. Now, where were we?'

She smiled. 'You're sure?'

'Nothing that can't wait until after lunch.' Vincent beckoned to the waiter. 'Another bottle, please.'

'I'm working,' Vanessa said.

'So am I.'

Vanessa took her phone out of her handbag. 'You don't mind if I record?'

'Of course not, it's all on the record with me.' She selected the voice recording app, then took another sip of wine. 'You're one of Cape Town's biggest property developers, successful in business. Why the sudden interest in politics? Power?'

She was good, he thought, feeding him a premise, laden with an emotional word – *power*. Vanessa wanted him to repeat it in his answer. The waiter brought the wine and Vincent sat back, waiting for the man to fill both their glasses. Vincent thanked him.

'I'm at a point in life where I want to give something back to my community, to those in need, those who have not been as lucky as me.'

She narrowed her eyes. 'With respect, I don't think luck had much of a part in your success. You've said in other interviews that it's good old-fashioned hard work that got you to where you are.'

He spread his hands wide. 'True. People make their own good luck, don't you think?'

'Though your work wasn't always on the right side of the law, was it? There was the time in prison, in Pollsmoor, when you were younger.'

He put his hands together as if in prayer and slowly lowered his nose to his fingertips before he spoke. 'As I've said in the past, and have never tried to cover up, I was raised amid poverty and disadvantage – mind you, I am most definitely not using those as excuses for turning to a life of crime. I was young and foolish and I regret my actions. I paid my debt to society and came out of prison a better man, I like to think.'

She nodded as though she had heard it all before. She probably had, Vincent mused, as he'd said it enough times to the media these past few months since his candidature had been announced. The public relations firm he had hired had encouraged him to be honest, 'on the front foot' as they put it, about his past, and to make a virtue of it.

'I *know* about the overcrowding in our prisons, the gang culture, what turns young people to crime,' he said before Vanessa could ask another question, and ensuring he communicated his key messages. 'And that will help me give a voice to the disadvantaged and help a future government develop strategies not only to fight crime, but to prevent it.'

'You sound very passionate.'

'Thank you.'

'You were never affiliated with one of the gangs? The Americans or the Hard Livings? None of the numbers, the 26s, 27s or 28s?'

He shook his head resolutely as she reeled off the names. 'Just because I am a coloured South African male who grew up on the Cape Flats does not automatically mean I am a gang member, Vanessa.'

'Of course, I didn't mean that, and please do accept my apology. I certainly didn't mean to infer –'

He held up a hand and smiled. 'I'm joking, and not offended. However, I can see why you need to ask. For many people the only way to survive in prison is to be initiated into one of the gangs, to kill someone, in order to survive their incarceration.'

'Not you?'

He took a sip of wine. *If only she knew*, he thought. 'I like to think I was strong. I will not sit here and tell you I am a saint, Vanessa, because I'm not, but sometimes it is the weak who will resort to the worst violence, because they fear the bigger, scarier predators in this jungle we call life. It is the strong who stand up for themselves, fight off the bad people, even if they must suffer alone. That takes real courage.'

'I see.'

Did she? Could this woman, well educated, from a family rich enough to afford her tuition, perhaps a nice apartment in the city, understand what it had been like for him?

She carried on with the interview, asking about his plans for redeveloping part of Mitchells Plain, a grand development part-funded by government, partly by him, to build new housing which through its design would hopefully minimise crime and provide hope and protection for the residents.

Parroting his lines bored him, but they were a means to an end, whether that be making money, achieving political power or bedding a pretty woman. 'Tell me about you, Vanessa. I'm assuming someone so charming – I hope you're not offended by a compliment – has a prince waiting at home?'

She tittered, a little colour coming to her cheeks. 'Really, I'm the one who's supposed to be asking the questions.'

'I bet he's a Springbok.'

She laughed and took another big sip of wine. 'I wish. No, just a cat.'

'I find that very hard to believe.'

'And you?' she said, nodding to the phone on the table, reminding him why they were here. 'Please accept my condolences for the loss of your wife.'

His head dropped. 'Over a year and yet it still feels so raw.'

'I'm sorry, I didn't mean to upset you . . . Vincent.'

He left one hand on the table, and wiped his eye with the other, still looking down. He didn't look up when he felt her hand slide over his, the skin of her fingers soft and cool, the nails expensively manicured.

'Thank you.' At last he looked up, and in the same moment gently squeezed her hand. He left it there. 'You know, she was part of the reason I decided to run for parliament.'

Vanessa nodded, saying nothing, a compassionate look on her face.

'She always encouraged me to think of others, to do more, to ensure young people did not end up in prison, as I had.' He thumped the table with his free hand, loud enough for the diners nearest to them to look over, yet his face told the onlookers, many of whom would have recognised the high-profile candidate, that he was showing sorrow, not anger. A woman at the next table gave a sympathetic frown.

'Tiana was my rock.'

She squeezed his hand back, tighter. 'I'm so, so sorry.'

He forced a smile. 'Thank you. I thought I could hold it together.'

'I had a boyfriend,' Vanessa said.

He looked up, took the pocket square handkerchief from his sports coat and wiped his eyes, regaining his composure. He waited for her to go on.

'He was killed last year, as well, in a drink-driving crash.'

Vincent shook his head. 'I'm so sorry. It's all so senseless – yet at the same time preventable, and needless, like Tiana's death. *We* have to work together to make our country better, safer, Vanessa. People like you and me, we need to drop the history and the labels and prejudices and find solutions.'

'I couldn't agree with you more,' she said.

He held her gaze, both of them now half smiling, with sympathy, empathy for the other, and perhaps something more.

She was, he thought, ten years younger than he, and pretty. He knew his effect on women, always had done. Whether he was the toughest boy on the street – without gang support he'd had to be – or the well-dressed, wealthy businessman, it didn't matter; he knew women liked a mix of both.

Vincent nodded to her glass. 'More wine?'

She looked at her watch. 'I have to drive back to Cape Town and, well, as you can imagine, I never drive if I've had too much.'

He raised his eyebrows. 'Why?'

'Why what?'

'Why do you have to drive back this afternoon? Deadline?'

She leaned forward and pressed pause on her phone. 'No. This is for next month's magazine. I've got plenty of time to –'

'To research me? Dig up my sordid past?'

She laughed, and it was easy, not nervous. She twirled a finger around her hair. 'No. You've been open about that. Time to, I don't know, get to know you?'

'You mean this isn't just a one-off interview?'

'I know you're a busy man, but maybe I could come with you on the campaign trail, get a photographer to get some shots of you meeting people, perhaps around Mitchells Plain?'

He nodded, considering her words. 'I'm staying here, in Franschhoek; there's a political fundraising cocktail party I have to attend tonight.'

Vanessa picked up her glass, swirling the wine in it while she looked at him over the rim and smiled. 'Any "events" planned for the rest of the afternoon?'

'No, but I've got a coffee maker in my suite . . .'

'I don't drink coffee in the afternoon,' she said, finishing the rest of her wine in one go.

'Waiter?'

The young man hovering nearby came straight to Vincent.

'A bottle of your finest champagne, to go, please.'

*

Vincent made full use of the mirror in his hotel suite.

He knelt on the bed, behind Vanessa. He enjoyed watching her, them, and Vanessa didn't seem to mind. In fact, she looked to be enjoying watching herself as Vincent held her hips from behind.

Their eyes met in the mirror and he grinned. He wasn't smiling at them, though, but at a memory. He'd caught Tiana in this very same position. She was with Coetzee, one of his rivals, in a hotel at Sea Point when Vincent had used the key card sold to him by a domestic to silently walk in.

He'd stayed out of sight, behind the corner of the hotel room's built-in wardrobe, and carefully taken aim with the silenced .22 pistol, a tool quiet enough to stop anyone in an adjoining room or hallway hearing. Vincent had put a bullet in the back of Coetzee's head as he'd climaxed inside Tiana.

He'd been careful not to mark his wife as he and one of his men tied and gagged her and smuggled her out of the hotel via the staff elevator. If a post-mortem had revealed the high levels of opioids in her bloodstream he would have later tearfully confessed to the media that his beautiful wife was a drug addict and that he'd thought she was getting on top of her addiction.

Vanessa moaned.

The sound of it, whether in pleasure or pain, always did something for him, to him. His fingers gripped her harder, his pace increased.

Vincent remembered Tiana by the deserted roadside, watching her figure grow larger through the windscreen of the stolen BMW as he accelerated towards her, the thud and the bump as the car hit and then went over her.

He had stayed by Tiana's side until she died of her injuries. His man had taken the BMW a few kilometres away and torched it. It was, he thought as he stared into the mirror, the perfect crime.

*

Vanessa lay on her back, mouth half open, asleep. Vincent pulled on his boxer shorts, opened the French doors and walked out onto the balcony. He turned on his phone and it vibrated, several times, with maybe half a dozen messages.

Looking at the screen he saw that four were from the same policeman who'd called during lunch, a compulsive gambler, Vincent knew. He dialled the man's number rather than wasting time listening to voice messages.

'It's me,' was all he said when the call was answered.

'Sorry to say sir,' the detective said, 'but it's your son.'

Vincent had three of them, and two girls, but the detective would only be calling about one. 'Denzel.'

'Yes, sir.'

Vincent closed his eyes and pinched the bridge of his nose with his free hand. 'Just tell me.'

'I'm very, very sorry, sir, but he's dead.'

Vincent drew a deep breath. He had known it, as soon as the man had said 'your son'. 'How?'

'Gunshot wound, sir, to the head, close range. The detective who's investigating is thorough and smart, sir. She's saying that there was another wound, a cut to the leg, but she thinks that was done earlier. He'd been in the water, sir.'

'Poaching.'

'He was in a wetsuit, sir.'

Vincent ended the call and shook his head. Denzel had wanted for nothing in his privileged life, except risk and to prove himself to his father. This, Vincent thought, was why young men went to war. In its absence they found other ways to risk their lives and prove their courage. Because of the way *he* had spent his youth he was an expert at not showing his feelings but felt the fuse of rage sputtering inside him. He went back inside and closed the balcony door too loudly.

Vanessa opened her eyes and saw his face.

'Vincent? What's wrong?'

The mirror on the wall, in a hand-crafted ethnic African lace-work frame of wire and coloured glass, shattered under the blow of his fist.

CHAPTER 5

The vultures rose reluctantly from their feasting as Hudson Brand got out of the Land Cruiser game viewer and walked towards the elephant carcass. Giant wings audibly cleaved the air as the big birds fought for altitude.

Hudson worked the bolt of his .375 rifle, chambering a round. Where there were vultures there would be other scavengers.

He approached from upwind, to avoid the already-ripening smell of sun-baked flesh and to allow his own scent to deliberately reach any predators that might be feeding on the elephant; if there was a lion or leopard there, he didn't want to surprise it. His heart was heavy, thinking of the tragic loss of an impressive bull in his prime. The tusks were gone, hacked out of the head.

Hudson had no proof that the workers at the Chinese-owned mine, nor those who had been discovered drilling for new deposits inside Hwange National Park, were responsible for the recent upsurge in elephants being killed for their ivory, but he felt it was more than a coincidence. Getting proof would be the hard thing.

How a mining company had been given permission to explore within the boundaries of Zimbabwe's flagship game reserve was anyone's guess. When confronted by some people from a local non-government organisation that looked after the park's waterholes, the miners had claimed they had a permit signed by the president. The president's office was refuting that, but the drilling was still going on in the meantime.

Nantwich Lodge's resupply vehicle, bringing rations and a staff member back from leave, had spotted the vultures in surrounding trees that morning and Hudson had gone out to investigate. Kills were good for business, and this one was in reach of Nantwich. Guests loved seeing critters eating other critters.

Mostly.

He remembered one drive, a mad chase after he'd seen the telltale puffs of dust of a cheetah at full sprint, way off in the distance on the *vlei*. He'd been standing on the deck by the swimming pool and bar, on the hill that overlooked a dam on one side and the open grassy floodplain on the other. When he'd seen an impala taken down he ran to the middle of the three accommodation units and knocked on the door of the suite the two American women were sharing.

'Quick, there's just been a kill,' he'd said.

Roused from their midday siesta they'd rushed out and the three of them had driven down the hill to the *vlei* as fast as they could. When they arrived, however, they found that a pair of hyena, normally nocturnal, had been woken by the sounds of death. They were tearing the pregnant impala apart while the cheetah perched on a nearby termite mound, robbed of its feast.

'Take me back, please,' one of the women had said, her face in her hands as she sobbed.

The thrill of the hunt, the drama of life and death was something that people told themselves they wanted to see, but the reality was different from television. It was the same with war. He'd chased action as a young man in the US Army, but been scarred by the sights, sounds and smells of it.

Brand approached the elephant carcass, rifle raised and ready. Up close, the smell wasn't as bad as he'd imagined, more fresh blood and meat than decay. He caught sight of movement in his peripheral vision and saw a hyena bobbing its head up and down. The animal started to come towards him.

Brand fired a shot in the air, scaring the predator off. He knelt and touched a dark stain on the ground by the massive head. The blood was still sticky.

He circled the scene of the crime, looking at the ground. He picked up tracks and, like the blood, they were fresher than he had expected. Surprisingly, they led into the bush, towards the national park, rather than away from its border. Brand went back to his Land Cruiser, got in, and drove into a grove of trees so the vehicle was out of sight of the road. He took the keys and slung the carry strap of a water bottle in a canvas pouch over his shoulder then set off in the direction he'd seen the footprints heading.

The bushland where the elephant had been killed was a safari area, a government-administered hunting zone on the periphery of the national park. Shooting elephants was legal here, with a permit, but this had not been done by trophy hunters – Brand had already called the lodge which held the concession for hunting on this block and they said they had no clients at the moment. By rights he should have waited for the Zimbabwe Parks and Wildlife Authority rangers or local police to show up. He'd alerted both, on hearing the news of the dead elephant, but with their perennial shortages of fuel, manpower and money, there was no telling how long it would take them to arrive.

With a fresh lead he couldn't wait.

Brand felt a jolt of adrenaline as he set off. While he never hunted big game, he had made a living finding animals for tourists and tracking down people in his role as a private investigator.

Studying the dry, red-brown earth he made out the tracks of three men. Judging by the size of the elephant, two of them would each be carrying a tusk of some twenty or more kilograms. At least one would have a firearm, and one or both of the others would at least have an axe.

Commercial poaching – for a high-value commodity such as ivory – was usually rare in the remote northwest of the reserve, where Brand worked, so the recent increase – two elephants had been killed in as many months – was worrying. The hunters just outside the park kept a close eye on their properties, discouraging poachers, and rangers patrolled the area, which bordered Botswana. Brand couldn't shake the thought that the killing was related to the new drilling.

Brand stopped, knelt and picked up a cigarette butt. The tip was warm. These men were much closer than he had dared to hope, and either ill-disciplined or lazy, making no attempt to cover their tracks. He could feel himself gaining an advantage over them with every step, with every clue they casually revealed. However, he warned himself not to get cocky; these men would kill to protect themselves, knowing that just being seen with a firearm in the national park would be justification enough for a ranger to shoot them on sight.

Brand squinted up at the sun, then looked at the hands on his watch. The tracks were heading west. Once more, he thought it unusual that the men were going *into* the park, instead of north towards Victoria Falls or the town of Hwange, to the east.

While he didn't yet know if he was outgunned, he was certainly outnumbered.

A zebra snorted somewhere ahead of him and he heard the thump of hooves as the skittish animals ran off, even before he saw them. Had they seen him, he wondered, or had the men he was following spooked them?

Brand was still debating whether to do the right thing and return to his vehicle to wait for the cops, or to follow his natural instincts as a tracker and guide and pursue his quarry, when he heard voices.

He slowed, watching his front and, at the same time, monitoring every step he took. The snap of a dry twig could give him away. He moved from cover to cover, one large teak tree to the next. The chatter became louder and he smelled cigarette smoke on the breeze.

The three of them had stopped at the edge of an open area, a wide ring of dry earth pounded to dust by the relentless passing of elephants and other game visiting a nearly dry, muddy pool of water about a hundred metres away in the centre of the beaten circle. Brand crept to an old termite mound; the grey sandy structure made of insect excreta was as tall as him. Carefully, he peered around it, rifle up and at the ready. There were three men, two African and one who looked Chinese; the tusks of the dead elephant were at their feet. The Asian man was wearing a camouflage shirt and trousers, which looked to Brand like the uniform of China's People's Liberation Army. He was carrying a heavy-calibre hunting rifle, which he handed to one of the other men in exchange for an AK-47 assault rifle. The third man, who Brand thought might be a tracker, was unarmed. He was pretty sure he knew who the man in camo was.

Brand worked through some quick scenarios. He had the drop on them, but if he stepped out of cover and one of them opened up on him, he might very likely come off second best. He had never been in the business of shooting first and asking questions later. The assault rifle could fire on automatic, but Brand could only fire one round before he had to re-chamber. Better, he decided, to keep shadowing them and find out where they were headed or based.

A herd of elephants filtered silently out of the bush on the far side of the pan, as waterholes were known in Hwange. Immediately, the matriarch in the lead raised her trunk and sniffed the air. Others in her herd of fifteen or more also began to sniff. Their leader must have picked up the men's scent, perhaps even that of the bloody tusks. She shook her head and from across the open ground came a low rumbling sound emanating from her belly. Her family heard the warning and she moved them on, big legs marching quickly, almost at a trot, as she led them around the far side of the pan, away from the danger and off in the direction Brand had come from.

The three men watched the elephants, then sought the shade of a large tree. Brand sweated in the sun, ignoring the tiny mopane flies that tried to invade his nose and ears.

With time to survey the land, Brand could see that the spot where the men were waiting had probably not been chosen randomly. He could make out the indentation in the ground of an old road running across his front, skirting the edge of the cleared area around the pan. Hwange had plenty of these rough roads – old fire trails used by rangers in past decades or new trails blazed through the bush in times of heavy rain when main roads became blocked or impassable because of bogged vehicles. Looking closer he could see where young trees had been driven over; some had not sprung fully upright.

He was considering changing positions himself when he heard a vehicle's engine, confirming his suspicions.

The vehicle which came into sight around a stand of trees was a Land Cruiser *bakkie*, a pickup rigged with a bench seat across the load area in the back, and a bar across the cab fitted with two spotlights. It was a hunting vehicle, and Brand knew it had no place inside the borders of the national park. The man driving it looked middle-aged, baseball cap and red sunburned cheeks above a bushy grey and black beard. He looked familiar, but Brand couldn't place him at this distance.

The man pulled up next to the trio and touched a hand to the peak of his cap. He went to the rear of the *bakkie* and opened the tailgate. The two African men loaded the tusks into the rear while the driver conversed with the Chinese man in uniform in a low voice.

Brand stayed in cover, though he wished he was closer so he could hear what was going on. The men's conversation was interrupted by a burst of static and a voice coming through a radio speaker in the *bakkie*. It was loud enough for Brand to catch the most important part of the message.

'*Check behind that anthill. Armed man!*'

At almost the same instant Brand heard a buzzing noise. He looked up and saw a drone, descending from altitude and heading down towards him.

The hunter, for that's what he looked like, ran to his vehicle; the Chinese man cocked his AK-47.

'For crying in a bucket,' Brand said to himself. He raised the barrel of his rifle skyward, pulled the butt into his shoulder and fired. The heavy-calibre slug wreaked a satisfying amount of damage on the flying snooper; Brand was aware of pieces of drone shearing off and falling to the ground and the whole thing tilting crazily on its side and starting to spin as he got up and started running.

There was shouting behind him and a burst of fire from the AK, the distinctive popping sound of three rounds coming his way.

Taking out the drone had robbed the enemy, whoever they were, of their eye in the sky, and brought him a moment's diversion, but now he was running for his life. They'd decided to fight rather than get away. He heard the growl of the Cruiser behind him; the driver had started her up and was ploughing off-road, after him.

Brand re-chambered on the move. He was leading them on a tangent, north, away from where he had left his vehicle and deeper into the thick vegetation. Although the Land Cruiser was making hard work of it, judging by the sound of high revolutions and pauses to change gears, he knew they would probably catch him if he kept going in a straight line.

He turned and ran back towards them.

As he suspected, there were looks of surprise from the driver and the three others as Brand burst from the cover of the trees no more than ten metres in front of them. Brand stopped and put a round through the *bakkie*'s radiator. A jet of steam shot up, partially obscuring him, but Brand was sprinting past the Cruiser before either of the armed men in the back could draw a bead on him. The Chinese man with the AK fired anyway, chasing him with a wild burst of fire as he sprinted for his life.

The ruse might have bought him a minute or two. Brand disappeared into the bush again then broke left, judging and hoping he was heading towards his own vehicle. That was his only chance now, although again he reloaded as he ran, then focused on speed.

He was not a young man, though he kept himself as fit as a man in his fifties who lived in lion country could. Running was dangerous, but he tried to get some exercise in when he visited Victoria Falls for supplies for the lodge. All the same, he was breathing heavily as thornbushes whipped and scored his bare arms and legs.

At least there was no sound of the vehicle behind him. Brand was sure the driver would not risk blowing the engine by driving without water. That didn't mean they weren't following him on foot. Brand had to figure the driver was armed, so that made three rifles to his one.

Brand heard trumpeting off to his right and glanced in that direction. Never in his life had he been so glad to see a charging elephant. The matriarch had her head down, big ears pinned back and her trunk curled between her tusks. She was running in from his right flank, trying to intercept him, and she had killing on her mind.

He raised his rifle again, pointed it towards her and fired a round into the ground. The bullet sent up a puff of dust about ten metres in front of her. The old cow knew humans, and weapons, and she slowed to a halt. Brand ran on, then, judging that he was far enough from her, turned and fired again, a shot over her back.

The elephant panicked and turned and ran off, away from him, but towards Brand's pursuers. Her herd chased after her.

'Good luck, old girl,' he said as he carried on.

He still needed more than his own share of luck, but he was banking on the elephants either scaring the hell out of the men chasing him, or at least delaying them.

Brand charged on, lungs burning, legs suffering. Not even adrenaline could overcome fatigue, sore knees, and the strength-sapping heat of the African bush. He imagined the man with the AK drawing a bead on him as he pushed on.

His own game viewer came into sight, more welcome than any desert oasis to a lost man. Behind him he heard the screech of the elephant matriarch. She sounded properly furious and he hoped she was stomping someone right now as he burst from the bush onto the main graded road. He was clear of the national park and seconds away from freedom.

Brand hit the bodywork of the Cruiser like a charging rhino. He tossed his rifle on the front passenger seat, jumped in behind the wheel and was fumbling for the keys in his pocket when he felt the cold steel of a pistol barrel against his right temple.

'Out of the vehicle, now!'

He raised his hands instinctively, and when he tried to turn his head the man rammed the pistol in harder.

As Brand eased himself out of the driver's seat he could see, looking down, the leather boot and gaiter of a Zimbabwean police officer.

'On the ground.'

'Wait, man –'

'Shut up, you are under arrest.'

'No, listen.'

He felt the blow on the back of his head, and his eyes start to roll backwards as he pitched face first into the dirt.

'Stop . . . there are poachers . . .'

A boot went into his ribs. 'I said shut up. *You* are the poacher.'

'No –'

'You have the right to remain silent.' The man was on one knee next to him, wrenching his arms behind him. Hudson felt the metal snap of handcuffs on one wrist, and then the other. 'You are under arrest.'

'I'm innocent, you –'

The officer, who was as well spoken as he was brutal, slapped Brand in the back of the head. '*You* should know, Mr Hudson Brand,' the officer dragged him painfully to his feet, 'that we could have shot you on sight, seeing you decamping from the national park with a rifle. You were clearly guilty of an infraction of the law.'

'I'm a professional guide and this is a registered, licensed firearm.'

'Yes, which you used to kill an elephant.'

Brand took a deep breath, doing his best to project calm and reason, even though he'd just been assaulted. 'One of my workers saw a dead elephant on his way to Nantwich, where I work, and I came to investigate. I trailed the real poachers. They're armed and following me. They'll be here any minute.'

The policeman, young but stern-faced, shook his head. 'You can tell the magistrate. We received a call saying that you were caught in the act of removing the tusks and you then fled. A professional hunter from Victoria Falls says he and some other men with him chased you into the bush and that you opened fire on them, shooting down their drone and disabling their vehicle.'

Brand nodded and smiled. 'Yep, see what they've done. They just called you – let me guess – ten minutes ago.'

'Yes,' said the policeman, 'they called me a few minutes ago to tell me about the drone, but they also called the station more than two hours ago.'

'What?' That didn't make sense.

'And then I saw on the station log that *you* also called, not more than one hour ago.'

'Yes . . .'

'Yes, Mr Hudson Brand, you are the one who is guilty here, the one who is obfuscating. You are the miscreant in this case, trying to deflect attention onto the man who called in the elephant's demise in the first place.'

'Holy shit,' Brand said.

'You have the right to remain silent . . .'

Brand tuned out as the officer led him to a white Zimbabwe Republic Police Land Rover Defender. As soon as the policeman had said that it was a professional hunter who'd made the allegation against him, the pieces fell into place. Brand pictured the man he'd seen in the distance. He was now sure he knew who he was.

'The guy who called you was Allan Platt, right?'

The eloquent officer squeezed in next to him in the back

seat of the vehicle and delivered a short, sharp punch up under Brand's ribs. 'I am not at liberty to discuss the names or details of witnesses or complainants, Mr Brand, as I'm sure you would appreciate, being an amateur sleuth yourself.'

Brand was going to protest some more, but he figured he would do better in the cells with all his ribs intact, although he suspected one might already have been cracked from the kicking he'd received on the ground.

They drove past the carcass of the elephant and Brand could see four people there, a mix of uniformed and plain clothes police. The driver accelerated, so the Land Rover's tyres could skip across the countless mini crests of the badly corrugated road. Brand was aching from his injuries and his run through the bush, and he sagged in his seat as the adrenaline wore off. He'd been beaten and arrested before – these weren't his main concerns – but someone had gone to a lot of trouble to set him up today. He wondered if the plan had been to kill him and plant the ivory on him, in the bush. The presence of the drone spoke of money and technology, things a mining company would have at their disposal.

He had guessed they were heading for the town of Hwange. It had always been a coalmining town, the headquarters of the Wankie Colliery Company, but in recent decades the under-ground mine had been supplemented with an open-cut operation.

They drove through the mine site. Brand had never been able to fathom why the mine's engineers had decided their workings should straddle one of the main access roads into the country's biggest and best-known national park. There had been no attempt to hide the mine out of sight or minimise its impact on tourism.

The police driver didn't slow as a troop of vervet monkeys raced to cross the jet-black surface of the road and avoid being hit by the Land Rover. Brand shook his head as he noticed their coats, normally pale grey and white, stained the same colour as the hellish landscape.

Brand had taken a lead role in the fight against drilling in the park and his name had been plastered all over social media. He'd even been interviewed by international programs, including CNN and BBC World, and it was these, he suspected, that had drawn the ire of the Chinese mining company. Was that why he was set up? he wondered.

The Land Rover's air conditioning was broken, so the occupants opened the windows. Sandwiched between two officers, Brand found the hot air blowing in did little to cool him. He was sweating and dirty from being on the ground. It was almost a relief to get to Hwange town. The tar road was potholed and too many of the people who idly stared at the police vehicle were probably unemployed. They waited at a railway crossing for a coal train to pass, a rare sign of economic activity.

Arriving at the station, Brand was at least able to stretch his legs. He was shoved and cajoled inside, where his cuffs were unlocked and he was fingerprinted, processed, then led to a cell.

'How about my phone call?' he said to the verbose officer who had overseen his booking-in.

'Regrettably the lines of communication are down.' He smiled and locked the door.

Brand lay down on the concrete slab that passed for a bed, ignored the graffiti-scratched walls and the lingering, foul smell of the cell, and closed his eyes.

CHAPTER 6

Brand woke an hour later to the sound of a key scraping the inside of the metal lock. He blinked and sat up. A woman thanked the uniformed officer who had opened the door and stepped inside.

'Please excuse us, Sergeant,' she said.

Hudson recognised her immediately. She was pretty, early thirties by now, he thought, braided hairdo, well dressed in jeans, boots, a snowy white T-shirt and blue fitted blazer. She carried a cardboard folder under her arm.

'Sergeant Goodness Khumalo,' he said.

She gave him a small smile. 'Acting Inspector now.'

'Congratulations on the promotion. You've come up in the world.'

She looked around the cell. 'Sometimes I wonder. I'm surprised to see you here,' she lowered her voice, 'Hudson.'

'Can you get me out of here, Goodness?'

'Acting Inspector, Mr Brand. We need to keep this formal, given the circumstances.'

He leaned back against the cell wall. 'I gave you a pretty good break on your first big case.'

She looked over her shoulder, through the open door. 'We can keep that between ourselves as well. I wouldn't have picked you as a poacher, I must say. Is the tourism business still that bad?'

'Come on, Good– Inspector, you know this is a crock. I've been framed.'

'This is not an American gangster movie, Mr Brand. I don't have time for conspiracy theories.'

He held up one hand. 'OK, you know about the drilling inside the national park.'

She nodded. 'I read the newspapers, yes, and your opposition to the granting of further coal leases is well known, but this is not police business unless someone breaks the law and from what I have seen that has not happened yet.'

'Apart from me being set up, oh, and beaten up by Sergeant Webster's Dictionary out there.'

'Come with me.'

Brand got up, again grateful to stretch his legs, and Goodness led him out into the corridor, away from the cells and through to the main part of the station. It had a 1960s feel to it, with the lingering smells of nicotine and sweat, peeling paint, faded wood panelling and grimy linoleum floors.

Goodness was too smart for this rural backwater, but he guessed it was a step on the promotion ladder for her. It was true that he had helped her, though when they'd first met he'd been suspected of murder – two killings, in fact, in South Africa and Zimbabwe, and he'd been on a missing person hunt, the fallout of a life insurance scam.

She ushered him into a small office, lined with battered filing cabinets topped with piles of manila folders. The former British colony's paperwork fetish was clearly still going strong. Goodness placed her own folder down in front of him. His name was on the front, and the contents looked bulky already. They sat either side of an old government-issue metal-topped desk.

'I'd offer you coffee, but . . .' she began.

'Let me guess, *hapana* ZESA?' he said. She nodded. No electricity, due to the Zimbabwe Electricity Supply Authority's generation and distribution failures, was part of life in the country. It was why Brand had convinced the owners of Nantwich to cough up for solar power back-up.

She sat across from him, silent.

'You know I didn't kill the elephant.'

She opened the folder in front of her and took a plastic zip-lock bag from it. She held up the brass bullet casing for him to see. 'My crime scene people found this by the carcass; it's .375 calibre, the same as the rifle the officers took from you.'

'It's probably from my weapon.'

She raised her perfectly sculpted eyebrows. 'Really?'

'I fired a warning shot when I got to the carcass to scare off some nosey hyenas. When you find the slug that killed the elephant, you'll see it's not a match.'

'There is no bullet in the carcass.'

'What do you mean?' he asked.

'The crime scene technicians used a handheld metal detector but found nothing. They located the bullet entry hole, a clean single-shot kill into the heart, but the skin had been cut and the bullet retrieved.'

Brand processed the information. 'That proves it wasn't me.'

'How so?'

'Do you think I'd be dumb enough to go to all the trouble of digging out a bullet, but still leave the empty casing at the scene of the crime?'

She pursed her lips, saying nothing for a moment, then said, 'Just supposing you're right and someone set you up, who would go to such lengths, and why?'

Brand didn't have to think too hard. 'Allan Platt. He was driving a hunting *bakkie* that picked up the guys who killed the elephant – he came after me.'

'What's Platt got against you?'

'You remember Cecil the Lion?' Brand said.

'How could I forget – the hunters who lured the famous big male lion out of the national park so that an American dentist could shoot him with a bow and arrow. I was a junior detective then, working at Hwange. I was part of the investigation.'

Brand nodded. 'Platt was doing the same thing, up near Nantwich, where I'm based now. All the other hunters in the Matetsi Safari Area are honest and ethical, but ask any of them and they'll tell you Platt's a cowboy; he gives them a bad name. I caught him and his boss and took a video.'

'I think I remember seeing that one on social media as well,' Goodness said.

Brand smiled. 'Platt knew I'd filmed him and he came after me, threatening to get even. The video went viral and cost him and his outfit hundreds of thousands of dollars, according to Platt.'

'Setting you up on a poaching charge would be a good way for him to get even; and if it doesn't stick he'll probably go to the media, and online, with the news.'

'Yup.' Brand winced. 'Be surprised if he hasn't already.'

'I think the elephant was killed by Carrington Wu, the Chinese businessman who's into mining and tourism around here and the Falls. I saw an Asian guy wearing camouflage – Wu used to be a general and I heard he still likes to dress up. My guess is that Platt was his professional hunter, and they made an illegal hunt inside Hwange National Park, not in the safari lands on the border of the reserve.'

'I see,' Goodness said.

'You gonna bail me, at least?'

Goodness's phone beeped and she took it from the pocket of her blazer. She read a text message and sighed. 'I think you'd better organise a lawyer from Victoria Falls.'

'How come? This charge is bullshit, pardon me, and you know it.'

She looked up from the screen of her phone. 'The tusks from the elephant that was shot have just been found at Nantwich Lodge, in the back of your private vehicle, an old Land Rover.'

Brand rolled his eyes.

*

Sonja had called Nantwich Lodge on WhatsApp from Cape Town airport, where she had been able to book two business class tickets on the spot, on the Kenya Airways direct flight to Victoria Falls, in Zimbabwe.

Hudson had been away from the lodge on business, but Brighton Ncube, the assistant manager, had said he would meet their flight and drive them to the lodge. By then, he was sure, Hudson would be back.

Emma had been quiet, in a surly way, which in turn ruffled Sonja. After leaving Kelvin with his cousin's body, they had hurried back to their holiday cottage and packed quickly, with Sonja's orders, tone and stare telling her daughter not to talk back or argue. Sonja had raced to the airport in their hire car. She wanted to be out of the country before the police dragged them both into the investigation of the killing of Denzel Hendricks.

Her holiday with Emma had gone tits-up, as her sometimes foul-mouthed and very British daughter would have said. The stupid boys – the bad one and the good one – had intruded and ruined the short-lived bubble of friendship and relaxation they had enjoyed for a few days in the Cape.

Hudson, Sonja knew, would be all over Emma as soon as they were reunited, hugging her, laughing with her at private jokes, asking her all about Cape Town's bars and restaurants and the beach. She sometimes – often – thought that the two of them got on with each other better than she did with either of them.

Brighton was waiting in the arrivals area of the terminal when Sonja and Emma completed the laborious process of buying Zimbabwean tourist visas and having their luggage checked for commercial goods. They emerged through sliding doors and walked past a rampant, but stuffed, lion.

Emma pointed to a mobile phone kiosk. Sonja had given Emma her mobile phone back at Cape Town airport; explaining the reason why she had searched Denzel's body on the beach. 'I'm going to get a local SIM card.'

'Fine.' Sonja turned towards the man in khaki who was walking towards her, smiling. 'Hello, Brighton, how are you?' she said as a group of Ndebele men, chests and limbs bare in their traditional dress, broke into song and dance as soon as she passed them.

'I am fine. Let me get a trolley for your bags,' Brighton said.

The performers continued their routine and when Emma had completed her purchase she stopped to take pictures and video of them with her phone, which resulted in an increase in volume.

Sonja wanted to tell Emma to hurry up – she still felt a sense of urgency as though she were being pursued – but she knew that doing so would rob the young men of some much-needed tourist dollars, and probably provoke the angry reaction that had been building up inside her daughter. Sonja would rather take on a machine gun than face Emma's ire.

Sonja reached into her cargo pants pocket and took out twenty dollars, which she crumpled into a bowl in front of the men. While Zimbabwe had its own currency, US dollars were accepted and prized in the tourist town of Victoria Falls.

'Thank you, God bless,' one of the men said.

Brighton loaded their luggage onto a trolley then led on, with Emma making a point of lingering a little longer and taking a selfie with the song and dance troupe.

'Is Hudson in camp yet?' Sonja asked.

Brighton took her Bergen rucksack and dive bag and lifted them into the Mercedes Sprinter transit van. 'He was still out when I left. He'd gone to check on a report of an elephant which had been killed, apparently by poachers.'

'Typical.' She climbed in after the luggage. 'He can't keep his nose out of trouble for five minutes.'

'Look who's talking.' Emma moved down the narrow aisle between the bus's seats to the rearmost row, as far away from Sonja as she could manage, and then sat looking pointedly out the window.

Sonja felt the stirring of anger. Brighton closed his door, started the engine and drove out of the car park. 'Please can you turn the air con up, Brighton?' she asked.

'It's cold enough in here already,' Emma called from the back.

Brighton glanced up in his rear-view mirror. 'There are separate controls for each zone of the vehicle.'

'Thank you,' Sonja said, opening the vents nearest her to full.

'You're just having one of your hot –'

Sonja snapped her head around to glare at Emma, who knew better than to complete her sentence. Satisfied Emma had shut her cakehole, as the British would say, Sonja calmed herself and asked Brighton about the weather.

'It *is* very hot here in Zimbabwe,' he said, placatingly.

'How has the game viewing been?' Sonja asked.

'Oh, marvellous. We are seeing lions often, and we hear them every night. The elephants are becoming more relaxed all the time and drinking at the dam now the water elsewhere in the park is drying up. Of course, we get our roan and sable antelope nearly every day.'

She took a breath, held it a few seconds, then slowly exhaled. Deep breathing helped; so did being in the bush.

'You are from South Africa originally?' Brighton asked.

Her accent was a mishmash, so people often assumed she was an expat South African. 'I was born in Namibia.'

'Ah, so you speak German?'

'Yes, my father was Namibian-German, but my mother was English. When I was young, we moved to Botswana and I grew up in the Okavango Delta.'

'Ah, yes, a wildlife paradise.'

'Exactly.' She left out the part about her father being unable to stay in the country of his birth because of his hatred for the new rulers, the South West Africa People's Organization, whom he had fought when Namibia was still known as South West Africa. He had waged a total, bloody war against his enemies.

Brighton pointed to the left and Sonja saw a small herd of kudu, beautiful grey antelope with chalky stripes, bound away into the bush. This country, Zimbabwe, had endured a long war as well. It seemed to Sonja there would always be conflict somewhere in Africa. Even on her botched holiday, she'd had Andrew Miles asking her to join him and Steve Oosthuizen in their latest mini war in Mozambique.

Sonja looked over her shoulder. Emma had her wireless earpods in and was listening to music. This time, the anger ebbed and she felt her daughter drifting away from her again. She was a crap mother. Sonja had not been around for Emma's formative years, spending her time chasing money and adrenaline working as a military contractor and bodyguard in the world's worst places. And now, on top of all that baggage, Emma thought Sonja was a murdering vigilante.

An hour and a half after leaving the airport they entered Hwange National Park via a thatch-roofed gate at the crest of a hill. Beyond them, the view of the game reserve stretched away forever. Sonja had some good memories of this place. Hudson had more or less taken on the role of lodge manager fulltime and she had found that far from hurting their relationship she had settled into the routine of seeing him for a week at a time, with a month's break in between. Sonja divided her time between her home in Los Angeles and, more often as her feelings for Hudson had grown, a house in the Hippo Rock Private Nature Reserve on the border of the Kruger National Park in South Africa. Hudson had been a live-in caretaker for some overseas owners in a house in the wildlife estate, where locals and foreigners lived in the bush among the wildlife, and Sonja had decided to make her African base there.

Nantwich Lodge was just a kilometre inside the gate and Brighton took them along a narrow dirt road through thick bush which opened onto a broad, open grassy floodplain with a dam. A family of warthogs, a mother with two of her young from the previous year's litter, lifted their heads and stared at them as the van pulled up.

Emma had removed her earphones, and once out of the bus

she strode onto the lawn in front of the long, thatched dining and lounge building, one hand shielding her eyes as she watched the warthogs trot away. She loved it here, and Sonja was pleased that she had been able to bring Emma to Africa often enough for her daughter to fall in love with Sonja's ancestral home continent. For all of its fucked-up politics and conflict there was nowhere else Sonja could truly call home. It didn't matter to Sonja if she was in South Africa, Namibia or Zimbabwe – she was African.

Brighton had gone into the building, which Sonja knew had once been the executive safari retreat of the local coalmining company, before being renovated as part of the new lodge development. He came out a minute later, wringing his hands in front of him. 'Hudson is not here.'

'What's wrong?'

'It seems the police were here earlier.'

'And?'

'They found two elephant tusks in Hudson's Land Rover. He's in prison.'

*

Sonja borrowed the lodge's runabout vehicle, a short-wheelbase Land Cruiser which had been converted into a panel van. She and Emma drove through the national park, stopping at Robins Camp, about ten kilometres down the road from Nantwich, to pay the entry fees.

With no time for sightseeing they drove past a grazing herd of cape buffalo, perhaps a thousand or more animals that dotted a golden grassy plain all the way to the horizon. The sky was a smoky blue, discoloured by a layer of dust which hung over the veldt at this time of year.

They bypassed popular dams and picnic sites – Deteema and Mandavu – on their mission to get out of the park before dark. They were both tired from their non-stop transit from Cape Town, but Emma made no complaint.

'I hope he's all right,' Emma said as they exited the park.

'He's been locked up before. He's tough.' Sonja was pleased that at least Hudson's predicament gave her and Emma something to talk about. She scanned the bush and the road as she drove. Sonja told herself she was keeping an eye out for wildlife, particularly as she was able to drive faster outside of the game reserve, but she also knew full well that she had just caught herself checking the road for disturbances which might indicate a buried IED. Unlike in Iraq or Afghanistan, where she had worked, there was no threat of an improvised explosive device here in Zimbabwe, but in times of stress she sometimes felt her present switching back to her past. She gripped the steering wheel harder.

Emma glanced across at her. 'Breathe, Mum.'

Sonja ground her teeth. She knew Emma was just worried for her, but she was also hypersensitive to anything she perceived as criticism. 'I'm fine.'

'Well, I wouldn't be fine, after what we've both been through.'

Did danger follow her, Sonja wondered, or did she chase it? She could have turned the other cheek after letting the police know about Denzel's assault on Emma, but instead she had gone after him, into the water, and taken the meting out of justice into her own hands. She was wild, feral, above the law.

Between Sinamatella Camp, where they exited the park, and the town of Hwange, they drove through an open-cut coalmine.

'This is what Hudson is fighting against,' Emma said. 'Now I understand why he's so passionate about it. At least he's fighting for a noble cause; these mines are an environmental disaster and an eyesore.'

Sonja felt the implied criticism of her work, serving as a contractor in conflicts that Emma had pointed out to her on more than one occasion were, in her eyes, unjust. What Emma tended to forget was that she had benefitted from the time Sonja had spent in those war zones with a first-rate, expensive education.

Emma used her phone to discover the location of the police station, which was on the main road from Victoria Falls to Bulawayo. When they reached it, they saw in the car park a

Land Cruiser game viewer with the Nantwich Lodge logo on the side – Hudson's work vehicle.

Sonja pulled into the compound and they both went inside. A bored-looking constable sat at a desk texting on her phone.

'Good afternoon, how are you?' Sonja said.

The woman looked up at her through hooded eyes.

'I'm looking for a man who was brought here and charged today, Mr Hudson Brand.'

The officer looked like it was too much of an effort to speak when another, dressed in smart casual clothes, came through a door behind her. 'Hello. Hudson Brand, you say?'

'Yes.'

'May I ask who you are?' the woman asked.

'My name is Kurtz. I'm his –'

'She's his partner, common law wife,' Emma piped up.

The woman looked at her. 'My name is Inspector Goodness Khumalo. I'm the member in charge here.'

Sonja nodded. 'I've heard of you. Hudson knows you, right, from past cases?'

'Yes,' Goodness said. 'We are acquainted.'

'Then you know this is bullshit, right?'

'Mum . . .' Emma broke in.

'No, it's fine,' Goodness said. 'I understand you're emotional.'

Sonja sneered. 'I. Am. Not. Emotional.'

'Mr Brand went before a magistrate a short while ago,' Goodness said. 'Bail was set at two thousand US dollars.'

'I'll pay it,' Sonja said.

Goodness raised her eyebrows. 'You have cash?'

'Yes.'

The police officer looked at her watch. 'It will take some time to process his release.'

'I need to see him, now,' Sonja said.

'Miss Kurtz . . .'

'You *know* him, and you know he wouldn't do this. Something is going on here.'

Goodness paused, then nodded. 'Constable Moyo?'

The uniformed officer looked up from her phone. 'Ma'am?'

'Start on the paperwork for Brand, H. I'll be back with him soon.'

The constable sighed. 'Yes, ma'am.'

'Come with me,' Goodness said to Sonja.

'You wait here,' Sonja said to Emma.

Emma saluted. 'Yes, *ma'am*!'

Sonja followed Goodness down a grimy corridor through a series of turns until they reached a row of cells with iron doors.

'I'll leave you alone for a few minutes while the paperwork is processed. A constable will come for you when it's ready and he can collect his things.' Goodness unlocked the door, opened it and stepped aside.

Brand stood up, came to Sonja and hugged her.

She felt uncomfortable with his public displays of affection at the best of times, but then again, he was part American.

'You stink,' she said.

He held her at arm's length. 'You're beautiful.'

She blushed. 'Enough. What the fuck is going on here, Brand?'

'Your guess is as good as mine.' He nodded to the concrete bed. 'Care to sit down while we wait?'

'I value my health too much. Besides, I've been sitting and travelling all day.'

Brand lowered himself slowly down.

'You're hurt?'

He touched his ribs. 'An overzealous police officer gave me a kicking. They don't take kindly to poachers in Zimbabwe. As he pointed out, technically, I could have been shot on sight. They brought me here in a police vehicle and one of the officers drove my game viewer.'

'But you're not a poacher.'

'No, but I was inside Hwange National Park and carrying a gun. I was stupid.' Brand told her how he had found the dead elephant, followed the tracks and discovered the men.

'Yes, stupid, and gung-ho. Typical American.'

'Thanks.'

She sighed. 'A Chinese guy, you say? Tied up with the mining exploration you've been going on about on Facebook lately, I suppose?'

'Since when did you start looking at social media?'

'I haven't. Emma keeps me updated.'

He shifted and winced. Sonja relented and sat down beside him. He put his hand on her thigh and she looked at it.

'Why are you here, anyway? Didn't you have another week planned on the beach?' he asked, breaking the momentary silence.

She looked up and waved a hand in the air. 'A little trouble down south. I thought it was best we cut the seaside holiday short.'

'Something to do with the guy you punched in the temple on the beach?'

'Yes. He found Emma later, when she was out for a run, and stole her phone. He assaulted her.'

He sat up straight, pain forgotten. 'What? Is she . . .?'

'Emma's fine, Brand. A little bruised.'

'The guy?'

'Dead.'

He stared at her a long minute, his jaw shifting side to side, like he was mulling over a question he wasn't brave enough to ask. Sonja said nothing. Let him think what he wanted, she thought. Emma certainly did.

'Abalone, you say,' he said at last.

She nodded. 'What of it?'

'I've been digging into the drilling company that's exploring for coal inside the park. It's called Giraffe Holdings Private Limited, but that's just a front. It's Chinese owned and backed. They've got a mine outside the park, and have apparently been given a special permit to drill inside Hwange, but that's going to be challenged in the courts by a coalition of lodges and environmental groups.

Anyhow, Giraffe Holdings is also in the export business, and not just coal.'

'Abalone? Shellfish?'

'Yep.'

Sonja shook her head. It didn't make sense. 'But Zimbabwe's a landlocked country. How can that be possible?'

Brand took his hand off her leg and slumped back against the wall. He'd been through the wringer, clearly. 'It's illegal for anyone in South Africa other than the companies with state-granted leases to export abalone. However, huge quantities of the stuff is shipped out of South Africa by road to Mozambique, concealed or labelled as something else, then shipped to Asia by sea, or trucked via Botswana to Zimbabwe, where it's flown out direct to markets in Hong Kong and mainland China.'

Sonja processed the information. 'So, it's illegal to export this stuff from South Africa, but legal to send it out of Zimbabwe?'

Brand nodded. 'By the ton – all of it dried in underground factories in Cape Town, Port Elizabeth and other coastal towns before it's smuggled out by road.'

'That's a hell of a big loophole.'

'Y'all got that right. It's big bucks, millions of dollars' worth.'

'And the Chinese pay for it with drugs or the raw chemicals to make Tik,' Sonja said.

'Sounds like you've been doing your research as well.'

'What do you think?'

'About the drugs? Anything's possible. The guy who owns Giraffe Holdings is a businessman from Shanghai called Carrington Wu. Personal net worth of a billion US dollars. He uses his anglicised name these days, but he's also a former general in the People's Liberation Army. There's a lot of info about him online. Plus he's a big game hunter.'

'Elephant hunter?'

Brand nodded. 'Could be. I saw a Chinese guy in camo fatigues – PLA uniform – with the group I tracked from the elephant carcass. I've never met Wu in person, but I'm 99 per cent sure it was him.'

'That's risky for a billionaire, to be out shooting elephants to frame some two-bit private investigator.'

Brand smiled and winced. 'Maybe he likes risky.'

'He wasn't alone?'

Brand shook his head. 'A part-time professional hunter named Allan Platt was with him. He's one bad hombre, plays dirty, does *not* like yours truly. He's in bed with Wu somehow, maybe just as his professional hunter, but he also holds a grudge with me for spilling the beans about his unethical lion hunting.'

'*Ja*,' Sonja said. 'My daughter read all about that episode on Facebook. She said your video got something like a quarter of a million likes, whatever that means, and went sick.'

'Viral, I think the word is.'

Sonja shrugged. 'Whatever. Where does Platt live?'

'In Vic Falls,' Brand said.

Inspector Goodness Khumalo came back to the door. 'Your release is delayed, Hudson.'

They both looked to her.

'How come?'

'We can't contact the magistrate,' Goodness said.

'No phone signal?' Hudson asked.

She shook her head, then lowered her voice. 'He's playing golf.'

'With the president?' Sonja asked. 'This isn't good enough. I'll go find him.'

'No, his clerk says he's with a local businessman,' Goodness frowned. 'Carrington Wu.'

'Sheesh,' Hudson said.

Goodness continued: 'She says the magistrate never takes his cell phone to the golf course, but she can get him to sign the bail forms in a couple of hours.'

Brand looked at Sonja. 'Do *not* even think about going to the golf course.'

CHAPTER 7

Sonja arrived in Victoria Falls after dark. She had agreed to not go looking for the magistrate, but she was not prepared to sit back and let what passed for justice in Zimbabwe hopefully acquit Hudson. He had been framed and she was going to make this fit-up go away.

It was never wise to travel regional roads in Africa once the sun had gone down, as Sonja was reminded when she had to slow down for a herd of buffalo crossing the main road into town.

She passed the large Zambezi Lager billboard welcoming her to the tourist town, carried on past the Cresta Sprayview Hotel and turned left off Livingstone Way into the car park near the OK Supermarket.

The Falls was a tourist town, with the main road, Livingstone Way, running down to the bridge over the Zambezi River and to Zambia beyond. Side streets and small shopping arcades were lined with shops selling wood and soapstone carvings, safari-wear and T-shirts, paintings and other curios; tour businesses and an army of street touts offered white-water rafting on the Zambezi and bungee jumping.

As she turned off the engine, a young man with dreadlocks, dressed in a Shearwater T-shirt, board shorts and rafting sandals emerged from the shadows, holding out a carved stone hippo in one hand and a clutch of pendants, carvings of the snake-headed river god Nyami Nyami, protector of the river, in the other.

She wound down the window. 'Not interested.' The air outside was heavy and warm; it was always hotter here than in Hwange.

'Where are you from, madam? Germany?' he asked, trying to drum up conversation. 'Would you like to go white-water rafting tomorrow?'

'None of your business, and no. How long have you lived in Victoria Falls?'

'All my life, twenty-two years.'

'You know people?'

He grinned, sensing an opportunity. 'Everyone. It's a small town.'

Sonja took her phone out of her pocket, opened the Facebook app – she did have it, just to keep tabs on Emma – and found Allan Platt's profile. She selected one of the pictures and showed it to the tout. 'Do you know this man?'

He leaned in closer. 'Yes.'

'Name?'

He smiled at her. 'I am very hungry. Business is so bad. The tourists are coming back, after COVID, but it is taking some time.'

Sonja reached into her breast pocket and took out one of the twenty-dollar notes she'd cached there, for just such an eventuality. She held it out to him.

'Allan . . . Plett, or something like that.'

'Close enough.' Sonja let the bill slip from her fingers into his. 'Want another twenty?'

'I can take you to him.'

'You know where he is right now?'

The man nodded. 'I know where he is every Friday night.'

'Tell me.'

He shook his head. 'I'll take you there for fifty dollars.'

'Forty.'

'Deal.'

*

The Three Monkeys bar was buzzing – loud music competed with even louder chatter and laughter from backpackers and groups of hard-partying locals finishing their working week.

The bar and bistro had a semi-industrial feel, one red-brick wall decorated with a big *I love Vic Falls* sign, with a heart, and no roof over the dining area other than a series of khaki shade sails. The kitchen and serving area were in an old train carriage, which was fitting as the place was situated on the railway line, adjacent to where it bisected Livingstone Way.

Normally places like this – any crowd, really – made Sonja jumpy. Tonight, she felt mission-ready, calm. She scanned the crowd: a group of guides; some young travellers doing shots and laughing; two couples in their sixties, in new khaki safari clothes and clean white sneakers – most likely from the Victoria Falls Hotel up the line, Sonja thought; a young Nordic-looking couple studying a map over pizza; and a woman alone, head down and reading a book, her black hair tied back in a ponytail under a green baseball cap.

The tourist tout – she'd learned his name was Benjamin – grinned and waved to a barmaid, who gave him an eyelash flutter in return as a waiter found them a table.

'That's Plett over there.' Benjamin nodded his head as they sat at a high table on barstools and the waiter left them their menus.

'Two Zambezi lagers, please,' Sonja said, casually registering Allan Platt.

'Thanks,' Benjamin said.

'Drink quick,' Sonja said when the beers came. 'You're leaving me soon.'

'All right. It's your money, but . . . be careful of him.' Benjamin rested an elbow on the table, his hand casually covering his mouth. It was as though he was worried Platt might be able to lip-read. 'He's violent. I once saw him beat the crap out of a kid who had tried to steal a loaf of bread off the front seat of his Land Cruiser. People are hungry, you know?'

'Yes.' She eyed the hunter. He was holding court at the head of a table of half a dozen men and women – the guides. Like the older tourists, they all wore safari gear, but their clothes were faded, with threadbare collars, well-worn Courteney boots or rafter sandals. These were bush people, with deeply tanned skin; half the table was smoking. 'What else do you know about him?'

'He's a hunter, but he was in the news recently for baiting a lion, just like that famous cat, Cecil, the one –'

'I heard,' Sonja said, sipping her beer. 'More information.'

'You got your forty dollars' worth.'

Sonja stared at Benjamin. He received her message, loud and clear.

'He takes hunters into the bush sometimes, and also drives a game viewer as a tourist guide. Also, he deals.'

'Drugs?'

'*Yebo.* Dagga – marijuana – sometimes coke for the people with money, diesel when it's in short supply. I also heard he can get you a gun.'

Sonja noticed that Platt wore a lightweight green jacket; everyone else was in short sleeves. She guessed he was carrying a shoulder holster which, in a country well known for its tough gun laws and lack of crime, confirmed the picture Benjamin was painting. 'Women?'

'Guy's got a new girlfriend every week. They never seem to stay.'

Sonja reached into her shirt pocket and took out another ten-dollar note, which she slid across the tabletop under her palm. Benjamin took it. 'Thanks, you can go.'

'I can stay, if you like; help you.'

She shook her head. 'No, you don't want to be here.'

He looked into her eyes again, then drained his beer and got up and left.

Sonja, alone, crossed one leg over the other, sipped her drink, and took the rubber band from her ponytail, shaking her hair free. She fingered a lock and, glancing towards the noisy table, waited for Allan Platt to notice her. It didn't take long.

She took her time over her beer and, fortuitously, Platt's party started breaking up. When the goodbye fist-bumps and kisses had finished there was only her target and one other man left. Platt said something to him and went to the bar.

Sonja took out her phone and pretended to check it. A waiter appeared at her side.

'Ma'am, the gentleman over there,' he nodded to the bar, 'asked me to bring you another beer.' He set the condensation-covered glass down on her table and took the empty.

Platt came to her table. 'Howzit?'

'You're being presumptuous, assuming I wanted another beer, and that I would accept a gift from a stranger.'

He held up one hand in surrender, the other clutching some kind of spirit mixed with Coca-Cola by the look of it. 'If you want to be like that then . . .'

She smiled, coyly, and slid the beer away from her. 'Klipdrift and Coke Zero. Double.'

He grinned and snapped his fingers. A waiter came over and he ordered. Sonja noticed that he slurred a little when he spoke.

Platt bowed. 'May I, my lady?'

She faked a titter. 'Of course.'

He pulled out a seat and sat opposite her. 'German?'

'Is my accent that strong? I live in England now.'

'You are – how can I put this diplomatically? – quite direct.'

She played with her hair again. 'I like to make my intentions clear, to dispense with small talk, particularly when time is short.'

His eyes widened, as did his smile. He was handsome, in a sun-damaged way, but his even teeth and semi-drunken wobble couldn't mask the coldness in his eyes. He was calculating, even as they bantered. Her drink arrived and they clinked glasses.

Platt leaned back in his chair, as if to get a better view of her as he looked her up and down. 'Let me guess – wildlife photographer?'

She smiled. 'What makes you say that? Maybe I'm just a tourist.'

He shook his head. 'You're wearing black pants, navy shirt and sneakers, for a start. Holiday-makers think they're on safari in the bush twenty-four/seven. No bum bag or other clutter, no camera and no selfies with your phone. No piercings or dreads, so you can't be with a bloody NGO.'

Sonja laughed and sipped her drink. 'If I was, this would be the shortest date ever, since you've made it clear what you think of tourists and do-gooders.'

'Oh, so it's a date now, is it?'

She took the straw from her drink and sucked it.

He swallowed. 'What was Benjamin doing here?'

So he wasn't drunk enough to have missed new arrivals in the bar, Sonja thought. 'He came up to me on the street. I asked him where I could score some dagga and he said he'd find some for me. I told him to find me somewhere I could have a drink while he went off in search.'

He glanced around the bar, then back at her, lowering his voice. 'We can cut out the middleman.'

'Maybe.' She mirrored his actions, leaning back and appraising him. 'Let me guess – safari guide?'

He ran his hands down the front of his jacket. 'What gave it away?'

'So, I'm right?'

He took a drink. 'I'm also a professional hunter. Is that a problem for you? So many foreigners, and even locals, are against it these days. I always like to check.'

'Always? Like when you meet a new woman?'

He shrugged.

'In answer to your question,' she slowly traced her index finger up and down the side of her glass, 'no. I think it would be quite thrilling, to be out in the bush, facing some real danger instead of just riding around in the back of a Land Rover.'

'Hmm, it is thrilling.'

Platt was, she thought, almost salivating. She needed more information from him, though.

'Tell me, does it pay well, hunting? Guiding?'

'You *are* direct, aren't you?'

'German.' She smiled again.

He took another drink. 'If you get the right clients. There's a lot happening around Vic Falls, new investment, and enough people with enough money to keep the hunting industry afloat.'

'Chinese money?'

His eyes narrowed and she wondered if she'd pushed too hard, too fast.

'It's just that I see them, Chinese people, everywhere,' she continued. Sonja looked down and slowly slid a finger into the open front of her blouse. She could tell his eyes were on her breasts. She looked up. 'Sorry, thought I might have been bitten by a mosquito.'

'You need to be careful of malaria,' he said, 'though I don't bother with prophylaxis.'

She looked into his eyes. 'Protection is overrated.'

'About that smoke . . .'

Sonja grinned. 'You've got a joint on you?'

'At my house. It's not far.'

'Full of trophies? Animal heads?'

He shook his head. 'I leave that sort of thing to my clients.'

Sonja pushed her drink aside. 'Ready when you are.'

He gulped his down and looked, pointedly, at hers. 'You're not going to finish that?'

'I want to get mellow, not wasted, if you know the difference.'

He nodded, not needing any more hints.

He led her along the road parallel to the railway tracks, away from Livingstone Way. There were no street lights, but the darkness didn't worry Sonja; this was her natural environment. They passed closed curio market stalls, their merchandise covered by tarpaulins, and the N1 Hotel. It didn't look like a residential area to Sonja.

Platt's right hand brushed against her left, and she sensed that it wasn't the result of a half-drunk lurch.

'What's a hot chick like you doing by herself in town anyway?'

'Looking for fun.' She flashed him a smile. 'You said some locals are anti-hunting? I would have thought people born in Zimbabwe would be smarter than that, appreciating the income that hunting brings to rural communities, the benefits in terms of boots on the ground in deterring poaching.'

He looked at her, as if surprised she was not just a pretty face. 'Exactly, except some of those protesting the loudest on Facebook and stirring up all that social media bullshit aren't even born in this country.'

'Where are they from? Europe?'

'America, mainly. There's this one guy, a *goffal* – coloured, so that might explain his lack of brains. Some half-American, half-Angolan –'

The punch to his throat, fast and hard with the pointed knuckles of her right four fingers, took the filthy words and foul wind out of Platt as he staggered and fell to the ground. In the darkness below the broken streetlight Sonja let loose.

She fell on him, smashing a fist into his nose, not because it was a particularly effective way of disabling him, but because she wanted his friends, cronies and potential conquests to see him with a flattened nose and black eyes. Her aggression was redlining, but still controlled. Even as he was finally gathering the presence of mind to remember he had a weapon, Sonja had her hand inside his jacket and was pulling it out.

Sonja kicked him in the ribs, hopefully hard enough to crack a couple, then racked the Makarov pistol. Platt groaned and writhed as she put a foot on the back of his neck.

'It's not nice to use racist terms.'

'Go fuck yourself, bitch.'

She leaned over and rammed the tip of the pistol barrel into the back of his skull.

'Tell me about the Chinese guy.'

'Fuck off, coon lover. You're not going to shoot me here in the street. Fucking white trash pussy.' She stood straight, took aim and fired a shot into his right calf.

Platt bellowed and tried to reach for his leg. 'What the fuck?'

Sonja lowered herself down again so her knee was on his back. 'Apologise.'

'I'm sorry, OK. Ow, that fucking hurts. I need a doctor.'

'The Chinese guy.'

Sonja looked around. A dog had started barking, probably from the noise of the gunshot, but no one else seemed to be stirring and there were definitely no houses this close to the railway line. With the number of elephants and baboons that passed through Victoria Falls from the nearby Zambezi National Park it probably wasn't unusual for the odd warning shot to be fired.

Sonja put her foot on Platt's bleeding leg. The wound was superficial, but he yelped again.

'Enough!'

'Tell me.'

'He's a client. His name's Carrington Wu. He likes to hunt and I do some business with him, that's all.'

'What kind of business?'

'Get off my fucking leg.'

She increased the pressure.

Platt gasped. 'He needed a Zimbabwean citizen to set up a company, import–export, so he paid me to be one of his directors and to take care of . . . administration and logistics stuff for him around Victoria Falls.'

Sonja scoffed. 'Yes, you sure do seem like the admin and logistics type. Why did he really pick you?'

'He likes to hunt, OK? I'm good at my job, I get him whatever game he wants and he looks after me in return.'

'Sure, by illegally luring lions out of the national park into the hunting areas. People like you are sick, and give hunting a bad name.'

'That's all bullshit, made up by that coloured –'

She leaned on his leg again, prompting another scream but shutting him up. 'What kind of import–export?'

'Stuff to Asia. For God's sake, get me a doctor, woman. I'm going to bleed out if I don't get my bloody leg seen to.'

Sonja glanced down at the wound. 'I've done worse than that shaving my legs. Grow a set of balls, man. More information.'

He sniffed.

Sonja took out her phone and selected the video function on the camera and held it to his face.

'What are you doing?' Platt whimpered.

'I'm going to film the big tough hunter crying like a little baby.'

He stifled a sob. 'Wu's in the abalone trade. It's legal, in case you're wondering, and in return he imports medical supplies into Zimbabwe.'

'I don't see any rocky ocean shores around here, do you, Platt? How does the abalone get here?'

'I told you, it's all legal.' He sniffed again, tears staining his cheeks. She moved the phone closer to him and took a picture, then put the camera back in her pocket. She knew he might clam up if he really thought he was being videoed.

'Do you want me to shoot the other leg?'

He flailed a hand out, as if that would stop a bullet. 'I should let you kill me. If I tell you more I'm going to die anyway.'

'Road or air?'

He turned his head sideways and licked his lips, like a snake sniffing the air with its tongue. He watched her take aim again. 'Road.'

'Where? When?'

'The stuff comes up from South Africa, via Botswana, then the drivers take a right at Pandamatenga and cross into Zimbabwe there. Technically, that border crossing isn't supposed to be used for freight or heavy trucks, it's just a gravel road through the bush, a track in places, but he uses tourist trucks, so the border officials let them through.'

Sonja nodded. It was a clever strategy; Pandamatenga was about a hundred kilometres south of Kazungula, the much busier crossing between Botswana and Zambia, where a random search by customs officer was more likely. 'Now, when's the next shipment due?'

'For God's sake, woman, if he finds out . . .'

'He won't, trust me,' Sonja said. Once someone had started spilling the beans in an interrogation, she knew, it was almost impossible for them to stop. One just had to be patient. 'I've got some painkillers with me. I'll bandage you before I go. You'll have a *lekker* scar to show your next conquest.'

'Tomorrow. They'll probably cross the border as soon as it opens, after eight in the morning.'

'What type of vehicle?' Sonja asked.

'A Hino truck, converted into an overland tour bus.'

'Company name?' Sonja asked. 'Any branding?'

Platt sighed. 'Flame of Zimbabwe tours.'

'What happens to it after it gets here?'

He shook his head, as if ashamed of himself. 'It's transferred to a locally registered commercial lorry, trucked to Harare, and flown out from there, usually to Hong Kong, but also Shanghai.'

'Who's Wu's contact in Cape Town? Who does he get the abalone from?'

'As if I'd know?' Platt whined.

Sonja put the top of the barrel of the pistol against the back of his good leg and Platt squirmed.

'A coloured dude from Cape Town flew up to go on a hunt. The *oke* had money, dressed well. They were talking business, about shipments and what-what-what, but didn't say much in front of me. I saw him on DSTV, on the news from South Africa a couple of weeks ago; he's like running for parliament or something.'

'Name?' Sonja said.

'Hendricks. Victor, or Vincent, something like that. Please . . .'

Fuck, Sonja mouthed silently. She composed herself. 'OK. Anything else I need to know about Wu?'

He sneered up at her. 'Take him on, I dare you. He's a martial arts master and a killer. They say he was responsible for the *cleansing* of those ethnic Muslims in China. You think you're tough, lady, but he'll fucking cut your liver out and take a bite out of it. Just you try.'

Sonja heard a police siren and back towards Livingstone Way she could see a blue light coming from up the hill. She grabbed one of Platt's wrists and pulled it up behind his back, causing him to yelp again, then secured his hands together with one of the cable ties she'd taken from the Land Cruiser's toolbox.

She knelt down, lowering her mouth to his ear. 'I'm not going to hear from you again, and nor is anyone I know, am I, Allan?'

He swallowed hard. 'I'll –'

'You've got plenty of bullets left in this little Russian peashooter, but only two legs, Allan.'

'No, all right, you won't hear from me.'

'And you'll withdraw your statement against Hudson Brand, won't you?' She put the gun back to the rear of his head, pushing hard enough to drive his face into the concrete.

'OK, yes. I will.'

'Good. Otherwise, Wu will hear who snitched on him.' Sonja frisked Platt, quickly, and found a spare magazine of ammunition in his jacket. She took it and put it in her pants pocket. The siren was getting louder. She stood and started to move deeper into the shadows, along the railway line, away from town. When she looked back, she saw that Platt was starting to get up.

She took aim, and fired a single shot.

CHAPTER 8

'm worried about Mum,' Emma said as she took a bite from her omelette. She and Hudson sat on the long, wide verandah of the dining and lounge area at Nantwich Lodge, shaded by the overhang of the thatch roof.

He was eating muesli and yoghurt and Enoch, the chef, brought another plunger of coffee to the table. 'Thank you, Enoch.'

'Sure,' Enoch said.

Hudson poured for both of them. 'How come? You know it's not unusual for her to go off-reservation.'

Neither of them had seen Sonja since she'd left them at Hwange Police Station the previous afternoon. Hudson had, as Goodness Khumalo promised, been bailed thanks to Sonja's cash, but they did have to wait for the magistrate to finish his round of golf, plus drinks at the clubhouse. It had been nearly 10 pm by the time they made it back to Hwange National Park.

A herd of roan antelope, handsome, sandy-coloured creatures with clownish black and white faces, walked cautiously down to the dam to drink. Blue waxbills, tiny, beautiful birds, drank from the waterhole just on the other side of the lawn in front of the *stoep*.

'No, I'm more worried about her mental health,' Emma said.

Hudson set his cup down. 'Like we were saying the other day, this is all most likely a side effect from her post-traumatic stress.'

Emma nodded. 'Sure, but she's acting screwy, even for her. Hudson, I think it's more than that.'

'I'm not sure that *screwy* is a recognised term in psychology, but tell me what's wrong, Emma.'

'She went apeshit about what happened with the guy at Silver Sands.'

Hudson pursed his lips. 'You know, kiddo, if I'd been there I would have gone after the guy as well.'

'Would you have shot him in the head?'

'Emma, I'm sure your mom didn't execute the guy.'

Emma pursed her lips. 'She took her gun when she went out looking for him.'

'Sonja always has a weapon.'

'I know, but she had those crazy eyes the next morning. You know what I mean?' Emma said.

He frowned, but did not say no.

'That's why we left in a hurry. I found the guy, Hudson, the one who attacked me. I was with his cousin and we came across him on the beach, with a bullet in the back of his head. Mafia style.'

Hudson sat back in his chair and exhaled. 'Emma, your mom is one tough woman, we both know that, and she has her issues, but one thing she is not is a cold-blooded murderer.'

It was Emma's turn not to answer. She understood how protective her mother was, and that Sonja had no doubt set out to find Denzel and give him an arse-kicking – that would be classic Sonja. However, what else had gone on? Kelvin had pointed out that Denzel had also been wounded in the leg – a knife cut or stab wound – so there had been a fight of some kind. However, that didn't explain how Denzel had ended up being shot in the back of his head.

Had Sonja finally snapped?

Her mother had been at war, or in war zones and low-intensity conflicts, for as long as Emma had been alive. She'd served in

Northern Ireland with the British Army, then, later, as a mercenary in Sierra Leone, Iraq and Afghanistan. She'd also been part of a failed uprising against the government of Namibia, leading a force of separatist rebels opposed to the construction of a dam, and had been involved in anti-poaching operations from South Africa to Tanzania. In addition, Emma knew her mother had been contracted on several occasions by the US Government to do jobs that she would not talk about.

All of that, Emma knew, had taken a toll on her mother, physically, mentally and emotionally. Sonja struggled to connect with people, or form lasting relationships; she had seen friends – lovers – killed in action. And while Emma was sure her mother loved her, and would probably die for her, Sonja had missed most of her daughter's childhood, entrusting her to Emma's English grandmother; and that had hurt. Emma sometimes wondered if there was more to her mother's problems, something deep-rooted that she couldn't tell Emma, something that maybe she'd even suppressed in her conscious mind. Sonja had gone through a rough childhood; Emma's Namibian-German grandfather, Hans, had been an alcoholic and had beaten Sonja and Emma's grandmother, but Hans had found God later in life and tried to make amends before dying. Emma knew other soldiers who had seen and done the things that Sonja had, but who had managed to lead relatively normal family lives. Whatever the reason, Sonja struggled with people.

The relationship between Sonja and her own mother had been difficult, as well. When Emma's grandmother had left her grandfather, Sonja had rebelled against her mother and decided to stay on with Hans, who was working as a maintenance manager at a safari lodge in Botswana. It was only when Hans had hit Sonja that she finally left him. Emma didn't know for sure, but she felt that her grandmother had never forgiven Sonja for not coming with her to England in the first place.

Emma sometimes wished she could just have a regular, normal relationship with her mother, where they could go on a relaxing holiday together and nothing eventful would happen. Even with what had transpired at Silver Sands, if Sonja had not killed Denzel then she could have just stayed and let the police handle it. Emma imagined it would have been a simple matter of checking the ballistics of the bullet that killed Denzel with Sonja's pistol, which she was licensed to own. Sonja had run, which was not like her – unless she was guilty of killing Denzel in cold blood.

'What are you thinking, kiddo?' Hudson asked.

'How screwed up my family is – what little there is of it.'

He smiled. 'Every family is screwed up, Emma, in its own way. That's because families are made up of people.'

'I know she's human, trust me,' Emma said. 'But that doesn't give her an excuse to go around killing people.'

'Have you had any word from her?' Hudson asked.

Emma checked her phone, which was connected to the lodge's satellite wi-fi internet.

'Nothing.'

*

Sonja lay in the meagre shade of a mopane tree, atop a small rise cluttered with granite rocks and small boulders, about thirty kilometres northwest of Nantwich Lodge. Platt was Carrington Wu's lackey and it was time for her to exact a little payback on the man she was sure had masterminded Hudson's framing.

Given what had gone down on the beach, it was also karma, she thought, in a non-Buddhist way, that Wu was tied to Denzel's father, Vincent Hendricks, via the illegal abalone trade. She now had an excellent opportunity to fuck them both over and disrupt a poaching operation. Sam would have been proud, which pleased her. Also, one more day alone in the bush was one less day she would have to endure of Hudson and Emma asking what was *really* wrong with her.

She was a few kilometres from Zimbabwe's unfenced border with Botswana, in the Matetsi Safari Area. Looking through the telescopic sight atop the Barrett .50-calibre anti-materiel rifle, she watched the dirt road from the Pandamatenga border post.

She lay on a carpet of red-gold mopane leaves, which had fallen during the long, dry, sunny winter months. Through her scope she watched an elephant feeding by the roadside.

The rifle had been an unlikely, but lucky, find. Its owner, Johnsy, was an old soldier she had served with as a private military contractor in Afghanistan. Needing somewhere to stay in Victoria Falls after finishing with Platt, she had called him.

'Sonja, howzit!' Johnsy had bellowed into his phone when he answered the call. In the background she could hear ancient music, Engelbert Humperdinck, blaring. Clearly, she hadn't woken him. '*Lekker* to hear from you, my girl, where the flip are you?'

'Vic Falls.'

'All right. Party. My place, now.'

She'd followed his directions, moving through the night, skirting the main street and the extra two police Land Rovers that had appeared after she left Platt.

Johnsy was wearing a pair of too-short denim shorts, sandals and a Springboks T-shirt. The rugby had been on that night, she recalled. He had a cigarette in one hand and a bomber, a 750-millilitre bottle, of Lion Lager in the other. 'Give me a kiss, my girl.'

She navigated away from a mouth-to-mouth kiss and allowed him to hug her. 'Hello, Johnsy,' she said.

'Come in, come in. Klippies and Coke Zero, right?'

'Sure,' she'd said.

The sixties music was blaring from an LP on the turntable of a radiogram in a wooden cabinet. 'Vintage,' Johnsy said as he turned the volume down to a bearable level, 'like me, babe. Sheesh but it's *mushi* to see you, my g–'

'Call me "my girl" again, Johnsy, and I'll shoot your balls off.' She lifted her blouse a little to show him the pistol grip of the Makarov in her belt.

'Yeah, baby.' He lifted the bottle to his lips, swigged, then burped. 'Pistol-packin' momma, that's my . . . Sonja.'

Johnsy's whole house was mid-twentieth-century vintage, though Sonja suspected that rather than being a collector he'd never moved out nor seen the need to update the home he'd had since he served as a horseman in the Rhodesian Army's mounted infantry unit, Grey's Scouts. The scouts had patrolled the border with Zambia and Botswana during the Bush War, which later became known as Zimbabwe's war of liberation, and took part in incursions in Mozambique. Sonja glanced around the living room. On the nicotine-stained walls were pictures of young men in uniform, and their horses.

'How have you been?' she asked.

He'd shrugged, suddenly more sober and sombre. 'All right, I suppose. Not many wars these days.' He sounded regretful. 'I got on one of the last C-17s out of Afghanistan.'

'*Ja.*' The gravy train for contractors had ground to a halt with America's decision to pull out the last of its combat troops in Afghanistan and Iraq.

'Some action brewing in Mozambique,' he said, hopefully. 'I'm heading there in a few days' time. Those Islamic State gooks are tearing up the north of the country, cutting off heads and stopping fuel and gas production. You should come, join the party. It'll be a *jol*, just like old times, hey?'

'I'm getting sick of being asked,' Sonja said.

'Sure. What do you need, Sonja? Somewhere to stay? I heard you were hooked up with that old 32 Battalion Yankee, Hudson Brand, down at Nantwich.' He raised an eyebrow. 'Trouble in paradise?'

'At ease, soldier,' she said. 'All is good between me and him. I'm stuck here in town tonight . . . on business. So, I wouldn't say no to a bed. Oh, and I need a weapon.'

He nodded to her belt. 'Seems like you're already partnered up.'

'I mean a proper gun, Johnsy.'

'*Lekker.*'

He'd led her outside, to the garage in his backyard. Inside, behind the flaking paint and rusty hinges of the battered wooden swing doors, was a new, purpose-built concrete strongroom. Johnsy used his body to shield a combination lock in a stout steel safe door from view and spun it until the lock released.

'Come into my parlour.' He grinned, reached inside and pulled on a light switch cord, then stepped aside.

Inside, in hand-crafted wooden racks lining the walls, was a collection of modern military weaponry which would have done an armaments museum proud.

'Mauser K98, .303, AK-47s, RPD machine gun, FNs.'

She'd been tempted to pick one or two up, but didn't fancy her fingerprints ending up at some future crime scene. The vault smelled of gun oil and tobacco. 'Where did you get all this shit, Johnsy?'

'Some of it's stuff I souvenired during the Bush War, also from Angola.'

Sonja had stopped at the end of one of the racks. There, like a giant exclamation mark at the end of this death sentence, was the granddaddy of all rifles, the Barrett. 'How the fuck did you get this into Zimbabwe?'

Johnsy had grinned. 'You know how to eat an elephant?'

She shook her head at the old joke.

He winked at her. 'One piece at a time. In my kitbag, every time I came home from the Middle East. I bought it off an Afghan Ktah Khas special forces dude. Hardest thing was getting the barrel back – I put it in a set of golf clubs I bought in Kuwait.'

Sonja picked the monster up. It weighed nearly fifteen kilograms. She brought it to her shoulder.

'Effective range, eighteen hundred metres, but it'll reach out to four kilometres or so,' Johnsy said. 'Semiautomatic, ten-round magazine, but those .50-calibre rounds are like gold here in Zimbabwe.'

'How many rounds you got?' Sonja asked.

'About thirty.'

'That should do me. I'll take them all.'

'Sonja, no . . .'

'Johnsy, yes. Remember Kandahar? I saved your life in that ambush.'

He'd rubbed his nicotine-stained goatee beard. 'True that, but if you're caught with that thing in this country you're going to prison and the Zimbabwe Republic Police and the Charlie 10s will beat a confession out of you. They'll put me away for life, too, I'm telling you.'

She lowered the massive rifle. Sonja had tangled with the CIO – Zimbabwe's Central Intelligence Organisation, also known as 'Charlie 10' – in the past and thought she could evade them easily enough. 'Why do you even have this cannon?'

Johnsy had shrugged. 'Because it's there?'

'Borrow me this thing, Johnsy. How much?'

'I can't –'

'You said it yourself,' she'd pushed, 'there's no work for the likes of us any more. I've got cash.'

'You're not going to shoot any humans with this, are you?' Johnsy had asked.

'It's an anti-*materiel* rifle, Johnsy. I'm going to shoot the shit out of stuff, not people.'

'*Ja*, but you and me both know it's one of the best sniper rifles in the world. There were Yanks slotting *terrs* at two kilometres-plus in Afghanistan and Iraq.' His eyes suddenly widened in a moment of apparent horror. 'Hell, you're not going to shoot an elephant with it, are you?'

She smiled. 'No, you big softy. No animals, no people. I've just got a little long-range payback in mind.'

'I heard Brand got arrested and has been charged with poaching.'

'That was quick-moving news,' she said, pulling back the rifle's cocking handle to look inside the breech. The action was smooth; the weapon was clean and lightly oiled, no rust.

'Small town,' Johnsy had scoffed. 'I also heard Al Platt caught Brand red-handed in the bush, near the carcass of the dead elephant.'

'You believe Hudson Brand is an elephant poacher?' Sonja looked at him over the rifle.

Johnsy laughed. 'No. That Yankee's greener than the army, babe. He's a bloody tree hugger; he wouldn't kill a mosquito. I'd say his big mouth, complaining about the mining exploration and the Chinese and causing a big Hondo – a war to you – has probably got him in too much *kak*. He's a big broad-shouldered target and he's not afraid to speak his mind on social media. That can be dangerous in a country like this. Also, Platt's got it in for him.'

'Well, trust me, Platt won't be testifying against Brand, Johnsy,' Sonja said.

Johnsy had said nothing to that, just looked her in the eye and given a small nod.

Now, up on the hill, Sonja let the tiny mopane flies have free rein on her face. Moving a hand could give away her position.

Johnsy had dropped her five kilometres to the east of her current position and then carried on. He'd never lost his interest in horses, and worked part-time at horseriding safari operations at Victoria Falls and for a lodge offering riding just outside Hwange National Park's Main Camp, about a hundred and fifty kilometres southeast of where she was now. Johnsy was towing a horse float, transporting a horse from the Falls to the lodge.

The walk in was not long, but burdened with the Barrett rifle, ammunition, water and some rations she'd prepared for herself, she was reminded of every ache and pain and old injury she was also carrying. She could feel, even lying down, that her knee had swollen again.

She hated getting old.

Sonja knew she could have done better, by Emma and by Hudson, and probably by Sam, her late husband. She'd made some bad decisions in her life, including one she'd tried to bury for many years, but which for some reason had come bubbling up again at Silver Sands. The one thing that did continue to give her purpose was protecting those she loved, and being here was a way of doing that.

Before her, stretching away on either side of the road, was a wide-open *vlei*. The floodplain was dotted here and there with pools and rivulets of water that glittered in the sun's rays. In the distance was a herd of sable antelope, little more than a grouping of black spots to the naked eye, classed as rare across Africa but plentiful in this part of the continent. She wondered if they were the same herd that sometimes visited Nantwich Lodge.

Closer, a warthog dragged his bottom blissfully through some mud, scratching and cooling himself at the same time. Off to her right a herd of waterbuck, dark grey with white 'toilet seat' markings on their rumps, grazed on the grass. Here, as opposed to the dry country either side of the lowland, the grass was bright emerald against the dull browns stretching to the horizon.

She heard the far-off hum of an engine, the grinding of an ageing gearbox. Peering through the scope she saw the truck come around the bend. On the side, as it came into view, was the logo of the travel company that Platt had mentioned to her.

Sonja checked the range and shifted her gaze to an ilala palm tree, checking its fronds for any wind movement. There was none. She focused on the vehicle again. She had chosen this particular rise as it allowed her to look more or less straight down the road, giving her a clear shot at the front of the truck without having to aim off to allow for the vehicle's movement.

She focused the crosshairs on the centre of the vehicle's radiator and took up the slack on the trigger. She inhaled, released half a breath, and squeezed. The giant rifle bucked into her shoulder, but she was leaning into it, expecting the recoil.

The crack of the shot rolled across the plain, sending antelope and the startled warthog fleeing for their lives. As residents of a hunting area, they knew that sound all too well. A jet of steam erupted from the front of the truck and the panicked driver slewed from side to side. Sonja shifted her aim and, as the driver turned the wheel in order to pull over, she squeezed again, sending a copper-jacketed projectile into the fuel tank this time.

Sonja got up, leaving the Barrett resting on its bipod – speed was of the essence now and the heavy weapon would slow her down. She ran, her right knee protesting at every jarring downhill step. She dodged mopane trees, shredded to splintered bushes by elephants, and jumped over the larger rocks. She drew the Makarov pistol as she ran.

The driver of the truck climbed down out of the cab and took a quick look at the hole in his external fuel tank. Diesel was gushing out of it and splattering on the dusty road below. Realising that this was no accident, and no doubt having heard the slug hitting the tank, if not the radiator, the driver simply turned tail and ran down the road in the direction he'd just come from, towards the Botswana border. Sonja knew this was lion country, and although the driver was probably aware of that too, he must have figured that he was better off running from a gunfight than worrying about the old African adage of not running from natural predators. Sonja hoped, for his sake, there were no big cats lurking in the shade of the trees fringing the floodplain.

Sonja slowed, pistol raised on the off-chance there was a braver co-driver lurking somewhere. The vehicle, however, was empty when she arrived. She looked in the front. In a folder she found the vehicle registration document. The truck was owned by Giraffe Holdings Private Limited.

She clambered into the back, where the tourists would normally sit, two to each side of the passenger compartment. There was no cargo immediately visible, but when she lifted a rubber mat running down the centre aisle between the pairs of seats, she found a latched, hinged hatch. She opened the door to the hidden compartment; inside were a dozen cardboard boxes, and when she ripped one open she found plastic packets full of dried abalone. The little sea creatures had shrivelled up in death. Sonja shook her head. Fixed to the rear of the truck were two jerry cans. She popped the lid on one and found it was filled with spare diesel fuel.

Sonja took a moment to consider reporting the crime to the Zimbabwean police. She shook her head – Wu was well connected and as it was not illegal to export abalone from the country. She couldn't help but think this valuable consignment would not spend long in an evidence lock-up, if she reported it. As much as she hated the idea of wasting food, she was here to send a message. She took a can from its cradle, climbed into the rear of the truck again and emptied the contents over the boxes.

Sonja had chosen the site of her ambush with care. This was a low-lying area and even though it was the end of the dry season, this area was green and boggy with year-round water that seeped up from underground. A fire would not catch and spread here. She used her cigarette lighter – she always carried one – to get the diesel going, and soon the storage boxes were alight, spewing foul chemical smoke. Even if the vehicle didn't burn down to its axles, the cargo would be ruined and the message sent.

Sonja backed away from the radiant heat of the growing blaze in the back of the truck. Then, over the crackle of the flames she heard another engine. Looking towards Botswana she saw a white Land Rover appear. Quickly raising the binoculars she'd borrowed from Johnsy to her eyes, she saw the blue and gold stripes on the bonnet and roof that marked it as a police vehicle.

'Shit.'

She ran, but stumbled in the marshy ground by the road as her weak knee gave out. She yelped in a moment of pain. The police driver put on his siren and lights and accelerated.

Sonja hauled herself to her feet again and set off. She cursed herself for being rash. She could have just left the vehicle stranded, or waited a little longer to make sure the coast was clear. The cops were bearing down on her and it was uphill all the way to the rifle.

She did not want to get into a gun battle with the police, but nor did she want them to find the Barrett. It would have been easy for them to deduce where she had fired from, and to follow her clear-as-day trail down the hill. Sonja couldn't tell if she was getting lazy or crazy in her advancing years.

She figured, also, that even the hardy Land Rover would make slow work of the swamp and then the loose rocky surface of the knoll. She stumbled again as she ran on.

Bloody knee. She picked her way as carefully as speed would allow, avoiding rocks the size of softballs; if she stood on one of them that would be the end of an ankle in a split second.

The police driver was abreast of the burning truck now, swerving to avoid the smoke and flames. He turned off the road. As she had hoped, the vehicle was slowed to walking pace by the muddy ground as soon as it left the raised embankment of the sometimes-graded dirt and gravel road.

The doors opened and two officers got out. Younger than her, they made easy work of the marshy ground, their boots sending up geysers of mud as they ran. One carried an AK-47; the other drew a pistol as he moved. They wore the dark blue fatigue trousers and lighter shirts of the Zimbabwe Republic Police and old-style brown leather boots with buckle-up gaiters. Sonja could see there was another man in the Land Rover, besides the officer still at the wheel; she imagined it was the truck driver. Unluckily for her the police must have been on a regular patrol or responding to a call-out when they came across the trucker fleeing on foot down the road.

'Hey, stop! Police!' one of the officers called.

Sonja was breathing heavily, trying to ignore the spreading pain in her knee as she focused on putting one foot in front of the other. She decided not to turn and fire on the police – she had no beef with them and could only imagine her fate if she shot one of them. She could, she imagined, be shot on sight as it was, being armed and fleeing from them after setting a truck alight in a wildlife area.

Glancing back, Sonja could see that the men were clearly gaining on her. She pushed on, the crest of the low hill in front of her. She heard the Land Rover's engine rev hard as the driver coaxed the four-wheel drive out of the bog. It would be bouncing through the mud now – the muddy layer was not too deep – and trundling up the hill after her any minute.

Sonja felt the slope start to ease and tried to think of a way out of this mess. This was not like her. She'd been foolish, impetuous, blinded by her desire to seek revenge for Hudson, just as she'd gone after the boy at Silver Sands. This was the work of a madwoman, not a trained professional soldier. She felt rage building inside her, not at the men following her, or those who had wronged the people she loved, but at her own stupid self and her failing body.

Pop, pop, pop. She heard the distinctive sound of an AK-47 and then the *crack-thump* of rounds flying over her head.

Sonja risked another glance over her shoulder. The rifleman was standing, taking aim. She heard more shots, but lost her footing again and stumbled. The fall probably saved her, as a round zinged into the ground and ricocheted off a rock a few metres in front of her face. She scrambled to her feet again.

In front of her was the Barrett. She stooped and grabbed the heavy rifle, dragged it over the other side of the crest of the hill, where she was temporarily out of sight of her pursuers, and shrugged it over her shoulder. Its angular metal corners banged and stabbed her back as she ran down the hill, but she ignored the pain. If she was going to be cornered in a gunfight, she at least wanted superior firepower. The trick, however, was to stay at long range.

The first of her pursuers made it to the top of the hill and fired a shot at her. This time it was a pistol. Sonja found herself in a shallow valley, on rocky ground amid desiccated trees. She had another low rise to negotiate ahead of her, and knew, with a sickening feeling, that she would not have the strength or speed to stay ahead of the lightly armed and unencumbered policemen.

'Halt!'

She heard two more shots, this time from a different direction, though small calibre, as if from another pistol. Then came a wild yell. 'Hah!'

Sonja looked up and to the left and heard the sound of rapid drumbeats. From over the rise came a man on horseback, urging his mount on with a one-handed slap of the reins on either side of the big black animal's neck. The man fired twice more, into the air like a Wild West cowboy, then slid his pistol into a shoulder holster.

'Arm up, babe!' Johnsy yelled as he galloped obliquely towards her. The stallion beneath him grew in size with every full-length stride. Dust and small rocks flew in the horse's wake, creating a mini desert storm.

The man with the rifle was struggling his way to the top of the hill and taking aim as Johnsy bore down on her, his right arm out and crooked at the elbow as he gripped the reins with his left hand and urged his horse on with more whoops.

As he passed her, Sonja reached up and outwards and Johnsy grabbed her and swung her up onto the saddle behind him. 'Hah!'

Sonja landed awkwardly behind the saddle, the barrel of the Barrett smashing into the back of her head, but she managed to keep her balance.

They thundered down the rocky little valley, in front of the officer with the pistol. He got off a shot at them, which went wide. The officer with the AK-47 chased them with bullets along the depression, but within seconds Johnsy was pulling his mount to the left, up and over the hill Sonja had been heading for and out of sight of the officers and the Land Rover, which was still making slow work of the rock-covered hillsides.

'How's that for the bloody cavalry?' Johnsy yelled over his shoulder.

'Yee-hah!' Sonja screamed into the hot African wind. 'Ride 'em, cowboy!'

CHAPTER 9

Vincent Hendricks stood by his son's coffin, looking down at Denzel's serene face. His firstborn was dressed in a white suit and tie, holding a single red rose. It was Denzel's aunt's doing, Kelvin's mother. She wept inconsolably. Kelvin nursed a glass of water, standing alone on the fringe of the crowd, not looking at his cousin or his uncle.

Vincent's phone buzzed on silent. Surreptitiously, he checked the screen.

'Where are you going?' his sister Isabelle said, looking up from her clutch of friends, dark eyes burning away her tears.

'I need fresh air, a cigarette.'

Isabelle shook her head.

He shook a couple of hands en route and went to Kelvin. 'Outside, now, boy.'

Kelvin handed his empty glass to a passing waiter. 'Yes, Uncle.'

Vincent loosened his tie once he was outside of the funeral home, took out his cigarettes and lit one. 'Tell me how Denzel died.'

Kelvin quickened his pace to catch up with him. 'He was shot, Uncle Vincent, you know, a single . . .'

Vincent aimed the cigarette at Kelvin, its glowing tip stopping just a few centimetres from the point between his clever nephew's eyes. 'I know you're studying to be a doctor, *jong*, but I don't need a medical examiner's report. What happened?'

'I don't know. I only found him, his body.'

'I know.' Vincent waved the cigarette around and noted how the boy cowered back, ever so slightly. 'I've read the police report, spoken to the investigating officer. She said Denzel had been cut before he died and that a woman had filed a complaint against him.'

Kelvin licked his lips.

Vincent ran his free hand through his hair. Kelvin was holding back, which was interesting. Vincent had the investigating officer, February, on his payroll, so he knew all there was to know about his son's death and the events leading up to it. But he wanted to know more about the woman and her daughter who Denzel and Kelvin had encountered on the beach. 'Denzel was hot-headed – we both know that. The complaint against him was that he assaulted an English tourist and stole her phone – supposedly because the girl took pictures of him on the beach.'

Kelvin shrugged.

'The police said you were with a girl when you found him – and that they took statements from both of you.'

'Yes, Uncle,' Kelvin said.

'The same girl Denzel allegedly assaulted.'

Kelvin looked at the ground.

Vincent stared at his nephew. The boy was weak, like his mother. The father had been killed young, the victim of a gang war, when Isabelle was pregnant, unmarried. Isabelle had vowed that her only child would never be involved in crime. And yet here he was, Vincent thought, the coloured boy from the Cape Flats, son of a hardworking sales assistant in a Waterfront fashion store, who could have lived a life of leisure if she had taken the money Vincent had offered her. Instead, Isabelle had cut ties with her own blood, choosing to raise Kelvin in isolation from his family. Yet, Vincent knew, Kelvin had been on that beach with Denzel for one reason.

'You're a poacher.'

Kelvin looked him in the eye now, and shook his head. 'I took nothing from the sea.'

'The police also said the girl had the same surname as the woman who laid the complaint against Denzel – Kurtz. Emma Kurtz; Sonja Kurtz.'

Kelvin shrugged. 'I went to her, tried to smooth things over. She was fine.'

Vincent noted how Kelvin tried to look him in the eyes again, but couldn't hold his gaze. The boy was hiding something, maybe trying to protect the girl.

'The mother?' Vincent said.

'I only met her once.'

'What's she like?'

Kelvin looked away again. 'Like any mom, wants to protect her kid.'

'She and her daughter flew to Victoria Falls.' Vincent's network of corrupt informers extended to the Department of Home Affairs, as well as the police and environmental agencies. Kelvin looked up, clearly surprised, perhaps even disappointed.

'You didn't know? Why would they up and leave like that? The police want to talk to the mother.'

Before Kelvin could answer, Vincent's phone rang. He took it out of the inside pocket of his suit jacket. Carrington Wu's number came up on his screen. Kelvin used the opportunity to go back into the funeral parlour.

'I'm burying my son today.'

'Please accept my deepest condolences, Vincent,' Wu said.

'Thank you.'

'I knew of your loss, and am sorry for it. I would not have called you unless it was important.'

'What is it?'

'You haven't heard?'

'If I had, I wouldn't be asking you.' Vincent balled a fist. Denzel's death was hitting him harder than he imagined.

'Your latest shipment was destroyed.'

'Where, how?'

Wu recounted an improbable story of a sniper, heavy-calibre rifle, and a woman torching the abalone and fleeing on horseback in Zimbabwe.

'A woman?' The mounted escape was novel, but he was more interested in the gender of the enemy.

'I know, crazy, right?' said Wu.

Although the Chinese man had been an officer in the People's Liberation Army, Vincent sometimes wondered if Wu had learned English from watching too many American movies, or screwing too many blonde prostitutes in Shanghai. He gathered information on his partners, just as he was sure they had sources providing them with intelligence on his every movement.

'Maybe.'

There was a pause. 'A scorned lover, Vincent?'

'Do you have a description?'

'Caucasian. Auburn hair, I am told, pulled back in a ponytail. Broad shoulders. Age: late forties to early fifties.'

Vincent chewed his lower lip. February, the investigating officer, had described the mother in almost exactly those terms. 'Alone?'

'Yes, until she was rescued by a man on horseback. The police have an idea who that might be – a mercenary from the old Rhodesian regime, living in Victoria Falls. Who is this woman, Vincent? Is she going to be an ongoing problem for us?'

His son had been killed and now someone – a woman of very similar description to the one involved in his son's death – was disrupting his business. Like a police detective, Vincent rarely believed in coincidence.

'See what you can find out about a woman named Sonja Kurtz – she's recently arrived in Victoria Falls.'

'Rest assured, I will be conducting enquiries of my own,' Wu said, 'but at the moment you are the one who is out of pocket.'

'I'm expecting your next delivery tomorrow.'

'Ah, regrettably I foresee a delay in the shipment. There are problems in Mozambique, as you may have read online or seen in your news.'

Vincent held it together. Wu was threatening to block his next shipment of Tik, and the chemicals his people needed to manufacture it locally. This was because the abalone had been intercepted; it had little to do, he reckoned, with the upsurge in fighting in northern Mozambique, where ISIS-affiliated guerrillas were running amok in coastal towns, disrupting legal and illegal port traffic in the process.

His phone began vibrating in his hand.

'Vincent? Are you still there?'

Vincent looked at the screen. Another call was coming in, from a number he did not recognise. Few people contacted him on this, his second phone. He kept it for regular business associates, such as Wu, and lovers, such as the journalist, Vanessa. He'd had enough of Wu's games for now.

'I'll call you when I know more. You do the same, Carrington. I have to go now.'

'Of course. Condolences.'

Isabelle appeared at the door of the funeral home. He held up five fingers to her. She shook her head and went back inside.

The number had gone through to voicemail, which he never checked. He dialled it.

'You called me?' he said.

'Mr Hendricks, hi. My name's Rosie Appleton. I'm a friend of Vanessa's.'

'Are you now?' A smile played across his lips, the first since he'd last seen Vanessa naked.

'A *journalist* friend, though she did mention what a nice guy you were.'

Vincent narrowed his eyes. He knew when he was being played, and flirted with. 'I'm sorry . . .?'

'Rosie.'

'Rosie. I'm busy with some family matters and not able to give any interviews just now. You can call my campaign office if you'd like to schedule –'

'Vincent, if I may call you that?'

'*Ja*, sure.'

'I'm not calling to interview you, not just yet anyway. I have some information for you.'

He looked back at the funeral home. He needed to get back inside. 'About what?'

'About the woman who killed your son.'

*

Sonja, Emma, Hudson and Johnsy sat around the dining table on the Nantwich Lodge *stoep*. Frogs croaked in the dam and a jackal wailed as the sun set.

'You sure Count Yorga will be OK in the courtyard?'

'I'm sure,' Hudson said. He'd met Johnsy a couple of times before, at Shoestrings, a backpacker joint in Victoria Falls where they both liked to take in a beer and burger. He knew how passionate the man was about his horses, especially his own black stallion, Count Yorga. It was only because he'd saved Sonja, though, that Hudson had agreed to stash the horse in the walled courtyard behind the dining area. This was where guests eating in the main part of the lodge went to use the bathroom, but the lodge was empty this night. It was now the O.K. Corral. 'It's probably the only place around here the lions won't be able to get to him.'

They had stashed the horse float trailer in the bush, in case the police came knocking, but so far, they had not been visited. It seemed Sonja had got away scot-free.

'I'm telling you, those bastards won't be smuggling any more abalone through that border post,' Johnsy said, setting his beer glass down on the table and nearly losing the contents.

'Sonja, you can't go around shooting up vehicles in a national park,' Hudson said.

'It was in a safari area,' Sonja corrected him.

'Yeah,' Emma weighed in, 'isn't that what people do in a hunting area, shoot shit up?'

Johnsy slapped the table. 'Yes! Sure, I haven't had that much fun since that convoy got shot up in Afghan on the way to Kandahar. You remember that, Sonja?'

She smiled and nodded.

Emma's eyes widened. 'Getting shot at in Afghanistan was fun?'

'You had to be there.' Sonja was on her fourth brandy and Coke Zero.

'Your mom was bodyguarding some Muslim woman from the UN, in the second vehicle,' Johnsy said, arranging the salt and pepper shakers and sugar bowl into a line of vehicles. 'Pow! The lead vehicle gets hit by an RPG.'

Hudson watched as Johnsy tipped over the pepper grinder and Sonja flinched, just a tiny movement, but noticeable.

Johnsy ran his fingers across the tablecloth. 'We were in a choke point, coming into town, down a narrow street. *Bam!*' He knocked the lid off the sugar bowl, trapping the salt shaker – Sonja's vehicle. He ran his first two fingertips across the tablecloth. 'Our Sonja gets out and takes the fight to the *jundis*. *Pow, pow, pow*. She opened up on them and the gooks, the Taliban, or al-Qaeda or what-what-whats, just take off and run for it. She had them terrified, I'm telling you.'

Hudson saw a new look on Emma's face, one of open-mouthed adoration, or awe.

Sonja swallowed. 'Happy days,' she said.

'*Eish*, she must have slotted, what, three or four of them, hey, Sonja?'

'Two. Wounded a third, I think.'

Johnsy shook his head. 'I'm sure it was more than that, but the rest of us boys were just pouring out covering fire.'

'I should have stayed with the principal, the person I was supposed to be looking after,' Sonja said to Emma.

'But you took the fight to the enemy instead.' Johnsy raised his glass. 'Cheers to that!'

They all clinked glasses, Sonja half-heartedly.

'You can stay here as long as you like, Johnsy,' Hudson said, seeing Sonja's discomfort and wanting to change the subject. 'Until things cool down at least.'

Johnsy waved a hand in the air. 'Nah, thanks, Hudson, I'm fine. The cops were too far away to get a good look at me and if I get stopped and asked about my horse I'll tell them one looks the same as another, and pay a nice fat bribe. In any case, I've got to get Count Yorga down to Main Camp in the morning. There's a posse of American cowboy tourists coming in a couple of days' time. After that, I've got to go back to the Falls and get ready for Mozambique.'

'Well, OK. Sonja?'

She looked at him across the table. 'Do you want to get rid of me?'

'Of course I don't. It's great to have you here.'

'If we can't be in the Cape on holiday,' Emma said, sipping a glass of wine, 'then this is just as good – even better.'

Hudson reached out and put his hand on Sonja's, on the table. 'It's good having you both here.'

She forced a smile, it seemed, then gently extracted her hand. 'Yes.'

Would it kill her, he thought, *to show some emotion?*

Emma yawned and covered her mouth with her hand. 'I'm exhausted.'

'I'll drive you to your room,' Hudson said. Nantwich was spread out, having been built on the footprint of an old national parks camp, where the accommodation units were meant to be secluded from each other. To walk back to a room here was to invite a nocturnal encounter with a pride of lions on the hunt or a patrolling leopard.

'It's cool, I can drive myself, maybe take the spare game viewer.'

Sonja looked to Hudson and he shrugged.

'Sure,' he said.

Johnsy belched. 'I'm sleeping down here, if that's all right. Near my horse.'

'You'll find some blankets in the lounge room, Johnsy,' Hudson said. 'We keep them for the guests for when they sit out by the fire on cold nights.'

'*Lekker.* I'll sleep on the couch.'

'There's a camp bed in my office,' Hudson said.

'Still more comfortable than out in the bush on patrol in the bad old days, hey?'

'Y'all got that right,' Hudson said. ''Night.'

Hudson and Emma headed outside and Hudson used a powerful handheld spotlight to check the area around one of the game-viewing vehicles.

'Where's Mum?' Emma asked. 'I thought she was behind us?'

Hudson looked around. 'I'm not sure. Bathroom maybe?'

'I'm still worried about her,' Emma said.

'Let's talk in the morning.' He completed his scan. 'All clear.'

Emma got into the nearest Land Cruiser, started the engine, waved, and headed up the hill to the turnoff to the accommodation units.

Hudson went back onto the *stoep.* 'Sonja?'

There was no sign of her. He switched on the spotlight again and shone it out into the blackness. He saw her, about fifty metres away, silhouetted against the surface of the dam, which glittered in the beam. His first instinct was to yell at her, to admonish her for being out in the dark alone. Instead, he switched off the light and walked out to her, until he was by her side. She did not look around at the sound of his boots on the dry ground. He looked up and saw stars blazing overhead, smelled the earthy, musty elephant-odour of the dam.

'Looking at the stars?'

'That's for romantics and children,' she said.

'What are you looking for, then?'

'Peace.'

'One-way ticket into a lion's belly, if you're not careful.'

As if to reinforce the point they heard the far-off, low, almost sorrowful call of one of the big cats.

'Wouldn't be such a bad way to go,' she said. 'Quick.'

'And dirty.' He put an arm around her. She was strong, still mostly muscle, but there was a brittleness to her, like she might snap if he held her too tight. She didn't melt into him, but nor did she wriggle out of his embrace or pick him off her skin like she usually did.

He exhaled, trying to let out a little of the stress he was feeling.

Sonja tilted her face to him. 'What's wrong? People are always asking about me. How are *you*?'

She was perceptive. 'It's the whole coalmine thing. A few of us are running a campaign on social media, and if I can catch Wu illegally hunting elephant we might be able to force the authorities to reconsider his permit and lease.'

She shook her head.

'What?' he said.

'For a combat veteran you're a boy scout, Brand. Wu's in cahoots with that gangster, Hendricks, in Cape Town – the one whose son attacked Emma; it was his abalone that was on the truck I shot up. The pair of them are nothing more than criminals. They understand only one thing – violence.'

He looked into her eyes. 'Sonja. No.'

'Don't worry.' She yawned. 'I'm tired.'

'I know. I've been there; that place where the adrenaline's worn off, the rush is gone, and you wonder if it's worth it after all.'

She stared up at him. 'If what's worth it?'

'Peace.'

She looked back out over the dam. 'For a long time, forever, I used to think I'd die in battle, in some war-torn shithole.'

He could have said a dozen things, most of them about Emma, but he'd learned when to shut up. He *had* been there, wondering if anything could ever compete with the rollercoaster ride of combat.

He'd chased big game, booze and girls at different times – hell, sometimes all at once – to try and find something as thrilling or fulfilling.

Sonja wasn't romanticising it, he knew. She was smart enough to know that she didn't want to leave Emma without her last surviving close relative or, he hoped, him. But that didn't mean Sonja wasn't lost.

'Better people than me have died, Brand. Even in that ambush Johnsy was talking about. There was a guy, one of the other contractors; we were – what's the word? Close? He had two little kids and had just left his wife. He wanted to be with me; those kids now have no father. One of the other principals, not mine, also got it. He was a politician, but a good one, could have been a peacemaker in that fucked-up place. The other thing Johnsy didn't tell in his war story is how a kid was killed, an eleven-year-old girl, in the crossfire.'

He tried hugging her tighter. He looked down at her face and saw a single tear escape and roll down her cheek. She didn't wipe it away – she was probably pretending it wasn't there.

'Could have been me who killed her. I don't know. All I know is I don't deserve to be here.'

'Sonja . . .' He couldn't help himself.

She held up a hand. 'Don't. I'm not going to kill myself, but the fact is, the world would be better off if I wasn't here. Emma could get on with life, and so could you. I know I'm a shitty girlfriend, Brand. You know, I don't like you mooning around, waiting for me all the time.'

He smiled, pleased she couldn't see his face. 'I know.'

She looked up at him again. 'Which part do you know?'

'That you're a shitty girlfriend.'

She laughed. An actual, honest-to-goodness expression of mirth, but it was gone like a shooting star.

Sonja took a deep breath, then exhaled. 'There's some stuff I need to tell you, about my past. It's been preying on my mind.'

'OK, I'm all ears,' he said, encouraged that she might open up to him. She carried many wounds, old and deep, but he suspected not all of them were battle-related.

She shook her head. 'Not now, but soon. It's late.'

He knew better than to push her. 'All right. Now, don't go getting any ideas about wreaking any more havoc up here – you got your payback on Wu and Hendricks today.'

'Whatever,' she said.

'Come to bed, Kurtz.'

'All right, Brand.'

CHAPTER 10

Sonja barely slept. At three in the morning she got up. The moon had risen and was heading back towards the horizon, shining its light through the glass sliding doors leading onto the balcony.

Somewhere outside a Scops owl chirped. Brand lay like a soap-stone sculpture, darkly perfect against the crisp white linen. She slid open the door, the cool morning air raising goosebumps on her skin.

She remembered the feel of him inside her, making her whole again, putting her back together for a little while. She wanted to get back under the mosquito net and bend down and kiss his forehead, to get into bed and spoon him. Instead, she gathered up her clothes, daypack and boots and went outside, closing the sliding door as quietly as she could. Still naked she walked on the flagstones to the outdoor shower. A lion called in the distance. The hot water from the shower washed away the love and the grime from her skin until she was ready for work again.

She dressed quickly, outside. Brand was a heavy sleeper – yet another thing she envied about him and one more of their many differences – but she didn't want him waking and trying to stop her. Hudson was being framed and his lodge, and tourism in general, were under threat from Wu and his coal-mining venture. She wanted to defend Hudson – hell, protect him – but sometimes the best form of defence was attack, not social media.

There were no lights on in Emma's room. Sonja wondered if she should leave her daughter a note, then chided herself for being melodramatic. She would be home for dinner.

Unchallenged, she skirted the ridgeline in front of the accommodation and then set off down the gravel path through the long, wintertime-yellow grass to the main communal building down on the flat, where they'd had dinner.

Her earlier foray out at the dam aside, she was not blasé. She focused on all her senses to give her advance warning of any nocturnal predators that might be lurking or hunting. This part of Hwange National Park was widely acknowledged as having the highest density of lions in the country. In addition, there was a resident leopard who sometimes stashed his kills up by the water tanks that were silhouetted on the crest of the hill high and to her right as she descended.

As she neared the lodge's main building, she heard a lowing noise, like cattle. Walking onto the *stoep*, she peered out into the darkness. Next, she smelled them. As her eyes adjusted to the faint light of the setting moon, she realised the darkened *vlei* in front of the lodge was alive; a herd of maybe a thousand buffalo, their black coats hiding them, was grazing in front of the lodge. Sonja let herself into the courtyard behind the lounge and dining area via the staff entrance at the rear. Count Yorga, the big black stallion, whinnied at her approach.

'Shush, big man.' She stroked his muzzle.

From somewhere inside she heard a buzz-saw. Johnsy had consumed enough booze to give an infantry squad a serious hangover. Hopefully, he wouldn't stir. Sonja saddled the horse and retrieved the Barrett rifle and ammunition from where they'd hidden the weapon the afternoon before, under a stack of thatching grass destined to repair some parts of the roof that had been attacked by baboons. In her daypack she had a couple of bottles of water, bread rolls and some cooked meat she'd secretly wrapped in serviettes and squirrelled away during dinner, ostensibly when she'd gone to the bathroom.

She led Count Yorga out of his makeshift yard and walked him halfway up the hill on the access road before mounting him and giving him a gentle kick in the ribs. It felt good to be moving again with a sense of purpose, even though she felt a little guilty for taking Johnsy's horse. If all went well, she could ride Count Yorga part of the way towards where he should have been heading anyway, and call Johnsy to come pick her up after she'd completed her mission.

Sonja checked her watch, verifying she was on course. She had treated herself to a new Garmin, with maps and navigation function, and used her phone to enter a waypoint she had found on one of Hudson's Facebook posts. Both Hudson and Emma thought she was a Luddite and anti–social media. The second assumption was true, but she used the internet to keep track of those she loved.

Count Yorga seemed to be enjoying himself and was clearly at ease around most wild animals. A herd of zebra was spooked by their approach as they came down the hill and onto the floodplain, but settled after bolting a hundred metres and watched them pass. Dawn broke, bringing the promise of another perfect dry-season day, clear blue skies and temperatures in the late twenties Celsius.

Sonja relaxed as best she could, enjoying the wide-open expanses of Africa as they moved from the *vlei* through areas of half-eaten mopane. She avoided the few roads in this part of Hwange, not wanting to bump into tourists or park rangers on patrol. Her greatest risk, she knew from the dinner table conversation with Hudson and Johnsy, was running into a foot patrol. Perennial shortages of fuel and money meant that most anti-poaching operations here were done silently, by men patrolling in the bush, rather than by rangers charging about in vehicles.

The other good news – for her if not the local wildlife – was that the national parks rangers here had no access to helicopters or other air assets.

There were lions, however. Sonja recalled a story her father had told her when she was a little girl about Harry Wolhuter, one of the early rangers in South Africa's Kruger National Park. Wolhuter had been patrolling the reserve on horseback when he was attacked by a pride of lions. The cats took down his horse and Wolhuter himself was grabbed by a lioness who fastened her jaws around his shoulder and upper body and began dragging him along the ground.

'Harry pretended to be dead,' Hans had told her, 'but he took a small knife from a sheath on his belt, and reached up and stabbed the lioness in the heart.' She remembered being astounded and curious at the same time. How, she wondered, had a man who had already been savaged by a lion had the presence of mind to play dead, and then calculate the exact means of defeating his opponent? 'Always carry a knife in the bush, Sonja.'

She had her Leatherman in a pouch on her belt. It had saved her more than once.

She scanned the tree lines and grass for the telltale twitch of a furry ear or the flick of a tail. The horse, she figured, would smell a cat long before she saw one, assuming the direction of the wind was in their favour.

Elephants took refuge in the shade of trees as the sun rose. She had learned from her stays at Nantwich that in this hot, semi-arid park, the big pachyderms preferred to drink at night, when it was cooler. Elephants had never caused her grief, personally, but growing up in Botswana, in the Okavango Delta, she had developed a healthy respect for the seemingly gentle giants.

'Nothing, other than a human being,' her father had cautioned her, pointing to a bull elephant with impressive tusks, 'can fuck you up quicker and more completely than one of those bloody things.'

She thought about Hans as she rode. He was a tough old

bastard – cruel, even. He'd beaten a prisoner to death during the war in Namibia – South West Africa, as it was when she was a child. Although the man had been part of a gang of insurgents that had terrorised the farm where Sonja and her mother had been living, that did not give her father the authority to commit a war crime. However, after seeing Emma hurt and Hudson unfairly jailed, she finally thought she knew how her father had felt.

Sonja looked to the horizon, where specks in the sky caught her eye. It looked like an airborne tornado or dust devil but was, in fact, an impressively large flock of vultures circling in an updraft. The birds were so big they needed to wait for the earth's surface to warm each morning, to generate enough lift to get their bodies airborne.

In the shade of a giant leadwood tree, she checked a tourist map of Hwange National Park which she had souvenired from the lodge's small library. Her path was taking her north of Robins Camp, another old government rest camp that had been privatised, towards the Tshowe River. When she reached the mostly dry watercourse she heard the *ting, ting, ting* of blacksmith lapwing, indicating the presence of water. The black and white birds strutted around on their long legs on the bank of a remnant pool. A reedbuck gave its high-pitched, squeaky alarm call and darted from the cover of long grass. Sonja dismounted, easing her sore legs as she led Count Yorga to the water to drink before they headed out again.

*

Two hours later, with the sun climbing towards its merciless zenith, she spied a glint in the distance. The mining exploration camp was right where Hudson's post had said it was.

Sonja found another shady tree, tethered the horse, and set off on foot. She'd found good water for him on the way, so he would be fine to wait for her.

She unslung the Barrett and cocked it, chambering a round in the process. Sonja carried the heavy rifle cradled in her arms, scanning the dry bush as she walked. The mopane trees had been shredded by elephants and she knew from her youth in Botswana how silently the giant creatures moved through the bush.

As with her ambush of the truck carrying the abalone, she looked for high ground. She headed for the crest of a hill and when she made it to the top, she found a circle of stones, piled into the shape of a wall about a metre and a half high and two metres across.

Sonja wondered if this was related to other historical sites in the park, which Hudson had told her about. There were significant stone ruins at Bumbusi, near Sinamatella and Mtoa, not far from Main Camp. Was this, she wondered, an ancient outpost or defensive position? There were the remains of a small campfire, cold when she touched it, which was a sign that either poachers or a national parks anti-poaching patrol had camped on this vantage point – tourists were not allowed to camp at remote spots such as this.

She had approached from the rearward slope, so she lowered herself to her hands and knees to survey the far side. There, perhaps seven hundred metres away, was a camp carved out in the bush. There were two prefabricated huts, perhaps accommodation and/or an office, and a smaller building that looked like an ablutions block. A cyclone fence of wire mesh had been erected around the compound. A Toyota HiLux double cab was parked nearby and in the centre of the cleared area was a truck-mounted drilling rig, its boring arm vertical like a mast.

Sonja pulled back into the shade of the stone wall, unslung the Barrett, and unfolded its bipod legs. She set her daypack down beside her and laid out the second magazine Johnsy had supplied with the rifle and some spare loose rounds. She took out a water bottle and drank half its contents.

Through binoculars, Sonja saw two workmen emerge from one of the huts, and a third from the toilet block. One of the men went to the rear of the drilling rig and pushed some buttons, and from across the dry, thorny bushveld between them, Sonja heard the machine rumble into action. The other two men readied themselves near the opening in the earth where the giant drill shaft began spinning.

The noise would act in her favour. Sonja settled down behind the Barrett. This was a case of the right tool for the job. She had already formulated a plan and she set about executing it.

As a curtain-raiser, she swung the weapon's long barrel so that it was pointing at the four-wheel drive. Her first shot went into the fuel tank and, using her binoculars, she confirmed that fuel was pouring from it. Above the far-off whine of the drilling machine she heard the faint blaring of a siren. Sonja realised the heavy thud into the body of the vehicle had triggered its alarm.

For a moment she thought she had lost the element of surprise. One of the workers moved away from the drilling shaft, looked over at the HiLux, and saw that its hazard lights were flashing. He took a set of keys out of his pocket, pushed a button on a fob, and the noise stopped. Perhaps he thought the vibration of the drill rig had set off the alarm – whatever the case, it seemed the men could not hear her gunshots over the noise they were making.

The man, Sonja saw now, was Asian, as was the one controlling the drilling rig. The others, including two more men who exited one of the huts and joined the drilling team, were African. While the Asian men – she guessed they were Chinese – monitored the controls and machinery, the others took it in turns to remove heavy bags of soil excavated by the rig and replace them with fresh sacks.

Sonja found her second target. On top of one of the buildings was a satellite dish. With the workers oblivious to the sound of the rifle, she destroyed their means of communication with the outside world with a single shot.

She smiled to herself. Sitting on the ground next to the administration building was a generator. She put a round into it, and an instant later saw a flash of orange.

Her bullet had hit the fuel tank and, being petrol, it had

ignited, perhaps from a spark. The generator began smoking and this caught the attention of one of the workers, who dropped the bag of soil samples he was carrying from the rig and ran into the nearest building.

Sonja bided her time. Just as she hoped, the man operating the drilling rig left his controls and ran to help with the fire. She shifted her aim to the drill's operating panel and put two rounds into it, in quick succession.

Another African labourer must have seen the bullets impacting because he waved and shouted to the others.

One of the Chinese men went to the HiLux and opened the driver's side door. Even though there was a spreading dark patch on the sandy ground where fuel had been spilling out, there might be enough diesel in the tank for him to reach help and bring reinforcements. Sonja took aim at the right front wheel and squeezed the trigger. The tyre exploded and the man cowered for cover behind the dashboard, now fully aware someone was shooting at him.

Glancing back at the drill, Sonja saw that the drilling arm was still spinning. She took aim at a fat hydraulic hose on the rig and fired but missed. She drew a breath, calmed herself and refocused. The next severed the hose and fluid gushed out and the drill wound down to a stop.

She put the last two rounds of the magazine into what looked like a generator and auxiliary fuel tank on the drilling rig truck and was rewarded with the sight of more diesel fuel spilling out onto the ground.

Sonja set the butt of the Barrett down, rolled onto her side, and quickly changed magazines and cocked the weapon again.

Looking through the binoculars again she saw that the men below were temporarily paralysed by fear and inaction. They had all taken cover where they could. One of the Chinese men peeked from around the corner of the toilet block.

The man in the Toyota opened the door and made a mad dash for the hut with the ruined satellite dish. Sonja liked to think he was desperately trying to contact his superiors.

When he re-emerged, however, it was with what looked like a tentative sense of bravado. He now carried an AK-47 assault rifle. Sonja tracked him through the crosshairs of the telescopic sight. The man had the rifle up, but he was not pointing it directly at her. He clearly had no idea where she was, but he might spy her hill and take a guess. She had to be careful, now. If he had any shooting or military training he might be able to get a fix on her if she fired again.

She was torn between the desire to wreak more havoc and the quiet voice that told her to do the sensible thing, which would be to retreat in good order.

The other Asian man, who had been cowering behind the drilling rig, cautiously emerged from cover and waved to the man with the rifle. The pair came together at the control panel, animatedly checking the damage. They pushed a few buttons and the unarmed man pointed up at the severed hose on the drilling arm.

'That'll teach you,' Sonja said to herself.

The man with the rifle set it down, propping it upright against one of the wheels of the drilling truck.

Sonja couldn't resist. She pulled the butt of the Barrett hard into her shoulder, took aim and squeezed the trigger. The bullet smashed into the AK-47, sending it spinning off into the dirt and, as an added bonus, the round carried on into the tyre, puncturing it. The heavy vehicle settled a few centimetres on the flat. Both men took cover once more, terrified all over again.

Sonja rolled onto her back and looked up at the clear blue sky. She started laughing, safe in the knowledge that no one would hear or see her. It was like a release, knowing that she had got some payback for Hudson and, temporarily at least, stopped this ridiculous prospecting in a national park. Today had gone better than yesterday's attack on the truck, which had been foiled by a stroke of bad luck – the random police patrol.

She felt like her old self again, complete, charged by the smell of cordite and the familiar ache of recoil in her shoulder, warmed by the sun and almost happy that when she made it 'home' there would be people waiting there for her.

Then she saw the helicopter.

*

The Zimbabwe Republic Police Land Rover trundled down the access road to Nantwich.

Sonja had disappeared, and so had Johnsy's horse. Hudson was worried. Riding was not allowed in this part of Hwange National Park and, in any case, he doubted Sonja had headed out on horseback just for fun.

Hudson had heard the approaching engine and came out of his office to investigate. Johnsy was sitting on the *stoep*, a beer and a paperback on the table in front of him. He looked over the top of his sunglasses, bloodshot eyes enquiring.

'Maybe you should make yourself scarce,' Hudson said.

'Me?' Johnsy croaked. 'I'm the victim of a crime here – grand theft horse and rifle. I'm not going anywhere. Besides, I'm incapable.'

Emma had not come down from her room yet. The last stragglers of a big herd of buffalo were wandering off the *vlei*, to the north. Hudson walked out from the shade of the overhanging roof and into the bright sunlight.

The vehicle stopped and Inspector Goodness Khumalo got out. 'Mr Brand.'

He nodded. 'Goodness.'

'Let's keep it formal.' She said something to the uniformed officer who had exited the vehicle from the driver's side. He nodded and squatted down in the shade of a tree next to the lodge building.

'Would you like tea? A cold drink? I'll organise something for your officer, as well,' Hudson said.

She gave a short, sharp shake of her head. 'No, thank you. Where is Miss Sonja Kurtz?'

He spread his hands wide. 'Honestly, I have no idea.'

'She is the woman who came to the police station at Hwange, the one who bailed you out, yes?'

'You've got the paperwork.'

'What is your relationship with this woman, exactly, Mr Brand?'

Good question, he thought. 'To tell you the truth, I'm not exactly sure. We're friends, I guess you'd say.'

'Close friends?'

He shrugged. 'What's this all about, Goodness . . . I mean, Inspector?'

Goodness exhaled, almost as if the business of keeping up a formal exterior was too much for her, or maybe it was an expression of exhaustion, or disappointment. 'Allan Platt was found dead in Victoria Falls the night before last, in a back street near the railway line, not far from the main road.'

'He was?' Hudson was surprised, and instantly worried. Sonja had stayed with Johnsy at the Falls that night, though Hudson was unsure of her timings.

'Is there somewhere we can sit?'

Hudson led her through to the *stoep*. Johnsy had summoned the strength to move away, which was probably for the best.

'Brighton,' Hudson said to Brighton, hovering nearby, 'can I get a cup of coffee, please?' He looked to Goodness.

'All right, tea, please,' she said.

'And take a pitcher of ice water, please, out to the officer under the tree.'

'Sure,' Brighton said.

Hudson gestured to a pair of wicker cane armchairs. They sat as a herd of kudu, four females and a male with spiral horns, walked towards the dam from the far side.

'It is beautiful here,' Goodness said, as if only just noticing.

'What happened to Platt?' Hudson asked.

'Shot in the back of the head. He'd been carrying a pistol by the look of the empty shoulder holster he was wearing under a jacket, but the gun was gone.'

Sonja had shown up with a Makarov, but Brand had assumed Johnsy had sold or loaned her the weapon. She had told him she had cached her own pistol back in South Africa, in a long-term luggage locker at Cape Town airport. 'And you think, what, Sonja shot him to avenge my honour or something like that?'

'Or to stop him testifying against you,' Goodness said. 'I Googled your friend. She's a mercenary.'

He shook his head. An investigative journalist named Rosie Appleton had done a piece on Sonja and a couple of other female private military contractors a few years back and it was critical of them, especially Sonja, questioning their morals. What wasn't mentioned in the magazine article was that Sonja had killed Rosie's then lover, a crooked ex–army officer and poaching kingpin.

'She *was* a PMC, although most of her work was as a body-guard,' Hudson said. 'But semantics aside, executions are not her style. She's a warrior, Goodness, not an assassin.'

'There were signs Platt had been roughed up – bruises, a broken nose, another gunshot wound to his leg and dirt marks on his pants like someone had trod on the wound, maybe torturing him.'

Now *that* sounded more like Sonja. The information about the abalone shipment that she had destroyed had come from Platt. But would she really have killed him? The guy would have been left in fear of her, maybe with even more of a grudge, but unless he'd made a move on her – and a bullet to the back of the head did not indicate that – Hudson knew she would not have shot him in cold blood.

'Has she been acting strange lately?'

Hudson stared out over the dam, watching the kudu, thinking about the question.

'Mr Brand?'

He blinked and looked back to her as Brighton brought a tray with their drinks.

'No,' Hudson lied, 'she's been just fine.'

'Do you have any guests staying here in the lodge at the moment?'

'No.'

Goodness looked over at the table and chair where Johnsy had been and saw the empty glass and green bottle of Zambezi Lager, also empty. 'Getting an early start on the day?'

'Not a guest, just a friend who was here. I'm not sure where he is right now, unless you want to question everyone here.'

Goodness sipped her tea, crossed her legs and regarded him. 'You seem anxious.'

'I do?'

'Where did you go after you were released from the police cells?'

'Straight here. You'll find a record at the entrance gate, where you came in just now, of my time of arrival.'

She nodded. 'I checked already. The gate guard told me he remembered you arriving, after dark. He did you a favour, letting you in.'

'There you go.'

'There is no record of Miss Kurtz entering or leaving the park via the Robins Gate since the morning of the day of your arrest.'

'She drove through the park and exited at Sinamatella,' he said. 'You should find the record there.'

'But she never re-entered?'

He looked her in the eyes. 'Like you said, no record.'

Any debt she owed him had been cancelled by her working overtime to get the magistrate to allow his bail. Goodness stared back at him.

'Where is she?' Goodness tried again.

'I don't know, Goodness, and that is God's honest truth.'

She stared him down for a few seconds, but he didn't blink. 'May I use the bathroom, please?'

He led her inside, through the dining area and past the display kitchen. Enoch, the chef, waved. 'Welcome.'

'Inspector Khumalo's just using the bathroom.'

Hudson opened the door to the courtyard and showed her the bathrooms, then went back out to the *stoep* to wait for her. He did not want to lie to the police, and while he hadn't, technically, he felt himself becoming angry at Sonja for pulling one of her disappearing acts.

He had a pretty good idea where Sonja had gone and mentally kicked himself for bleating again last night about Wu drilling for coal inside Hwange National Park. He thought it likely she'd set off like some cowgirl on another revenge mission. And she'd taken the Barrett with her.

'There is horse manure in your courtyard.'

Hudson turned around and saw Goodness, hands on hips, confronting him.

'Probably a zebra,' he tried. 'They're smart critters. They seek out shelter from the sun and rain; we've even had poop on the *stoep.*'

'So now you're a poet. Tell me what's going on, Brand.'

'I told you, I don't know where –'

'There was a truck ambushed on the road from the Pandamatenga border post yesterday. Someone fired two bullets into the vehicle, one into the fuel tank and another into the radiator, then burned the contents of the vehicle. From what the investigators can so far ascertain, the truck was carrying seafood – dried abalone. The driver of the truck is not saying much.'

'Seafood?'

'Don't play dumb. You must know that this stuff is smuggled into Zimbabwe from South Africa. A police patrol came across the driver of the vehicle and chased the assailants – a man and a woman on horseback.'

He sighed. 'I'm not saying she was here, or that the poop out there is a horse's, but I'll work with you on this, if you want me to.'

'Why should I do that?' she asked him.

He took a deep breath, then exhaled. 'Because I'm a part of this, I think. At least I'm pretty sure I'm responsible.'

'How so, Mr Brand?'

'I've been poking about in Al Platt's affairs, and those of his boss, Wu, who's been drilling for coal. I've heard he's also involved in exporting abalone from Zimbabwe.'

'Are you telling me now that you killed Platt?'

Brand shook his head. 'No, but if he's turned up dead and someone has torched one of Wu's trucks full of abalone, then you can bet someone's going to put two and two together and come up with me. It's the same reason those tusks turned up here. Even you must be able to see that was a frame-up?'

'I believe in evidence and procedure, Mr Brand. That is what solves cases and the verdict is still out on you – but I am listening.'

'Platt was crooked, up to his eyeballs in stuff a lot worse than unethical professional hunting. You know he was a gun runner?'

She gave a small shrug. 'I cannot comment on ongoing investigations.'

'Ongoing?'

She gave a small smile. 'Let's just leave it at that.'

'What about Wu?'

'As you saw from his golf game with the magistrate, Mr Wu is well connected. His company is investing a lot of money in Zimbabwe. We need foreign investment and jobs in this country.'

He shook his head. 'Now you're just towing the party line.'

She lowered her voice. 'If I have evidence of criminal activity, be it poaching or whatever, you know I will act. I think you know me well enough.'

He nodded. 'I do.' She was a good cop, and straight up and down.

'If your girlfriend killed Allan Platt out of revenge over you, she deserves to feel the full weight of the law, Mr Brand, no matter what Platt was up to.'

'Agreed,' he said.

She carried on back out to the courtyard, put the bag inside out and delicately grabbed some chunks of manure.

Goodness was clever – he knew that already – and while

she'd found Count Yorga's manure, she had not gone looking for the horse's tracks. Hudson had been about to do that himself when the police arrived.

'If collecting dung hasn't put you off your tea, shall we at least finish it?' he said.

He escorted her back out to the *stoep* and she placed the sample on the floor, under her chair.

'I'm no fan of the Chinese investors,' she said, sipping her tea. 'They do bring money into the country, but they take out more than they leave. They are stripping our country of natural resources – coal, timber, gold, and our wildlife.'

'You said it, not me,' Brand said.

'Wu has a company involved in abalone export from Zimbabwe. It's a loophole, which I'm sure you know about,' she said.

'It's illegal to export the stuff from South Africa to Zimbabwe, but legal for it to be shipped out of Harare.'

She nodded. 'The vehicle that came through Pandamatenga should not have used that crossing; it's meant for tourist and private traffic only, not commercial freight. Also, the driver was unable to provide any paperwork for his cargo.'

Hudson felt for the guy – shot at by Sonja with a modern-day blunderbuss and then arrested by the cops.

'The driver is not going to talk. I'm convinced of it; he's too scared. I do believe he'd rather go to Chikurubi than tell us who his bosses are.'

'Serious?' Chikurubi was a notorious maximum-security prison in the capital, Harare. Hudson had spent a short amount of time there once himself – it was no picnic. 'He must be scared.'

'Victoria Falls is our number-one tourist town, as you know, and has a reputation for being safe. I've got a safari guide-cum-hunter with a bullet in his head in the morgue. I'm under incredible pressure to solve this case.' She set her cup down. 'You could help me.'

He raised his eyebrows. 'How so?'

'You want to see Wu's mining company stopped from exploiting in the national park, yes?'

'You bet.' Brand gestured out to the kudu, who were now drinking. 'Otherwise it's the end of all this. No wildlife, no tourists; no tourists, no money – and that's money that would stay in the country.'

'Then help me.'

'As I said, I'm willing to work with you,' he said.

'Even if it's your girlfriend who killed Platt?'

'It wasn't,' he said.

'Are you sure?'

Hudson looked out over the dam.

CHAPTER 11

The helicopter came in low, following the contours of the earth, heading towards the mining exploration camp. Sonja took a quick look at the compound through her binoculars and now noticed that the man who had been cowering in the HiLux was talking into a radio handset.

She had no time to chide herself. If she'd thought more about alternative means of communication she might have tried to put a couple of .50-calibre rounds into the dashboard of the *bakkie*, through the windscreen, but it would have taken a lucky shot to neutralise a target as small as a radio set, and she did not want to kill the man who had been hiding in the cab.

She gathered up the empty magazine and spare ammunition, stuffed them in her daypack and folded the Barrett's bipod legs. She looked for cover; the circle of stones would conceal her – a tree shaded the ruin as well – and would give her some protection if anyone started shooting at her. Sonja crawled inside. She could also observe the compound below through chinks in the rock wall.

The helicopter slowed to a hover near the compound and the man in the HiLux was now brave enough to stand outside the vehicle. He had pulled the handset cord to its full extension and was talking and gesticulating, pointing her way, up the crest of the hill where she was sheltering.

'Shit,' she said to herself. They had got a bead on her. Trapped in the ruined enclave was a deep pile of dried mopane leaves; she scooped up handfuls of them and spread them over herself as she burrowed into the litter.

The helicopter pilot dipped the nose of the aircraft and headed her way. It was a small machine, a Robinson, she thought. It buzzed towards her like an angry red wasp and went into an orbit as it approached her hill.

Sonja lay dead still, knowing that movement, more than anything else, would give her away. The chopper went around once, then again, then moved off, tracking the same way as she had approached. She crawled to the opening of the circular redoubt and risked a glance around the wall.

Count Yorga obviously had no inclination to stand still; if anything, he was probably spooked by the low-flying helicopter. Sonja couldn't see the horse, but she could tell where he was and cursed as the helicopter went into a hover and then began descending. She lost sight of the Robinson as it dipped beneath the brow of a hill in between her and where she'd left the Count, but she remembered, clearly, the open grassy area near the tree where she had tethered him.

'Shit,' she said again. They were going to do what she would have done, cut off the enemy's escape route. She prayed they didn't shoot the horse, but rather just untied it and gave it a slap on its rump. Count Yorga, however, was the least of her problems now.

Her mind raced.

Her options were few.

In case of an ambush, the drill she had learned as a young soldier was to turn into the hail of fire and charge the enemy. It was counterintuitive, but there was method in the madness of the instructors who'd taught her.

She figured she only had a couple of minutes before the

helicopter was back in the air. Sonja stood, shrugged on her daypack and hefted the Barrett. She charged down the hill, towards the drilling encampment.

For a start, this was the last place those on the chopper would be expecting her to head. Secondly, the men on the ground would, hopefully, still be shaken and in disarray. If any of them found a weapon and tried to shoot her, then they would be fair game for her and her .50-calibre elephant gun.

Running downhill was hard on her bad knee, but Sonja's overdrive was being injected with adrenaline. Even so, she scanned her front and watched where she placed her feet. She could not afford a twisted ankle, especially carrying the significant weight of the rifle.

Behind her, though she did not dare to stop to look, she heard the whine of the helicopter's engine spooling up. Unencumbered she could still crank out a kilometre in five and a half minutes, but with her pack and rifle it would be more like six. With seven hundred metres to cover to the compound she mentally counted down the time she had left. Quite what she would do when she got there, she didn't know, but at least she was moving – to sit still and do nothing was to die.

She briefly thought of Emma and Hudson. She was here, indirectly, because of both of them. If she was going to be killed today then she would make it her mission to take down the threat to them.

Sonja ignored the sting of dried, thorny branches whipping her arms and face and the pain in her joints. Her arms ached from carrying the weighty firearm, but she blocked that out too.

Ahead of her, through the leafless winter trees, she made out the fence of the compound and the first of the drill site buildings. The structure shielded her from view of the men still milling about the compound.

Sonja dropped to her knees as she reached the fence and set down the Barrett. She took her Leatherman from the pouch on her belt and used the wire-cutter blades at the base of the plier jaws to snip a vertical line through the diamond mesh fence. When she had cut a metre-long slit she pushed the rifle through then crawled after it; the bare metal ends of the links ripped her shirt and drew blood, but she felt nothing.

Cradling the Barrett in her arms she leopard-crawled through the dried yellow grass until she reached the first building, which was the portable shower and toilet block. Above her she heard the increasing crescendo of the approaching helicopter engine and actually felt the first of the rotor downwash on the backs of her thighs and calves as she crawled under the raised building.

Dust billowed around her as she edged towards the other side of the building, where she could view what was happening in the compound. The Robinson settled just outside the perimeter fence.

A man in camouflage fatigues jumped down from the chopper. From his gait and pace it looked like he was pissed off. He marched to one of the Chinese workers, the man who had been operating the radio, Sonja thought.

The worker stood smartly to attention, making Sonja wonder if he was also military. The man in uniform slapped the worker in the face, hard enough for the other man to reel back and have to fight to keep his balance. A stream of what sounded like shouted abuse in Mandarin followed.

Sonja looked around. The three African men were standing back, out of reach. When the angry man in uniform turned on them, they all took a further step backwards.

Sonja wondered if this was Carrington Wu.

The other Chinese man came to him and saluted. Sonja was now sure the newly arrived man was the boss, and he was not happy. He gesticulated to the drilling rig and the others followed him to the machine. He was shown where the damage had been inflicted and the group then walked to the HiLux where the boss squatted down and inspected the sizable bullet hole Sonja had punched in the fuel tank. He stood, looked around and shielded his eyes to look up at the hill where she had been based.

Then she clearly heard him say the word 'Barrett' amid another sentence spoken in his own language.

'You!' The boss went over to the tallest of the African men and stabbed a finger in his chest. 'You track.'

The man nodded.

'Now!'

'Must we walk to the hill? There are some ruins there,' the African man said.

The boss rubbed his chin and looked around him again.

'No. Start here, immediately around our perimeter,' he said, switching to English for the benefit of the locals. 'We saw no sign of the shooter from the air. I suspect he or she may be close.'

'She?' said the Zimbabwean.

The man nodded. 'There was an incident near the Botswana border yesterday. A truck was fired on by someone with a heavy-calibre rifle. The police gave chase and believe that it could even be a woman.'

The African shook his head incredulously, as if he did not believe such a thing was possible.

Sonja felt a grudging respect for the boss – he was clearly not someone to be underestimated. A blind man would find her tracks into the compound. She had to think fast.

The two local men and one of the Chinese workers, who seemed to have found an undamaged AK-47, walked out of the compound via the main gate and started circling back around the fence, towards where Sonja had entered. They would find the hole she had made in the next few minutes.

Sonja dragged the Barrett up beside her and unfolded the bipod. She needed a diversion, and quickly.

The other Chinese worker and the boss were standing in the open, in the centre of the compound not twenty metres from where she was lying. She could kill them both in a few seconds, but that was not a realistic course of action. Soon there would be men behind her, either crawling under the building, if they were stupid, or spraying the cavity with automatic rifle fire.

Outside the compound the helicopter's rotor blades were slowly coming to a full stop. Over her shoulder, Sonja could see the legs of the men who were walking around the perimeter, looking for her tracks. They were moving to the far side of the administration building. Quickly, leaving the Barrett, she crawled out from under the ablutions block on the side closest to the perimeter fence. Along that wall were two large, forty-eight-kilogram gas bottles, which fed an externally mounted instantaneous gas hot water heater. Also protruding from the wall were outlet pipes, for washbasins inside the building.

Sonja wrenched one of the PVC downpipes from the wall, exposing the open outlet. Next, she checked the regulator atop the gas bottles. A quick shake of the bottles confirmed each was full, or almost full. Only one bottle supplied the heater at a time, so she unscrewed the rubber hose leading to the bottle that was not being used and pushed the end of the hose into the open outlet pipe. Next she flipped the regulator switch over and opened the cock on top of the bottle. Gas began shushing out, under high pressure, into the water outlet pipe.

Sonja made her way along the back wall of the building until she came to a window. She slid it open and found a shelf above a sink, with a roll of paper towel. She lifted out the towel, tore off several sheets and wadded them. Then she took her cigarette lighter from her pocket and held it to the paper until it caught. Once it was burning she reached up again, tossed the burning towel into an empty basin and closed the window.

Sonja dropped to her belly, crawled as fast as she could back under the building to where she had left the rifle and folded the bipod legs, ready to make a run for it.

The boss finished berating the underling then came towards the ablutions block. Sonja hardly dared to breathe as his booted feet came within a metre of her face. She shook her head; he would smell the gas and see the burning paper inside – assuming it hadn't gone out – and she would lose the value of her diversion.

She grabbed the pistol grip of the Barrett, ready to go out fighting, taking whatever and whomever she could with her.

'Goodbye, Emma, my love,' she whispered, in case her plan failed completely. She closed her eyes and thought of Brand.

As the boss opened the door to the toilet block, the burning paper ignited the gas and the building exploded. Windows shattered and blew outwards and Sonja saw the man thrown backwards, off his feet, and land on his rear end in the sand of the compound.

Sonja had her diversion. She crawled from under the building, emerging in the centre of the compound, dragging the Barrett, then picked it up with her left hand. She needed to get to the chopper as fast as possible. She drew Platt's Makarov pistol as she ran across the open ground and fired two shots at the remaining Chinese guy, who made a move towards her. He was unarmed, so she sent the rounds over his head; he fell to the ground, scrabbling at the sand with his fingers.

Sonja made it to the helicopter, where the pilot was climbing out of the cockpit.

'Get back in!' She pointed the pistol at him.

The man stared at her, wide-eyed, then raised his hands. 'Don't shoot.'

'For fuck's sake, start this thing and I won't have to.' She backed up to the co-pilot's seat and started to slide her bottom in, her gun hand still menacing the poor pilot. As well as being heavy, the Barrett was an exceptionally long rifle and Sonja was struggling to get it into the cramped cockpit one-handed.

The boss was on his feet. He shrugged off the other man, who had made it to him and was fussing over him, and started coming towards Sonja. Likewise, the man who had taken the Africans in search of Sonja's tracks had returned to the entrance of the compound. He pointed his AK-47 towards them, perhaps not sure whether he should fire on the helicopter or not.

The boss ran to the man with the assault rifle and took it from him.

The helicopter's engine began to whine and the blades over Sonja's head started to turn.

'Come on, come on!'

The pilot nodded as his shaking hands roamed over his control panel.

The boss opened fire, a burst of three rounds on automatic. Sonja heard one round hit the fuselage of the helicopter behind her, but another went through the fabric of her bush shirt and grazed her left arm. It wasn't a serious injury, but it hurt and surprised her enough to make her drop the Barrett; the rifle tumbled out of the cockpit onto the ground.

The pilot, now seeing that his former passenger had no qualms about shooting at him, lifted off.

Sonja twisted in her seat and fired down towards the boss with her pistol, but the pilot was banking away, spoiling her aim. She looked back at him. 'Get us the hell out of here.'

'I'm with you!' Any need for coercion was long gone.

Sonja leaned out of her side – the doors had been removed from the chopper, which she guessed was probably for sightseeing reasons – and the slipstream tugged at her ponytail. Pulling herself back in, she sank with relief into the co-pilot's seat.

However, although the pilot was beginning to put distance between them and the compound, Sonja now saw that the boss had discarded the AK-47 and picked up the anti-materiel rifle. He had it braced on the roof of the HiLux.

'Evasive action!' she yelled.

'What?'

Sonja leaned over and rammed her hand against the cyclic control, forcing the helicopter to lurch violently to the right. 'He's still fucking shooting at us.'

The pilot began to protest, but a .50-calibre slug erupted up through the cockpit floor, between Sonja's legs, and smashed a fist-sized chunk out of the clear Perspex front canopy. The pilot got the hint and pushed his controls down and to the left.

Sonja buckled her safety harness as they dived and closed her eyes.

'Emma,' she whispered to herself.

They would be all right, she told herself. Every second they were moving out of the boss's range.

Bang. Bang.

'Shit!' The pilot checked his gauges.

Sonja had felt the two sickening blows to the airframe.

The pilot was levelling out.

'What's happening?' Sonja smelled smoke.

A siren was sounding inside the cockpit as they began to lose height.

'I've lost control. Autorotating. Brace, brace, brace!' The pilot then made a mayday call over his radio.

'For fuck's sake.' Sonja stuck her pistol back in her belt, put her head down, chin on chest, and grasped the sides of her seat. In her peripheral vision she was aware of the sight of the ground rushing up to meet her.

Sonja heard another gunshot and was spattered with blood and gore as the top of the pilot's head disappeared.

*

Emma, Hudson and Johnsy had decided to go looking for Sonja, as soon as Goodness Khumalo left and Emma discovered her mother missing. The three of them, guided by Hudson, followed Sonja's footprints and Count Yorga's hoof marks up and over the hill at Nantwich Lodge and far enough out on the open *vlei* beyond for Hudson to be sure of his theory.

Emma was feeling angry at her mother. After Goodness was gone, Hudson had told her about the man being killed in Victoria Falls and Emma felt Hudson had been too charitable when he said Sonja was innocent until proven guilty. Two people who had threatened the people Sonja loved had both ended up with a bullet in the head.

They had been walking for less than half an hour, but Emma's shirt was already soaked with sweat. Hudson stopped, then turned around.

'Let's head back,' he said.

'You know where she's gone?' Emma asked. She had been trying to learn as much as she could about tracking from him as they walked.

'Yep. She's headed for the drilling site,' he said as they started making their way back to the lodge.

A pair of reedbuck watched them from a distance and the male snorted a high-pitched, squeaky warning call as he and his mate took off. Their hooves raised puffs of grey ash from beneath the bright green grass shoots that had popped up after a recent fire.

'You're sure?' Emma said.

Hudson held up his wristwatch. 'I punched in the coordinates for where the Chinese have been looking for coal and the horse's path has been following the exact course since we left the lodge. Sonja and I were talking about the impact of a mine in the national park last night. I think your mom's doing this for me, dammit.'

'*Ja*, she could do a helluva lot of damage to a drilling rig with that Barrett of mine,' Johnsy said. 'I told her, if she gets caught with it and tells them it's mine then it's tickets for me in this country.'

Emma wanted to tell Johnsy to think less about his rifle and more about Sonja, but she could also see it from his side. Her mother's impetuous need for revenge would not only land her in trouble; there would be collateral damage.

'What do we do?' Emma asked.

'I'm going to drive to the drilling compound, see if I can find her, or stop her, or whatever.'

'I want my horse back, and my gun,' Johnsy said.

'And what about me?' Emma said.

Hudson waved a hand. 'You stay at the lodge until we get back, Emma. I need you to keep an ear out in case she calls or shows up out of nowhere.'

Emma stopped. 'No.'

Hudson carried on walking. 'I don't want to risk losing you as well.'

When she didn't answer he and Johnsy eventually stopped and looked back.

'Emma . . .'

She put her hands on her hips and glared at him.

Hudson sighed. 'Come on, now, we've got to get back.'

She nodded. 'Yes, and when we do, you're taking me with you. I'm not a kid, you know, Hudson. For God's sake, I'm nearly thirty and I know how to shoot a gun. Whose daughter do you think I am, anyway?'

Hudson locked eyes with her, but Johnsy snorted and grinned. 'I don't think there's any doubt which tree this rosy little apple fell out of.'

She looked to Johnsy. 'Careful.'

He held up his hands in mock surrender.

'I need a gun,' she said to Johnsy.

'Whoa there, little lady,' he said, trying to imitate Hudson's accent, 'come on now, we've got to get back.'

She wagged a finger at them. 'You two better start taking me seriously.'

Hudson sighed. 'OK, maybe it would be better if you were with me. I can keep an eye on you.'

'I'm not your fucking child, Brand.'

Hudson looked to Johnsy, who looked back at him and mouthed the word *Brand*. The men set off, making plans between themselves as they walked.

Emma stomped after them. They were treating her like a kid, but she also realised she had just called Hudson by his surname; that was how her mother always addressed him, even though they were lovers. Was she turning into her mother? She fumed as she followed in their wake.

They walked back to the lodge. Emma stopped in her room to quickly prepare a daypack with a fleece, beanie and leggings, in case they were out late, as well as her binoculars and a water bottle. When she made it down to the main lodge building, as quickly as she could in case the men decided to drive off and abandon her, she found them preparing for war. They stood either side of the dining table on the *stoep*. Hudson was loading a magazine for his Colt .45 and Johnsy was racking a Glock 19.

'I'm just going to the bathroom.' Emma went through the door at the rear of the lounge, but instead of heading to the toilet she deviated right into the manager's office, where Johnsy had spent the previous night. There was an open rucksack. Emma quickly rummaged through it until she felt the angular steel shape of a pistol.

It was a Browning nine millimetre, old, probably ex-military, she thought. As a battlefield archaeologist Emma knew a thing or two about weapons, but unbeknown to Sonja she had also paid attention to her mother's life and times. As far as Sonja knew, Emma disdainfully abhorred her choice of occupation, but Emma's guilty secret was that she had scoured the internet as she grew older, searching for information to fill in the gaps in Sonja's story.

She'd found a book about a woman who had served in the British Army and joined 14 Intelligence Company, and then gone on to work undercover against the Irish Republican Army in Northern Ireland. She'd found websites devoted to mercenaries and even old copies of *Soldier of Fortune* magazine on eBay that recounted, with almost sycophantic devotion on the part of the journalists, the exploits of guns-for-hire in Sierra Leone and other conflict zones where Sonja had worked.

Emma did not aspire to be like her mother; she wanted to understand what drove someone to follow a path such as hers. As she racked the Browning to check it was clear, then fished about in the pack for a couple of magazines full of ammunition, she now wondered if she perhaps wanted some of the excitement Sonja had experienced in her life.

Emma slapped one magazine into the butt of the pistol and pocketed the second. She tucked the pistol into the waistband of her jeans, then untucked her blouse so it covered the weapon. Johnsy would eventually notice the Browning was missing, but that was his problem. Emma left the room and went to the bathroom. By the time she came out, Johnsy and Hudson were ready to go.

'Johnsy's got his horse trailer and vehicle parked just outside the national park, hidden in the bush, so we'll drop him there. You'll come with me,' Hudson said to her, 'and we'll call Johnsy if and when we find his horse.'

They took one of the Land Cruiser game viewers, dropped Johnsy at the nearby entrance gate so he could walk the short distance to his vehicle, then headed deeper into Hwange National Park, via Robins Camp.

Hudson looked grim as he drove. He sat on the speed limit, the warm air rushing through the open vehicle.

'Why do you care so much about her?' Emma said into the silence.

He looked over at her. 'I love her.'

'She treats you like shit,' Emma said.

Hudson returned his eyes to the road and said nothing for a while, as if considering this. 'I've never met anyone like her.'

'She's a one-off, all right. Is that the attraction, her – what – uniqueness?'

He shrugged. 'She's the toughest woman I've come across in my life, hell, a better warrior than most men I served with. But there's also a fragility about her.'

'"Fragile"? Not a word I'd use to describe my mother.' *Unbalanced, maybe*, she thought.

'Brittle, then.'

Emma nodded. 'You think she's going to break? Or maybe, has snapped? For real?'

He chewed his lower lip as he drove, but didn't answer.

The pistol dug into the small of Emma's back, but she didn't dare move or adjust it, in case Hudson saw it and forced her to hand it over. As uncomfortable as it was, there was something reassuring about its heavy bulk next to her body. She regarded Hudson in her peripheral vision as the vehicle rattled along the corrugated gravel road, still trying to work out the connection between them.

She guessed Hudson could have had his pick of women, but why had he chosen Sonja? Her mother clearly didn't want to settle down to a quiet suburban existence, so maybe that was the key. Sonja went through the motions of being nice and playing house sometimes, but Emma guessed that she was more at home as she was now, out in the middle of nowhere, on a stolen horse with a gun. Brand might be fine with that, but where did it leave her daughter?

Would things have been different between her and Sonja, Emma wondered, if her mother had married younger and had another child? The fact that she hadn't made Emma think that her mother had few innate maternal instincts and led her to question, once again, whether her mother resented the fact that Emma had come along.

'Has my mum ever talked to you about my father?'

Hudson glanced at her again. 'Only in passing. I asked her, early on, if your dad was still on the scene.'

'And what did she say?'

'That he was a truck driver in Northern Ireland. They'd met when she was on operations there, with the British Army, but he died in the Troubles. I didn't push it.'

Emma bit her lower lip. Sonja had clearly told Hudson just enough to make him not want to ask more – even the slightly theatrical reference to 'the Troubles'. The fact was, Sonja had been in Ulster in 1994, serving undercover in the British Army's intelligence corps. Emma's father, Danny Byrne, was her target, the supposed mastermind of a horrific bomb attack. According to Sonja, while Danny had been a member of an extreme IRA splinter group, he'd had enough of the struggle and wanted out of the movement. It was his brother, Patrick, who had been responsible for planting the bomb. Sonja learned all this by getting close – too close – to Danny, but both the Byrne brothers were killed in a raid by the British SAS. Nine months after Sonja met Danny, Emma was born.

Emma gave Hudson a sympathetic smile. 'It's OK, Hudson. She told me it was a one-night stand. She only found out he was dead after she learned she was pregnant and started asking around. For a while she thought my father might have been another guy she started sleeping with around the same time, her former commander, a British SAS officer.'

Hudson raised his eyebrows. That bit, it seemed, was news to him.

'Don't worry,' Emma added, 'he was a creep.'

'Are you looking for some kind of pattern here, Emma?'

She laughed. 'No. You're a non-creep, like –'

'Sam. She sure loved him.'

Emma thought she caught a note of regret, perhaps even jealousy. 'You and he were alike, where it counted,' she said. 'Kind. And she gave him plenty of shit as well.'

He exhaled and smiled. 'Thanks. I think your mom's the once bitten, twice shy type. She gave her heart to Sam; now she's so scared of getting it broken again that she keeps it locked up – at least part of it.'

And yet, Emma thought, Hudson had stuck with her. She didn't know whether that said more about Hudson or her mother.

'Are you trying to save her, Hudson?'

He mulled that over. 'I think in some ways she saved me. I wasn't always "kind", as you put it. I drank too much, broke too many hearts myself, and ended up hurt. The things we do, the stuff we see . . .'

'In the military?'

He nodded. 'And even just in life, on this continent. Those things change us, stay with us long after we think they're done. I think your mom and I found each other at the right time.' He looked over and smiled at her. 'She just doesn't know it yet.'

'I hear you.'

Emma thought of what she knew about where Sonja had served and worked as a contractor, and the things she must have seen and done. She knew only a fraction, a snippet picked up from a conversation here and there, a shouted line from a nightmare, a mention in a newspaper article.

The question was not whether Sonja's experiences had affected her, but how much. Had it all finally become too much for her? Sonja struggled with her demons all the time – that was clear for anyone close to her to see. It manifested itself in her temper, her drinking and her inability to form or maintain close attachments.

However, had Sonja crossed the line from warrior and protective mother bear to murderer?

CHAPTER 12

Sonja came to in near total darkness, a chink of light just enough to illuminate a smokescreen of dust particles whirling around her.

She was encased in a rattling tin box, her ears assaulted by the bang and shudder of metal on metal. Sonja reached out and pounded on walls less than a metre on either side of her. She kicked away, but met similar resistance at the other end.

And it stank. Of fish or old seafood.

As disoriented as she was, she realised she was in a vehicle, probably low down given the pounding her body was taking as the wheels bounced over corrugated roads. A pothole or deep rut caused the truck to become almost airborne and she felt herself lifted then slammed down. Her head hurt and she felt nauseous. In her mind was the memory of falling, a robotic warning voice inside the cockpit of a helicopter, the rush of the ground coming up to meet her.

Her world went black again.

*

Hudson had planned on parking off in the bush some way from the drilling site and walking in, with Emma, to take a look at the place from the hill nearby, the one with the historical rock ruins on the summit.

The plan changed, however, as the green Zimbabwe Parks and Wildlife Authority Land Rover came around the bend towards him and flashed its lights, indicating he should stop.

'Prosper, how are you?' he said as the man in khaki uniform pulled up next to him.

Prosper Sibanda, the area manager for this part of the park, was normally a smiler, but he looked grim. 'I am fine, and you?' He didn't even wait for the customary reply before continuing, 'The police, they are at the drilling compound.'

'What's happened?'

'Someone has caused a great deal of damage, and a person has been killed.'

'Male or female?' The words tumbled out; Emma was wide-eyed.

'A man, a helicopter pilot.'

Hudson closed his eyes for a second, then opened them.

'There is a detective there, from Hwange, Inspector Khumalo. She told me she had been to see you, and asked me some questions about a woman and a horse. Is there something you need to tell me, Hudson?'

He shook his head. 'No, Prosper. Nothing at all.'

'You know, of course, that it's illegal for people to be on horseback in this part of the national park. Permits are needed for that sort of thing.'

'I understand. I know the rules, Prosper.'

He pursed his lips. 'Just make sure you continue to follow them, my friend, and we will have no problem.'

'Of course. You said something about a horse?'

Prosper nodded. 'Yes, we found a horse, wandering in the bush. One of my men can ride – he's taken it to Sinamatella. I don't suppose you know who the owner might be?'

'Um, no.' Hudson said. 'Are there many police there now?'

'Yes. They are searching the area. They think someone was shooting from the hill with the ruins.'

'I see. Thanks, Prosper. Have a nice day now.'

'You as well.' Prosper engaged gear and drove off.

'What do we do now?' Emma asked.

'Well, we've lost the element of surprise. I think we'd better go see what your mom's been up to.'

Emma nodded.

They drove on, taking a recently graded road with a *No entry* sign.

The drilling site had been a surprise even for Prosper and the rest of the rangers in this part of Hwange National Park. It was such a big, wild expanse of Africa that the Chinese miners and their labourers had been able to set up, truck in their demountable buildings and start drilling well before they were detected. Hudson drove along the access road, and the open gate of the compound, which was now filled with three police vehicles, came into view.

'Smoke,' Emma said.

Hudson looked to where she was pointing, off to the west.

As they pulled up Hudson saw Goodness Khumalo emerge from one of the site's portable buildings. Hudson had visited the compound a couple of times in the past, when organising his protest activities, and he noticed that the satellite dish on top of the office had been destroyed. He knew what sort of rifle did that kind of damage.

Hudson pulled over just outside the perimeter fence and turned off the engine. Both he and Emma got out.

'We meet again,' Goodness said to him as she approached them. 'Miss Kurtz.' She nodded to Emma.

'Hello, Inspector,' Emma said.

'What's gone on here?' Hudson asked.

Goodness put her hands on her hips. 'You tell me.' She pointed over to the column of smoke in the distance. 'A helicopter was shot down and the pilot killed by a large-calibre, high-powered rifle, and this drilling camp was rendered useless, probably by the same weapon judging by the holes and damage everywhere.

Also, someone got into this compound and blew up the toilet and shower block.'

'Suspect?' Hudson asked.

'Maybe the same woman who shot up and burned a tourist truck smuggling abalone on the Pandamatenga Road, using a big gun, Mr Brand. What do you think?'

'Similar weapon used in both incidents?' Hudson asked, already knowing the answer beyond a shadow of a doubt.

Goodness looked to the hill overlooking the compound. 'You know the ruins up there?'

He nodded.

'Someone with a .50-calibre sniper rifle,' she pulled a plastic bag from her jacket pocket and showed them an empty brass casing the length of Hudson's middle finger, 'the sort of thing the American military uses, opened up on the camp from up there. The shooter, either a small man or a woman judging by the size of the boot imprints, then came down here, cut the fence of the compound and crawled under the ablutions building. We think they then came out shooting and took down the chopper from here.'

Hudson closed his eyes for a second. 'Who called this in, Goodness?'

'The company that owns the downed helicopter. The pilot sent a mayday just before he went down and they called parks and wildlife, who called me. There are the footprints of several people all over this compound, and some tyre treads, but there's only one body, the pilot.'

'Where's the shooter?' Emma asked.

Goodness shrugged. 'We haven't found tracks leading from here, yet, but whoever this was knows the bush, and probably knows a thing or two about counter-tracking strategies. My men are searching, but they are not expert trackers. Where is your mother, young lady?'

Emma squared up to the detective. 'I don't know.'

Goodness turned to Hudson. 'And yet you, the friend of this

mystery woman, and her daughter, show up at my crime scene. Why is that? What brought you to this very site, here and now, in the wake of this slaughter?'

Hudson was rendered temporarily speechless, his mind reeling.

'Can we see the tracks, please?' Emma asked.

Goodness regarded her.

'We'll be careful,' Hudson said, 'not to trample anything.'

'This is a police crime scene.'

'Goodness,' he lowered his voice so the other nearby officers wouldn't hear, 'you and I go back a ways. We may be looking for the same person. Like we said this morning, let me help you, OK? I promise not to get in the way.'

She exhaled. 'Before I do, I want you to tell me everything you know about this female friend of yours.'

Hudson knew he would have to give her something. 'Let's walk.'

They moved away from the others, although Emma followed them. Goodness pointed to the fence line closest to the hill. 'She came down and snipped through the wire there.'

'I wonder why . . . someone,' Emma checked herself, probably, Hudson thought, because she had almost followed Goodness's lead and said *she*, 'would come into the compound if they were sitting up on a hill shooting?'

Hudson, hands on hips, looked up at the hill, then to the fence. 'Counter-ambush drill.'

'What is that?' Goodness asked.

'You run into the danger, not away from it – it's the last thing your enemy expects you to do.'

'So your friend has military training,' Goodness said.

'Let's be clear,' Hudson said, 'I am not saying that I know who did this, or why that person was here. For the record, I was doing OK lobbying the government to review the lease on this drilling operation and to have it shut down. I did not, and would not, advocate sending someone with a gun here to shoot the shit out of this place.'

Goodness nodded. 'For what it's worth, I believe you, but I currently have four crime scenes – a dead elephant not far from here, the shooting death of Allan Platt in Victoria Falls, this mess, and a shot-up, burned-out truck full of fried abalone near Pandamatenga – with you as the only common denominator, Hudson.'

'I didn't shoot the elephant.' She had at least dropped the 'Mr Brand' routine, he noted. Hudson looked at the ground. He could see where Sonja had crawled under the first of the buildings.

'She hid under there,' Goodness said, following his eyes. 'Then emerged from the other side, into the centre of the compound.'

Hudson cast about the compound and saw a crime scene marker, a stick in the ground with a small flag attached. Next to it were what looked like two .50-calibre cartridges.

'There are signs on the ground, indentations, showing where a helicopter landed,' Goodness said.

Hudson pointed to the brass casings. 'And someone here shot it down.' Hudson could see a pair of policemen walking through the bush, looking at the ground as they walked. 'Have they found any tracks yet?'

'No,' Goodness said. 'But we will.'

'You think she swept the ground as she left? Really?'

Goodness shrugged. 'At first I thought she might still be here, somewhere,' she gestured around her, 'but we have searched everywhere and it is, as you say, a small camp.'

Hudson walked across the open square between the buildings. He noticed footprints leading out the open gate, past the wrecked HiLux, along the access road and then into the bush, towards the smoke. 'And these?'

'My men and I walked to the site of the crashed helicopter.'

'Tell me, Goodness, where was the chopper hit? What part of the airframe?'

Goodness frowned and paused, but must have decided it couldn't hurt to tell him. 'It looked like one round entered from below and to the rear, exiting through the front of the cockpit and smashing some stuff on the way through. Two other shots went into the engine from behind, and the pilot was hit in the head.'

'Thanks.' Hudson started to follow the tracks left by Goodness and her officers, with Emma trailing him.

'That's also a crime scene,' Goodness called, though she did not follow him because one of her officers was hovering nearby, clearly waiting to talk to her.

Emma quickened her pace to catch up to Hudson. 'What do you think?'

'There's plenty not right about this,' he said as they walked side by side, following the tracks.

'Yeah, like my mother shooting up a mining camp and a helicopter, for a start,' Emma said.

Hudson shook his head. 'Nope. That doesn't make any sense; no way would Sonja shoot down a civilian chopper. I get why she might have come down off the hill and snuck into the camp – that's the last thing they would have expected her to do. But why would she break cover from under the building and then get up and shoot down a helicopter that was flying away from her?'

'How do you know it was flying away, and not towards her?'

He raised a hand to point to the smoke. 'Look how far it is. That Barrett rifle's got a hell of a range on it, and from what Goodness said the chopper was hit from below and behind – it was bugging out of here. If the helicopter wasn't orbiting overhead, with someone shooting at her, why would Sonja waste ammo shooting down a civilian chopper trying to get away? It doesn't make sense. Also, there are none of her tracks leading from the compound.'

'Yeah,' Emma said, 'that is weird. You don't think she just covered her tracks?'

'No. If what Goodness says is true then Sonja had just shot down a chopper and killed a man in cold blood. It's not like she was going to carefully creep away, sweeping the ground behind her with a branch or something. No, there has to be another explanation, and if there were witnesses, they've all vanished.'

They cut through the bush, the smell of smoke becoming stronger in their nostrils. Through some mopane they came to a clearing, a depression which would have held water during the wet season but was now like a dusty bowl in the bush, its centre nothing but dried, cracked mud. It had obviously looked like the perfect place for the pilot to try a forced landing.

A Zimbabwe Republic Police officer was using a fire extinguisher, presumably from the stricken helicopter in front of them, to put out the last embers of a grass fire.

The chopper was on its side, its blades snapped off and lying in the dust. The fire, Hudson saw, had started where the engine or exhaust had hit some tufts of grass at the edge of the clearing. The tail boom had slammed into some stunted mopane trees. The fire looked worse than it really was and the absence of ground cover meant that it would have petered out naturally.

The officer came to them. 'This is a crime scene, who are you?'

'How are you?' Hudson took out his wallet and withdrew a business card, which he handed to the policeman.

'I am fine.' The officer read the card. 'Hudson Brand, Investigator?'

'Zimbabwe Civil Aviation Authority,' he lied. 'I'm working with Inspector Khumalo on this case. My colleague and I got here as quick as we could. Goodness knows we're here. We just need to take a look around.'

'Ah. All right,' the man said.

Hudson nodded his thanks and went to the cockpit. He held up a hand to keep Emma back. 'You maybe don't want to come around here.'

The pilot was still strapped into his seat, though someone, presumably a police officer, had covered his body with a green plastic rain poncho. The interior of the cockpit was sprayed with blood.

Emma came up behind him and stopped short. 'I need to –'
She walked away, into the bushes, and was sick.

Hudson started circling the wreck. He stopped and looked
over the engine area, then got down on one knee to check underneath. There, punched into the metal skin, was a hole he could
put his finger into. From the location and entry angle, which he
confirmed by feeling inside the hole and noting the way the metal
had been bent, he was now sure, as Goodness had also deduced,
that the chopper had been flying away from the shooter.

Running his hand over the panels some more he found a second
bullet hole. Oil was oozing from this one and had sprayed out over
the skin of the aircraft – the killer blow for this flying machine.
The trajectory was more or less the same. If Sonja hadn't shot
down this helicopter, then someone who was an equally good
shot had done so. He wondered if the shooter had intended to
kill the pilot as well.

He stood and dusted off his hands and knees and continued
on to the front of the Robinson. There were three holes here, in
the Perspex canopy, one round entering from below by the look
of the damage inside and the bullet's trajectory. From its location
and the presence of blood, Hudson guessed the third hole was
where the bullet that killed the pilot had exited; at a guess, he
thought the projectile might have come through the open side
of the cockpit, where the door had been removed. Hudson got
up on his toes and, steadying himself by holding on to one skid,
looked inside.

The passenger's seatbelt was unclipped. Did that mean
anything? he wondered. If there was no passenger, would the belt
have been left unclipped or fastened? On the headrest he noted a
long strand of hair, which he took.

Hudson boosted himself up with two hands and leaned as
far as he could into the interior. He looked around. Something
metallic caught his eye and he reached down into the footwell,
below a dual set of pedals on the co-pilot or passenger side. He
stretched and got his finger around the used cartridge case.

Easing himself out, he inspected his find. It was made of copper and steel, rather than brass, and on the base, as he suspected, were stamped numerals telling him it was Russian 9x18-millimetre ammunition, the same make and calibre that would have come from the Makarov pistol Sonja had sourced for herself.

Emma came to him, wiping her mouth. 'Sorry.'

'Don't be,' he said. 'Shows you're human.'

She leaned over, looking into his palm. 'What have you got there?'

He showed her the first of his finds, the pistol cartridge. 'Your mom.'

'You sure?'

Next he held up the hair he had found, auburn-coloured with a grey root. He closed his fist around the cartridge case and put it in his pocket. 'Some things are making sense here and some aren't.'

'So, you think she was in the chopper, maybe, and someone else shot them down? Why?'

'She knew they were on to her, so maybe she went to the compound, then hijacked the helicopter, and whoever was still on the ground was pissed and took her out, using Johnsy's Barrett rifle, which Sonja must have ditched.'

'Oddly, hijacking a helicopter does sound like something Mum would do,' Emma said. 'What do we do now?'

'We hunt.'

Emma picked up his meaning straight away and they both began circling the helicopter, searching the ground.

'There are footprints everywhere,' Emma said.

'Cops,' Hudson said, also looking down, 'and maybe whoever was at the drilling site would have come to look for survivors.'

'And maybe drag them away.' Emma had stopped. 'Come take a look at this, Hudson.'

He went to her. 'Footprints and drag marks, like two people carrying someone who's unconscious, or . . .'

'Dead?'

155

'Why bother?' he said.

There were two furrows scored in the dirt where a person had maybe been carried by two others, their hands under the person's arms, heels dragging in the dirt. Hudson looked over his shoulder; Goodness was approaching, busy conferring with the officer who walked beside her. 'Let's go,' he added.

Hudson and Emma set off into the bush and he continued to read the ground as they moved, as quickly as they could while still picking up the tracks.

'The two men headed to the crash site from this direction,' Emma said, pointing at the boot prints.

'You're good,' Hudson said.

'There were a few things she taught me, growing up,' Emma said.

He glanced at her and saw how she bit her lower lip. These two women in his life could be as prickly as all hell towards each other but he knew, deep down, there was no doubting the love between them.

'You know how tough she is, right?' Hudson said.

Emma nodded and they carried on, heading away from the drilling site and the helicopter crash. Eventually they came out onto a road and found vehicle tracks.

He looked around, getting his bearings from an outcrop of boulders. 'This is the main road through the park in these parts.'

'Tyre marks go both ways, same vehicle,' Emma said, pointing. 'And there are different tread marks, too.'

Hudson looked at them. 'Bigger than a car. Some type of light truck or touring vehicle, plus another car, maybe a private or rented tourist vehicle.'

'What makes you say that?' Emma asked.

He bent and pointed to the patterns in the dust. 'The bigger vehicle's tyre tread is worn; the other one's got wide tyres, deep tread, new and expensive – definitely not the sort of rubber you'd find on a national parks Land Rover or some jeep jockey's HiLux from the Falls.'

'Want me to go back and get the Land Cruiser?' Emma asked.

'Yep. Please. Goodness is less likely to want to stop you and grill you. I'll keep following the tyre tracks. Pick me up.'

'You think she's still alive?' Emma asked.

He looked up the empty road. 'I know she is.'

CHAPTER 13

Sonja's body and clothes were wet with sweat and blood.

She was ready for them.

Continually battered and bruised as the truck bounced on its way, she had used her time to prepare her escape. She assumed the Chinese boss had found her unconscious in the wreck of the helicopter – if she had been awake and able she would have killed him – and bound her hands behind her with a plastic zip tie. He had also wrapped duct tape around her ankles.

On the punishing road trip she had worked at the ties until the skin was stripped from her wrists and blood flowed over her palms and fingertips. She'd also shredded the duct tape.

It had taken her over an hour, but now she was free.

The battering stopped as the truck lurched onto a tarred road. From here on there was only the occasional thump and judder when the driver went over a pothole. Sonja had no way of knowing for sure, but she guessed they were heading towards Victoria Falls. They had clearly left the rough gravel roads of Hwange National Park and its surrounds and had to be on the main north–south road. The Falls, to the north, was a major tourism hub with an airport linking it to destinations in Africa and the wider world, and Botswana, Zambia and Namibia were all just short drives away. Bulawayo also had an airport, but if the driver headed that way then he ran the risk of a thorough search by one of Zimbabwe's ever-present police roadblocks.

Sonja waited, suppressing her anger at being caught and the pain from her injuries, and channelled them into a quiet fury, ready to be unleashed. In an hour, by her best estimate, she felt the vehicle slow and turn off the main road onto another dirt or badly potholed track. A short time later it stopped, idling, and she heard the screech of a metal door being slid open. The vehicle drove off again, then stopped. She heard the door bang closed again and wondered if they had just entered a warehouse.

She lay on her back, hands hidden, as though they were still tied, and replaced the shredded duct tape loosely around her ankles.

The silence made her ears ring. She waited in the dark, every muscle tensed, her body a coiled spring.

The truck rocked, slightly, suspension creaking as first one, then another person got out. Next she heard a sliding door attached to the vehicle open and a scrabbling noise above her.

'Careful,' someone outside said.

You don't know the fucking half of it, she thought to herself.

There was a rattle of metal on metal like a padlock being undone. The roof of her coffin-like prison swung up and open. Although it was not bright outside – her suspicion that they had entered a shed or warehouse of some kind was confirmed – the sudden influx of light was enough to make her blink.

An Asian face tentatively showed itself. Sonja mumbled something incoherent. When she noticed the man drop his guard, ever so slightly, and turn his eyes to someone else, she engaged her core and launched into a lightning-fast sit-up. She slammed her forehead into the man's face. Luckily – for her, not him – he was starting to look back down at her so she was able to break his nose.

The man reeled backwards and Sonja sprang up from the box. She saw now where she was, in a hidden compartment fitted beneath the floor of the passenger area of a truck that had been converted to an overland tourist vehicle. It was a similar model to the one she had disabled with the Barrett near Pandamatenga. She registered that the man she had just head-butted had been at the drilling site.

She surveyed her surroundings with a mix of instinct and experience, searching out threats and opportunities. Another man who looked Chinese was bringing an AK-47 to bear. Behind and above him, on the rear wall of the building, was a mezzanine gantry level, with an office with a window, where supervisors were meant to oversee whatever should have been going on below. There was no sign of life up there.

Sonja vaulted out of the truck and grabbed the man with the bleeding nose by the shirtfront. Just as she had at the drilling compound, she charged towards the threat, fearless, screaming a war cry as she propelled the injured man backwards.

The man with the AK tried to take aim, but hesitated, not wanting to shoot his comrade. The man she was pushing had a pistol, which he tried to raise. Sonja batted it aside with her left hand, let go of the man's shirt and stabbed two fingers into his eyeballs.

In a second, the gunman with the assault rifle would have a clear shot. Sonja grabbed her victim, now screaming, by the wrist, pirouetted and threw him over her shoulder. As she rolled to the floor in a judo throw, her captive pulled the trigger on his pistol and a shot clanged off a metal wall somewhere. Sonja wrapped her right hand around his as they fell, and as they hit the concrete floor the man with the rifle opened up.

Bullets ricocheted off the floor beside her as Sonja wrenched her man's arm around so it was pointing at the other man. One of the AK rounds went through the struggling man's leg, eliciting an even louder howl and forcing him to relax his grip on his pistol. Sonja was able to get a better hold on the weapon and put two rounds into the chest of the man shooting at her.

Sonja rolled the now seriously suffering man off her and scrambled towards the fallen man. She wanted that rifle.

When she reached him, she saw he was finished; blood was gurgling from his mouth. He'd dropped his AK-47 but as she was reaching for it, she heard footsteps behind her. She turned, pistol still in hand, and saw the man with the broken nose, half-blinded eyes and bleeding leg coming towards her. He had pulled a knife from a sheath on his belt. She felt a mix of sorrow and respect for him as she put a bullet between his eyes.

She stuffed the pistol in her belt and picked up the AK.

A new noise made her spin around. The front driver's-side door of the truck, on the far side of the vehicle to where she was standing, was flung open and beneath the chassis she saw feet hit the ground. The driver, young, with dreadlocks, bolted away from her towards the shed doors.

Sonja ran around the front of the vehicle, bringing the rifle up. 'Stop!'

The man ignored her, almost colliding with the sliding door as he went to open it. Sonja took aim and put a bullet through the corrugated iron less than thirty centimetres from his head.

He got the message and turned to her, raising his hands. 'No, please.'

'Come!'

'I'm sorry,' he said.

She saw the way he cocked his head, looking over her shoulder.

Sonja turned, and, too late, saw a man who had just emerged from the upstairs office standing on the gantry, a rifle of some type resting on the handrail in front of him, pointed at her.

'Shit.'

The projectile flew at her, slower than but just as true as a bullet, and the dart embedded itself near her left collarbone.

Sonja tried to bring the rifle up, but it suddenly felt impossibly heavy. She crumpled, her knees hitting the unforgiving floor. She looked up at the man who had shot her; he was the boss from the drilling site.

'Wu . . .'

*

Emma and Hudson drove to the Sinamatella Gate, the nearest entry and exit point to the drilling site. This was the route the truck they were following had taken.

Emma knew Hudson had driven as fast as he dared, mindful of the presence of wildlife and the state of the roads, which deteriorated as they passed Mandavu Dam and climbed towards the mesa on which Sinamatella Camp and the gate of the same name were located.

The camp itself was rundown. 'It was an old national parks rest camp,' Hudson told Emma as they pulled up at the gate, 'but then another Chinese-owned mining company took out a lease on it.'

At the gate Hudson asked the ranger on duty about the last vehicle that had come through.

'A tourist vehicle an hour ago, but only one other passenger on board,' the ranger said.

'Local?'

The man shook his head. 'Chinese. The driver was a man I know, Bheki.'

'This Bheki, is he a guide?'

The ranger nodded. 'Yes. He is the son of a friend of mine, a very good guide if you have a job for him at your Nantwich Lodge. He's twenty-five and willing to learn.'

'What's wrong with the job he's got?'

The ranger looked away. 'He is not happy.'

'Sure thing, I'll do what I can,' Hudson said. 'Can you give me his number?'

The ranger took out an old phone with a cracked screen and asked for Hudson's number. He sent him a message.

'They're an hour ahead of us,' Hudson said.

'Then let's hit it,' Emma said.

He nodded and drove at a terrifying pace now they were clear of the park and its restrictions. Once on the tar road, clear of the mining town of Hwange, the warm wind howled through the open vehicle as Hudson pressed on towards Victoria Falls.

At a police roadblock Hudson confirmed that they were on the right track when the officer on duty told him that his 'friends', a guide named Bheki and a Chinese man, were in a vehicle that had passed through an hour earlier.

'They're moving as fast as we are,' Hudson said.

'You think she's with them, smuggled somewhere in their vehicle?' Emma asked.

He shrugged. 'As sure as I can be. We know they're using overland tourist trucks for smuggling, so it makes sense your mom could be on board.'

At Victoria Falls, however, they drew a blank. It seemed to Emma that every second vehicle was a khaki or green-painted tour vehicle of some shape or size and no one Hudson spoke to, from a tourist tout to the pump attendant at a fuel station, or a pretty girl outside a souvenir shop, remembered a vehicle with an African guide and a Chinese man on board.

They had both tried ringing Bheki's phone as soon as they came into range of the Victoria Falls cell phone towers, but each of them was answered with the same recorded message saying the phone was not in use or out of range.

Hudson drove them down to the entry to the Victoria Falls, where they slowly cruised the car park, then did a U-turn and headed back up the hill into town. He pulled over near the Three Monkeys bar.

'Any ideas?' he said to Emma.

She thought for a moment. 'How old did that ranger say Bheki was?'

'Twenty-five, I think,' Hudson said.

Emma took out her phone and selected the Tinder app.

Hudson leaned over from the driver's seat. 'You have Tinder?'

'Don't look so shocked – you are not, actually, my father.' She opened her account and searched for single men nearby. She read down a list of names. 'Robert, Brett, Justice, Shadrack, Martin, Kenny, Charles, Sipho . . . here we are, there's one Bheki.' She clicked on his picture and showed it to Hudson.

'Dreadlocks, khaki shirt, Nyami Nyami pendant, fit, good-looking. He looks like a safari guide to me.'

'Here goes nothing.' Emma swiped right.

They sat there, waiting, scanning vehicles coming down the street. A few minutes later Emma's phone dinged.

'Hellooo, Bheki,' Emma said, and started tapping out a message.

'He responded?' Hudson said.

'Sure did.'

'Wow!'

'Hey!' she said in mock anger. 'I'm reasonably hot.'

'That's not what I mean, Emma, it's just that . . . well, hell, you know.'

'It's OK.' She kept an eye on the screen. 'He's replying.'

Emma sent him a message. *In town for a couple of days. I am looking for some fun. Are you?*

Bheki replied: *for sure.*

Now good?

'What's he saying?' Hudson asked.

She read the new message, putting on a German accent when she spoke her lines. 'He's just told me he's busy right now, and can we meet tonight.'

'Busy, hey?'

'I need to bring out the big guns, I think,' Emma said. She undid the top two buttons of her blouse.

'Wait!' Hudson leaned over to grab her phone, but she shifted out of reach, pouted, exposed the lacy bra under her shirt and took a selfie.

'If that doesn't get him all hot and bothered, I'll –'

'You'll do no such thing,' Hudson said quickly.

'Relax,' Emma said. 'I was just going to say I'll flirt some more.'

Emma's phone dinged. 'Gotcha.'

'You got him on the hook?'

'About to land him. He says he's changed his plans and wants to meet in twenty minutes.'

'Where?' Hudson asked.

'He says at the Pick n Pay shopping mall.'

'I know it; we're close.' Hudson started the engine. 'And he must be close as well. Tell him . . . well, tell him you're in kind of a hurry.'

Emma grinned and started tapping a message as Hudson pulled away from the kerb and headed uphill, away from the Falls. 'What are you writing?'

She glanced demurely at him. 'Trust me, you don't want to know.'

Hudson shook his head and accelerated.

Emma received another message. 'He's on his way, just finished work.'

'Ask him what company he works for, and for his phone number. We need to make sure he's the right Bheki.'

Emma did and Bheki replied. 'The number's a match, he's our guy. He must have just been ignoring our calls as he didn't recognise the numbers, or maybe he was busy. He says he works for Flame of Zimbabwe tours.'

Hudson nodded. 'Figures.'

'How so?'

'They were bought out by a Chinese company. A lot of companies changed hands during COVID. It could be part of the Giraffe Holdings group of companies. Flame of Zimbabwe had a warehouse where they stored their overland vehicles. They were in the industrial area, not far from the Pick n Pay. Let's still meet him at the mall anyway – that way we know he'll be alone.'

Hudson went on towards the open-air mall dominated by the big supermarket, then turned left.

Emma saw workshops and garages, some occupied, but some abandoned. A troop of baboons scampered along the roof of an empty hardware store, while a family of warthog, an old sow and two adolescents, ferreted and snuffled about on the unkempt roadside.

Hudson pointed. 'Young guy with dreads there.'

Emma turned her head and saw a tall man in khaki. 'It's him.' He was really quite handsome, she thought, though not as good-looking as Kelvin. Why, she asked herself, was she thinking about Kelvin?

Hudson slowed, but crept closer. 'How do you want to play this?' he asked.

'You're my safari guide, showing me around town,' Emma said, banishing thoughts of boys from her mind. She scrambled over the back of the front passenger seat into the first tier of game-viewing seats, behind Hudson.

'Bheki?' she called out.

He stopped and looked around at the sound of his name.

'Bheki!' Emma waved. 'Over here.'

He grinned and crossed the road to them. 'Hi . . .'

'Emma.'

'Yeah, right, Emma, how you doing?'

'I am fine, thank you very much, and all the much better for now seeing you.' She had turned on her German accent. 'Please come and join us.'

Bheki looked to Hudson, who said: 'Howzit?'

'Cool, man, mind if I jump in?'

Hudson shrugged. 'Like she says, all aboard.'

He climbed up onto the side ladder, then looked at Hudson again and narrowed his eyes. 'I know you . . . Harrison?'

'Hudson. I knew your old boss at Flame, Brett.'

'Yeah, he had to move back to South Africa.'

'Good guy. How's the new regime?'

'Oh, you know . . .'

Hudson left it at that.

'I am so glad I found you,' Emma said.

Bheki grinned. 'Made my day. Where to?'

'Well,' Emma leaned closer to Bheki, 'I know we talked about a drink, but I have got Mr Hudson here for the rest of the day, so how would you like to go into the bush, on a game drive with us?'

'Um, sure. Cool.'

Bheki had his eye on her – in fact he was very interested in her cleavage – but in her peripheral vision Emma saw Hudson's look. He, like her, knew Bheki was less than impressed at the prospect of going on a game drive for a few hours.

'First time to Zimbabwe?'

He was forcing a grin and lapsing into his tourist spiel, Emma thought.

'Oh, yes, I love it here,' she said, continuing in her faux German accent, wondering what her mother would make of it. 'All the *wild*life, and the bush, but I want to also see how the real people of Zimbabwe live and work.'

'There's a village near the Stanley & Livingstone hotel,' Bheki said, 'we could go there and do a tour.'

Emma put her hand on his thigh. 'I think I would like to see where you live, Mr Bheki.'

'Um, it's pretty humble . . .' There was a new look in his eye and his tongue darted over his lower lip.

'Perhaps, Mr Hudson,' Emma leaned forward, 'you can take us on a behind-the-scenes tour of Victoria Falls, somewhere quiet?'

'It's your dime.'

He started the Land Cruiser and carried on down Pioneer Road into the light industrial area. Bheki looked around, like he was unsure that what they were doing was sound, but Emma threw back her head and laughed. 'Oh, "it's your dime". This is like being in a movie, yes, Bheki?'

'Um, sure, I guess.'

Hudson was scouting ahead, Emma noticed, eyes moving left and right. He accelerated, as if working out exactly where he wanted to go. The industrial area was the busy, dusty heart of Victoria Falls, beating away behind the facade of the cafes, guesthouses, hotels and souvenir shops. They passed mechanics' yards with busted, rusted vehicles parked outside; wholesale fruit and butchers' stores supplying the hospitality industry, and dozens of other small businesses dependent on the tourist dollar.

He took a left up a short drive and stopped outside a tall, free-standing, tin-clad shed with a faded sign that read *Flame of Zimbabwe Tours and Travel*.

'Wait a minute,' Bheki said. He leaned towards Hudson. 'What's going on?'

Hudson reached under his seat and drew out his .45-calibre Colt 1911 pistol. 'This.' A baboon, fossicking in some rubbish, looked up, saw the gun, screeched and scampered off.

Bheki reached out an arm to grab Emma, probably to use her as a human shield, but she was ready for him. He stopped moving when he felt the Browning nine-millimetre pistol dig him in the ribs.

'Where's my fucking mother?' Emma dropped the German accent.

He put up his hands, meek, now, with two guns on him. 'I don't know what you're talking about.'

'He's lying.' Hudson got out of the truck. 'Cover him.'

'Hudson, no,' Emma said as he started to walk towards the sliding front door.

Emma looked to Bheki, fidgeting in his seat. 'Don't try anything or I'll shoot you, I swear to God.'

'OK, OK.'

'Where's my mother?'

'I don't know where anyone's mother is,' he said. 'What are you, some kind of psycho?'

'You'd better think again.' Emma levelled the gun at him. 'What's waiting behind the door over there?'

'If you're smart, you'll tell Hudson to get back in the truck, let me go and just drive away.'

'You saw a woman, right? You picked her up from Hwange National Park and brought her here. We confirmed you were in the reserve today.'

'What if I was?'

'The woman,' Emma said again. 'Where is she?'

Bheki ignored her and looked over to where Hudson was

inspecting a chain hanging from the front sliding door. He took aim and shot the padlock. Hudson grabbed the door, wrenched it open and ducked inside, gun-hand up.

A minute later he re-emerged and walked back to the vehicle.

'Anything?' Emma said.

'Two bodies. Asian males.'

Emma motioned with her pistol to Bheki. 'Get out of the truck. Into the building.'

'Emma,' Hudson began, 'you don't want to.'

'Don't tell me what I want and don't want, Hudson.'

He stared at her but said nothing. He was a good man and they'd never argued about anything, nor had she ever spoken to him in that way. Emma felt a change. It was as though her body and mind were fired by rage, but at the same time she felt an almost icy calm descend over her. Clearly, Bheki was reading her, because he complied, climbing down from the Land Cruiser.

'Inside.' She urged him on at gunpoint and he went into the building, keeping an eye on them but glancing at the ground every now and then. Hudson trailed them.

Bheki shook his head when he saw the two dead Chinese men. Dust particles danced in the beam of light that had been let in by the sliding door.

Emma smelled the blood; it was coppery, just as it was described in books. The gore and the covered body of the pilot in the helicopter had shocked her, but she viewed these corpses clinically, forensically, wondering if her mother had been responsible for their deaths. One man had what looked like a broken nose and a wound in his leg, but he'd been finished off with a bullet between the eyes. The other a few metres away had two bullet holes in the chest.

The 'double tap', her mother had called it, when she'd taught Emma to shoot properly, on a firing range outside of Los Angeles. Mother and daughter bonding – how to kill, 101.

Hudson just stood there.

'Talk to me,' she said softly.

Bheki looked unsteady on his feet. He stared at the cobwebs in the roof rafters. 'I know nothing about any of this.'

'Yet the tracks from your rafting sandals are as clear as day and fresh as these corpses, on the ground outside, leading to and from this place,' Emma said. 'You came from here, to meet me.'

He glared at her now, nostrils flaring. Hudson had his pistol hanging loose at his side. Bheki appealed to him: 'She's crazy, man. I had nothing to do with this. I'm a guide.'

'You got one outta three of those statements correct, partner,' Hudson drawled.

'Tell us where she is,' Emma said. 'Last chance.'

Bheki sneered at her. 'Go fuck yourself, woman.'

They were not, Emma decided, the words of some innocent safari guide. She took aim with the pistol and fired.

Bheki crumpled to the ground, screaming and clutching his leg. Blood welled between his fingers as he writhed on the concrete floor.

Hudson looked at the roof. 'For crying in a bucket, Emma.'

'He told me to go fuck myself.' She closed the distance between herself and Bheki and looked down at him. 'Man up, you wimp.'

Hudson shook his head. 'Where have I heard that before?'

Emma ignored Hudson's jibe. Bheki looked up at her, summoning the strength to reply, but her stare silenced him.

'One more time,' Emma took aim between his eyes. 'Tell me where my mother is.'

'I don't . . .'

She pointed her toe and rested it against his hands. The bullet had gone through the flesh of his calf; he winced and tried to scoot away from her on his bottom.

'All right, all right,' he continued. 'I was in the park and got a call from my boss. I went to the place where they've been drilling.'

'Your boss?' Emma said.

He nodded.

'Carrington Wu?'

'Don't make me say his name,' Bheki said. 'Please,' he added in a softer voice.

Emma kept the pistol on him. 'Go on.'

'He flagged me down as I got close, off the road. He jumped in my truck and directed me towards some smoke. It was a helicopter crash. There was a woman there, unconscious, on the ground. He told me she had hijacked the chopper.' Bheki looked to Hudson. 'Get me a bandage or something, man.'

'In good time,' Hudson said. 'Keep singing.'

'The pilot?' Emma said. 'What happened to him?'

'He was dead. The boss said the woman shot him in the head after the crash. Something about not wanting to leave witnesses, but then she must have passed out afterwards. She looked a bit banged up, like maybe she wasn't wearing a seatbelt or something.'

'That pilot was *not* killed by a shot from the pistol that woman was carrying,' Hudson said.

'Why didn't you suggest calling the police?' Emma asked Bheki.

'The boss said the cops were on the way,' Bheki replied. 'Besides, it's not my job to ask questions or make suggestions.'

'What did you do with her?'

'We put her in the vehicle.'

'The ranger on duty at the gate would have told us if he'd seen an unconscious woman in your vehicle. He's a friend of your family.'

Bheki exhaled and looked down.

Emma put the barrel of the pistol under his chin. He started, then looked up, fear in his face. She would not have said she enjoyed the power she had over this man, but it was there, undeniable, like a force within her. She needed to harness it, to understand it, and control it.

'Tell me,' she said.

'We put her in a place, in the truck, a box down low in the chassis. We use it for –'

'Smuggling,' Hudson said.

Bheki gave a small nod.

'Smuggling what?' Emma prompted.

'Abalone.'

She clenched her jaw. They had treated Sonja like a piece of dead cargo.

'And you thought this was OK, kidnapping an injured woman, when you knew the police had been called.'

He shrugged. 'It wasn't my decision. Like I said, the boss told me she'd hijacked the helicopter.'

'What happened to whoever else was at the drilling site?' Hudson interjected.

'The boss had another vehicle pick them up – told the local guys to make themselves scarce. The Chinese workers came back here.'

'You didn't think that was suspicious, that they didn't stay to give statements to the police?' Emma asked.

Bheki glared at her. 'I don't get paid to think.'

'What happened when you got here?' Emma said.

Bheki gestured to the two bodies with his head as he rocked, clutching his leg. 'That happened.'

'She got away?' Hudson asked, his voice rising with hope.

'No,' Bheki said. 'The boss shot her.'

'What . . .' Emma began, her feeling of power instantly disappearing, like a light switched off.

'With a dart gun. She was knocked out. He took her.'

Emma swung the pistol into the side of Bheki's head. 'No!'

'Emma . . .' Hudson said.

She hit the young guide again.

'I'm sorry, I'm sorry, I'm sorry.' Tears rolled down Bheki's cheeks as he lay in the foetal position on the warehouse floor, his body racked by heaving sobs.

Emma felt Hudson's big hands clasp her upper arms from behind and although at first she wanted to shrug him off, she felt her rage dissipate and her body crumple in the next instance.

'Bheki,' Hudson said, his tone demanding attention. The young man looked up at him, his eyes red. 'Tell us where you think Wu's taking the woman or, God help me, I'll let Emma finish you off, here and now.'

He blinked, then nodded. 'There's a shipment of drugs heading to Cape Town via Botswana today. They pick the stuff up at Vic Falls airport – the boss uses it to pay for his abalone. They'd normally drive through Pandamatenga, but since a truck got ambushed there, they were going to use the Kazungula crossing today. They might be sending her south in a hidden cargo compartment in the tour vehicles, with that shit.'

'Timings?' Hudson said.

'I don't know, man. I just get told when and where I have to drive,' Bheki sobbed. 'Don't let her kill me.'

Emma composed herself and saw the blood where the butt of her pistol had cut Bheki's skin, at his temple. She glanced at his bleeding bullet wound. *Did I do that?* She shook her head, knowing very well that she had, and how easily it had happened. 'How do you track your vehicle?' she asked Bheki.

'There's a tracking service the company uses,' he said. He gestured with his head to the gantry walkway and upstairs office. 'The number, login and password are on the wall upstairs. The vehicles all have names. The one the woman was in is called Takunda; its registration number is upstairs.'

'I'll go,' Emma said. She needed to get away from Bheki right now, before the rage overtook her again.

CHAPTER 14

Hudson bandaged Bheki's wound and put fifty US dollars in his shirt pocket. 'Get out of town, now, and don't let me see you back here again – ever.'

They left the warehouse and dropped the sullen, limping guide at the Pick n Pay. Emma was on the phone, on hold with the vehicle tracking company.

'Are you thinking what I'm thinking?' Hudson said.

Emma nodded. 'I think so. We know that Wu and Vincent Hendricks are in business together. I think that maybe they've been talking and that Wu's delivering Sonja to Hendricks.'

Hudson nodded.

'Yes, hello, I'm calling from Flame of Zimbabwe,' Emma said into the phone. She gave the registration details of the vehicle they wanted, Takunda, and the password to access the system.

'They've got a lock,' Emma said. She waited, listening. 'Kazungula border post, just as Bheki said.'

'Bingo.' Hudson accelerated.

'Can we catch him?'

'That border post is busy with tourists these days, but we're lucky. Since the new bridge was built across the Zambezi, from Kazungula in Botswana to Zambia, most of the heavy commercial traffic heading north or south uses that route. Kazungula's mostly for tourists doing day trips from Kasane on the Chobe River to the Falls, and vice versa. Hold on to your hat.'

The wind blasted them in the open vehicle as Hudson pushed the Land Cruiser as fast as it would go.

'The tracking company's sending me a link, so I can track Takunda on the map online,' Emma said.

Before she could open the link, however, they lost phone signal as they drove through the bush – most of the route to the border skirted the Zambezi National Park and wild lands to the south of it. They passed some elephant and Hudson had to slow for a journey of giraffe crossing the road, but otherwise he kept up his blustery pace.

'Hide the guns good.' Hudson took out his .45 and handed it to Emma as he drove. She scrambled over the seat-back and found a toolbox rattling around under the rear tiers of seating. She hid the guns in it.

As they approached the border, Emma held her phone up, searching for a signal. 'Got it,' she said. 'Takunda has just passed through into Botswana.'

They hit the border post at a run, filling out paperwork to exit Zimbabwe as quickly as they could. Fortunately, they both had their passports with them, and there were only four people ahead of them. As soon as they finished, they sprinted back to the Land Cruiser, like racing car drivers at Le Mans, and beat some of their competition into the Botswana border post. There they went through a similar bureaucratic rigmarole.

'He's slower than us,' Hudson said as they finally drove through a boom gate and into Botswana.

'I'm losing signal,' Emma said, checking her phone, 'but he's definitely headed south.'

'That road only goes one way for a couple of hundred kilo-metres,' Hudson said.

They barrelled down the road that skirted the western edge of forestry land that in turn backed onto Hwange National Park.

The speed limit was 120 kilometres per hour, and while Hudson couldn't manage that, he was sitting above 100, the air rushing through the open vehicle and the canvas canopy above them flapping and snapping in protest. The verges had been cleared of vegetation so they had plenty of notice of elephants, which they saw a few times, as well as a herd of kudu that bounded across the road in front of them.

'Get the guns,' Hudson said.

Emma took a breath and nodded.

There was going to be no easy way to do this, Hudson thought.

Ahead of them was a semitrailer. Hudson passed it and then saw the Flame of Zimbabwe tour truck.

Emma passed him his Colt .45 and Hudson tucked it between his legs. Emma crawled over the seat again, positioning herself behind him.

'Don't just open up on him, all guns blazing,' Hudson said.

'All right. Who do you think I am?'

He grinned and shook his head. Hudson geared down and accelerated. The road was clear ahead, so he indicated and began to overtake the vehicle. Hudson checked the cab as he passed. The vehicle's name, Takunda, was painted on the driver's door. The man behind the wheel had earbuds in and was bobbing his head to the beat of whatever he was listening to. The man was alone, no co-driver, and there was no sign of anyone else in the rear of the truck, which had been converted to carry about fifteen tourists. He carried on, keeping his speed up.

Emma leaned forward. 'What now?'

'We see if he's innocent, and a good Samaritan.' A few minutes later they crested a hill and Hudson checked in his rear-view mirror. They were out of sight of the truck. 'Check in the back. You'll find ten litres of water in a plastic container.'

Emma dropped down behind the seat, then re-emerged. 'OK, found it.'

'Tip it out, slowly, and keep it running while I pull off the road.'

Emma unscrewed the cap and let the water flow out over the

side. It left a clear black streak on the road and Hudson slowed as he veered off onto the grass. As soon as he stopped he got out and went to the front of the vehicle and opened the bonnet.

'Wave at him as he approaches.'

Emma jumped down and took up a position by the roadside. 'Clever,' she said. 'He'll think we've got a burst radiator or a fuel leak.'

'Let's hope,' Hudson said.

He watched from the front as Emma stepped out onto the edge of the tar road and started waving her arms. Seeing her there, silhouetted against the sky, she reminded him so much of Sonja it almost hurt. In the rush of trying to keep up with Sonja and the chain of devastation she'd left in her wake, he hadn't had time to be truly afraid for her. He swallowed, trying hard not to think the worst.

His .45 was in the waistband of his shorts, cocked and ready.

The overland truck approached, but didn't slow.

'Hey!' Emma yelled, still waving as the truck passed them and continued on.

Hudson closed the bonnet with a thud and got back behind the wheel as Emma climbed up and over the side of the Land Cruiser, back onto the viewing seats. 'That arsehole deserves to be shot for not stopping for a fellow traveller.'

'Not quite,' Hudson said, checking over his shoulder and pulling back onto the highway, 'but it's kind of unusual for a safari guide, especially, not to help.'

Gravel flew from under the tyres as the Land Cruiser re-joined the tar road. Hudson floored the accelerator once again. He looked over his shoulder and saw that Emma had drawn her pistol.

'Put that away.'

She saw the look in his eyes and hid the weapon again.

He worked the stick shift and was soon behind the tour vehicle. He pulled out and drew alongside the truck.

The driver was still listening to his music. Hudson leaned

on the Land Cruiser's horn. Eventually the man looked over, surprised.

'Pull over!' Hudson pointed to the side of the road.

The man shook his head.

Hudson tooted again.

The man looked down at him from his higher vantage point and spat into the slipstream. Hudson dropped down to fourth gear to get his revolutions up and in the process dropped a little behind the truck. As he started to gain on the other vehicle the driver swerved hard and fast to the right, forcing Hudson to do the same. In the process he bled off some more speed.

'Want me to shoot him?' Emma yelled. 'He's clearly got something to hide.'

'Let me try and get ahead of him.'

Hudson attacked the gearbox and floored the accelerator again. This time he gave the other vehicle a wider berth as he accelerated, but the overland truck started drifting way over to their side of the road. When the other driver was close to them the man stuck his arm out of the cab.

'Is that a gun?' Emma yelled.

'No, it's a –'

The driver hurled the wrench at them and the heavy tool smashed into the Land Cruiser's windscreen. Hudson swerved, and Emma could see he was trying to look around the shattered glass.

She put a foot up on the side wall of the vehicle and grasped the vertical steel pipe that held up the game viewer's shade canopy. The other driver swung his steering wheel and rammed into them. Hudson was fighting to stay on the highway as the other man forced him closer to the edge. On the right-hand side the road dropped away over an embankment about a metre high.

Hudson put on the brakes, but the other guy did the same and came at them again. There were only millimetres to spare as Hudson fought off the other vehicle, physically turning into the bigger truck. The rear of the touring vehicle was just in front of Emma. There was the screech of metal on metal and Emma could feel the vibrations passing through the Land Cruiser as the right front tyre started to go over the edge of the road. The game viewer lurched sickeningly.

She jumped.

Emma landed with one foot on the extended rear bumper of the tourer and tried to grab hold of one of the two spare wheels fitted to racks on the back. At that moment the driver put on the brakes again, driving her chest hard into the big rubber tyre, and when he accelerated again she found herself leaning back. Hudson managed to get the Cruiser back on the road and rammed the big truck, and Emma lost her footing.

She scrambled for a handhold on the tyre, the rear door handle, anywhere she could get purchase, as one foot dragged and bounced on the black tarmac below. The driver was too preoccupied to notice as Emma fought to stop from falling to the road. He was picking up speed again.

Emma managed to grab hold of a high-lift jack bolted to one of the spare wheels, but a counter-blow by the tourer driver brought another collision with Hudson's vehicle and Emma's right foot slipped as well.

Now she was only holding on with her hands and had to heave her whole bodyweight up, fighting the constant ebb and flow of the bucking truck at the same time. The man swung to the right yet again.

'No!' Emma screamed as Hudson's Land Cruiser careened off the right-hand shoulder of the highway. She could see him wrestling with the steering wheel but then, as if in slow motion, she watched in horror as the Cruiser rolled. The roof structure crumpled as the vehicle went over a second time, before digging into the dirt.

Emma looked back but the blare of an air horn made her turn her head again. Through the empty passenger cab of the overland vehicle she saw a semitrailer hurtling towards them, the bulk of its big square front end filling the driver's windscreen.

The driver threw his truck over to the left so violently that it felt like they might roll as well. The g-force of the manoeuvre tossed Emma like a ragdoll; both her legs went flying out to the right, her arms feeling like they would be ripped from their sockets. As the semi roared past, horn still blaring, the driver of the overland truck straightened up and Emma was flung the other way. Finally, she was able to get both feet on the bumper.

Emma kept hold of the jack with one hand and drew Johnsy's pistol with the other.

'You son of a bitch.' She wrapped her arm around one of the spare tyres and wrenched open the rear door of the truck.

'Stop!' she screamed.

The driver glanced over his shoulder at her, then stood on the brakes. Emma went flying forward as the vehicle fishtailed to a halt. She slid down the centre aisle between the passenger seats in the back and banged her head on a fire extinguisher clipped to the front wall of the cab.

The driver reached to his belt, then leaned over the firewall, a knife in his hand. He slashed down as Emma raised her pistol. She cried out as the blade caught her across the knuckle and dropped her gun. The man unclipped his seatbelt and started crawling over the front seats into the rear. Emma rolled onto her back and kicked him in the chest. She tried to reach the pistol but it had slid out of reach.

Winded, the man fell back, but came for her again a moment later, knife in hand and murder in his eyes. Emma reached out and undid the catch securing the extinguisher. She grabbed the handle and held it up to block his downward slash. Then she wriggled back on her butt – the pistol was wedged up under a seat and to get to it she would have to roll over and crawl on her belly; but if she did that, he would stab her in the back.

The man came at her again. Emma pulled the safety ring from the canister and depressed the handle, letting him have a streaming jet of foam in the eyes. He bellowed and floundered, but still came towards her.

Emma remembered Sonja in action, and the self-defence tips her mother had tried to drill into a bored teenager. She knocked the man's knife hand out of the way and drove her fingers into his eyes. His skin was slick with white foam, but she did enough damage to him to make him stumble to his knees on the floor between the passenger seats.

Emma raised the fire extinguisher, then slammed it down onto his hand. He bellowed in pain and let go of the knife. She scooped it up with her free hand and stabbed him in the shoulder as he tried to get up. She staggered back. The man looked up at her, roaring with a mix of pain and fury, and started coming at her again. Emma brought the extinguisher down on his head.

She was exhausted, sore and bleeding from the hand, but she had to find Sonja, and get to Hudson. Emma checked the man on the floor; he was out cold. She gave him a kick in the ribs to make sure he wasn't faking, then grabbed him by the epaulettes of his safari shirt and dragged him down the length of the passenger compartment. When she got to the open door at the rear Emma pushed him out. He landed with a thud on the road.

Emma banged on the floor of the truck. She knew from Bheki that the compartment was below. 'Mum! Mum!' She put her ear on the linoleum.

She heard nothing.

'Shit.'

She felt for the edges of the floor covering and lifted it up. As she tugged it from under the chairs and to one side she saw a hatch. It was secured with a sliding bolt and a padlock.

Emma felt the panic rise in her. She had to think, about Sonja, Hudson and herself. First, she needed to get rid of the danger. She crawled back under the front seat and retrieved her pistol and then the driver's knife. She leaned into the front of the truck and took the keys from the ignition.

She started trying the padlock with the assortment of keys on the ring and got lucky with the fourth. Emma took a deep breath, steeling herself for the worst, as she removed the lock, undid the bolt and opened the hatch. It opened with a squeak.

'Mum?'

She exhaled. In the hidden cavity were two large green vinyl dive bags; at least they weren't big enough to contain a body, she thought.

Emma went to the rear of the compartment, jumped down and sprinted back up the road to where Hudson's vehicle had come to rest. She felt bad, now, that she had wasted time looking for Sonja, who was clearly not inside the vehicle.

'Hudson!'

The Land Cruiser had come to rest on its side, near where the cleared verge of the highway surrendered to the dry African bush beyond. She heard the *ping, ping, ping* of tortured metal, contracting in the heat. The vehicle's radiator hissed steam.

'Hudson?' She ran around the vehicle, seeing the crazed windscreen, blood smears, his Colt .45 lying on the ground. He hadn't been wearing a seatbelt.

Everything they had done had been crazy and it was bloody Sonja who had set them off on this mad, violent chase. As usual, she had left nothing but death and destruction in her wake.

And tears.

Hudson had been thrown from the vehicle and was lying on his back, ten metres away, his face a mask of blood, one leg bent at an impossible angle. He wasn't moving. Emma started to cry.

'No! Damn you to fucking hell, no!'

CHAPTER 15

Carrington Wu took out his Huawei phone and called Hendricks from the air. Normal airline restrictions about making calls didn't apply when one owned the aircraft, which in this case was a twin-engine Beechcraft.

'Hello, Vincent, how are you? Have I caught you at a bad time?'

'I'm fine, and no, I'm just playing a round of golf.'

'A fine game, which, as you know, I enjoy myself.'

'Carrington, I don't wish to sound rude, but I'm also talking business here on the fairway.'

'Of course. I am actually on my way to you, but wanted to give you a "heads-up", I believe is the term.'

'Where are you? In a car?'

Wu looked out the window at the dry expanses of Africa. Some saw emptiness there, but Wu saw money, a vast, still mostly untapped well of resources to feed his own country, hungry as it was for raw materials.

'I'm flying, not far out of Cape Town International.' He gave Vincent his arrival details. 'I have a gift for you, Vincent. Boxed and ready for you to open.'

'Really?'

'I was annoyed that certain personal matters have resulted in the loss of a shipment of abalone, but I have no desire for some third party to come between us, my friend.'

'And I feel the same.'

'I bring this present to you not just as a show of good faith in our business relationship.'

'That is good.'

Wu looked back at the cargo hold, beyond the webbing net, at the crate. The thought of the woman in there was mildly arousing to him. He wondered what Hendricks, a well-known devotee of the sins of the flesh, would make of her.

'This gift,' Hendricks continued with a chuckle, 'is it bigger than a breadbox?'

'About five-ten, auburn hair, blue eyes.'

'Ah, just my size. I'm indebted to you.'

'Vincent?'

'Yes?'

'She is like a caged lioness, this one. Handle with care.'

*

Hendricks ended the call, excused himself once more to the man he was playing golf with, and made another call, to a SARS officer at Cape Town airport who received a fat bundle of cash from his network every month.

'South African Revenue Service, Gerald speaking. How can I help?'

Vincent gave the man Wu's name and the details of his flight. 'Make sure he and his cargo are not delayed.'

'Of course, sir,' Gerald said.

Hendricks ended the call.

'You've got the best golf courses in the world outside of Ireland, Vincent,' his playing partner said to him with a broad smile.

'Thank you, David. I'd love to come to Ireland sometime in the future and play some of yours.'

'If you've a taste for the finer things in life, like a good Irish whisky, you'd love it.'

Vincent put a ball and a tee on the ground. 'So, David, our mutual friend in the UK tells me you're here to do some shopping, for more than carved wooden giraffes.'

The Irishman, David Rafferty, was dressed well, casual but stylish, like a successful businessman nearing the end of a good career, perhaps with an eye on an early retirement. His build and complexion spoke of a life well lived; the broad shoulders, crooked nose and the white scars on his knuckles hinted at another side.

'That's true, and I appreciate you seeing me.'

Vincent swung his driver.

'Good shot, Vincent.'

Hendricks retrieved his tee and both men got into the buggy, with Vincent at the wheel. 'What's on your shopping list, David?'

'Assault rifles. AKs, as long as they're not made in some Yugoslav tractor factory in the 1950s – something more modern if you've got it; RPG-7 grenade launchers, and some Dragunov sniper rifles.'

Vincent raised his eyebrows. 'And what makes you think that I, an honest Cape Town property developer, would have access to such weapons?'

'Honest property developer? Sure, and that's an oxymoron if ever I've heard one. No, you're a man with an eye for a deal, Vincent, is what I hear, and also one with a bit of a soft heart for the oppressed. Is it true you were a foot-soldier in the ANC in the old days?'

They stopped where David's ball had landed. David selected an iron and Vincent nodded at his choice.

'I did my time,' Vincent said. 'My people were forcibly evicted from their homes in Cape Town and moved out onto the flats by the apartheid regime. We had to do whatever we could to survive.'

'Then you know what it's like to be oppressed, to have your identity taken away from you.'

'I always thought it was the Catholics who were the underdogs in your country?'

'It's my people, the Protestants, who've been left in the lurch since this whole Brexit mess happened. We want to stay part of Great Britain, but now with the hard border in place it's as though our enemy has won and we're locked out of our own country. It suits the Tories in Downing Street to court my people when they need our vote, but they care nothing for us. Trouble's brewing again, so it is.'

'Governments are all cut from the same cloth, favouring their own supporters over anyone else,' Vincent said. 'My people have not fared well since Mandela. I myself left the ANC.'

'Sure, and now you're a big man in the Democratic Alliance, isn't that right?' David took his shot, and they both watched as his ball reached the green. They got back in the buggy. 'Running for parliament, I hear.'

'I'll do my best.' Hendricks had been contacted by a man he knew in England, a former Capetonian, whose tourism business had been crippled by the COVID pandemic. The man had 'pivoted' during the outbreak to importing illegal drugs, cocaine from South America, shipped via South Africa. The man had dealings in Northern Ireland and it seemed that the extremists on both sides of the political and religious divide were no strangers to the drug trade. 'You're UVF? Ulster Volunteer Force?'

'More of a splinter group. So, you won't sell me some guns, Vincent?'

'No.' Out of habit he made as if to scratch his chin, placing his hand over his mouth, just in case there was some anti-gang squad surveillance team, or even someone from State Security, snooping at the behest of the ruling party, trying to lip-read. 'I said I was an honest man.'

'Yes, so you said,' David said. 'Though your old pal from Cape Town, Engels, said you were still in the, shall we say, import–export business.'

They walked the short distance to his ball. 'Tell me, David, why are you reaching out to me for guns? Like you say, I'm a businessman and aspiring politician.'

David grinned. 'And, from what I hear, one of the largest exporters of abalone out of South Africa. Got a licence for that, have you, Vincent?'

Vincent narrowed his eyes. Engels had told him via an encrypted messenger service that this Irishman wanted 'hardware'. Engels had gone quiet these last few days, but that wasn't unusual. Vincent knew his old friend from the Cape Flats was sometimes too fond of his own merchandise, as well as English girls, and every now and then dropped out of contact on a drug-fuelled bender. Engels had said that 'David Rafferty', whatever his real name was, would pay for contacts.

'No comment,' Vincent said. 'But perhaps I can facilitate an introduction for you. There is a person I can put you in touch with who will have the hardware you want.'

'I'm guessing there'll be a fee for this introduction.'

'A million rand.'

David whistled. They stopped the buggy, and Vincent got out and took his next shot.

'Sure, and that's more than I expected to pay for the whole shipment,' David said. 'I'm looking for the best deal I can get.'

'I thought you were looking for guns and rocket-propelled grenade launchers at short notice, in the face of a volatile situation in your country.'

'Aye. I'll give you half a million for an introduction.'

'Eight hundred thousand, not a rand less.'

David hesitated for a moment, then nodded. 'All right.' They got in the buggy and drove to the green. 'When and where can I meet the dealer?'

'X is in Mozambique,' Vincent said as they got out and went to his ball.

'"X"? Bit theatrical, isn't it? What do you know about him – or her?'

Vincent looked the Irishman in the eyes. 'What makes you think X could be a woman?'

David grinned. 'It's a new world, Vincent. By rights I should be asking you what pronoun you prefer to be addressed by. In my business I've come across some hard women, as well as tough guys.'

Vincent held the other man's stare. He didn't let on, but Wu, who also dealt with X at arm's length when he needed firearms, had recently voiced an opinion that he thought the supplier could be a woman. It was, Wu said, a feeling he had picked up from the tone of X's messages. 'I've never met X in person. I'm told they are from Africa, originally, but served in the British Army in the 1990s. For that reason, I doubt they would see you if you were from the IRA. In any case, you'll be meeting an intermediary in Mozambique.'

'And how, exactly, will all this take place?' David asked.

'X's man – or woman, or whatever – is in Palma in the north of Mozambique.'

David raised his eyebrows. 'Palma? Isn't there a wee war going on there, with ISIS taking over the place?'

'Correct,' Vincent said. 'And it's awash with guns right now. It's said X has contacts everywhere, on all sides of all conflicts. There's a mercenary crew headed by a man named Steve Oosthuizen based just outside of Palma at the moment. They're flying out expat workers from the liquefied natural gas plant there. I know you're ex–British Army yourself – I had you checked out – and I've recommended you to Oosthuizen.'

'You seem to be a few steps ahead of me, Vincent.'

'When Engels told me you were coming, I took the necessary steps.'

'You and this Oosthuizen . . . is he in your line of business also?'

Vincent shook his head. 'No. Some members of a criminal gang, nothing to do with me, assaulted his mother, badly, in a robbery. Steve came to me and I gave him the names he needed. He owes me a favour.'

'Fair enough. How will I know who to contact? When? Where?'

'Do you have a satellite phone?'

'I do,' David said. 'I wasn't sure in which far-flung part of this continent I'd end up.'

'SMS me the number. You'll get a message when you're in Mozambique. Check every hour on the hour once you arrive. How do you intend to move your hardware out of Africa, once you buy it?'

'I'd be expecting this X to have a plan.'

'No,' Vincent said. 'Let me introduce you to a man who specialises in import–export, flying certain goods out of Zimbabwe.'

'Zimbabwe, you say? All right. Thanks.'

'All part of the service.' Vincent selected his putter. He lined up the ball as David waited by the flag. They had deliberately avoided having a caddy along for this game. Vincent looked up from the ball to David. 'That was my import–export contact on the phone, earlier. He'll be in Cape Town later this evening. I'll introduce you.'

'That'd be grand.'

'Just do me a favour,' Vincent said.

'For sure.'

Vincent put one hand over his mouth again. 'Say nothing about guns. If I tell him you want to ship "product" from Zimbabwe to the UK or Ireland, he'll assume it will be something else.'

'Abalone?'

Vincent smiled. 'No comment. I'm thinking of staging a little event, if everything aligns. It's something of a sporting fixture, with a little wagering and partying thrown in. You can come along and meet my guy.'

'Wild horses wouldn't keep me away, Vincent. Can I bring a friend? She's a real little pistol, one of those hard women I was talking about.'

'Of course.' Vincent took his putter in both hands again, looked from the ball to the hole and played his stroke.

David lifted the flag just as the ball spun around the edge of the cup and landed with a satisfying *plop*.

David fished Vincent's ball out and handed it back to him. 'Well played. I concede. I didn't say anything earlier, when we met, but I understand you've some family issues. I'm sorry for your loss.'

'Thank you, David. My heart is heavy, but the man I've been speaking of has brought me a gift that will help ease my burden.'

David shook his head. 'What could possibly make up for the loss of a child?'

'The woman who killed him.'

*

Emma crouched over Hudson and felt at his neck for a pulse.

'Thank God.'

He blinked, looked up at her and tried to sit up.

'Stay down.' She put a hand on his chest, gently. 'You got shot out of the truck like a fucking human cannonball. You might have a neck injury.'

'My leg.' He was a big, strapping safari guide, but when he tried to move his right leg he cried out in agony.

'Broken,' Emma said. 'I told you, stay still.'

He gritted his teeth. 'Bossy. Just like –'

'Don't fucking talk to me about her.' She swallowed hard, trying to maintain the authoritative look, but her lower lip started to tremble. 'She's not in the truck.'

He reached out and gripped her hand, squeezing it. 'She's tough. You have to be as well. What . . . what *was* in the truck?'

'A couple of big bags, hidden in the compartment where Bheki said they'd put Mum.'

'Go take a look at what's in them. Must be something valuable . . . why that guy didn't want to stop. Emma, is he . . .?'

She frowned. 'Out cold. Don't worry – I didn't go full Sonja on him.'

He tried a small laugh, but his body thought better of that. 'She's alive. We've just got to find her.'

'*We* aren't going anywhere any time soon, cowboy. Let me get the first aid kit.'

She went to the rolled Land Cruiser and ferreted about under the seats until she found the kit, and the remnants of the water container she'd tipped onto the road. She heard a car and ran to the roadside.

Emma started waving, but the driver, in an expensive-looking SUV, was already slowing.

'*Dumela*,' said a man in a suit, greeting her in Tswana as he got out. 'My goodness. I will call an ambulance.'

'Thank you so much,' she said. 'Can you also call the police, please? There's an unconscious man by the other vehicle. He ran us off the road.'

'Really?' The man's mouth and eyes were wide open. 'All of this, in Botswana?'

Emma gave Hudson some painkillers and took a golf umbrella from the Land Cruiser to give him some shade. She asked the businessman to wait with him, took a bandage from the first aid kit, then strode across the road. The other driver was still lying on the tarmac where she had last seen him. She rolled him onto his belly, and as she began to draw his arms together behind his back he started to come to. He struggled against her.

'Lie still, you stupid fucker.'

She knelt on him and wrapped the bandage around his wrists, tied it off, then used the excess to bind his ankles, effectively hogtying him.

'I need a doctor.'

'You need the cops.'

She stood, brushed her hands on her shorts, then climbed up into the truck. She went to the hidden compartment, reached in and unzipped one of the dive bags, silently praying she was right about the bags not being big enough to hide a body, and that she did not find pieces of her mother wrapped in plastic.

Instead, she saw dozens of plastic-wrapped bundles. She took one out and hefted it in her hand; it weighed about a kilo, she thought. She took the driver's knife and sliced the package open.

Inside were more plastic bags, sandwich sized, but packed with a crystallised white substance. 'Ice,' she said to herself. At least Bheki had told the truth about the drug shipment, even if Sonja wasn't on board. Emma groaned as she lifted out the first dive bag; she thought it must weigh thirty or forty kilograms. Underneath was some rubbish. She fished out some broken cable ties and old duct tape. When she held it up to the light streaming in through one of the passenger windows she saw blood.

Sonja's?

She stuffed the tape in her pants pocket, walked back through the compartment and jumped down to the road. The driver was moaning.

'Help me . . .'

She ignored his pleas, instead rolling him over again and searching him.

His wallet contained a driver's licence, credit card and five hundred US dollars in cash. She took the contents and dropped the wallet on the road. In his shorts was a phone, which she also pocketed.

Emma paused for a moment to collect her thoughts.

'Please . . .'

Emma looked at the man, who was craning his neck to look up at her.

'An ambulance is coming. They'll have a look at you.'

'Please, he would have killed me if you had stopped me.'

She put her hands on her hips. 'We did stop you, in case you hadn't noticed.'

'He will kill me, now.'

'In prison?'

He gave a small nod. 'No one is safe from him, anywhere.'

'Carrington Wu?'

He just stared at her, but his look said it all.

Emma knew now what she needed to do. She turned and climbed back up into the vehicle. She lifted one of the heavy bags from the hidden compartment and dragged it to the rear of the truck. Emma jumped down and slid the dive bag from the truck onto her shoulders, using the handles like pack straps.

'No,' the man on the ground said to her. 'Leave it. He will kill you if he knows you took it.'

'Touching,' Emma said. 'And how's Wu going to know that I've got his drugs? Won't he think the cops have just impounded it all?'

The man shook his head, quickly. 'I won't tell him, I promise. Just cut me loose. I'll disappear and you can let the cops take the stash.'

She smiled down at him. 'We both know that's not going to happen, and that when Wu comes to visit you in prison you're going to tell him I've got half of his "stash".'

'He won't visit me, he will send someone.'

'I need to find him. Where is he?'

The man shook his head.

'I need to find him,' Emma said, 'so I can do a deal to get his drugs back to him, and maybe then he'll let you live. Where is he? Vic Falls?'

The man seemed to think a moment, then shook his head. 'Cape Town. He has a private plane; he came to the airport in Takunda, the truck, and left from there.'

'Did he have a woman with him? Some sort of cargo? A big box maybe?'

The man shrugged. 'I have no idea. My job was to wait outside the cargo area. I did not see him. I collected Takunda when I was phoned and told to do so.'

Emma decided he was probably telling the truth. They had missed Sonja, but she thought it likely that her mother was on that aircraft bound for Cape Town. She adjusted the weight on her shoulders and took a plastic bottle of water that had rolled out of the back of the truck. She walked across the road to where

Hudson lay. The helpful businessman had moved out of earshot and was talking on his phone, hopefully to find out when the police and ambulance would arrive.

'Where are you going?' His face was pale; he was probably suffering from shock.

'Cape Town. To find my mother, although at the moment I feel like bloody strangling her. From what the driver said, I think Wu is flying her there in his private plane.'

Hudson closed his eyes for a second, then opened them. 'I don't suppose there's any point in me trying to stop you.'

'You do know she's my biological mother, right?'

He smiled at that one, which was good.

'How . . .' He coughed and squinted through the pain. 'How will you find them once you get there?'

She tossed her head, indicated the bag of drugs on her back. 'They'll find me.'

'Shoot.' He reached into his shorts and pulled out a spare magazine of .45-calibre ammunition and tossed it to her. '*Vaya con Dios*, little lady.'

*

Emma was out of sight by the time the paramedics, a man and a woman, had splinted Hudson's leg, given him a shot of stronger painkillers and strapped him to a gurney. One of them had tended to the man on the roadside.

The businessman had left and Hudson raised a hand to point to the still-bound man as Hudson was lifted into the back of the minibus ambulance.

'What about him?'

'He'll be fine. We radioed it in,' the female medic said. 'The police are on their way; they got held up at another accident. We've told them about that guy. The cops will interview him then bring him to the hospital in Kasane; we only have room for you.'

Hudson had a view out the back window. As they drove off, the overland truck and the man lying behind it almost disappeared in the shimmering heat haze coming off the long black ribbon of tar. Hudson's brain was fuzzy and he'd been concussed or in shock when Emma was talking to him. He should have forced her to come with him, but he also knew enough about her, Sonja and their genes to know there would have been nothing he could have said to Emma to make her change her mind.

'How soon before you can get me patched up and out of hospital?'

'I am not the doctor,' the paramedic said, 'but I am guessing they will let you out once they have set your leg properly and examined you. Maybe tonight, maybe tomorrow.'

His private health insurance covered him for medical air recovery to South Africa, where he was a resident. He'd work on catching up with the Kurtz women in the next 24 to 48 hours, assuming Sonja wasn't still in Zimbabwe.

A black four-by-four with tinted windows raced past the ambulance and Hudson watched it, noticing a flash of red as the brake lights came on. He couldn't be sure, because of the haze, but it looked like the vehicle was stopping at the crash site.

CHAPTER 16

Sonja woke up in a cage, naked.

She registered that she was in an aircraft, propeller-driven judging by the noise and vibrations, but she was blindfolded and gagged. She tried kicking, but found her ankles were manacled to the steel mesh of her prison. Likewise, her wrists were encased in handcuffs, not cable ties. Carrington Wu was a fast learner.

Normally cool-headed, she fought to control a rising surge of panic. She tried to focus her mind. She remembered a warehouse, two men down, one trying to get away.

If. It was a senseless word, but if she had shot that man who was trying to leave instead of taking the time to decide to let him live, to do the *right* thing, as Hudson would have said, she might have been able to dodge the dart that had felled her and finish the man who had fired it.

She wiggled her toes and fingers, feeling through the steel mesh. The cage was inside a wooden crate, she now realised. Even Houdini would have had trouble getting out of this set-up. Reasoning that she had no chance of escape at the moment, she had to think about what was going to happen next.

Someone wanted her alive. Why? Wu was going to great

lengths to transport her somewhere, by air, which probably meant another country.

Wu and Hendricks were in business and she had, deliberately, got between them and disrupted their plans. Both men were utterly ruthless, of that she had no doubt, which made her wonder, again, why she was still alive. Was Wu taking her to Hendricks?

She thought of Emma. Her thoughts were not motherly. Rather, she thought about what she might do if she were in the gangsters' situation. If they wanted to hurt her, they could do their best to cause her pain, but she could absorb punishment. The surest and quickest way for them to debilitate her, or get her to do whatever they wanted, would be through her daughter. Emma was, Sonja realised coolly, her one weakness.

If it came to that, Sonja thought, she would die trying to protect Emma. She would also kill for her. Anyone. Anytime. Anywhere. Emma represented all that was good in her life – perhaps the only thing she had ever done right. At the same time, as hard as it was for her to admit it even to herself, Emma was also living proof of the mistakes she had made, including the worst decision of her life. That did not stop her loving her daughter, nor make her any less prepared to die for her; instead, the thought of Emma being harmed both gnawed at her and strengthened her resolve. A calmness descended over Sonja – if she died, it would be for Emma, and that would be better than living with the knowledge that she had lost her.

The steel dug into her flesh. For once she was grateful for those few extra kilos that had attached themselves to her thighs and butt and refused to leave, no matter how hard she exercised. *Look for the positive*, she told herself. *Embrace the suck.*

She didn't need to ask herself why she was naked. It was fairly common practice to strip a captive, the sort of thing the Americans would have done at Bagram, in Afghanistan, or Guantanamo Bay. Removing her clothes was meant to make her feel vulnerable. Time would tell how sophisticated her captors' interrogation techniques were.

Sonja heard and felt a change in the pitch of the propellers, then the *thunk* of landing gear being lowered and locked into place.

There was a rattle and the squeak of metal on metal as her environment changed. She felt the temperature rise, and the background thrum of engines became louder – someone had opened the lid of the crate she was in. She lay still, not wanting to betray the fact that she was conscious.

That was a mistake. Before she could arch or writhe away, she felt the sting of a needle in her butt. She passed out.

*

Emma hitched a ride with a South African couple in a four-wheel drive who were towing an off-road caravan. They had been to Victoria Falls and were headed for the Okavango Delta. They dropped Emma at the turnoff to Maun, at the dusty town of Nata, after dark.

She'd told them the truth, that she had been involved in a car accident, but left out the parts concerning guns and drugs.

Nata was a refuelling town, a place to stop on the way to somewhere else. She sat outside the Shell service station, drinking a Coke. She'd SMSed Hudson and now her phone rang.

'Where are you?' Hudson said.

'Nata.'

'Stay there. Check into a room at Nata Lodge – or anywhere you can find.'

'Save it,' she said. 'What do you really want?'

He sighed, audibly. 'Did you see a black Mercedes four-by-four, maybe ten minutes after the ambulance took me away?'

Emma searched her memory. 'No. I definitely would have tried to flag down a Mercedes. As it was, I got stuck in a Land Cruiser talking to Ouma and Pa Kettle from Pretoria for nearly two hours.'

'Hmmm.'

'What does that mean?'

'Maybe nothing. I'm not sure.'

'How are you, anyway?' A young man bearing arms full of beaded bracelets and necklaces approached her, but she waved him away. A truck flashed its headlights and honked its horn in a vain attempt to get a donkey to move off the road.

'High, I think. I'm not feeling any pain. My leg's in a moon boot. Emma, I shouldn't have sent you on your way. Please come back – not now, tomorrow. I don't want you hitching a lift in the dark.'

'Bye, Hudson.' She ended the call.

The phone she had taken from the overland truck driver buzzed in her pocket, making Emma start.

She answered it, but said nothing.

After a few seconds a voice said: 'Who is this?'

Emma bit her lip. She tried to think what Sonja would do in this situation. Probably, she thought, her mother would start abusing the caller, or threaten to kill him or cut his balls off. Something like that.

'My car tracking service sends me updates of where my tourist vehicles are.'

The voice was Asian, by the sound of the accent.

'If you are not Blessed, my driver, then I am simply asking you if he is all right. If you have him and my vehicle, please do not hurt my man.'

His *man*? Emma wondered if Wu could track his staff's phones as well as their vehicles, but then a quick glance at the device in her hand told her, no. It was not a smart phone – most likely the drivers were issued with cheap burner phones.

'Hello?'

Emma took a deep breath, then exhaled, trying to slow her racing heart. 'Carrington Wu?'

Silence.

'Your driver put up a good fight,' she continued.

'And he was beaten by a girl, by the sound of it.'

Misogynistic, paternalistic pig, she wanted to say to him. 'I'll save us both some time. I've got your drugs.'

The briefest of pauses. 'I'm sure I don't know what you're talking about, Miss . . .'

'Kurtz. Like my mother.'

'Sorry, the, ah, name is not familiar to me. I'm merely a businessman enquiring about one of my touring vehicles, which appears to have been abandoned or involved in an accident between Kazungula and –'

'I want an exchange,' Emma said.

He kept her waiting and Emma's heart refused to slow down. She wondered if Sonja was like this, a ball of nerves and fear behind her cool exterior. Probably not, she thought to herself, on reflection.

'You say you have my . . . cargo.' His cold tone indicated he had dropped the pretence of ignorance.

'You can have half of it.'

'Why half?'

'I'll give you half of it,' Emma said, making it up as she went along, 'when you give me my mother back, and I'll arrange to get the other half to you once we're out of Africa.'

'No, all of it, now. I have a better offer for her on the table already.'

'What's to stop me just going to the police now?'

'Do you want me to send you a picture of your mother's head? Detached from her body?'

'All right, all right,' she said. 'What are you doing with her, anyway?'

'I am not the only one your mother has wronged.'

Denzel, Emma thought. 'Hendricks. The abalone kingpin. You're delivering her to him.'

There was a pause before he answered, 'I am saying nothing to you, certainly not until I see my cargo.'

Emma felt that Wu's momentary hesitation meant she was on the right track. She thought of movies she'd seen about kidnap and ransom. Sonja wasn't one for television, but there was a film that her mother absolutely loved – she'd taken

Emma to see it when she was eight years old. 'I want a proof of life.'

'Prove to me you have my cargo.'

Emma looked around to make sure no one was close enough to see the contents of the dive bag, then unzipped it. She took a picture with the stolen phone – at least the piece of junk had a camera – then SMSed it to Wu.

'Where is the rest of the shipment?' he asked.

'It's safe,' she lied, although Wu would probably not agree given it was likely in a police lock-up by now. 'Where are you?'

'Come to South Africa, Cape Town. I will send you instructions of where we are to meet.'

'That's still a long way from where I am. What if I get caught with all this stuff?'

'Then you will end up in prison and your mother will die a slow death.'

Emma swallowed. 'Send me a picture of her, or I'm going to the cops now. With the bodies in your warehouse and drugs I've got, there's enough evidence to make things very unpleasant for you, Wu, even with all your friends in Zimbabwe.'

There was a pause on the other end of the line.

The phone dinged and buzzed. Emma opened the photo and had to close her eyes and turn away. It was Sonja, lying in a box in what looked like a cage. She had no clothes on and was handcuffed.

'You're fucking sick. Is she . . . is she even alive?'

'I'll send you details,' Wu said.

The call ended. Emma took a deep breath. She was sick to her stomach with fear.

'Hey?'

She looked up. A tall man in khaki shorts and shirt, with dark wavy hair, was silhouetted against a streetlight. Emma blinked at him.

'Howzit? Are you OK?'

'Um . . .'

'You waiting for someone?'

She shook her head. 'Not really, no. I mean, yes. I'm looking for a lift, down south. That's what you say for South Africa, right?'

He smiled. 'Hundreds. Hundred per cent. Yes. My name's Bryce. I work for a tour company and I'm towing one of our vehicles back to South Africa.' He gestured with a thumb and she saw a Land Rover Defender towing a car trailer with a Toyota on the back. 'I'm headed all the way to Cape Town, if that helps.'

'That would be too good to be true.' She narrowed her eyes, staring up into his face.

He read her vibe, because he lifted his left hand, showing a wedding ring. 'Wife and a baby boy at home. I'm happily married, I promise. Not a serial killer.' He pulled out his driver's licence and Emma read the name.

She managed a small smile. 'All right, Bryce Duffy, thank you.'

He went to pick up her bag, but Emma noticed that the zip was still partially open. 'No, no, I'm fine.'

'OK.' He laughed as he pointed to the heavy bag she was lugging. 'As long as you haven't got body parts or a load of drugs in there, then we're all good.'

*

Goodness Khumalo did not waste any time.

Hudson Brand had called her and told her that he had been involved in an altercation with the driver of an overland truck owned by a subsidiary of Giraffe Holdings, the company owned by Carrington Wu.

She'd thought it worth the time to drive to the Pandamatenga border post, wake up the staff, show her credentials and her passport, which, fortunately, she always carried, and then enter Botswana. A short way down the main road towards Nata she came across a crime scene attended by four local police cars, officers and plain-clothes detectives and lit up by portable floodlights. There was also a medical examiner's vehicle present. About three hundred metres away a bull elephant browsed contentedly, feeding in the tree line on the edge of the cleared zone that flanked each side of the main A33 highway.

'Move along, please,' a uniformed constable said to her.

She took out her ID. 'I'm Inspector Khumalo, Zimbabwe Republic Police. I need to speak to whomever is in charge here.'

The constable pointed to a tall man in an open-necked blue shirt and chinos. 'Inspector Mpho.'

She went to him, letting herself under the cordon of blue and white police tape.

'Hey,' the officer said.

She introduced herself again, ID once more on show.

He smiled. He was handsome, she thought. 'Inspector Maxala Mpho.' He held out his hand and they shook. 'But my friends call me Poster. To what do we owe the pleasure of a visit from our colleagues across the border?'

She looked to the medical examiner's van and a body on the ground, covered with a blanket. 'I thought this was a motor vehicle accident?'

'Sorry,' he said, 'Inspector . . .?'

'Khumalo . . . Goodness.'

'A beautiful name. Goodness, please, what's your interest in this?'

'There has been a string of incidents in Zimbabwe, all linked to this company, Flame of Zimbabwe,' she pointed to the tour truck, 'and its parent, Giraffe Holdings. One of these vehicles was destroyed yesterday, not far from Pandamatenga; it was carrying illegal cargo – abalone. Giraffe Holdings is an umbrella company owned by a Chinese man named Carrington Wu. He has fingers in everything – tourism, mining, import–export. The driver of the illegal cargo truck is locked up, but he's not talking – scared, I think. Two other men who had dealings with the same company – a helicopter pilot at a mining exploration camp and a professional hunter in Victoria Falls – are dead. Also, just before I crossed the border I got a call from my colleagues in Victoria Falls ZRP; they're investigating a double homicide at a warehouse belonging to this same company, Flame of Zimbabwe tours.'

'Ah, these Chinese.' Poster shook his head. 'As colonialists they are worse than the British were.'

Out of habit, Goodness did not talk politics – and Chinese investment in Africa fell into that category – with strangers. Not even good-looking ones. In her country, one never knew who was listening.

'I'm not into racial profiling, Inspector Mpho,' she said stiffly.

'Of course not . . . I merely . . .'

She smiled. 'It's fine. This Wu, he is raising red flags with us, not because he is Chinese but because I think he is up to no good. I came because I think your incident here might be related to those I'm investigating.'

Poster nodded. 'I see. Then I suppose I can tell you that this guy,' he nodded to the body, 'was shot in the back of the head, execution style, and we found what we think is several million pula worth of crystal meth in the vehicle.'

Hands on hips, Goodness said, 'It seems we've got a war of some sort going on here, Poster.'

'May I ask how you heard about this incident?' he asked.

'The man driving the Land Cruiser,' she pointed to the wreck on the other side of the road, 'is a private investigator. I know him; he filled me in on some of the details.'

Poster checked his notebook. 'A Mr Hudson Brand, I believe.'

'Yes, that's him. He's not a bad guy, but trouble has a habit of following him, or vice versa.'

Poster gave a comical grimace. 'A well-meaning amateur?'

'Yes and no. He's actually a good man, at heart, although he *is* on bail for elephant poaching. For the record, I think he was framed for that crime, maybe by the dead professional hunter who worked for Wu.'

'You're right, this Brand guy sounds like a trouble magnet.'

'He believes a friend of his has gone missing,' Goodness said, 'supposedly kidnapped, and he thought she was being carried in this overland truck. He thinks Carrington Wu is involved.'

The detective shrugged. 'As you can see, my crime scene team is crawling all over it now. Come, let's take a look from outside.' They walked to the rear of the Flame of Zimbabwe truck, which was open.

'If you look inside,' Poster pointed, 'you'll note how the crime scene tech is down in a hollow.'

A woman in white hazmat overalls turned and gave them a wave.

'It's some kind of hidden compartment,' he said.

'Anything in it, other than the drugs?'

He opened his mouth to answer, then seemed to think better of it.

'Poster,' she gave him her best smile, although his was a hard act to follow, 'I don't suppose you'd consider cooperating on this matter? Like I say, I know Brand and I'd be happy to sit in on your interview with him. I'll happily share all of the information I have from my investigations so far.'

He held off, thinking again. 'All right, on one condition.'

'What's that?' she asked.

'That you have a drink with me at the Chobe Safari Lodge after we finish interviewing this Hudson Brand.'

Not such a hardship, she thought. 'Deal.'

A uniformed female constable came up to them. She had been manning a roadblock, stopping vehicles as they approached the crime scene. 'Sir?'

'I've told my people to ask motorists if they've seen anything unusual or suspicious,' Poster said to Goodness, then turned to the young woman. 'Yes?'

'Sir, I just spoke to a man who said he passed a young white woman earlier. She was hitchhiking at Nata, at the Shell station. He thought it was unusual – you know most tourists are either on tours or in their own rental vehicles. He thought she was not local, maybe British. He spoke to her, asking if she was OK.'

'Description?'

'He thinks late twenties, auburn hair. He said she looked "sporty".'

'Anything else?' Poster asked.

'The man said she was sitting on a green vinyl bag, not like a backpack, though.'

Poster looked to Goodness, who glanced back at the touring truck. They had both seen the dive bag in the hidden compartment.

'Thoughts?' Poster asked.

'Brand was travelling with a young woman named Emma Kurtz – she is the daughter of the friend he believes has been kidnapped, one Sonja Kurtz.'

'I see. Have you taken Carrington Wu in for questioning?'

Goodness frowned. 'He is very well connected – he plays golf with judges and entertains senior politicians.'

'That's not an answer,' Poster said.

Goodness felt a flash of anger, not at the handsome inspector but at herself and how easily she had slipped into the slow lane of compliance. 'He'll have an army of lawyers and well-connected friends. We need to catch him red-handed.'

Poster raised his eyebrows. 'We?'

She cleared her throat. 'A figure of speech.'

'I like the sound of that.' He smiled at her, then looked down the road, into the distance, then back to the truck carrying the drugs. 'I see these vehicles quite often. They use this route from South Africa to the Okavango and Kasane, and into Victoria Falls.'

Goodness nodded. 'Yes, an easier run than trying to cross the chaotic border into Zimbabwe, at Beitbridge.'

'There are police roadblocks on the main road regularly,' he said, 'and veterinary control points where Department of Agriculture inspectors look for fresh meat, dairy products and the like, to prevent the spread of foot and mouth disease.'

'The perfect place to catch the next load of smuggled abalone, or drugs,' Goodness said.

'You read my mind. I think I'm going to enjoy working with you.'

Enough flirting, for now at least, Goodness thought. She went to the covered body and bent over it. She looked to Mpho. 'May I?'

'Be my guest.'

Goodness took a breath to steel herself then lifted the blanket. 'One round, back of the head, and out the forehead.'

'Execution style. Cold blood. This young woman, Emma?'

Goodness looked at him.

'She seems to have fled the scene, perhaps with a bag of drugs similar to the one in the truck,' Poster said. 'You think she is capable of something like this?'

Goodness replaced the blanket. 'If she is anything like her mother, then yes.'

CHAPTER 17

Among his extensive property portfolio, Vincent Hendricks owned a disused warehouse at Cape Town, at the Duncan Dock. He had earmarked it for redevelopment as a future luxury apartment block, once approval was granted – which, as with most things, was just a matter of money.

He parked outside and stepped from the warmth of his new model Range Rover into the night; a brisk breeze was coming off the Atlantic. He took the camel-coloured cashmere overcoat from the seat-back and put it on. Vincent breathed in the clean salty air, tinged with the pungent odour of old fish. It was the smell of his childhood.

The soles of his handmade polished Italian shoes, worth more than he might have made in a year as a boy working on his father's fishing boat, slapped in the small pools that had formed on the pitted tarmac of the dock. Parked near the edge of the dock was a HiLux *bakkie* with a rotating blue light on top and *Department of Agriculture, Forestry and Fisheries, Marine Anti-Poaching* emblazoned on the side.

Tied to a bollard was a sleek-looking jet-black RHIB, a rigid-hulled inflatable boat, with an impressive pair of outboard motors on the back. One uniformed officer was in the boat, assisting the last of a trio of handcuffed men onto the wharf. Two others were being questioned or processed by two other inspectors.

One of the inspectors saw him. The man hitched up his gun belt under his beer belly and walked towards him.

'*Goeie naand, Meneer* Hendricks, *hoe gaan dit?*'

'*Goed dankie*, and you, Charl?'

'Fine, sir, fine,' he replied in Afrikaans, their shared language.

'Looks like you've caught a few minnows here tonight, Charl,' Vincent said.

'Yes, sir, do you know them?'

Vincent nodded. 'One of them is the son of my cousin. Give them a slap on the wrist, Charl, and send them on their way.'

Charl looked over his shoulder, then back at Vincent. He moistened his lips with his tongue.

'What is it, Charl? Do we have a problem?'

He glanced back again. 'We've got a new guy on the team. The Zulu.'

Vincent looked past the portly fisheries inspector. The tall dark-skinned man was now lifting dive gear – cylinders, fins and BCDs – and tossing it onto the wharf with ease. He worked quickly, without a break.

'And?' Vincent said. 'Have you not been sharing your wages from me with him?'

Charl shifted his belt again. 'That's the thing, sir. I raised it with him, like making a joke, telling him there'll be a little something for him each month if he's a team player and, well, he threatened to report me to the anti-corruption people, sir.'

As he watched the young men in wetsuits being processed, Vincent remembered this life – not the dangers of the sea, including sharks, nor the law enforcement officers, some of whom would deliver a beating in lieu of a fine, and still steal one's fish. He reminisced, instead, about the simple pleasures of taking a haul of abalone from nature, of the beauty of the undersea world, of a few beers and a girl after a long night under water. He was removed from all of that now, a wealthy man, a politician.

There was no need for him to get his hands dirty any more, no need for him to even be talking to a man like Charl. He had his foot-soldiers to do his muscle work, his lieutenants to collect his money and enforce discipline. All the same, he was still drawn to this world, and the danger.

'He's a fit-looking guy,' Vincent said, looking the man up and down.

'That he is, sir,' Charl said. 'He tells me he works out almost every day, sir, in the gym.'

'Nice. A worthy opponent.'

'Sir?'

'Something I have in mind. SMS me his name and his home address, Charl, and the names of any family or dependants.'

There was the slightest hesitation before Charl answered. 'Yes, sir.'

Vincent waited longer, his eyes searching Charl's, seeing the fear, which was good, but wondering if there was more, perhaps a spark of loyalty to his Zulu colleague, or a moment's thought of his duty to the state and to the environment.

Charl took his phone from his pocket and began tapping out the required information.

Vincent smiled and clapped him on the arm. 'Good man, Charl.'

The other man pressed send and Vincent felt his own phone vibrate in his pocket.

'I prize loyalty above all else, Charl. You'll be rewarded for this, my friend, don't worry about that.'

'Thank you, sir.' He adjusted his belt again.

'Your conscientious Zulu –' Vincent took his own phone out and read the message, 'Mr Jacob Dlamini, won't be bothering you in the future.' He forwarded Dlamini's details to one of his more ruthless employees. Time was of the essence – the honest young fisheries inspector would not be going home this evening after work.

'Sir?'

'No more questions, Charl, and get rid of that RHIB. I need privacy at my warehouse for the next couple of days. No disturbances. Understood?'

'Understood, sir.'

*

Sonja shivered. She was still groggy, hungover from whatever drug they had given her. She had regained consciousness as her cage swayed, and vehicle springs creaked somewhere beneath her. She remembered being on an aircraft, but now she was in a vehicle.

Chilled air infiltrated the cracks in the box, along with the hum of traffic, the hoot of a horn, the far-off wail of a siren. The sounds of a city. There was a lurch and the squeak of air brakes, then, muffled through the timber of her prison, the rattle and screech of roller doors being opened, just as there had been at the first warehouse.

The vehicle moved again. Sonja shook her head, trying to clear it. She needed to be ready for whatever awaited her. Something or someone knocked against the timber above her, then her small world rocked crazily and she was thrown hard into the steel mesh of the cage within the crate. The box was being lifted, by a crane of some kind. They were taking no chances with her, no men lifting her out or escorting the crate at gunpoint.

Good, Sonja thought. They were afraid of her. She was being treated like a predator, to be caged when not sedated.

The crate was lowered to the ground, and there was more fussing above her. Voices, hushed, maybe cautious, removed a hook. She looked up and saw the hard steel tongue of a crowbar poke its way between two slats. Sonja thought of the Afrikaans word for the tool – *koevoet* – which was also the name of a police paramilitary unit her father had served with during the Border War, in Namibia. He'd passed on so much to her, without even knowing it.

The nails protested; the lid was lifted. The light, as weak as it was, made her blink. A nylon sling was threaded through the steel mesh. She would have bitten those brown fingers off if she'd been quicker, and the man probably feared the same fate as he almost jumped back out of reach once a new hook was fitted. A motor whirred and the cage was lifted a metre and a half off the ground, until it was swinging clear of the walls of the wooden crate.

'She's *mooi*, but she stinks.' The man laughed behind the safety of his ski mask.

Another, behind her so she couldn't see him, wolf-whistled, then turned on a fire hose. Cuffed and on her side, the steel mesh biting into her skin, Sonja could do nothing but endure the blast of ice-cold water that assaulted her body. But she embraced it, relished it. She was, as the man had said, filthy after her confinement. Perhaps, she thought, lying in her own waste, naked, was supposed to break or weaken her, but it hadn't. The water revived her as it sluiced her clean.

'Get her ready for the boss,' the ski-mask man said. The other one, his face also covered, moved around her with the hose. The water smacked her in the face and she lapped up what she could – that also made them laugh.

The force of the water was making the cage spin under the swivelling hook, allowing her to look around her. On each revolution she glimpsed a car, a top-of-the-line Range Rover with dark tinted windows, and another two cages. One, in a corner, was bigger than hers, but high enough for the tall African man inside to stand up. He clenched the upright bars.

'Give her some clothes, you fucking animals,' he yelled at the masked men. He wore a uniform of some kind.

The man without the hose strode over to the caged man, reached in through the bars and touched a hand-held taser to his skin. Sonja heard the crackle of electricity and the man crumpled to the concrete floor.

The second cage was much bigger again, the size of a suburban lounge room, she thought, but freestanding. Next to it was a stepladder. The man with the hose shut off the water flow, then went to the ladder, climbed it, walked out onto the steel mesh roof of the larger enclosure, then used a key to unlock a padlock. He swung open a hinged section of the roof. The other man used a hanging remote control to activate the hoist and Sonja was lifted higher.

She swung, again, as the man used the gantry control to manoeuvre her cage until it was hovering over the larger one. He pressed the 'down' button and she was lowered inside. The man above climbed in, removed the hook from the sling and then dropped a key inside her cage. 'Use this to unlock your cuffs,' he said.

Sonja glared up at him.

He blinked. 'Do as you're told.'

He then unlocked the lid of her cage and quickly scampered up onto the roof of the larger enclosure before locking the hatch closed.

Part of her was determined not to cooperate with these people in any way, but she knew that she would stand no chance without the use of her hands and feet. She rolled onto her back and managed to pick up the key on her second attempt with her cold, wet fingers. She fumbled, twice, to get the key into the lock and turn it. The man watching her, now safely outside, laughed at each attempt she made.

With her wrists finally freed, she sat up and undid the cuffs on her ankles. She stood, trying not to show pain as the blood flowed through her cramped limbs, and sneered at her captor, who unashamedly looked her up and down.

'Like what you see?' She stood straight.

'You're a little old for my tastes.'

She would kill him for that, Sonja thought. 'Who's in charge of this fucking rock show?'

A Judas gate door in the larger entry to the warehouse opened and a smartly dressed man in a camel-coloured coat stepped inside. 'I am.'

His voice echoed in the otherwise empty space. *First mistake*, Sonja thought. She now knew there was a microphone some-where in or near the cage, because Mr Tall, Dark and Handsome wouldn't have heard her otherwise. It was a small piece of infor-mation to file away.

Close on his heels, stepping through the door, was Carrington Wu. Sonja climbed out of her small cage and took hold of the bars of the larger one. She stood, making no attempt to cover herself with her hands, and watched the two men approach. They stopped a few metres away.

'I hope you like your gift,' Wu said to the other man.

'From what I've heard of her, you did well getting her here.' The man looked from Wu to Sonja. 'Allow me to introduce myself. My name is Vincent Hendricks. You killed my son.'

Her first instinct was to deny his allegation, but if she started pleading with them then she would automatically be at a disad-vantage. Also, Hendricks and Wu were making no attempt to disguise their identities. That meant she was most likely going to die in this warehouse.

She now had a playing field, with the goalposts set. She thought about what Hendricks had just said, about his son, Denzel. She had cut his air hose and his leg, but he had made it to shore. She remembered *thinking* about killing him. It had seemed the most natural thing for her to do. Denzel had threatened and then physically abused Emma. For that he deserved to be arrested or, in lieu of that, have the shit beaten out of him. She had punished him. But she was sure she'd stopped short of killing him.

A thought occurred to her, though even as it did, she wondered if her mind might still be affected by the drugs they had given her. *Wait, did I kill him?*

'She's like a caged lioness,' Wu said, breaking into her thoughts. 'I wonder if she will start pacing. See how she looks at us, wondering how and when she will get the chance to kill us. I like that she is not afraid of us.'

'You're lucky she didn't kill you,' Hendricks said to Wu.

'She took out several of my men,' Wu said. 'She has probably done me a favour – Allan Platt was a dangerous madman, and the others were clearly incompetent, to let a woman get the better of them, but she still needs to be taught a lesson.'

The two men began walking around the cage, inspecting her. She stood where she was, looking straight ahead, calculating, planning, and also wondering at Wu's reference to her killing several men.

'You say the daughter is on her way?' Hendricks said.

They were behind her. She gripped the bars of the cage until her palms hurt, but she would not give them the satisfaction of turning around.

'Yes. She says she has one of the bags of cargo, that she will exchange that for her mother, and then give us the other,' Wu said.

Hendricks laughed. 'Do you think she has any idea at all what she is playing at, who she is dealing with?'

Sonja heard the click of a camera phone.

'We should send the daughter this picture,' Hendricks said.

'What do you want?' Despite telling herself to be quiet, she knew that the mentions of Emma had set her off.

'Aha, it speaks,' Wu said. 'We want our property. You and your daughter have cost us money already and we need retribution.'

'You can do what you want to me,' Sonja said, 'and I have money. Just leave her out of it.'

They completed their circuit and came around to face her again. She stood there, naked and defiant, even as Hendricks took his time looking her up and down again.

'You will serve a purpose for us – you and our Zulu fisheries investigator friend over there.' He nodded to the other cage. The man inside was back on his feet, also holding on to the bars, watching them, listening.

'You have, stupidly, entered our world at a bad time,' Hendricks said. 'We have enemies who would divide us, and word will have got around of the fact that Wu has lost a truck full of abalone, and

I half of a drug shipment. Such cavalier behaviour, Miss Kurtz, encourages others to think that they, too, can steal and destroy at will. A message needs to be sent. Plus, you killed my son.'

She spat on the ground. 'Your son was an animal. Someone needed to put him down.'

Hendricks reached into the pocket of his coat and took out a taser. He came close to her, though she noticed he stopped just out of arm's reach. For all his bluster, and his taser, he was scared of her. He was a smart man.

'Why did you have to kill my son?' he asked her.

She locked eyes with him. 'Who says I did?'

'Are you denying it?'

'Would it matter?'

'Probably not,' he said.

'I went after him, tracked him, went into the sea and scared the life out of him. I cut his air hose and gave him a scratch on the leg while he was diving. I saw the fear in his face; I hope he pissed himself.'

Hendricks clenched his jaw and his fists, but said nothing.

'He's a typical bully. He could act the big man around his friend, or cousin or whoever it was, when he thought he was taking on a couple of women, but he was no fighter. He gave up.'

'Enough.'

She had him. 'Did he want to be as tough as you?'

He came a few centimetres closer. 'You have no idea who I am, what I have done. I could skin you alive.'

Sonja smiled. 'Look at you. You're too scared to even come close enough to touch me. The only way you'll be skinning me is when I'm dead. Where's the fun in that, big man? Now tell me . . .'

Hendricks stood there, trying to regain his composure.

'Your boy wasn't worth the price of a bullet. Tell me,' Sonja continued, 'who else might want to kill your son, either out of revenge, or to hurt you?'

He glared at her.

'I know you're going to kill me,' she said matter-of-factly. 'Why else would you allow me to see your face? You can threaten my daughter, but there's not much I can do about it here, now, is there?'

He cleared his throat. 'My son was impetuous.'

'More like trying to prove to Daddy what a big tough man he could be, just like his gangster father.'

'You taunt me,' he smiled, 'but I could simply put a bullet through your head right now, if I wanted to.'

'You think that scares me?' Sonja said. 'You'd probably be doing me, and my daughter, a favour. Don't you sometimes think Denzel would have been better off without you, that he might have taken another path in life, if his father wasn't a criminal, a killer, someone who keeps women in cages to help him get off?'

Although he maintained eye contact with her, he yelled: 'Bring the screens.'

His two men in ski masks disappeared into a row of downstairs offices.

Sonja could see that Hendricks was seething, his hatred and impotence boiling inside his skin. He had some grand tough-guy plan for her and, presumably, for the poor guy locked in the other cage.

'Going to put some porn on to warm yourself up?' she taunted.

He stood, tantalisingly out of reach of her. He'd have a gun, probably in a shoulder holster like some TV thug, she thought. And there was that bloody taser. She let him see her smile as she imagined giving it to him. 'What do you really want? Revenge?'

He looked at her for a moment. 'You're going to help me send a message.'

'Really?'

One of the two men wheeled two large flat-screen monitors on a trolley to a point near Sonja's prison. The other unspooled a long extension cord from a reel. He connected the power to the monitor. Hendricks's phone rang; he answered it, then checked the phone's screen and smiled.

Hendricks turned his back on her and walked closer to the television monitor. Wu moved a short distance away, made a call of his own, then returned to Hendricks. Wu glanced over at Sonja, then addressed Hendricks: 'We estimate that her daughter, Emma, will be in Cape Town tomorrow afternoon.'

'Good. Just in time.' Hendricks stood in front of the screen, phone out, tapping on the screen. 'I'm pairing,' he said to Wu.

The plasma screen came to life. It was a video, shaky, being streamed from another phone or camera. A woman sat on a red sofa with two little children, one on each side of her.

'Hey!' the African man in the other cage called out. Sonja looked around and saw that the man was looking their way and could see the screen. He bellowed: 'Sibongile!'

Hendricks turned to Sonja. 'Sibongile Dlamini, the wife of Jacob, the man over there, as you can probably tell.'

Dlamini was screaming now, almost incoherently.

'Soon enough we'll have visual contact with your daughter, Sonja. Wu has his own problems with her – she killed one of his drivers in Botswana. He's got someone on her tail.'

'What?'

'Yes.' Hendricks nodded. 'Shot him in cold blood, in the back of the head. He was already down on the road, in Botswana, his arms and legs tied.'

'No,' Sonja said, 'that's not possible.'

Hendricks shrugged. 'What am I to do? I have a mother and a daughter causing havoc, and a cleanskin fisheries inspector who is too high and mighty to take a simple bribe.'

'I'll do it!' Jacob called from his cage. 'Hey! I'll do whatever you want.'

Hendricks walked over to him. 'Yes, Jacob,' he said slowly, loud enough for Sonja to hear. 'I know you'll do whatever I want, but you took too long coming around to our point of view and, as a result, your family has had to suffer.'

'No!'

'I'm cold,' Sonja said to Hendricks, hoping to distract him.

She stood, full-frontal nude, feet slightly apart, making no move to cover herself.

'I've got something for you to wear,' he said.

'What are you going to do, dress me in latex and whip me?' She nodded to the second screen. 'Kill me in front of a camera for some sort of perverted snuff movie, for fun?'

'No.' Hendricks shook his head and pointed to Jacob. 'That's why he's here.'

CHAPTER 18

Bryce Duffy, it turned out, knew Hudson, and had been involved on the periphery of one of Hudson's private investigation cases. The drive had been long and tiring, with an overnight stop at a self-catering camp Emma couldn't even remember the name of. They had slept in separate rondavels.

'Something on your mind?' Bryce said now, as Table Mountain came into view.

She'd had a message, on the phone she had taken from Wu's driver, instructing her to let Wu know when she was at the Victoria & Alfred Waterfront shopping precinct. 'I'm fine.'

'What's in your bag, Emma?'

She looked at him, feigning innocence. 'Just clothes and stuff.'

'You're one of the few women I've met who wears the same clothes two days in a row.'

'Are you saying I stink?' she said, trying to deflect.

'No, but you do have a tomato sauce stain on your shirt from breakfast at the Wimpy this morning.'

'All my other tops are dirty. I need to find a laundry.'

'And you hid that dive bag of yours, properly, before we crossed the border.'

She *had* been paranoid that some customs officer might conduct a random inspection. Bryce was kind and seemed genuine and honest. She did not want to drag him into the murky mess her mother had got her into. She recalled the two large Pelican waterproof cases she'd seen in the back of his Land Rover, hidden under a tarpaulin, where she stashed the dive bag. She needed to change the conversation.

'What were *you* smuggling in those serious boxes you've got in the back?'

'Camera gear, and a drone,' he said. 'The most expensive things I own, so I keep them out of sight of any thieves, or thieving border control officers.'

'You're into photography?'

He nodded. 'And video. A lot of the lodges like aerial vision for their social media and advertising.'

'You should talk to Hudson about that – maybe do something for the lodge he's managing.'

'Good idea. Are you meeting someone at the V&A?' he pressed.

She sighed. 'Bryce, it's time for me to go my own way. I'm a grown woman.'

'Who was hitchhiking through Botswana, but not dressed like your typical backpacker, and with a scuba-diving bag full of what – drugs?'

'What makes you say that?'

He glanced at her, then back at the road, concentrating. The traffic was getting heavier as they passed the airport. Her guns – Johnsy's and Hudson's – were in the bag as well. She felt the danger encroaching on her, the larger the flat-topped mountain loomed through the windscreen.

Emma wished there was some way she could prove to the gangsters that Sonja did not kill Denzel – even if she did. She wasn't one hundred per cent sure in her own mind, either way. Like Hudson had said, Sonja was tough, but she was not the sort to execute prisoners in cold blood. On the other hand, she had been acting weirder than normal. If Sonja didn't kill Denzel, though, who did?

There was no excusing what Denzel had done, either on the beach or afterwards, when he had assaulted her. Violence against women – anyone – was unforgivable, but it did not warrant summary execution, Emma told herself again.

'What are you thinking about?'

'My mother.'

'Oh. Do you miss her?'

'No. She's a pain in the arse and a borderline psychopath.'

Bryce nodded, like he was taking that in. 'So, basically, what you're saying is you love her, right?'

'That's not what I said.'

'No, but you've been sitting there stewing for the last two hours, and grinding your teeth.'

'She annoys the hell out of me.'

'Yes. But you'll miss her when she's gone.'

She looked at him. 'You?'

'I lost my mom a few years ago. Tell her you love her when you see her, Emma. Even if she is a pain in the arse and a psychopath.'

Emma shook her head. 'It won't do her any good; she's virtually incapable of showing any human emotion.'

'No, but it will do *you* some good.'

He was right. She remembered from their rare 'girly' shopping trip to the V&A – Emma had bought a floral mini dress, Sonja a pair of black cargo pants – that they had felt closer than they had in years. She wrung her hands in her lap.

'How can I help you, Emma?'

'Just drop me off, please. I'll be fine. Why do you care, anyway?'

'Hudson helped me once – helped my wife, in fact. You're close to him.'

Emma had, she knew, gone on and on about Hudson, much more so than about her mother. He'd been a good friend to her. 'It's weird to think of him and my mother – dating, or whatever it is they do. I've never really thought of Hudson as a father, more as a friend, but I suppose, in a way, he's been the closest thing I've had to one.'

'Then let me help.'

She looked at him. Whoever his wife was, she was a lucky woman. 'You're lovely, Bryce, and thank you, but I have to sort this shit out with my mother on my own.'

He seemed to get the message, and they said little more until he pulled into the car parking area of the V&A Waterfront. It was busy; tourism was returning to South Africa and Emma heard a few different European languages around her as she slid the heavy bag from the back of the Land Rover.

'Take care,' Bryce said to her, and helped her adjust the bag on her back.

'Thank you.' She shook his hand, then gave him a peck on the cheek and turned away.

Emma set off, walking past a stone-built pub. She found a quiet spot behind the building, unzipped the dive bag and took out the Colt and put it in the waistband of her pants. She closed the bag and emerged into a crowded open area by the edge of the water. She took out the stolen phone and sent a message.

I'm here.

A minute later the phone vibrated. *Walk towards the One&Only Hotel.*

She looked around, saw the building, hitched up the bag's straps and started walking.

*

Bryce Duffy had driven a short distance, to Mouille Point. He parked, quickly opened the back of the Land Rover and took out the cases containing his commercial-grade drone and camera gear.

A couple of families with small children stopped their walk along the coastal path to watch as the machine raced up into the sky, its four battery-powered motors bearing the weight of a high-definition video camera. Bryce fitted Bluetooth earbuds and connected them to his phone as he worked the drone's controls and watched the screen of his iPad, which was linked to the now-airborne camera. Bryce had the iPad slung around his neck in a harness. Keeping the drone steady with one hand, he took out his phone and searched WhatsApp for Hudson Brand's number. He dialled.

'Bryce Duffy,' Hudson said. 'How the hell are you, buddy? It's been a long time.'

'Fine, Hudson, but I'm sorry, man, I don't have time for pleasantries. You know a woman called Emma Kurtz?'

'Shoot, Bryce. Have you seen her? Where the hell is she?'

'Cape Town.'

'Figures. You with her now?'

'Not exactly; I can . . . yes, I can see her now. She's got a big green bag of something and she's set off into the crowds at the V&A looking for someone. I only just got to know her and she says she knows you –'

'You get hold of her, Bryce, please, for me. Round her up and tie her down if you have to.'

'I think that's going to be a little difficult, Hudson. Is she in some kind of trouble?'

'Plenty. So's her mom, a . . . friend of mine. She's gone missing.'

'*Ja*,' Bryce said. 'She said something about her mother.'

'She needs to get to the cops, Bryce, turn herself in, along with the stuff she's carrying. You may as well know, there's millions of rands' worth of drugs in that bag she's toting. She's going to try and do a deal with a Cape Town gangster and a Chinese guy to get her mom back.'

'*Eish.*'

'Exactly. You say you can see her?'

'I've got a drone, with a camera on her. She's walking along the dock, heading towards the hotel, the One&Only.'

'Yeah, I know it. Bryce, listen to me, these people aren't going to play nice. If they've got the mom, they want the daughter. The only way they'll be able to hurt Sonja – the mother – or get anything out of her, is if they take Emma.'

'So, what do you want me to do?'

Hudson paused. 'Hell, call the cops, Bryce. Emma's better off in prison, cooling her heels in a cell than out there at the mercy of these people. I feel bad. I was banged up – Emma and I were in a car wreck – and I kind of gave her the green light to go off-reservation. I was concussed.'

'She's moving down a laneway, out the back of the hotel.'

Bryce had his phone in his pocket now, talking to Hudson on Bluetooth. He concentrated on steering the drone, which he had to fly between buildings in order to follow Emma.

'What do you want me to do,' Bryce said to Hudson. 'Stay on her or call the police?'

'Keep her in sight, Bryce. I'll contact the cops.'

Hudson rang off, then called back a few minutes later. 'Tell me what you're seeing, buddy,' he said.

'There's a black van, a Sprinter, tinted windows, at the end of an alley.'

'Shoot. What's she doing?'

'She's put the bag down, stepping back from it.'

'How many bad guys?'

'One, no, make that two, getting out of the van, coming towards her.'

'Any sign of anyone else in the van, like maybe a hostage? Woman, around fifty.'

Bryce manoeuvred the controls, bringing the drone down lower. He didn't want to alert the men in the alley to its presence, nor have Emma look up and give him away, but he needed a lower angle to see inside the van. 'Could be. Wait a minute, yes, I can see a leg or something. Some movement in the van. Just checking. Yes, there is someone, but I think it's a man. I can see him holding an iPad or some other tablet.'

Bryce changed the drone's position.

'What's Emma doing? Talk to me, Bryce.'

'OK, she's made contact. One of the men is pointing inside the open door of the van, like he's telling her there's something or someone inside. She's shaking her head. She's picking up the bag again.'

'Darn it, she should just leave that shit there.'

'I can't get word to her, Hudson. You want me to head there now?'

There was another pause. 'Bryce, you stay out of that situation, you hear? You got a wife and kid now. I don't want any more collateral damage from this war.'

'Sheesh, Hudson, one of the guys has just pulled a gun on Emma. She's dropped the bag.'

'Pistol?'

Bryce lowered the drone some more and zoomed in. 'Yes, with silencer. Shit.'

Bryce stared intently at his screen. The man was taking aim at Emma.

Just then, a black blur flashed across the screen of Bryce's iPad. For a moment he thought it was a bird, swooping past, but when he pulled the focus back out again, he saw, to his surprise, another drone.

*

'You see?' Hendricks said to Sonja, gesturing to the large monitor. 'The game's up. We now have your daughter.' Carrington Wu was by Hendricks's side, arms folded, smiling.

She'd been kept locked up through the night and the next day. Before he and Wu left for the night, Hendricks had ordered one of his men to toss a paper bag into her cage, after she had been hosed down. In it, she had found red satin boxing trunks and a black tank top. Dlamini had been given new clothes as well, all-white shorts and a T-shirt. They had been fed, takeaway from a Spur restaurant.

'You'll both need your strength,' was all a henchman had said to her.

Sonja looked at Emma, her image captured from above, most likely via drone camera. Emma was walking down an alleyway of some kind, carrying a dive bag. Sonja gripped the bars of the cage and wanted to wail, just like Jacob Dlamini had, when she saw her daughter put the bag down and raise her hands. Hendricks had obviously put Jacob's family under guard as soon as they nabbed him, so that his wife could not alert the authorities to him being missing, and Hendricks could exert maximum pressure on Jacob. She now fully understood what Jacob had been going through.

Hendricks took his phone out of the inside pocket of his overcoat and dialled a number. He hit the speaker function and turned up the volume. Sonja could see the man on the screen, holding the pistol with a suppressor screwed to the end, covering Emma. With his other hand the man took his phone out and answered it.

'Boss?'

'Reuben, I see you have her.'

The man gave a little laugh and Sonja saw him shrug his shoulders as he did so. 'It was too easy, boss.'

'Good work, Reuben. Is there anyone around you?'

Reuben shook his head. 'No, boss, just us. We can do it now, if you want.'

Hendricks looked to Sonja. 'What do you say? Quick and clean? I can't promise you that we'll be kind to Emma if you don't do what I want.'

Part of her wanted to scream, but a bigger part of her wanted to kill.

'Talk to me, Sonja,' Hendricks said. 'I don't have all day.'

'Still got a clean shot, boss,' Reuben said. 'She's asking for her mother, for proof of life.'

The drone had shifted and Sonja could see Emma's face, and her lips moving. The sight of her felt like a bayonet piercing the scar tissue of her heart. Sonja looked across to the other cage, to Jacob. It was the big man's turn to see her anguish, her impossible dilemma.

Sonja moistened her lips with her tongue.

'You look like a cobra, sniffing out its prey,' Hendricks said.

'I'll do what you want.'

Now Hendricks looked to Jacob, then back to her, his eyebrows raised in a question.

'Yes,' Sonja said, 'and I'll swear my loyalty to you. In exchange for my daughter's life, and no contract on her head, from you or Wu.'

Hendricks turned to Wu, who nodded.

'Boss?' Reuben said, the phone still clamped to one ear.

'Yes, Reuben?'

'I can hear sirens. I'm sure no one's seen us, but what must we do with her now?'

'Put her in the van. Bring her.'

On the screen Reuben advanced towards Emma.

Sonja snarled, like a leopardess, at Hendricks.

*

'They're grabbing her, Hudson!' Bryce flew the drone to the left and used his controls to swing the camera around. Having phoned the police, Brand was back on the line. 'They're using a drone as well – it's right below mine.'

'Cops are on the way,' Hudson said. 'That drone's the bad guys' eyes and ears. Can you take it down somehow?'

'I can see it. They're bringing it down. It's close. The guy who was hiding in the van is coming out now, probably to guide it in.'

'Don't let them get away, Bryce. The cops just messaged me. Two minutes out.'

The man with the gun had Emma by the arm now, his pistol pointed at her. He dragged her to the van and said something to her. She turned, put her hands against the van and spread her legs. The third man came towards Emma, obviously planning to frisk her.

'You owe me, Hudson,' Bryce said.

'What?'

Bryce ignored Hudson. He used the controls to send his drone, bigger and heavier than the other, hurtling downwards on a forty-five-degree angle. He watched as the other drone and, now, the upturned face of its operator, both grew larger on his iPad screen. The operator had his mouth open, yelling a warning as the gunman came closer to the door of the van.

*

Emma screamed as the tangle of wreckage of two disabled drones clipped her shoulder and then slammed into the man holding the gun.

The one who had been about to frisk her stumbled backwards.

She had been cursing herself, knowing they would find the .45 tucked into her jeans. She reached around, pulled it out and brought it up into the stomach of the gunman who, even though his face and neck were bleeding and he was on his knees, a tangle of shattered machinery around him, was bringing his gun up to shoot her.

Emma fired first and he doubled over.

The man who had been going to search her was reaching for a pistol stuffed in his pants. Emma put two shots, a double tap, into his chest.

A third, younger man with a wispy beard and long hair was emerging from the van.

He put his hands up. 'Don't shoot. I'm just the geek. I don't even have a gun.'

Emma pointed the barrel at him, the foresight wavering; her heart was pounding.

'Where's my mother?'

'Who?'

'The woman, the one they took prisoner.'

He shook his head. 'I don't know anything about that. I was just here to work the drone and the feed.' He pointed to the wreckage on the ground.

Emma heard sirens, getting closer.

'I'll leave you to the cops. You can explain to them where my mother is.'

'Please,' he said, and she saw what looked like real fear in his eyes, 'I don't know where your mom is. But let me tell you, don't trust the cops. The boss – he's got them in his pocket. Anything you or I say to them will get back to him, I promise you.'

Emma heard a car's engine and turned. A black four-wheel drive, a boxy-looking luxury model, was turning into the alley towards them. It had dark tinted windows. There was something sinister about it.

'Where would he be?'

'They don't tell me anything. He has properties all over Cape Town. I know that some high-end screens and sound gear was delivered to some place at Duncan Dock, a wharf near here. They asked me if I knew anyone who could rent or sell some big AV around here for a rush job.'

She wanted to ask him the company name, but at that moment the driver of the vehicle coming towards her gunned his engine.

Emma ran off down a side alleyway. As she fled, she heard a single gunshot.

As Emma sprinted, she barely had time to process everything that had happened. Bryce must have been watching her with his drone, she realised. He'd saved her, but she had no idea where he was. One of the two phones she was carrying was vibrating in her pocket, but she didn't have Bryce's number, so it couldn't be him, and nor could she stop to check it.

She'd left the bag of drugs behind and in it was Johnsy's pistol. *Shit*. She had hidden it there in case something had gone wrong during her transaction and she had an opportunity to reach into the bag. Now the police would find a stolen gun, with her prints and Johnsy's on it, in a bag full of ice. Even if she did find the police she'd be tied up for hours.

Emma ducked left down another laneway and came back out onto the main promenade along the water. Shoppers and tourists were going about their business, although she could see the flash of blue lights from the first alley she had headed down.

She slowed to a walk so as not to attract attention, the .45 once more hidden under her shirt. *Think*, she told herself.

The gangsters had had a drone up in the air, presumably filming her, and the geek she had bailed up had said they had ordered high-quality screens and sound gear to be delivered to a place at the docks.

Why?

It had to be because of Sonja, she told herself. Emma knew that she was no threat to criminal gangs or the triads, but she also knew that if Sonja had one weakness it was probably her. They had filmed her approaching with the bag of drugs and they also wanted to get video of her being abducted. The young guy had talked of 'the feed'. Did that mean Sonja was somewhere, maybe nearby, watching Emma's supposed kidnapping live?

'Shit.' By evading them, and killing two men in the process, had she just signed her mother's death warrant?

One of the phones rang again. It was hers, not Wu's driver's.

'Hudson,' she said.

'Thank God you're alive.'

'There was a guy, Bryce –'

'Duffy. Good guy, I know him. He and I were just talking. Where are you? I'll send him to come get you.'

'No, Bra– Hudson.' *For goodness' sake*, she thought to herself. She didn't want to start sounding like her mother. 'Like you said, he's a goodie. I don't want him dragged into this any more. He's got a wife and kid. He saved me.'

'I heard he went kamikaze with his drone.'

'Yeah. She's alive, Hudson, I know it.' Emma told him about the geek who she suspected had been live-streaming from the other drone, and her theory about Sonja.

'Dammit, wish I was there.'

'Well, you're not. You're in Botswana with a broken leg.'

'I called the cops, in Cape Town.'

Emma nodded to herself. 'OK. I wondered about that. One of the guys who tried to kidnap me – he was their tech guy – told me Hendricks has cops on his payroll.'

'Figures,' Hudson said, 'but you'd be safer in custody.

231

Your mom's got enough money to get you the best lawyers in the country.'

'We might be waiting for her will to be read if I don't find her soon. Also, someone else turned up, before the cops arrived.'

'More gangsters?' he asked.

'I don't know. It was a black four-by-four. Not a Land Rover or a Cruiser.'

'Mercedes?'

'Could have been, I'm not an expert on cars, but it looked big and boxy. How did you guess?'

'Remember how I asked if you'd seen a Mercedes in Botswana? Well, I saw a black G-Class with dark tinted windows racing past the ambulance after I got picked up. Goodness Khumalo, the police inspector from Zimbabwe, came and interviewed me in hospital, along with a local detective. They told me that the driver of Wu's overland vehicle was dead, Emma, shot in the back of the head.'

Emma tried to take this in. 'But he was alive when I left. You know that wasn't me, Hudson.'

'The Merc man, maybe?'

Emma remembered hearing the single shot after she'd left the alleyway.

'Let me call my contact in the police at Cape Town, Emma,' Hudson said, breaking into her thoughts. 'Also, I can try audio-visual sales and rental places around Cape Town, tell them I'm waiting for my shipment of big-screen TVs and get them to check the address. I can't think of any other way to find out where your mom is. Can you?'

'Sounds good. I'll call you back.'

Emma ended the call before Hudson could protest.

Her other phone rang.

'The Cape Town police have just been sent some stills from footage taken by a destroyed drone. They show you at the scene of a crime in which three harmless delivery drivers were killed, by their van,' Wu said.

Emma thought fast. She had shot one man in the stomach and definitely killed the second – she shuddered at the memory and suppressed a wave of nausea. She had left the third, the geek, alive, but then she'd heard a gunshot as she left.

'The police are at the scene,' Wu continued. 'You'll be in jail soon. We'll make sure of it.'

So what? she thought to herself. Wu was in business with Hendricks and, according to the hipster technical guy, the gangster had the cops in his pocket. This was not news.

'We will kill your mother.'

'Good luck with that,' Emma said, 'especially now that you don't have a video of me crying and begging for my life.'

'It's not a problem. She saw enough before the feed was cut. As far as she knows we have you.'

'You've got your drugs. Let her go.'

'*Half* of my cargo. I want the rest. You have an hour or your mother dies.'

What the hell, Emma thought, *I may as well tell them the truth.* 'The other bag's in Botswana. It'll take me and a small army more than an hour to get it out of the Kasane police lock-up. We can pay you for the fucking drugs.'

'I'm afraid it's not just about the money,' Wu said. 'Trust me, Emma. If you want your mother to live, you should hand yourself in to us.'

'No way.'

She heard him sigh on the other end of the call. 'Very well. Then I must tell you, honestly, that if your mother is not one hundred per cent sure that you are alive, and that we are holding you as a hostage, then she will most surely die. She seems to have a great strength of character and that is about to be put to the test.'

'What do you mean, most surely –?'

Wu ended the call.

Around her, tourists blithely went about their business, taking selfies, laughing, eating ice-cream, queueing for restaurants.

Part of her wanted to scream: *All I wanted was a fucking normal life!* She stilled herself. The other part of her, the Sonja part of her, knew what she had to do.

CHAPTER 19

Sonja watched the warehouse begin to fill with cars and people. 'I want to see my daughter again,' she called out.

Hendricks was with a couple, an older man and a younger woman. Hendricks patted the man on the arm and walked towards her.

Sonja assessed the crowd. They were well dressed, but flashy. There was clearly a 'masque ball' dress code; Sonja didn't know if it was some kind of kinky theme, or for security, with some of the attendees preferring to remain anonymous. The men sported a style she would have described as 'gangster formal'. The women, although wearing cocktail dresses and insane heels, were rough around the edges. She saw homemade tattoos on exposed skin and when a pair of eyes locked on to her, they had the hardness of the streets in them. The one who had just been talking to Hendricks was staring at her.

'Be quiet, now, Sonja,' Hendricks said to her in a low voice. He was now wearing a Zorro mask tied behind his head. 'Not long to go.'

'I want to see my daughter. Proof of life.'

'You think we've killed her already? I'm not that stupid.'

'I think she might have killed a couple of your men by now.'

235

He laughed. 'She's an archaeologist, not an assassin, unlike you.'

Sonja ground her teeth.

Hendricks carried on, though he stayed a metre from the cage. 'It's quite simple: when the bell is rung, you and Jacob will fight, to the death. The one who loses will do so knowing his or her family will join them in heaven, see?'

She shook her head. 'I have seen some sick shit in my life . . .'

He smiled and spread his hands wide. 'Jacob has more to lose than you – two children and a pretty wife. You have one person. The winner will work for me, with their loved one – or ones – in protective custody for six months. After that period, he or she will be so compromised that they will have to continue in my service, or risk going to prison for a very long time. You and Emma already have a string of murders pinned on you the length of southern Africa. If you live, I should be able to make most of those go away. You should count yourself lucky I didn't just put a bullet in your brain, the same as you did to my son.'

'Listen to me, Hendricks.'

He looked over his shoulder and gave a small wave to another couple who had just arrived.

'I did not kill your son.'

He turned back to her. 'Really? Now you're lying? What next, begging?'

'I caught him, under water, cut his air hose, and stabbed him. To teach him a lesson.'

He shrugged. 'For that alone I would kill you.'

She seethed. 'And I could have – should have – killed him for attacking my daughter, but I didn't.'

He looked hard into her eyes. 'You know, I don't think you know what you did, there, or in Hwange or in Victoria Falls with Wu's people. Wu told me about the trail of executions you carried out, on people who wronged you and those you care about. I want you working for me. You're just the kind of controlled psychopath I need.' Hendricks started to turn back to his crowd of couture criminals.

'Someone else killed your boy,' Sonja called after him. 'You let me and Dlamini out of this zoo and I'll find out who.'

Hendricks ignored her and strode across the warehouse floor to a newly arrived Tesla. He embraced the man and woman who got out.

Sonja surveyed the crowd. Wu, distinctive by his height, hair and build, now had a tall blonde, pushing more than two metres in her stripper heels, on his arm. She was disguised with cat's ears, eyes and whiskers and had the look of a high-priced rental about her, Sonja thought.

A girl standing with an old guy glanced back at her every now and then. She was beautiful, even in a mask, with coffee-coloured skin, curls and a hint of softness about her. Sonja manufactured a smile for her and she turned back to her sugar daddy.

A Land Cruiser FJ entered the warehouse. Sonja noted that each time a new car came in, two guards in black suits, AK-47s slung over their shoulders, opened and closed roller doors. Sonja reasoned that even this lot of ostentatiously clad gangsters didn't want to attract attention by parking their equally flashy rides out on the dock – the smell of cold salt air and the occasional toot of a ship's horn told her she was by the sea. A man with a bleached mullet and another blonde got out of the FJ, which sported a Western Province number plate – local abalone dealers, she guessed.

The next couple walked in, perhaps after being dropped off outside. Uber or chauffeured transfer, Sonja thought. He was tall and broad, grey-haired, carrying a mix of old muscle and new flab. Under his cheap, simple bandit's mask was a red nose that had been flattened in a fight or two in a previous life. The woman on his arm was much younger than him, judging by her slim but muscled alabaster arms and long, straight black hair. She was clad in a lime-green shimmering sheath, her face fully covered by what looked like a Roman or Viking death mask, which would make it hard for her to do drugs or booze. Even from a distance, and Sonja did not have her glasses or contact lenses, there was something familiar about her. She closed her eyes for a moment, trying to think where she might have seen the young woman, or, at least, her body, before.

Like everyone who entered, this couple paused to look at her then moved on to assess Jacob, as though she and the Zulu man were racehorses or cattle at auction. Jacob caught her eye every now and then, and searched her face for some kind of answer or way out of this madness.

The thugs had set up the room with rows of seats like a concert venue, and were now doubling as drinks waiters. They had wheeled in trolleys of food from outside – clearly the caterers were not going to be treated to the sight of cage fighting. The criminals reverted to type, jostling at the tables for oysters, canapes and mini cardboard boxes of something hot.

The curly-haired sugar baby, champagne flute in hand, drifted closer to Sonja while a circle gathered around Hendricks and Wu. The girl reminded Sonja of an impala, big dark eyes, twitchy, like she was worried about the predators in the room. She cast her eyes down at Sonja's upper arm.

'What's your tattoo?' She pointed to the ring of letters and numbers around Sonja's bicep.

Really? Sonja thought. Not: *What are you and that man doing in cages and why will you be beating the shit out of each other soon?*

'My home, or the closest thing I ever had to one.' Sonja glanced down at the letters and numbers. 'Latitude and longitude, like on a GPS.'

'Where?'

'Botswana. A place called Xakanaxa, in the Okavango Delta.'

She nodded. 'Your happy place, right? I saw it once, on DSTV. Lions in the water. Were you really happy there?'

'My first love was there, but my father beat me and my mother.' Sonja detected the slightest movement in the girl's eyes, back towards the old man she'd arrived with. 'I left.'

238

'You were lucky.'

Sonja nodded to the man. 'I'm guessing he's not your father.'

The girl lowered her voice and came half a step closer, almost within reach. 'He tells people he's my godfather.'

'Does he hurt you?'

Her long lashes blinked through the holes in her feathered mask, like a doll Sonja had bought for Emma as a child. Her daughter, however, had preferred digging in the sandpit to playing dollies – a promise of things to come. 'It was worse, where I grew up. Mitchells Plain. He saved me, from the drugs, you know?'

'It doesn't make it right,' Sonja said. 'I'm thirsty.'

The girl glanced behind her, quickly, then closed the gap between them and held her glass to Sonja's lips and tilted it.

Sonja took a sip, then got her teeth around the rim and bit down. There was the satisfying crunch of glass breaking.

'Hey,' the girl hissed, and snatched her hand away. The champagne flute slipped from her grasp as she stepped back and smashed on the concrete floor. Several people turned to look while others either politely or arrogantly ignored the mishap and kept talking. Hendricks strode over, followed by the girl's older companion.

'Laverne, stay away from there,' the old man admonished.

'Yes,' Hendricks said, snapping a finger in the air for one of his men, who had already raced off to find a broom. 'She's a wild animal, that one. She bites.'

Sonja held on to the bars and smiled. She turned away from him, wiping a trace of blood from her mouth with a finger.

'Let me see you,' Hendricks said.

She pirouetted, fists up in a mock boxing stance.

He regarded her as the couple moved back to the safety of the group, the older man now gripping his girlfriend's upper arm hard enough for her to try and wiggle away. Cocaine had been laid out on a silver platter on a table and two of the women in the group were indulging, via rolled-up two-hundred-rand notes.

Sonja's eye was drawn back to the girl with the full-face mask and long black hair, who was also, she noted, watching her. A cage fight to the death might be socially acceptable on the Cape Flats, but perhaps not in London or Berlin where this mismatched couple was from.

The black-haired woman broke from the crowd and went to Jacob's enclosure. Two other women were there, assessing him. Sonja continued to rack her brain. *The skin*, she thought. She remembered being on the beach at Silver Sands, scanning the other sunbathers. There had been the guy, the Silver Fox, and the one she had dubbed the 'European swallow'. Pale skin, black hair peeking out from under a broad-brimmed hat.

The woman came to Sonja and, standing back a respectful distance after what had just happened, looked her up and down, very slowly, as a flunkey swept away the shards of broken glass.

'Like what you see?' Sonja asked.

'I can see this is going to be an interesting evening.'

Her voice was muffled behind the mask, but the pronunciation of the 'I' gave it away immediately.

'You're from Belfast?'

The young woman nodded. 'Close enough.'

'You don't have the cheap tattoos to be a drug dealer's moll.'

The woman glanced at the crowd, then back at Sonja. 'Thank you.'

Sonja noted her body shape and remembered the structure of her face. She thought of the person on the beach, in the sunhat; then it dawned on her that she'd seen the same hair, but pulled back in a ponytail, under a baseball cap, worn indoors at the Three Monkeys in Victoria Falls. Her heart felt like a fist had just squeezed it. This girl had been following her. 'It wasn't a compliment.' Sonja tried to sound tough, but she wondered how long this woman had been on her tail.

'That so?'

'No, I think you're worse.'

'And what's worse than a drug peddler or junkie skank then?'

'A murderer.'

The woman laughed, then calmed herself. 'Going to preach to me, are you? You're the one who should be praying for salvation or making your last confession, looking at the size of your opponent.'

'What are you doing here . . .?'

'Fiona.'

Sonja stared at the mask, searching for the eyes, which usually gave away everything, but the woman was too far away. 'Following me.'

'Yes.'

The older, thickset man with the broken nose came to them, a beer in his hand.

'This is David,' Fiona said with a nod.

'A pleasure,' Sonja said to him. She turned on her own impression of a Northern Irish accent: 'Sure and I'm guessing it's not a first for either of you two, seeing someone bludgeoned to death.'

'It'll be the first time I've seen a woman killed in a fistfight,' Fiona said. 'I'm looking forward to it.'

'I bet you are.' Sonja looked to David.

'Not for me,' he said. 'Women make just as good combatants as men, in my experience, and as such they deserve the same fate. Some folks thought me very progressive on that front, a true advocate of gender equality.'

Sonja ignored his sick joke and nodded to the crowd. There were shrieks of laughter as the drugs and alcohol began to take effect. One of Hendricks's men had started taking bets, and wads of cash were being waved about. Sonja and Jacob were attracting more and more attention.

'What do you make of this rabble?' Sonja asked David.

'There's an honesty to the gangs here, and the triads. A kind of purity in a bizarre sort of a way.'

Sonja raised her eyebrows, but she knew what he meant. 'Loyalty.'

'Exactly. Tradition and structure. They call their leaders "generals", and salute. Just like an army, not just a bunch of thieves or mercenaries.' David lifted his mask, almost casually, and rubbed his eyes, or pretended to, then replaced it.

He wanted me to see who he was, Sonja thought. 'Who are you, David? Fiona's father?'

Fiona turned her back to Sonja and tilted her mask up onto the top of her head. She took hold of David's suit jacket lapels in her hands, drew him down to her and kissed him, on the mouth. She broke away from him, replaced her mask, and turned back to Sonja.

'Not your father, then,' Sonja said. 'At least I hope not.'

'Daddy, maybe,' Fiona said, 'but no, not my father.'

David shook his head. 'No fear.'

'I'm going to enjoy tonight,' Fiona said.

Looking through the eye slits into Fiona's soul, Sonja could see she meant it. Unusually for her, she felt a chill.

*

Emma's phone dinged. The sun was setting, the daytime shoppers being replaced with the after-work crowd and holiday-makers venturing out to one of the Waterfront's many restaurants and bars.

She went into Cape Union Mart, which was still open, and burrowed between shelves of camping gadgets and outdoor clothing.

'Evening, ma'am. Can I help?' a young assistant asked.

Emma grabbed a fleece jacket and a polo-neck top off the racks. 'Can I try these on?'

'Of course,' the man said, 'change rooms are out the back.'

'Thanks.' Emma made her way into a booth and slid her back down the wall until she sat on the small ledge seat. She exhaled. Her heart was racing. She closed her eyes for a second, trying to get the adrenaline coursing through her body under control.

I killed two people.

She shook her head and opened her eyes. On her phone was a cut-and-pasted message from Hudson. It was a report from News24.

Mother–daughter duo sought over murders
By Rosie Appleton

Breaking news: Police in three countries are looking for two foreign tourists suspected of involvement in a string of drug-related murders. Cape Town's organised crime unit confirmed it was working with counterparts in Botswana and Zimbabwe over a series of killings allegedly related to a cross-border drug-smuggling operation. Sources say American national Sonja Kurtz and her daughter, Emma Kurtz, a British archaeologist, are wanted for questioning over the brutal killings of three men in Zimbabwe, and the driver of an overland tourist vehicle in Botswana two days ago. Police spokesman Captain Derek Minnaar said today the pair was also sought for questioning in relation to the killing of three men at the Victoria & Alfred Waterfront. 'Police in Cape Town recovered a large quantity of crystal methamphetamine and a pistol at the V&A crime scene,' Captain Minnaar told News24.

'Shit.'

'Everything all right in there?' the male shop attendant called from the other side of the door.

'Yes . . . fine, thanks.' She was anything but. Emma put on the fleece jacket she had selected and ripped off the label. She emerged from the change room, took a beanie off a shelf and went to the cash register, where she grabbed the first pair of sunglasses she could reach. She paid for her purchases and put the beanie and glasses on too, then went out again.

Emma looked left, then right, and saw a pair of police officers heading her way. She ducked down another side alley and scrolled through the contacts in her phone. She dialled a number.

'Hello?'

'Kelvin, this is Emma.'

There was a pause. 'Oh, British Emma? Um, howzit? This is a surprise.'

'Cut the fucking chitchat, Kelvin, where are you?'

'At the Pick n Pay, working.' Kelvin sounded a bit taken aback.

'Good, I hoped so.' She'd remembered him telling her that he worked at the Waterfront. 'I need to see you, now.'

'Wow.'

'Don't get too excited,' Emma said. 'How do I find the supermarket?'

He gave her directions and she headed back to the main shopping mall precinct, skirting another pair of police officers on her way. She figured that in the crowded mall it would be just as hard, if not harder, for the cops to single her out.

Emma walked as fast as she could without drawing attention to herself among the shoppers and tourists who ambled about. She felt her fear growing inside her like a cancer, but at least it kept the images of the dead men out of her mind. It was odd, she thought, that the media report had claimed three people had been killed at the V&A. She only killed two, but she remembered hearing the single gunshot after she left. She made her way to the supermarket and hurried along the aisles, peering down each of them until she found Kelvin, crouching, opening a carton of Ouma Rusks.

He saw her and stood, smiling. 'Emma, this is a nice –'

'This isn't a social call, Kelvin.'

'OK, can I help you with something? Biltong's in aisle four.'

'No time for jokes,' she said. 'My mother's in trouble.'

He wiped his hands on the white apron he wore. 'What's happened?'

Emma gave him as much of a rundown as she dared.

'She's really pissed off your uncle and his Chinese partner in the drug-smuggling operation.'

Kelvin shook his head. It was a lot to take in, but he didn't challenge any of the assertions or assumptions Emma had made.

'I've stayed out of his way since Denzel's funeral. You know the police think your mom shot him?'

Emma nodded. 'So did I, but now I'm not so sure. She's screwed up, but not even Sonja murders people in cold blood, not even . . .' She saw the look on Kelvin's face. 'Sorry.'

He held up a hand. 'No. Denzel was family, but he was ruining his life, big-time. I hear what you're saying.'

'Your uncle Vincent is holding my mum somewhere, that much I know. Where would he keep her, Kelvin?'

He rubbed his chin. 'He owns plenty of properties; he's a very rich guy.'

'Wu told me to bring the drugs here, to the Waterfront. Would that mean that she was close by, if they were going to follow through with the exchange?'

Kelvin pondered the question for a few seconds. 'He owns an office block in the city, and an empty warehouse at the Duncan Dock, close to here. He's been trying to get permission from the planning authorities to convert it into luxury apartments.'

'We'll try the warehouse first.'

He looked to the box of rusks at his feet, and along the aisle. 'We? I can't just walk out of work, Emma. I'll lose my job.'

Emma looked into Kelvin's eyes. In the midst of the killing, poaching and drug trafficking she'd witnessed, here was a genuinely decent guy who had almost been corrupted by his cousin, but had returned instead to his job in a supermarket to fund his studies. She had no right to expect that Kelvin might help her. He'd seen Denzel's body and probably still believed Sonja had killed him.

'It's warehouse number twenty-four,' Kelvin said, 'if that helps. Just call the police, Emma.'

'There's no time.' Emma turned on her heel, her boot squeaking on the supermarket floor. She dodged a woman with a loaded trolley and angrily flicked a tear away from the corner of her eye as she weaved through some more shoppers and made her way back out into the mall.

'Emma!'

She stopped and turned. Kelvin was at the entry to the Pick n

Pay, a store manager bustling close at his heels wagging a finger at him. He shrugged the apron over his head, rolled it into a ball and tossed it to the man.

Kelvin ran towards her.

CHAPTER 20

A DJ holding headphones up to one ear squeezed a deep bass beat out of a digital turntable deck and the waves of sound reverberated off the walls of the warehouse.

The main lights had been turned down and lasers painted the cages and walls in garish hues. Some of the crowd, which now numbered about a hundred, were dancing, grinding. A cheer went up as the hook now attached to the top of Jacob's cage was raised and he was lifted off the ground, holding tight to the bars as his enclosure swayed.

Footsteps clanked above her as a man with an AK-47 walked on the steel mesh roof of Sonja's cage. The small cage, which she had been transported in from Zimbabwe, had been removed and now a second man steadied Jacob's enclosure from below as the operator lowered Jacob towards her.

Sonja craned her neck, looking up, hoping for an opportunity of some sort to open for her. The man with the rifle, however, kept the weapon trained on her as his comrade undid a padlock, then released a bolt. A roof hatch swung down and Sonja could see, immediately, that it was too high up for her to reach, even if she wasn't being covered.

Deftly, for Sonja was getting the distinct impression this was not the first time this bizarre ritual had been enacted, a floor hatch in Jacob's cage was unlocked and opened. The two structures then mated, with the opening and hanging door from the cage above connecting with the hatch in hers. The worker without the gun then used the two large padlocks he had just removed to lock the floor of Jacob's prison to the roof of Sonja's. Simple but clever, she thought.

'Get in there,' the man with the AK yelled to Jacob above the noise of the music. 'Jump down.'

'Fuck you,' Sonja saw Jacob mouth.

With his attention focused on the gunman, Jacob didn't see the worker slide up beside him, reach in, and press the taser to his ribs. There was another roar from the crowd, who had all been watching, as Jacob fell to the floor.

The gunman raised the rifle to his shoulder, aiming at Jacob as he struggled to his knees.

'Jump, jump, jump,' the crowd chanted.

Jacob clasped the bars, pulled himself upright and looked down at Sonja through the open hatch. They were in this together, whatever happened. She gave him a small nod. Jacob licked his lips, bent his knees, then jumped. It was a three-metre fall and he landed hard, trying to roll as he hit the concrete. Sonja reached down, offering her hand, and helped him to his feet. The crowd cheered its approval.

'Thank you,' he said. 'I am Jacob.'

'Sonja.'

'What the hell is this?' he said.

'Cockfighting for psychopaths, I'd say.'

Hendricks went to the DJ's station and spoke to the man controlling the music. There was sudden silence. Hendricks took up the microphone.

'Ladies, gentlemen, friends . . .'

He looked around the crowd and so, too, did Sonja. She saw more than a couple of smirks on the faces of the Rainbow Nation of criminals present in the warehouse.

'Welcome,' he continued. 'I know the past couple of years have been tough for all of us here, with certain restrictions put on imports and exports, but we have weathered the storm and we have emerged stronger.'

There were a few nods among the crowd now that he had dropped the irony.

Hendricks surveyed his audience. 'All of us know that in business, we must keep our friends close and our enemies closer.'

There was outright laughter now, but, Sonja thought, he was yet to elevate himself above the cliches.

'And someone,' he went on, 'has been doing their best to sabotage the friendship between Carrington Wu and myself.'

The senior Chinese gangster, Sonja noted, had his arms folded. He gave the slightest nod of his head. Others in the crowd looked to each other, as if trying to work out who Hendricks was going to point the finger at next.

'Whomever has done this has seen fit not only to attack my business interests, but also my family.'

There were respectful nods of assent as Hendricks's words hung in the cold, dank air.

'This woman,' he pointed to Sonja, 'is an assassin. A hired gun, masquerading as a tourist. She is the one who pulled the trigger on my son, destroyed one of Wu's shipments, and killed several of his men in Zimbabwe.'

Faces turned to Sonja. Some of the men, she thought, were assessing her in a different manner from the way they'd surveyed her, like a piece of meat, when they had arrived in the building.

'She is a killer.'

Sonja replayed the events of the past days. It had been a blur. Had she, she wondered, blanked some of it out? She *was* capable of killing, no doubt at all, but had she executed Denzel? Had she executed Platt? How did Fiona fit into all of this?

'Did you do what he says?' Jacob asked. 'Are you a criminal?'

Sonja looked to her fellow captive, momentarily lost for words.

She was sure he was searching for something, perhaps guilt, in her face. 'Yes and no.'

'*Yes and no* to which? Are you a killer? A criminal?'

Hendricks droned on about how he and Wu would survive their temporary setback, thanks to friends in high places, and yet more propaganda. Despite his words, his bravado, and even this ostentatious, risky piece of theatre, she sensed a weakness in him. Someone or something was undermining him, killing his son and disrupting his and Wu's business. She had to work out who or what that was.

'Sonja?' Jacob pressed.

'I've killed, yes, but I am not a criminal. Hendricks's son hurt my daughter, Emma, so I paid him back. I also took out a shipment of smuggled abalone and caused a bit of trouble for Hendricks's partner in crime, Wu. You?'

He squared his shoulders, puffed his chest out. 'I am an inspector with the Department of Agriculture, Forestry and Fisheries.'

Sonja nodded. He'd said it like he was an FBI special agent or a US Marine, with pride. He was honest.

'These two,' Hendricks's voice rose as he pointed to the cage and all eyes turned to Jacob and Sonja, 'are nothing. They are foot-soldiers, sent by those who would sabotage us, those who would rob us of our heritage and our right to share in the wealth of this country and all it has to offer.'

Seriously? Sonja thought. He was playing the apartheid era card now? She could understand honest fishermen and local communities feeling aggrieved, but not gangsters. Hendricks had let the line between criminal and politician become blurred – if there even was such a line.

'In the white corner,' that raised a laugh, 'weighing in at – well, a woman never reveals her weight in public – I give you Sonja Kurtz, hired killer and mercenary.'

There was a round of enthusiastic applause. Jacob looked at her as if he was only just now realising what was about to happen.

'And in the black corner, I give you Jacob Dlamini, honest, law-abiding pawn of the State. Jacob is a man of principles, who, unlike his colleagues, will not do business with us.'

There was a smattering of clapping. Sonja surveyed the crowd, looking for their reactions. The doe-eyed girl who had come to her with the champagne was looking down at her expensively painted toenails and shoes. She was new to this, Sonja thought, perhaps sickened by what she was about to see. Some of the men looked at Sonja and she thought they might almost be drooling. More than one of the escorts was trying to catch her eye. A tall brunette ran the tip of her tongue over glossy lips and winked at Sonja.

'The rules, as those of you who have been to one of our little events know, are simple. For the first-timers,' he looked to the cage, 'including our combatants, there is only one rule. The fight continues, until one of them is dead.'

He turned to the DJ, who started the music again, but even the thump of the bass and the wail of the rap was not loud enough to drum out the cheers and wild applause from the crowd.

Hendricks came close to them, staying a metre and a half from the bars, but even so he had to shout to be heard. 'The one who lives will have their family spared, and the opportunity to work for me. If you decline my offer, you will be put down, cleanly and humanely, as one would dispense with a dog, and you will have my word that your loved ones will be safe. Understood?'

'Your word?' Sonja shook her head.

'Don't mock me, Miss Kurtz.'

One of Hendricks's flunkeys rolled the two big-screen monitors closer to the cage, so that Sonja and Jacob could see them, but the crowd could not.

'A little incentive for you both.'

Jacob blinked as 'his' screen came to life again. A man off camera still had a gun pointed at the head of one of his little children. His wife wept.

Sonja looked at the screen in front of her. It showed a

darkened room. There was a figure in a pair of orange overalls, the kind often associated with American prisons, especially Guantanamo Bay. It was a woman, judging by the swell of breasts, but the captive's hands were bound behind her and she had a black hood over her head.

'I want to see my daughter's face,' Sonja yelled, but Hendricks had turned to face the crowd, now taking their seats, most with drinks in hand. If he heard her, he ignored her, and, instead, took out his phone and moved away from the noise of the speakers and the assembled criminals.

Hendricks went to one of his men standing at the edge of the crowd and spoke to him, but Sonja could not hear what was being said. The man shook his head and Hendricks poked him in the chest. Hendricks started to dial a number on his phone and ran his free hand through his hair as he walked further away. He was worried about something.

*

'Emma!' She had been striding ahead of him, through the mall, but Kelvin caught up to her, grabbed her arm and pulled her to him.

'Hey!' She tried to shrug him off.

'Shush, I'm not going to hurt you. Hold me. Hide.'

She squirmed in his grasp. He took her into a corridor that led to the shopping centre bathrooms, pressed her against the wall and moved his mouth to her ear.

'Stay still. There are men. I think they're looking for you.'

Now that she realised what he was doing, Emma put her face into his neck as though they were kissing. She peeked over his shoulder and saw two men, with tattoos and bling, clearly scanning the shopping crowds. Although it was only a ruse, she was acutely aware of Kelvin's presence – his strong arms, a whiff of nice aftershave, which no other guy she'd dated had ever worn.

'I recognise one of them; he works for my uncle.'

'Thank you,' she said, feeling her cheeks colour as she separated from him.

Kelvin's phone started ringing. He took it out of his pocket and looked at it.

'Shit.'

'What is it?' she asked.

'Uncle Vincent.'

'Answer it.'

He nodded and accepted the call. 'Howzit, uncle?'

Emma kept watch while Kelvin exchanged a few words, then ended the call. He looked distressed.

'What is it?' she asked him.

Kelvin frowned. '*Ja*, they are definitely looking for you. He knows I work at the Pick n Pay on the Waterfront and he asked me to tell him if I saw you. He sounded very agitated and there was music in the background, reverberating, like in a big hall or warehouse.'

'They're worried and they're close,' Emma said. 'Let's go.'

Kelvin looked around. 'We'll stick to the car parks. More places to hide there.'

He led now, but Emma stopped him. 'Kelvin, do you have a weapon?'

He frowned. 'We're not all gangsters here.'

She looked around then lifted her shirt a little, enough for him to see the hand grip of Hudson's .45.

'Sheesh, Emma.'

She thought fast. 'Come with me.'

Although Kelvin's idea about moving through the car parks and back alleys was good, she realised they needed more gear. She led him back to the camping and clothing store, Cape Union Mart.

'Hello again, ma'am, back again so soon?' the sales assistant said, smiling. 'Is everything –'

'What have you got for self-defence?' she asked, forgoing the pleasantries.

'Come this way, ma'am,' the attendant said, clearly affronted. He led them to the counter and started pulling out products from under it. 'Mace, pepper spray, ma'am; a stun gun; and a personal alarm.'

'I'll take them all,' Emma said, taking out her credit card as the attendant entered the purchases.

'They're all pink,' Kelvin observed, looking down at the weapons.

'I hope you're secure in your masculinity,' Emma said.

'These are very popular with women,' the attendant said.

Emma paid and they left the store. Retreating to the car park, Emma began opening the packets.

'OK,' Kelvin said, as he examined Emma's purchases. 'What's the plan now?'

'We go and save my mother.'

'Right,' he said. 'No problem.'

*

The DJ pumped up the volume as a cloud of purple mist enshrouded the cage from a smoke machine.

'Fight!' Hendricks yelled at them.

Sonja and Jacob faced off, a metre and a half apart, neither of them doing anything.

'Hit me,' Sonja mouthed at Jacob over the noise.

He gave a small shake of his head. Sonja took a step towards him. Jacob flinched. She shot her right fist out and aimed a jab at his nose.

Women screamed in delight.

The blow was not hard enough to draw blood, but Jacob rocked back, then closed the gap between them and grabbed her by the forearms.

She was close enough for him to hear her over the music and yelling. 'We've got to give them a show, Jacob, get them worked up. If they get within reach of the bars, we might be able to do something.'

'I . . . I can't,' he said in her ear. 'It goes against everything I know, everything I've been taught as a man.'

Sonja punched him hard, up under the chest. Jacob doubled over and released her.

'Yes!' a man cried.

Sonja faced the audience and flexed her muscles.

'Jacob!' Hendricks called. He had moved behind the screen showing Jacob's family. Sonja looked over and saw a man on the screen slap Jacob's wife, her hands bound behind her, in the face. Jacob came at her.

Sonja held up her hands and Jacob aimed a punch at her midriff. He was sloppy, giving her time to sidestep, which she did, then she spun, lifting a leg like a kickboxer and driving her foot into the side of his torso. He lurched away; the crowd applauded.

'Blood, blood, blood,' called a woman, starting up a chant, champagne slopping from her glass.

Jacob looked at the screen again. A man in a ski mask was grabbing one of his children. He let out an animalistic scream and charged at Sonja. She saw the rage in him, released as if a switch had been flicked. She half raised her hands to protect herself, but did not duck or weave as she saw the punch coming her way.

Sonja took the blow, on the chin. Jacob's knuckles grazed along her lower lip, and she did not have to fake falling to the ground.

Her head rang and she slid along the concrete, closer to the bars. Most of the crowd were on their feet now and two women and a man were coming to the cage, trying to get a closer view, urging the fighters on. Hendricks sidestepped from behind the screen showing Jacob's family and got between the onlookers and Sonja before they could reach the bars.

Sonja wiped her mouth with the back of one hand. She saw the blood, then spat on the ground. She looked up at one of the women; it was Laverne, the one who had been trying to make eye contact earlier. Sonja smiled and winked at her.

Jacob had pulled back, dancing from foot to foot like a prize-fighter.

'Finish the bitch,' one of the men yelled from the audience. His girlfriend punched him playfully in the arm.

Sonja got up, to applause and whistling. She took a breath and ran at Jacob. The DJ pushed the volume to the maximum. Sonja barrelled into the big man, surprising him with her speed. She hooked a leg behind his and tripped him, pushing him onto his back and straddling his chest. She punched him, again, in the face.

Hendricks was on his phone, by the monitor, his left hand over his ear as he tried to listen. When Jacob looked at the screen he saw one of his children being lifted, bodily, off the sofa by the masked man. Jacob reached up, another of Sonja's blows glancing off his arm, and grabbed her with two hands around her throat.

Men and women whooped. Sonja grabbed Jacob's arms, trying to prise them from her throat, but when she looked into his eyes, she saw he had changed. Any reluctance or unease was gone, and in its place was desperation and rage. He was serious.

Sonja raked his face and drove a thumb into one of his eyeballs. Jacob bellowed and Sonja rolled off him. As she jumped to her feet, she felt her bad knee click. All the same she delivered a couple of short, sharp but brutal kicks to his side. She jumped back, but her right leg was unsteady, the knee joint wobbly.

Jacob growled and got to his feet. Panting, he stared at her. She was the only outlet for the injustice that had been done to him and his family, and for his impotent rage.

'Come on,' she goaded him, wiping her lip again.

He charged her and at the last instant she took his outstretched arm, pivoted, and used his own momentum to throw him over her shoulder so that he landed again on his back, winded.

'Stomp on him!' a man yelled from the crowd.

'Kill him, kill him,' two women sang.

One of the men in the crowd booed her.

She looked to Hendricks. He gave her a thumbs down, like

a Roman Emperor delivering a death sentence at a gladiatorial match.

Fuck you, Sonja mouthed at Hendricks.

Hendricks smiled and looked at the screen of his phone. He tapped something and pointed it towards the plasma which had been showing the static image of the girl with the hood on. Seeing the way Hendricks had prodded Jacob into a rage by having his man torment Jacob's family, Sonja thought that if it really was Emma with the hood on, someone in the cell where she was being kept would do something similarly cruel to her, now.

Increasingly, however, she was becoming sure that Emma was still in the wind. The screen went blank. Sonja flashed a bloody-toothed smile.

Then her right leg gave out and she dropped to the hard floor. Sonja felt the pain as she realised Jacob had kicked her behind the right knee. He was bearing down on her, swinging his right arm. She rolled over onto her back as fast as she could, lifting her left foot. She kicked him in the groin, but it was hard for her to get enough force behind the kick to do damage. Jacob faltered, but carried on, half reaching, half falling. He landed on her, forcing the air out of her chest.

Jacob had hold of one of her hands, pinning it to the ground, and with his other he punched her in the face. Once, twice, three times. Sonja tasted more blood and her head rang.

'Kill her!' someone screamed. 'Finish her off.'

Sonja reached between his legs, for his penis and scrotum through his boxer shorts, grabbed hold and twisted. Jacob cried out and hit her again. She gripped harder, mercilessly. When he tried to arch back, she did a half sit-up and head-butted his nose with her forehead.

Jacob coughed blood, and half rolled off her. Sonja wiggled out from underneath him and tried to crawl away, but he took hold of her ankle in a big hand and the crowd laughed and applauded.

Sonja's vision was blurred. He had shaken her badly and she felt like she might be concussed. She tried to shut out the howls and music, and focus her thoughts. If Emma was dead, then she had nothing more to live for. If Emma was alive, then her daughter had a chance and Sonja would have to kill Hendricks. Sonja flipped herself over in Jacob's grasp and looked up at the live monitor, the one in Jacob's lounge room. The man in the ski mask had a finger hooked in the elastic waistband of Jacob's daughter's pants. The mother writhed helplessly on the couch, screaming silently into her gag.

Jacob snarled at her like a lion. Sonja closed her eyes for half a second and thought of Emma, and of Sam, the man who had been taken from her, and of the thing she wanted to tell Hudson. She pictured Hudson, sitting on the *stoep* at Nantwich Lodge, having a beer and reading a book.

When she opened her eyes, she looked up at Jacob. He had let go of her and was now standing over her. He was breathing hard, nostrils flaring, his shattered nose dripping blood on her.

Jacob hesitated, as if coming to his senses. He shook his head.

'Kill her!' the crowd began, 'Kill her!'

He looked to the screen showing his family. Hendricks picked up a remote and turned on the volume.

'Daddy!' his daughter cried.

Amid the blood, sweat and horror on his face, Sonja thought she saw a tear running down Jacob's cheek. He was a good man. She put a hand on the concrete floor and spun on her hip, kicking her leg around and driving her foot into the back of Jacob's knee. As he staggered she rolled out of his range, then got up, as fast as her knee would allow.

Sonja retreated towards the crowd, her back pressed against the metal bars, her face to Jacob, who had recovered and was coming towards her. Over her shoulder he could see his tormented family. He advanced on her like a robot, one heavy step after another.

She launched at him, her fists firing out jackhammer blows, left, left, right, like she was in the gym. Jacob's head rocked back each time, but he soaked up the punishment. Sonja knew her knuckles were split; her body was racked with pain. The crowd was loving it.

Sonja jabbed and weaved, but her arms were tiring. She tried another kickboxing move, but Jacob caught her foot and twisted her, so she was slammed against the bars, face first now. He grabbed a wrist, twisted it up behind her back, and put his other arm around her neck.

'Yes, yes, yes!'

Her eyes began to bulge and her head was swimming; from fatigue, the blows she had taken and the pressure on her windpipe. Sonja looked at the screens. The one that had showed Emma was blank. She looked to Hendricks. The gang boss was fiddling with his phone like a middle-aged man in need of a teenager. He was pointing the device at the empty screen. The crowd bayed, and Jacob obliged.

Jacob put his lips to her ear, as close as a lover, and croaked, 'I . . . am sorry.' On his screen, a child was struck in the head, and Jacob screamed in her ear.

Sonja reached an arm through the cage. The younger woman, Laverne whose glass Sonja had bitten, started to come towards her, as if to help, but her older gangster partner grabbed Laverne's forearm and wrenched her back into her seat. The woman looked up at him, and Sonja saw the fear in Laverne's eyes, even through the holes in the mask. The little display of an abuse of power made Sonja want to get out of this hold and beat the shit out of Jacob; to tear off one of his arms and use it to bludgeon Hendricks to death.

A knife was produced in Jacob's house; the little girl held down.

'Kill me,' Sonja said, loud enough for Jacob to hear.

Suddenly Sonja's screen came to life. Emma's face appeared large, on the screen, a pistol barrel jammed into her temple. The sight of her daughter, captured, changed her feelings in an instant.

CHAPTER 21

One of the guards armed with an AK-47 slung his rifle and spoke into a walkie-talkie. The other, who had been videoing Emma with his phone, put the device away.

The plan Emma had concocted had just passed its first test. She was pretending to be held captive, with Kelvin holding Hudson's Colt to her temple. The guard had just done a video call with Vincent Hendricks showing Hendricks's nephew 'delivering' Emma. Kelvin had called his uncle and confirmed that Vincent was at the Duncan Dock warehouse.

They could take the guards now, Emma thought – one man was talking and the other had his hands in his pockets – but they needed to get deeper inside the warehouse, and their plan had called for them to split up, once indoors. They might be able to kill these two, but then others could stop them getting closer to where the thumping music was emanating from. She forced herself to stay calm, while trying to look scared.

The man with the slung weapon slid open the heavy door enough for them to enter. 'Come with me.'

'I'll be fine,' Kelvin replied. 'My uncle's waiting for me.'

The man nodded and waved them through.

'It sounds like a rave in here,' Emma said over her shoulder as they stepped inside.

'Raving mad, more like it,' Kelvin replied.

They could see a crowd, a hundred or more, well dressed, all wearing masks and clustered around what looked like one large cage stacked on another. Laser lights painted the walls, smoke hung around the floor like fog, and speakers filled the cavernous warehouse with noise.

A young woman stumbled towards them. 'Howzit, do you know where the ladies' room is?'

Emma shrugged.

'I want to be quick. I think one of them is about to kill the other one and I don't want to miss it.'

Emma looked back at Kelvin as the woman teetered off. They moved forward slowly. Emma had her hands behind her back, loosely bound with a strip of torn plastic shopping bag, for show only. In one hand she held the taser, in the other the little pink canister of pepper spray.

All eyes were on the larger cage. Emma was shocked when she saw what was going on. She tore her eyes away from the fight and looked around them, then up into the rafters. She could see that a large crane ran the length of the warehouse moving on a set of rails, with its hook currently hanging over the uppermost cage.

'The crane,' she said to Kelvin.

He nodded. 'I see it. We need to lift the top cage off the lower one.' He stood on his toes to try and see over the heads of the crowd. 'There aren't any doors on the lower cage.'

'We need a distraction,' Emma said.

'Yes, but what?' He nodded towards the crowd. 'Here comes my uncle.'

Emma saw a tall, good-looking man in an expensive coat break from the crowd and stride purposefully towards them.

'Think of something, Kelvin.'

'OK.'

'Kelvin, good to see you, my boy.' He nodded to Emma. 'Vincent Hendricks. You must be Emma.'

She spat on the floor. Hendricks laughed, then gripped her forearm. 'Get yourself a drink, or whatever else amuses you, Kelvin. Come, enjoy the show. I'll take care of this one.'

Hendricks frogmarched Emma forward, through the crowd, to the edge of the cage. Her mother was on her knees, face cut and swollen; an enormous man had her in a headlock. Sonja did not seem to be resisting. Emma was horrified – at what was going on inside the cage and the bloodlust in the crowd. These sickos were getting off on Sonja's pain and suffering.

'Mum!'

The man who was holding Sonja had massive arms and hate in his eyes, but he blinked and looked up at the sound of Emma's one word, above the crescendo of calls for death and blood and the thump and grind of the music.

'Jacob, Jacob, Jacob,' the crowd was chanting, in unison.

Hendricks pushed Emma to her knees, and put the tip of the barrel of the pistol he'd just taken from a concealed shoulder holster to the back of her head.

Sonja saw Emma. She gave up her half-hearted attempts to break Jacob's hold on her and, instead, reached behind her back with her right hand. Relieving what little force she had been applying to the man's stranglehold just seemed to allow him to apply more pressure and Sonja's eyes bulged, literally, as Emma watched.

'No!'

Hendricks drilled the barrel deeper into her neck, but she fought to keep her head up and watch her mother.

It's OK, Emma mouthed.

Sonja blinked. Just when Emma thought her mother might pass out or die from a lack of oxygen, Jacob screamed in agony and released Sonja. Freed, she spun around and drove her fist into his already pulverised nose. He dropped to his knees.

Sonja followed up with a vicious kick to Jacob's stomach, and when her foot came down, ready for a second go, Emma saw blood on Sonja's foot and the man's stomach. Jacob clasped his belly as he doubled over. Emma saw a shard of broken glass in Sonja's hand.

'Come back from the cage,' Hendricks was saying to someone.

Although her head was being pushed down by the gangster's gun, Emma cast her eyes up as far as she could. A black-haired woman, young, in a tight-fitting green dress, was pressing herself against the bars of the cage. The woman turned her face, fully masked, to Emma. Something about the other woman's eyes, locking instantly onto her own, made Emma shiver.

These people were all sick, Emma thought, looking away, but she could use that to her advantage. So, too, could Sonja, who rounded on Jacob, delivering another kick-punch combination, her blows reminding Emma of the sound of Sonja working out on the punching bag at her mansion in Los Angeles. *Those eyes*, Emma thought again.

Emma moved her head slightly and caught sight of the big-screen TVs facing the two opponents in the cage. She could see a masked man pistol-whipping a woman, who rolled, bound, on a settee, not only to try and escape the blows, but to shield a child. A little girl wailed, her eyes filled with tears and mouth open in a scream, on the carpeted floor at the woman's feet.

Emma grasped what was going on. Hendricks was using a threat to the family – they had to be Jacob's – and to Emma herself, to get the fighters to go at each other. Sonja had found renewed vigour; she sent three rapid punches into the big man's kidneys as he tried to turn and retreat from her.

The fighters squared off against each other, both sweating freely and wiping blood from their faces. More of the crowd, emboldened by the black-haired woman's move to the cage, were surging forward, pressing into the space either side of Emma and Hendricks. The gangster, too, was enthralled by the fight, as Jacob came at Sonja, ducking, weaving and punching. A blow got past Sonja's guard and sent her head snapping back. She staggered, but would have regained her balance if Jacob hadn't kicked her. If this was a show fight, to buy them time, it was bloody realistic, Emma thought.

Sonja dropped, her knee seeming to give out, but she rolled and crawled, with Jacob coming after her. She hauled herself to her feet, then came at him again, kicking and punching. The big man was strong, but Sonja, even with her bad knee, was faster. As he closed on her she came at him like a wildcat, getting in under his guard and clawing and gouging at his face.

Hendricks had changed position, slightly, to get a better view of the action, and in doing so had relaxed some of the pressure on the back of Emma's head. She was able to look up and around. The gangster, she saw, was open-mouthed, almost salivating. He was fixated on Sonja's renewed offensive, and some of the other guests were grinding on the cage bars with excitement.

Where the hell is Kelvin? Emma wondered, as Jacob regained the initiative and punched Sonja in the side of the head with a lightning-fast right hook.

*

Kelvin had taken a beer, for pretences, and slowly drifted back, away from the cage and into the shadows behind the sound and light show.

He made his way to the rows of parked luxury cars until he found inspiration. On the back of a gaudy bright-yellow Toyota FJ Cruiser, a pimped-up version with tinted windows and too much external chrome, he found a jerry can. Probably more for macho image rather than the need for extended range on an off-road safari, the can was nonetheless full. When Kelvin popped open the lid he smelled inside – petrol.

He unfastened the jerry can from its holder and lifted it down. The FJ was unlocked. Kelvin opened the rear door and tipped fuel onto the leather seat. He let petrol cascade down onto the cement floor until it had pooled under the FJ and a neighbouring Porsche.

Kelvin picked up his beer bottle and, for some Dutch courage, downed the contents in a couple of seconds. He slopped petrol into the green bottle from the jerry can and then took a polishing cloth from the rear cargo area of the FJ and stuffed it in the neck of the bottle.

He ducked between the luxury cars at the sound of approaching footsteps, audible this far away from the freak show in the cage. Kelvin slowly raised his head and saw one of the guards from the front doors; probably disobeying rules, he was moving closer to get a look at the action.

Kelvin backed out of his hiding place, keeping an eye on the sentry, and melted even further into the shadows, to the side wall of the warehouse. He looked up, shifting his gaze through the rafters, tracking the progress of the gantry crane that was still hooked to the uppermost cage. He visually traced the path the crane's hook would make, and then noted the thick black snake of intertwined power cables that led across from the crane to the wall he was looking at, and then down. A control box swung about a metre off the ground.

The screaming, yelling, cheering and booing was almost drowning out the loud music and easily covered his soft footfall. Kelvin prayed Emma was all right. He took the .45-calibre pistol from his trouser belt and made his way to the hanging remote control.

*

Sonja's whole body ached; it was only adrenaline and anger that were keeping her going.

Jacob blinked and shook his head. They were both very likely concussed. She could not hate him, but she knew that she could probably kill him if she needed to, especially now that she knew Emma was alive.

Jacob staggered towards her, casting a quick glance at the active screen to see some new torture being inflicted or threatened on his wife and children. Hendricks was on his phone again, Sonja saw, perhaps planning something that would reinvigorate Jacob and push him over the edge.

Sonja risked a look at Emma, still kneeling like a slave at Hendricks's feet. She couldn't look at her daughter too long, or Jacob might blindside her again with another of his hooks to the side of her head; Sonja thought she would be lucky to survive one more of those.

Emma caught her eye and stared at her. There was nothing either of them could do to communicate, even covertly, but Sonja saw a steely calm in Emma's face. Her eyes shifted slightly upwards. Sonja thought of the hook, still connected to the upper cage. Emma then looked to her right, Sonja's left, and Sonja turned to see Jacob coming at her. Emma gave the tiniest of nods.

Now, Sonja thought, reading her daughter's mind. She was a clever girl. She'd evaded capture after the attempted kidnapping, Sonja was sure of it, and now Sonja caught a glimpse of the boy, Kelvin, who had come sniffing around Emma after the business at Silver Sands. Though she had been hard on him, Sonja had sensed a gentleness about Kelvin that his cousin had shown none of.

On the screen, Jacob's daughter was being held upside down by one tiny foot. He bellowed like a wounded buffalo being savaged alive by lions and ran at her. Sonja started out to meet him, then let her right knee buckle. Jacob bore down on her. He had perceived a weakness in her and slowed, ever so slightly, either because he was sure of finishing her off, or out of pity. It was a mistake.

Sonja launched herself, driving up using her left leg, and slammed a punch into his gut. As he stumbled, Sonja grabbed his outstretched hand and pulled him into a roll, taking him down with her. She ended up behind Jacob, he on his butt and she on her knees, turning him so that he was facing the mob. Sonja got one arm under his chin, and the other behind the back of his neck and proceeded to choke him.

The men and women, mostly drunk or stoned by now, were grabbing the bars of the cage, almost climbing them and each other to get a better look. They sensed that the end was near, and so did Sonja.

She saw the girl in the full-face mask, Fiona, again, and the older man with her, David, staring at her, the closest of all of them. Sonja applied pressure to Jacob's neck. He flailed at her, his short fingernails trying but failing to hook her skin. He slapped at her, but Sonja had suffered so many hits that she felt nothing now.

Hendricks, too, was looking over Emma's head, right at Sonja. He was smiling, sensing a victory of sorts. Sonja raised her eyebrows in his direction and he nodded, sending her the signal to finish Jacob off.

The harder Jacob fought, the more relentless her grip became. Sonja felt the power flowing through her, the pain and fatigue being replaced by the rush. Jacob's flailing became weaker, until, at last, it stopped, and he slumped in her arms. A hush descended over the audience as they hung on to the bars, as if they were inside, struggling to be let out, to experience what Sonja had just done.

Sonja locked eyes with Hendricks, the animal who had begun all this by siring his pig of a son. As she stared at him, she released her grasp and Jacob slipped from her arms, falling to the concrete floor, face up, not moving. There was a pause as the inebriated and stoned onlookers grasped the reality of what they had just witnessed. Even the DJ was transfixed, and had turned down the music as they all watched Jacob's fall.

Hendricks waved to the DJ. Sonja stood over Jacob and raised clenched fists in the air, playing to the crowd. The music exploded into life again, and the spectators turned as a ball of orange flame exploded from where the cars were parked.

Many of them cheered.

*

While nearly everyone else was looking at the explosion behind them, momentarily frozen to the spot, Emma looked up and saw the slack being taken up on the gantry crane's hook.

'My car!' a woman screamed.

Emma looked at her mother, who nodded to her, acknowledging she was good to go.

Sonja leapt at the cage bars, reached through and grabbed the suit jacket collar of a man distracted by the fire. She slammed him backwards, then reached around with her other hand and pulled a pistol from the shoulder holster under his left armpit. The man tried to take hold of her hand, but Sonja was too quick; she gave him a shove in the back and sent him sprawling, unarmed, into the crush of people.

Sonja racked her stolen Glock. Another man who had seen what was happening drew a pistol from a holster on his belt and raised it. Sonja shot him in the chest. Women screamed and two fell over each other trying to get away from the gunfire.

'Kill her!' Hendricks was distracted, yelling at his men, who were prevented from getting close to the cage by the crowd, as he raised his own gun.

Emma snapped the flimsy bonds holding her wrists together and raised the taser she had taken from her back pocket. She rammed it into Hendricks's groin and pushed the button just as he was taking aim at Sonja. He screamed and doubled over.

Looking down as she got to her feet, Emma saw that Hendricks had fallen with his gun under his body. By the time she rolled him over he would be aiming at her. Emma had the mace in her other hand and squirted pepper spray at Hendricks's face, causing him to wail even more.

Emma pocketed the taser and tried to run, but didn't get far because of the panicking crowd. She shoulder-charged a woman and knocked her off her stilettoes as she made for the man her mother had just shot. Emma bobbed down and picked up the gun he had dropped. As she rose she turned and saw the woman in the green dress with the spooky eyes. She alone seemed to be keeping her cool. The woman unzipped her handbag and took out a small pistol. Emma wondered for a moment if the woman was going to shoot her, but she kept her pistol down by her side. Emma raised the dead man's gun, aimed at Hendricks and pulled the trigger. Nothing happened.

'Shit.' Emma realised the man who'd taken aim at Sonja had forgotten to cock his own weapon.

Emma looked up as she racked the pistol and saw that the crane hook had stopped rising. Above the music she heard the screech of metal bending, then, a second later the *ping* of something breaking. The top cage tilted at a crazy angle; a gap had been opened in the roof of the main enclosure. Emma put the mace away and raised the pistol.

Hendricks was getting to his feet, wiping pepper spray from his eyes. He blinked, trying to focus on Emma, and pointed his weapon at her. Emma took a breath, aimed and fired. Her bullet hit him in the shoulder, spinning him around and knocking him to the ground.

'Emma!'

She turned to see Kelvin, who was standing away from the scattering crowd and the cars, holding a large cabled control box. Spooky-eye woman, Emma registered, had disappeared into the mob. Black smoke was filling the warehouse from the cars, two of which were now well alight. The first of the fleeing spectators were reaching their vehicles, and a horn sounded and tyres squealed on the floor as a Tesla streaked towards the doors. The driver sounded his horn again as two guards hurried to roll the doors open.

Kelvin still had his finger on the winch button. The top cage finally broke free and swung away from the enclosure below. Kelvin manoeuvred it to one side and then pressed a release button, which sent the smaller cage crashing and clanging to the floor.

Emma looked back at the cage. Sonja was on the ground, bent over Jacob. Emma hadn't had time, yet, to register what her mother had done to him. She blew an audible gasp of breath as she saw Jacob get to his knees. He was coughing, but Sonja was helping him to his feet.

Kelvin, keeping a cool head despite the chaos unfolding around them, operated the crane hook so that it was now hovering over the newly created opening in the roof of the main fighting cage. He hit another button and the hook, free of weight, raced downwards.

Emma surveyed the warehouse. More cars were leaving. She glimpsed an Asian man running – Carrington Wu, she guessed – but she had more immediate concerns. One of the door guards, the man with the AK-47, was coming through the smoke, heading for his boss, Hendricks. Emma saw the man at the same time as he recognised her. She raised her pistol, fired, but missed. The man raised his rifle and pulled the trigger. One of the three rounds he fired came close enough to Emma for her to feel the rush of air past her face. A woman in a cocktail dress ran in front of her, and one of the rounds punched her in the belly, sending her falling.

Emma tried for another shot, but a fleeing car obscured her view. When the man came into view again he was taking aim at her. Then he fell backwards, his rifle clattering to the floor. A Jeep Wrangler bounced over the man's body, crushing whatever life was left in him, as the driver and his partner raced through the warehouse doors. Emma looked around and saw Kelvin lowering Hudson's pistol and looking incredulous at what he'd just done.

'The hook!' Emma called to him.

Kelvin snapped out of his stupor and went back to the crane control panel. Sonja was clinging to the cable, one foot on the hook, and holding Jacob in a one-armed embrace. He, too, took hold of their lifeline. As Kelvin brought the hook up, the temperature of the fire below, which had now spread to four vehicles, set off the warehouse's internal sprinkler system.

'Emma, come here.'

Emma ran to Kelvin.

'Here.' He handed the control box to her and pointed to the buttons. 'Up, down, side to side. Easy.'

'Where are you going?'

'My uncle.'

'I shot him.'

Kelvin nodded. 'I saw him. He'll still be dangerous.'

Water was cascading down from above now as black, acrid smoke filled the warehouse and made her eyes sting. Kelvin looked at her for a moment.

Emma took his hand, rose on her toes and kissed him, quickly, on the mouth. 'Be careful.'

He smiled. 'You, as well.'

*

The water was drenching Sonja and Jacob as they rode the hook, washing the blood and the filth of this barbaric place from them, but Sonja did not relax. There was more killing to do.

Sonja had one arm wrapped around Jacob and that hand grasped the cable. She held the stolen Glock in the other.

'What . . .' Jacob coughed, 'what did you do to me?'

'Choke hold,' Sonja said. 'You passed out for long enough to convince Hendricks and the crowd that I'd killed you.'

'My . . . my family.'

'We'll get to them.'

Sonja held on tighter as Emma set them moving towards her, and they swung under the cable like a pendulum. Sonja looked down and saw the boy, Kelvin, moving quickly towards his uncle. Hendricks was sitting up and had his pistol raised, but lowered it as Kelvin approached. If Hendricks thought Kelvin was on his side, he was in for a surprise, as Kelvin put a gun to his head and forced his uncle to drop his pistol.

'Doorway,' Jacob said.

Sonja looked to the cavernous opening and saw another man with a pistol drawn heading towards Emma. Sonja opened fire at him, as did Emma. The man, perhaps seeing that his boss was now being covered by Kelvin, turned tail and fled back out the doors.

Smoke swirled around the warehouse. Most of the cars were gone now. Some people must have fled on foot, Sonja thought. The four burning vehicles were down to the steel wheel rims and even flying high above she could feel the radiant heat and smell the toxic odour of burning plastic, rubber and vinyl. It looked like Baghdad down there.

Emma lowered the hook and their swaying slowed. As they touched the ground Emma ran to her. Sonja wanted to tell her that there was still danger, that they needed to get out of here and go to Jacob's family, but her defences came crashing down as she felt her daughter's body meld into hers.

'Give me your gun, please,' Jacob said.

Sonja was about to protest, but she let him take it from her fingers and drew Emma even closer as Jacob moved away.

It was Emma who released her grip first. 'Mum, we have to get out of here.'

Sonja felt as close to crying as she had ever been since Sam's death, but she drew back a little, looked into Emma's face, and just nodded.

'No!'

They both looked over at the cry. It had come from Hendricks.

Sonja and Emma went to the men – Kelvin, Jacob and Hendricks. The gangster, his face pale, sat on the floor, his hands together, as if in prayer.

'Give me your phone,' Jacob said to Hendricks.

Hendricks's hands were shaking as he complied. 'Kelvin,' he said, looking up into his nephew's face, 'you need to help me get out of here. I'll make it worth your while, my boy.'

Kelvin said nothing.

Jacob kept his gun on Hendricks as he checked his phone. 'He's been communicating with the guys who have my family by SMS. Good.'

'Yes,' Hendricks said. 'Just send them a message from my

phone, using the code word, "mercy", and they'll let your family go, and they will disappear in an hour. I promise you.'

Jacob looked down at Hendricks and gave him a smile.

'Thanks,' Jacob said, then he shot Hendricks between the eyes.

CHAPTER 22

They drove fast through Cape Town in Hendricks's black Range Rover. Kelvin was behind the wheel, with Jacob in the front passenger seat. Sonja and Emma were in the back. Sonja winced in pain and Emma took her hand. Sonja thought they needed to all stay alert, so she tried to wriggle free, but Emma held on tight. Sonja relented.

Jacob looked around at them. 'I am sorry.'

Sonja shrugged. 'What for?'

'I was going to kill you, I know it.'

Sonja nodded. 'I was going to let you.'

'Why?'

'When the screen went blank,' she looked to Emma, 'I didn't know if she was dead. When they put that image of the girl with the hood on, I knew it was a fake – what use is holding someone's child to gain leverage over them if you can't see their face?'

Emma rolled her eyes. 'Mum . . .'

'It's true,' Jacob said, still looking at both of them, searching their faces. 'It's what made me want to kill, seeing my children being threatened, but all the same, I am ashamed of it.'

'Don't be,' Sonja said.

'Thanks.' Emma gave her hand a squeeze.

'I knew she was alive and free,' Sonja said.

'So you submitted because of that,' Jacob's eyes widened, 'because you thought she might be alive?'

'Either way,' Sonja shrugged, 'she didn't need me.'

Sonja felt Emma stiffen beside her.

'What's that supposed to mean?' Emma asked.

'It means your life would be better without me.'

Emma let go of her hand and placed it in her lap.

Sonja placed a hand on Emma's arm, and now it was Emma's turn to try and shrug it away. 'They were going to torture Jacob's wife and little children. I couldn't have that on my conscience.'

'Bastards,' Emma said.

Sonja wasn't one hundred per cent sure who Emma was talking about. Her daughter looked out the window of the speeding car.

'I haven't thanked you, both of you,' Sonja said.

'No problem,' Kelvin said from the front. 'Beats stacking shelves.' Despite his casual tone, Sonja could see in his eyes in the rear-vision mirror how the scene he'd just taken part in had shaken him.

'I'll write you a note,' Sonja said lightly.

'Thank you,' Jacob said, 'Kelvin and Emma. You saved us from . . . a fate worse than death.'

Hendricks's phone, which Jacob was holding, pinged. He read the message and looked back at Sonja. 'The men are asking for orders.'

'How far are we from your house?' Sonja asked.

'Five minutes, no more.' Jacob gave some last-minute directions to Kelvin.

'Message them, say: *Fight's over, I am bringing the man to you. Meet us outside.*'

'All right.' He sent the message.

Jacob put the phone down, hit the magazine release button on the pistol that Emma had taken, and slid the mag into his palm. Sonja could see he was checking the number of rounds left. She knew what he was thinking, and had no problems with it.

Kelvin glanced back from the road. 'Want me to call the police?'

'No,' Sonja said, before Jacob could speak.

'Can I have my phone back, please, Kelvin?' Emma said. She had given Kelvin her phone in case the guards on the warehouse door had frisked her.

Kelvin fished in a pocket as he drove and handed the phone into the back.

Emma worked the keypad.

'Who are you messaging?' Sonja said.

Emma glanced at her. 'Hudson. He's in Botswana – we were in a car crash. He's a bit banged up, but OK. Long story, I'll fill you in later.'

Jacob pointed to a turnoff and Kelvin took it.

'Slowly, now,' Jacob said. 'Fourth house on the right.'

As they approached Jacob's home they saw a man in the front yard, dressed in jeans and a black T-shirt.

'I know him,' Kelvin said. 'He's a friend of my cousin.'

'There might be another one inside, with the family,' Sonja said. 'Probably is.'

'Let me handle it,' Kelvin said.

Emma looked up from the phone. 'Be careful.'

Kelvin smiled at her and nodded. Sonja knew that look.

Kelvin got out and walked over to the man. They couldn't hear what he said, but they shook hands and it seemed the man was calling to someone else, still in the house, as Sonja had thought. The second man was concealing a firearm in a holster as he came out, and closed the front door.

'Standby,' Sonja said to Jacob.

Kelvin led the men to the Range Rover.

'Go,' Sonja ordered.

She and Jacob spilled from the Range Rover, pistols up.

'On the fucking ground,' Sonja said, training her pistol on one man's head. She went to him and grabbed him by the scruff of the neck for good measure and forced him to his knees. Sonja slid the man's weapon from his belt and tossed it to Kelvin.

Both men were kneeling, side by side, and Jacob now held two guns, one in each hand. Sonja saw the fury on his face and knew there was only one thing that would quell that rage. 'Kelvin?'

He turned to her. 'Ma'am?'

'Get in the car, in the back. Look after Emma.'

'Yes, ma'am.' He headed to the Range Rover.

'And Kelvin?'

'Yes?'

'Don't let her watch,' Sonja said.

'OK, ma'am.'

Kelvin opened the back door and got in.

'Cover them, please,' Jacob said to Sonja. 'I'll be back in a minute.'

'Sure,' she said. He had tried to kill her, but he was a gentleman. Sonja felt like his family was lucky to have him. Jacob ran to his house, opened the door and went in. Moments later Sonja heard screams and crying, but of joy and salvation, not of terror.

'Please,' one of the men said, trying to look around at her.

Sonja jammed the pistol into his head, forcing him to look forward. 'Please, what?'

'Please, we're just soldiers. We were only following General Hendricks's orders. What's that guy going to do to us?'

'The question is,' Sonja said calmly, 'two questions in fact. One: what were you two *soldiers* going to do to that family? And two: what would you do right now if you were in his position?'

The man started shaking. He sniffed and Sonja thought he was actually crying. Sonja checked her watch. They needed to get moving; however, she was enjoying watching these two sweat. A couple of minutes later, Jacob came to the front door. He was telling his wife to stay inside and that everything would be fine. He closed the door and came out.

'Thank you,' he said to Sonja.

'My pleasure.'

Jacob went to the man next to the one that Sonja was covering and placed the barrel at the back of his head. This one was more stoic than his comrade. He said nothing, but Sonja saw that his eyes were closed and he was mouthing some words, perhaps a prayer.

Sonja glanced at Jacob. One eye was puffy, and twin streams of blood had dried on his swollen upper lip, from where they had flowed when Sonja smashed his nose. He had a look of serene calm on his face.

'I've got this,' he said to her, 'you can go.'

'You sure?' she said.

'Better that you're not here, when it happens.'

She could have said something flippant, such as that she'd seen worse, or done worse, but the fact was that she did not go in for shooting unarmed prisoners. All the same, she bore him no ill will; the decision was his to make. Sonja backed away. She went to the Range Rover and opened the driver's-side door. Kelvin, she saw, was still in the back seat with his arm around Emma. Good, she thought.

Emma caught her eye in the rear-view mirror. 'Jacob's going to kill those men, isn't he?'

Sonja stared back at her for a moment, not sure if the inflection in Emma's voice was hope or horror. 'What would you do?'

The question hung there in the car. A phone rang outside. Sonja saw Jacob answer the call, which had come through on Hendricks's phone. Jacob pressed the gun hard into the back of the head of one of the men. The other whimpered his prayers.

'Yes, second turn to the right after you exit the motorway,' Jacob said into the phone.

They all heard the wail of sirens. Sonja pushed the start button, rammed the gear lever into drive and stood on the accelerator. In the rear-view mirror, she saw the first of the police cars screaming up the street.

Jacob looked at the disappearing car and gave her a small wave. He was a long way behind already, but she thought he was smiling as the police pulled up next to him and his captives.

*

'Mum,' Emma said once they were clear of the crime scene. 'Did you kill Denzel?'

She looked at them, still holding each other. 'No, but . . .'

'But . . . ma'am?' Kelvin said.

A thought had crossed her mind, about the people who had been killed in her wake. 'Nothing,' Sonja said to him, without turning her head.

'Ma'am, it's just that, at medical school, we were studying blackouts, like when people can't remember something they might have done. It can be associated with excessive alcohol consumption, or it can be psychogenic, linked to some trauma or horrific event a person's been through.'

'I hadn't been drinking when I went after Denzel,' she snapped back, 'well, no more than usual.'

'Then if it's not alcohol related, Ms Kurtz, what about past trauma?' Kelvin said.

Poor kid, Sonja thought, hooking up with a family who couldn't remember how many people they'd killed. However, the kid might be on to something – the one truly terrible thing she had tried to erase from her memory and life kept coming back lately. 'I remember what I did and didn't do, Kelvin.'

'The news media said that the police in Botswana were after us,' Emma said. 'You – for killing some guy in Vic Falls and others in Hwange National Park, and me for killing a guy in Botswana.' Emma brought Sonja up to date with what had happened on the road, when she and Hudson had tangled with Wu's drug courier. 'But I didn't kill him, Mum. He was alive when I left.'

'I shot up all that mining shit in Hwange,' Sonja said. 'But I *did not* kill Denzel, nor Platt, the guy who set up Hudson for killing an elephant.'

'OK,' Emma said, 'good to hear. They also said I killed all three guys who tried to kidnap me at the Waterfront. I didn't.' Emma sat back in her seat and whispered, 'I only killed two.'

Sonja glanced back at Kelvin. 'Would your uncle kill some guys for botching a kidnapping?'

Kelvin shrugged, talking to her via the mirror. 'For sure, he wouldn't be happy with them and they might pay for it, but I don't think he would have them gunned down in a back street of the Waterfront.'

'Hmm.' Sonja nodded. 'He was such a sicko he'd probably want to torture them first.'

'So, where does that leave us?' Emma asked.

'Still at risk. We need to leave the country. I need to get you to safety, Emma,' Sonja said. 'Give me a phone.'

'You're driving, Mum, keep your eyes on the road.'

Sonja turned her head and glared at Emma. Kelvin handed her his phone.

As she drove, Sonja typed in a number.

'Andrew Miles,' said the voice at the other end.

'Andrew, it's Sonja Kurtz. Where are you?' she said, getting straight to the point.

'I'm in Cape Town. You've been everywhere in the media. Where are you, in prison? Is this your one phone call?'

'Is that offer of work still going?'

'It is, but I'm flying out from Cape Town in an hour's time, late-night flight to Mozambique, under the radar, so to speak, with a new load of recruits.'

'Message me the details and don't leave without me.'

*

Hudson Brand checked himself out of hospital in Kasane, Botswana. It was after dark, but the air was still warm.

Emma had messaged then called, telling him that she and Sonja were free and giving him an at-times-breathless, at-times-teary account of her near kidnapping and the fight in the warehouse. He wished he could have been there for them, instead of laid up with a broken leg, but he realised he could not be Sonja's shadow all the time, even if she wanted that, which she did not.

He had no idea how he was going to get back to Zimbabwe. His own vehicle, the Nantwich Lodge Land Cruiser game viewer, was a write-off, and had been towed to an impound yard at Kazungula, at the border crossing into Zimbabwe.

Leaving the hospital grounds on crutches he turned left onto President Avenue, speeding up to avoid being hit by a police Land Rover from the nearby station.

He decided to head to the bar at the Chobe Safari Lodge rather than risk getting tangled up in the local justice system. He hobbled the short distance down the road to the hotel.

The main building was a large, thatch-roofed structure. Hudson went past the curio shop and reception and made his way through the foyer out onto the expansive deck overlooking the Chobe River. The dining tables were full of tourists having dinner after their late afternoon game drives or cruises. A hippo honked obligingly nearby.

A waiter greeted him and showed him to a table. 'Castle Lite, please,' Hudson said.

He settled himself into the chair, took out his phone and dialled.

'Inspector Khumalo, hello?' Goodness said.

'Howdy, it's Hudson Brand. How are you, Goodness?'

They exchanged pleasantries and she told him she was still in Kasane, but off-duty.

'Where are you?' Hudson said. 'I'm at the Safari Lodge.'

There was a pause and, he detected, a sigh. 'So am I. We're just coming in through the foyer. I see you.'

Hudson ended the call and saw Goodness walking across the deck with Inspector Poster Mpho, the Botswana Police detective who had interviewed him. He began hauling himself to his feet.

'Mr Brand. Don't get up,' Poster said, 'I was going to come visit you again in hospital. I actually called, not long ago, and the matron told me you had discharged yourself. You've saved me having to issue an all-points bulletin, or have you arrested at the border.'

Hudson looked down at his moon boot. 'I'm not going anywhere fast any time soon, Inspector. Join me for a drink?'

Poster looked to Goodness, who rolled her eyes and shrugged her shoulders.

Hudson waved to the waiter. 'I'm buying.'

'Sparkling water,' Goodness said, when the man arrived.

'Chivas, double, on the rocks,' Poster said.

Goodness looked at him.

Poster spread his hands. 'I'm off-duty. And we're on a date.'

'*Date?*' Hudson and Goodness said at the same time.

Poster put a hand to his mouth and cleared his throat. 'Business meeting, I meant.'

Hudson took his notebook out of his pocket and opened it. 'I made some calls, while I was in hospital.'

Goodness slumped back in her chair. 'The media has been calling me, from Zimbabwe and South Africa, about your friends, Kurtz junior and senior. It's been a long day.'

'You didn't release that information, about them being wanted for murder?' Hudson asked.

Their drinks came. Goodness shook her head, then sipped her water. Poster clinked glasses with Hudson.

'No,' she said. 'I was called by a reporter from News24, asking me for a comment on a multi-jurisdictional investigation into murders in Hwange, Botswana and Cape Town.'

Now it was Hudson's turn to shake his head. 'Let me guess, Rosie Appleton.'

'Yes, that was her name,' Goodness said. 'You know her?'

'Had a couple of run-ins with her in the past. There's bad blood between her and Sonja. Rosie'll do anything for a story.'

'Is she a good reporter, or is someone feeding her?' Poster asked.

'She's good,' Hudson said, 'but to piece all this together so quick means that someone's feeding her, or using her, maybe.' Hudson found himself warming to the male cop.

'Appleton's picked up what I have; the only common denominator I can see in all of them is Carrington Wu.'

'The abalone smuggler?' Poster asked.

Hudson nodded. 'Yep. He's got a finger in everything. It was one of his drug shipments that we upended on the road to Nata.'

'These Kurtz women . . .' Poster began.

'The mother is a psychopath, a trained killer and mercenary,' Goodness said.

Hudson sipped his beer. 'That's a little harsh, don't you think, Goodness?'

Goodness narrowed her eyes, and, perhaps out of habit, lowered her voice. 'I looked her up. The CIO, our central intelligence organisation, has a file on her. She's suspected of trying to assassinate the former president.'

'And the daughter executed the driver of the truck carrying the drugs?' Poster said. 'Meaning, what, she is a player in the drug trade?'

Hudson held up a hand. 'No, no, no. Emma, the daughter, is a good kid, and she was on the road, hitchhiking out, when the ambulance came for me. The driver was still alive then. No way did she double back to shoot that guy. I have a theory . . .' He reached for his notebook.

'About a mysterious black Mercedes four-wheel drive,' Goodness said, finishing his sentence for him. 'I've put the word out.'

Hudson flipped through some pages. 'I've been checking.'

'With whom?' Goodness asked.

'People I know – the gate guards at Hwange National Park, a contact at Pandamatenga border post; I'm always driving back and forth through there, from Zimbabwe to Botswana.'

Poster set his drink down. 'You really should leave police work to the police.'

'He's a private investigator,' Goodness said.

Hudson didn't know whether she'd said it as a compliment or an insult, but Goodness did nod to him, as if he should continue.

'In this part of the world, as you both know, Toyota is king, followed by a few old diehards, like me, who still own Land

Rovers as their personal vehicle, plus a few Nissans, Fords and VWs when it comes to four-by-fours, so a big, black Mercedes kinda sticks out.'

'Unless you're a politician,' Goodness muttered.

Hudson checked his notes: 'On the 24th, the day the shipment of abalone was discovered –'

'*Discovered?*' Goodness let out a laugh. 'Shot to pieces and burned by your girlfriend, more like it.'

Hudson cleared his throat. 'On the day that Carrington Wu's tour truck passed through Pandamatenga border post, my guy at the border says a Black Mercedes G-Class four-by-four passed through from Botswana to Zimbabwe about half an hour after the overland truck was *discovered* on fire by your cops, Goodness.'

'Interesting,' she said. 'Is there more?'

Hudson nodded, consulting his notebook again. 'The ranger on duty at the Robins Gate entry to Hwange National Park, right next to Nantwich, has a register of the same vehicle entering the park an hour after the abalone truck was shot up. Just like the border, they have to record make and model, and driver's name, licence plate, etc.'

'You have those details?' Poster asked.

'Yep, and I'll give them to you. It's a CA – Cape Town – registration. The name of the driver is given as Jane Smith.' He looked to both of them.

'Doesn't ring any bells with me,' Poster said.

Goodness shook her head. 'Nor me, but we'll run it.'

'Sounds like an alias to me,' Hudson said. 'The parks guys probably only checked the licence plate. The same vehicle exited the national park via Sinamatella later that next day and later that evening the professional hunter, Platt, who worked for Carrington Wu, was shot dead in Victoria Falls. That's all I've got on the car, but Goodness, maybe you can check with Kazungula border post if it exited Zimbabwe out that way.'

'I'll check with my people,' Poster said. 'I've seen those G-Class wagons online. They're built like tanks, but they're made for the

German autobahns, so they *move*. The road between Kazungula and the South African border has plenty of Botswana Police speed traps; if one of our officers caught them speeding, they might very well remember the vehicle.'

'Good thinking,' Hudson said.

'So, who's driving this Merc?' Goodness asked.

Hudson sipped his beer and sat back in his chair. 'All we know is that it was a woman. Maybe she was following the truck full of abalone.'

'Why do you think this vehicle has some connection to Wu or the smuggling business?' Poster asked.

Hudson took out his phone and tapped the screen. He passed it to Goodness so she could see the video he had just started and share it with Poster. 'That's a black G-Class wagon in Victoria Falls, heading past the Three Monkeys bar on the night Platt was killed. It's CCTV video from outside a curio and souvenir store – a friend of mine is the owner.'

'Interesting,' Goodness said. 'The time stamp is a close match to the estimated time of death.'

'Is this someone trying to disrupt Carrington Wu's illegal business?' Poster asked. 'Where's Wu now – we need to question him.'

'I just heard today that Hendricks and Wu were last seen together, in Cape Town,' Hudson said, 'partying hard at some bizarre cage fight. Word is they were talking about a brave new future in business together and all that kind of crap.'

'You can never trust gangsters,' Poster said. 'So, is this a rival gang, a third force trying to muscle in on the abalone trade between South Africa, Zimbabwe and China. Maybe they're trying to get Wu to turn on Hendricks.'

Hudson drew a breath. 'Well, if that's their aim, they're too late. I also just heard that Hendricks is dead.'

He filled Goodness and Poster in on the amazing events that Emma had relayed to him, about Sonja being drugged and flown to South Africa, Emma's near-kidnapping, the fight, and the appearance once more of a black Mercedes G-Class, the one that

Emma had seen lurking in the alleyway at the Victoria & Alfred Waterfront. As with the other killing, of the driver in Botswana, it sounded like the dirty work had been done after Emma escaped the scene.

'Where are Kurtz and her daughter now?'

'I don't know.' Goodness eyed him suspiciously so he put his hand on his heart. 'I swear. I tried to find out, but when I spoke to Emma her mother was not saying where they were headed and did not want to talk to me.'

Goodness shook her head. 'This is a lot to take in. But whatever the case, I've got multiple dead bodies and multiple murders to solve in Zimbabwe, even if they are mostly low-life criminals.'

'I'm under pressure as well,' Poster said, 'from my authorities. Botswana isn't South Africa. We don't get many murders here, and there's one other thing that separates us from our neighbouring countries.'

'What's that?' Hudson asked.

'Your girlfriend's daughter . . .'

'Emma,' Hudson reminded him.

'Emma, as the last person seen leaving the scene of a crime where a man was executed in broad daylight, needs to know that in Botswana, we still have the death penalty.'

CHAPTER 23

Sonja took the N7, sitting on 120 kilometres per hour, the maximum she could do without attracting police attention. She was headed north, out of Cape Town, towards Malmesbury.

She checked Emma in the mirror. Kelvin still had his arm around her. Sonja focused harder on the mirror.

'What is it?' Emma looked over her shoulder.

'I'm not sure, but I think we're being followed,' Sonja said.

Both Emma and Kelvin turned to check.

'Shit,' Emma said.

Sonja accelerated and weaved around the car in the middle lane. 'Talk to me.'

'Black Mercedes four-wheel drive. I think it's the same one that came into the alley when those guys were trying to kidnap me.'

'Wu?'

Emma clung to the seat-back, trying to see past the vehicle immediately behind them. Sonja had to keep her eyes on the road ahead.

'I don't know,' Emma said. 'It's got tinted windows so I didn't get a look at the people inside, but Hudson asked me on the phone

287

if I'd seen a black Merc after our crash with the drug smuggler in Botswana.'

Sonja searched her memory. 'Was there a vehicle like that parked in the warehouse? Did it come from there?'

'No,' Kelvin said. 'I would have recognised a *lekker* ride like that.'

'It's coming!'

Sonja heard the panic in Emma's voice and didn't even bother to look back. Instead she swung out into the oncoming lane. A truck coming towards her sounded its air horn and Emma screamed as Sonja passed the Audi in front of her and returned to her lane. The oncoming truck was so close its slipstream made the Range Rover rock.

Sonja stood on the accelerator, all thoughts of sticking to the speed limit gone as she checked the odometer. 'Morningstar's only five k's up the road.'

'Morningstar?' Emma asked.

'It's an airfield,' Kelvin said. 'One of my cousins takes flying lessons there.'

'OK, Mum, *now* is the time to let us in on the plan.'

Sonja ignored her and picked up the phone between her legs. She drove with one hand, again cutting in front of a car, whose driver honked his horn.

'*Give* me that bloody thing.' Emma reached over into the front and snatched the phone from Sonja as it began dialling. The phone was on speaker and Emma held it up near Sonja's mouth.

'Sonja, where the hell are you, girl?' Andrew 'Thousand' Miles, the pilot, asked.

'Two minutes out,' Sonja said. She checked the mirror. In a minute or less the Mercedes would be on her tail. The driver she had just passed was now honking at her pursuer.

'I was just about to leave without you. We're on a tight schedule. Oosthuizen said if it'd been anyone else he would have told me to forget them. I shouldn't even be flying out of this airfield at night. I've got three *boeties* in cars lighting up the runway for me with headlights. There's two cars mid-way down the strip with headlights on and one parked at the end with his taillights towards me. Head to the other end of the runway and you'll find me.'

She could hear the buzz of aero engines over Thousand's voice.

'Understood. Thousand, I'm coming in hot. I've got a black Mercedes G-Class on my tail.'

'Too expensive for SAPS, so I'm assuming it's not the cops?'

'Affirmative,' Sonja said. 'All I know is they're bad guys.'

'All right,' he said. 'I'll warn Steve, but I am not going to let you get the shit shot out of my plane, Sonja!'

'Stop panicking, Thousand, you sound like a scared old man.'

'I am *not* old.'

Sonja nodded to Emma to end the call.

'Where the fuck are we going?' Emma slapped the back of Sonja's seat.

'Stop having a tantrum.' Sonja ran a hand through her hair. She had been going to leave Emma and Kelvin behind, but there was no question of that now. 'Mozambique.'

'Mozambique?' Kelvin said. 'I don't have a passport.'

Emma shook her head. 'My mother often flies no-passport-required air.'

'We're flying to Pemba. It's beautiful there. You two lovebirds can get a beachside chalet, or I'll get Thousand to take you to Maputo, or somewhere else away from the fighting.'

'Fighting?' Kelvin's voice rose an octave.

'Don't worry. I'll be going on to Palma; it's about four hundred kilometres north of Pemba.'

'*Mum!*'

Sonja was about to tell Emma not to worry when she glanced in the rear-view mirror and saw that Emma wasn't worried about Mozambique, but, rather, the car behind them.

'Gun!' Sonja jinked the steering wheel to the right. 'Get down!'

A bullet clipped the left rear of the Range Rover, pinging off the bodywork with a spark.

Sonja could see a sign for Morningstar Airfield ahead, on the right. The strip ran close to the N7. The Mercedes was closing on her. She weaved again, but this time a bullet shattered the rear window of the Range Rover and passed to her left, through the front windscreen.

When Sonja was almost at the turnoff, she put on the park brake rather than using the pedal. The Mercedes, its driver taken unawares thanks to the absence of her brakelights, nearly rammed her. Seeing what had happened, the driver stood on their brakes. That gave Sonja the space she needed to swing hard across two oncoming lanes of traffic.

Emma, thrown about in the back, screamed as Sonja bounced up the access road to the airfield. The Mercedes had overshot and its driver was executing a clumsy U-turn. Sonja raced into the airport complex, speeding past administration buildings and a small terminal, looking to the flight line.

She saw the two cars lighting up the centre of the otherwise darkened airfield, and a twin-engine aircraft at the opposite end of the airstrip to the third car. As Thousand had said, his engines were running, turning and burning, though the rear hatch was open and the stairs down.

'Get ready to run,' she said.

'We don't exactly have check-in luggage.' Emma turned to Kelvin. 'Do you want to stay?'

He shook his head. 'Hell, no. This beats Pick n Pay any day.'

Sonja swung between two hangars and drove onto the taxiway. 'Get out!'

They all exited, and heard the sound of squealing rubber as the big Mercedes rounded the end of the next hangar along.

'Go,' Sonja ordered.

She aimed and fired three rounds at the Mercedes as Emma and Kelvin made it to the door of the aircraft. The driver was weaving, but Sonja was sure at least two of her shots hit the vehicle. Sonja braced herself across the bonnet of the Range Rover and fired again. This shot shattered the windscreen and the Merc slewed to the right and bounced off the closed metal door of the hangar before coming to a stop, fifty metres away. She squeezed the trigger. Nothing happened. Sonja turned and ran to the aircraft.

Kelvin and Emma were still at the bottom of the stairs.

'They won't let us on, Mum,' Emma yelled over the engine noise.

A burly man with a grey crewcut stood in the entrance door.

'Back the fuck up,' Sonja said to him.

'The pilot says we were expecting one person. Orders.'

'Fuck your orders.' Sonja raised her pistol and aimed between his eyes.

He glared back at her, holding her stare, but something distracted him inside – probably, Sonja thought, the pilot telling him to get a move on.

Sonja went up the stairs and jabbed the gun into his flank, telling him to move inside. Perhaps it was her bloodied, swollen face and knuckles, the look in her eyes, or a command from the front, but he relented. Sonja backed out and ushered Emma and Kelvin up the stairs. They got in just as a bullet punched a hole in the skin of the aircraft.

'Give me a proper gun!' She tossed the empty pistol inside as she grabbed the handrail of the entry stairs.

Crewcut-man bustled his bulk past Kelvin and Emma and handed Sonja an AK-47. Instead of the usual thirty-round banana-shaped magazine, this one was fitted with a circular drum, containing seventy-five rounds.

Perfect, she thought. Thousand started taxiing and Sonja, half inside and half on the stairs, yanked back the rifle's cocking handle and opened fire, on full automatic, on the Mercedes.

The Mercedes was moving again and was picking up speed, drawing parallel to them, about twenty metres away. A man in the back had the window open and his hand out, firing a pistol. Every now and then a shot found its mark as Thousand sped down the runway. The driver of one of the parked cars that illuminated the runway got out of his car to see what was going on, but then dived for cover as the Mercedes sped past him.

Sonja raked the side of the Mercedes, silver-rimmed holes appearing in its black paintwork. The driver lost his nerve, or was hit, and veered off. She kept her finger on the trigger until the big drum was empty, then heaved on the handrail cables, fighting drag and gravity to pull the door closed as the aircraft lifted off the runway and she slumped and fell backwards onto the floor.

The big man grabbed one of her forearms and helped her up. 'You OK?'

'Sure.'

He grinned and put out a hand. 'Good shooting. No hard feelings. I'm Wynand.'

Sonja shook. 'Nice to meet you.'

The last reserves of adrenaline in her system were almost depleted and every cut, bump, bruise and near fracture she'd received began to throb while her nervous system started to scream. Sonja half staggered, half crawled up the narrow aisle of the cabin. Eyes turned as eight hard men, all of them at least her age or older, looked her up and down. Sonja ignored them and dropped to her knees beside Emma.

'Are you all right?' she rasped.

Emma nodded. Her lower lip wobbled and Sonja reached out and stroked her hair. She drew her daughter to her breast and squeezed her as tight as her broken body could manage, for just a second, then let her go. Kelvin, who had found the last seat across the aisle from Emma, reached out and took Emma's hand as Sonja turned and made her way painfully forward.

She climbed between the pilot and co-pilot seats and strapped herself in next to Thousand, who was climbing into the night sky.

He shot a glance at her. 'Well, you're a sore sight for eyes.'

She couldn't even manage a smile at the joke. Sonja felt the sheepskin cover on the co-pilot's seat mould to her body like a spooning lover.

Thousand reached for a spare headset and passed it to her. Reluctantly, Sonja put it on.

'Want to tell me what that was all about?' he said.

'Tomorrow, Thousand.' Sonja closed her eyes and fell asleep.

*

They flew through the night, stopping once to refuel at an airstrip in the bush in Limpopo Province in the northeast of South Africa. It was warmer here, but Sonja was grateful that Wynand, the man she'd pointed the gun at, had given her a heavy German army parka to put on as they stood under the stars.

If big Wynand thought it strange that a woman had shown up in boxing shorts and a tank top, covered in blood and with two younger people, clearly civilians, he didn't comment on it. He fetched the first aid kit from Thousand's aircraft and helped her clean and dress the worst of her injuries.

'I was a medic in the Border War,' he told her.

Thermos flasks of coffee and sandwiches were handed out from a box in the aircraft. Sonja gripped a mug in two hands after eating. The food and drink and a couple of painkillers helped, though her ribs hurt every time she took a deep breath. She looked back at Emma and Kelvin, who were holding hands.

'You been to Mozambique before?' Wynand asked her.

'Only as a kid, once, on holidays,' she said. 'You?'

He nodded. 'Special forces. Beautiful place. Shame they're always killing each other.'

The irony was not lost on her, that she was heading into a battle to find safety. After one more refuelling stop, this time inside Mozambique as the sun breached the Indian Ocean, they arrived at Pemba mid-morning.

They all stayed on board, except for Thousand, who weaved between them out onto the runway where he met with two officials in uniform. A sizable zip-up wallet was handed over. Warm, heavy air filled the cabin.

Sonja was wide awake. While the long flight had allowed her to sleep, her multitude of injuries had been made worse from sitting for nearly twelve hours. When it was her turn to leave the aircraft she felt like her joints were barely able to move.

A rusty minibus swayed on protesting springs and shattered shock absorbers towards them. The passengers had clearly been instructed to bring one small bag each, so they were able to quickly transfer to the bus.

The driver took them out a remote gate in the airport perimeter fence, away from tourists and other customs and immigration officials, through cultivated fields and palm-lined roads to a low-key beachside resort which looked in need of an extreme makeover.

After the driver squeezed his way between two beach shacks made of palm thatch, they came to an open sandy area in front of the huts which looked more like a military parade ground than a holiday haven, despite being adjacent to a white-sand beach.

Steve Oosthuizen, dark hair now grey at the temples and wearing camouflage trousers and a black T-shirt that strained at his biceps, came to greet them. A dozen other men, similarly dressed, were milling about. Steve shook hands with each of the men and gave Sonja a hug.

'You remember my daughter, Emma? And this is her, er, friend, Kelvin,' Sonja said to Steve.

'I wouldn't have known Emma if you hadn't told me. I think the last time I saw you was when you were three. Your mom and I worked for Corporate Solutions in Sierra Leone at the time. Nice to see you both,' he said to them. To the others: 'Right, find a hut, get your heads down for an hour and have some breakfast. We move at twelve hundred hours.'

'It's good to see you, Steve,' Sonja said.

'Sure, you, as well.'

'How are Linda and the kids?'

'Fine, thanks. You look like you've been in the wars, or out clubbing in Cape Town.' He gave her a questioning look.

'I'll tell you about it later.' She looked around the camp. As with the passengers on the aircraft, the average age of the men in uniform, cleaning rifles, having a meal, or welcoming the newcomers, seemed to be between fifty-five and sixty-five years of age. 'What's with dad's army?'

Steve, a fit sixty, gave a small laugh. 'We all need the work, and you know Africa. Most of us our age or older have been to war. Come for a walk on the beach.'

Sonja waved to Emma and Kelvin, standing nearby under a palm tree. 'Get some breakfast. I'll be back soon.'

They left the grass, their feet squeaking on white sand. Sonja registered, for the first time since the fight, that she was still barefoot. 'How bad is the situation here?'

He shrugged. 'Pretty bad, though not exactly the war on terror the media makes it out to be.'

'You're not fighting ISIS?' A fisherman sat cross-legged on a tourist's cast-off frayed beach towel, mending his net by an old wooden rowboat. The sea glittered in the morning sun. It was beautiful.

'The insurgents are Islamic, and call themselves al-Shabab, like the extremist group in Kenya, but it's more a literal meaning of the term – "young ones". The fighters here are hotheads and the general feeling up in the north is that the locals have missed out on most of the wealth that's generated through mining and natural gas in this part of the country. It's more like politics dressed up as ideology. There's a sprinkling of jihadis, though, enough to give them some media cred.'

'You sound like you're sympathetic to the cause?'

He shrugged. 'They're still killing *okes* and I'm getting paid. It's chaos in Palma, Sonja, whatever the reason. Al-Shabab holds most of the town and the wild ones have been lopping people's heads off, sometimes settling old scores, or killing people who get in the way of their looting. There are a couple of pockets where workers from the LNG plant and their families are still holed up, under siege. That's where we're going.'

295

'Where can I get some clothes and boots?'

He looked her up and down as they turned back, retracing their steps. 'You can sit this one out if you like.'

'No. It'll do me good.'

Ahead of them, near where they had left Emma and Kelvin, a man walked towards them onto the beach. Sonja raised a hand to shield her eyes from the sun's glare. He looked familiar. As they got closer she recognised his fleshy face. 'What the fuck?'

Steve glanced at her, seeing the look on her face. 'You know David?'

'We met, briefly.' Sonja recognised the man from the fight, in Cape Town. David, the Irishman, had swapped his dinner suit for khaki bush wear and was carrying a Type 56, a Chinese-made AK-47 with a folding metal stock. She tensed up as David approached them, ready for anything. 'What's his story?'

'He's ex–British Army, Royal Irish Rangers. I had him checked out; he's legit.'

They met up on the beach. Steve excused himself, telling them they'd be leaving for Palma on their next rescue mission in two hours.

Sonja squared up to the big man. 'How did you get here so quickly?'

He smiled. 'Late flight to Maputo, then a connection up here. I was coming here anyway – fancy meeting you here. A coincidence?'

She ignored his question. 'Who are you, really?'

'I should ask you the same thing. X?'

'X what?'

'Are you X?' David said.

'I have no idea what the fuck you are talking about.'

David frowned. 'Hmm, I thought as much. Damn. Though, on second thought, I'm actually relieved.'

'Start talking in English,' Sonja said.

'To be clear,' David said, 'you're not working for X?'

'No. Nor Y, or Z. Would you like to tell me what's going on here?'

'First, I should clear up exactly who you are, today, Sonja Kurtz. Are you working for the CIA, or are you freelancing for someone else?'

'How do you know who I am?'

He slung the rifle over his shoulder and spread his hands wide. 'I won't kid a kidder, especially now I know you're not X.' He lowered his voice. 'I'm PSNI, Police Service of Northern Ireland.'

'What the fuck are you doing in Africa?'

'I could say enjoying the sunshine, but it's a bit gloomier than that. We're tracking a gun-running syndicate. They've been dealing with the ragtag bunch of wannabe jihadis here, shopping for AK-47s and RPG-7s. The local lads have upped their game after capturing half the Mozambican army's weapons and there's someone called X who's dealing guns and heroin out of Afghanistan, and probably helped the locals knock off a Portuguese police armoury.'

'Who's buying?' she asked. 'IRA? Is that why you were ringside in Cape Town, undercover as a buyer?'

David shook his head. 'Other side. The Protestants are up in arms over Brexit. They think the hard border between Ireland and Great Britain disadvantages them; they say old Boris and the UK hung them out to dry. A few of the youngsters who missed out on the Troubles are planning on kickstarting the UVF again and taking matters into their own hands. Scotland Yard picked up a South African drug importer, a former Cape Town gangbanger, and when he spilled the beans he led the Metropolitan Police and then my people to a UVF quartermaster in Belfast who was packing his bags for South Africa to meet with Vincent Hendricks and Carrington Wu. I fit the profile of the loyalist paramilitary, so I was called in to impersonate the buyer.'

'Is David Rafferty your real name?' Sonja asked.

'It is. The real buyer was also a David, and was only known to the people in Africa by his first name.'

'Have you been following me?' Sonja asked.

David's smile creased his face up into a wink. 'For a wee while, maybe. You served with the Brits in Ulster in an undercover surveillance role yourself, targeting an extreme faction of the IRA – you'll forgive us for thinking you might be sourcing guns for some old pals. Also, we got some intel that this mysterious X might be a woman who served in the British Army back in the nineties.'

'That's bullshit,' Sonja spat. 'I'd had enough of your ridiculous Troubles after two months there when I was young and stupid.'

He held up a hand. 'No offence meant. I worked out pretty quickly in the warehouse that your beef was with those gangsters, Wu and Hendricks, not the British Government.'

'What was their involvement?' Sonja asked.

'Oh, they're players, no doubt about it. We followed a typical path backwards from Belfast – drugs from Afghanistan and China, via Mozambique and South Africa. It's all tied up, as I'm sure you know. The same shipping routes and networks that carry heroin, ice and abalone also double up with guns. My partner's been playing Wu for a while – we're doing a bit of a double act, she and I – and it seems that both Wu and Hendricks buy guns from our mysterious X-man or X-woman.'

It sounded plausible to Sonja. 'So why tell me now who you really are?'

'If it comes to a shootout, here, when X's person contacts me, I'd like to think I have someone from The Det, with special forces training, backing me up.'

Sonja put her hands on her hips. 'Why the fuck do you think I owe you anything? You were going to watch me die in that cage in Cape Town.'

'I had the local cops on speed dial and was ready to slip out the back door with my partner and call the cavalry. I almost did when you choked out Jacob.'

'Your partner – Fiona? Tell me about her.'

He laughed. 'Fiona Mulqueen. She does the psycho well, doesn't she? Aye, and like me she's got a bit of an eye for the ladies. She put quite a sum of money on you for the fight, I'll have you know. Fiona still thought that you might really be X. Neither Wu nor Hendricks knows what X looks like – Fiona's theory was that you were on a solo mission to avenge the attack on your daughter, outside of your normal gun-running business.'

Sonja started to walk away, shaking her head.

'Sonja?'

She stopped and looked back at him.

'Fiona and I are security forces. We wouldn't have allowed a murder to take place in front of us – neither you nor Jacob Dlamini. From what I know of your file I'm sure you don't want to see industrial-scale killing return to Northern Ireland.'

Sonja closed her eyes for a moment, fighting off lingering fatigue and pain, and trying to force her brain to process the new information and to replay the hectic events of the past week or so. She had been thinking about Fiona; the woman on the beach at Silver Sands, the young woman with a black ponytail and baseball cap in the Three Monkeys bar in Victoria Falls. The PSNI had probably been bugging her or placing tracker devices on her gear. Why was she being followed? she had asked herself, over and over again. Now she knew exactly why.

'Tell me,' she said to David, 'were you driving a black Mercedes four-wheel drive during your surveillance?'

He shook his head. 'No. I've been flying everywhere just trying to keep up with you, Sonja.'

'Vehicle sound familiar, though?'

'Aye. Wu's got one. Several, in fact, in different locations. Our intelligence people told us it's his favourite vehicle. You'll like as not see one in Palma, as he ships his drugs in through there.'

'Was Fiona following me in Zimbabwe, and following my daughter?'

David said nothing; it looked like he was biting his lower lip.

'Who's running your investigation – you or her?' Sonja pressed.

'Like I said, she's, ah, following what you might call a parallel line of inquiry.'

'You don't know, do you?' He was obfuscating. She thought about what he'd just said. He had described himself and Fiona as 'security forces', not police. David had slipped up. 'She's a spook, isn't she? MI6 – UK Secret Intelligence Service?'

He spread his hands again. 'We're all on the same side, here, Sonja, you too, I hope.'

'Bullshit. Is Mulqueen her real name?'

David shrugged.

'Was she following my daughter and me, killing people in our wake?'

David gave a small laugh. 'Like I say, she does a good impersonation of a madwoman, but she's not a serial killer. Wu, on the other hand, is a butcher, from what Fiona's learned about him. His idea of human resources management is to put a bullet in the brain of underperforming staff and then use the body to set up an enemy.'

'My daughter and I have a string of those murders pinned on us at the moment.'

'There you go,' David said, as if that was the end of the discussion. 'Well, perhaps in return for a bit of cooperation with the police, I can get Interpol to have a word to the local fellas in Zimbabwe, Botswana and South Africa and have these matters cleared up. And you should know, Sonja, that Wu was on his way here, to Mozambique, after the fight.'

She stared at him. Sonja did not like being manoeuvred into a position or decision by anyone, but she sensed David was genuinely trying to help, and was man enough to admit he needed back-up. His undercover operation was leading him into an African war – small, but dirty. She'd brought Emma to Mozambique to escape Wu, but it seemed his tentacles spread here, as well.

David had also pushed one of her buttons. She had left the British Army under a cloud, having fallen for a target and then been forced to kill him. It had signalled the end of her career and she'd felt bitter and betrayed for many years. She had at least been able to take some measure of consolation from the fact that she had helped prevent more needless killing, and the Good Friday Agreement had ended the fighting in Northern Ireland in 1998. The thought of a new generation having to go through what she had horrified her. Plus, Wu, with his spider's web of repugnant businesses, needed taking down. Until he was locked up or, preferably, dead, Emma wasn't truly safe, wherever she was in the world.

'All right,' she said at last, 'but I want a couple of things in return.'

'What's that?' David asked.

'You keep Fiona away from my daughter and set up a time for me to meet her. I want to tell her who I really am. And I want to know everything you can tell me about Fiona.'

He rocked his head from side to side. 'All right.'

'Good,' Sonja said. 'Now let me find some fucking shoes so we can go to war.'

CHAPTER 24

'No!' Emma said. 'Please, please don't go.'

'I'll be fine,' Sonja said, knotting the tails of an over-sized camouflage shirt Steve had found her around her midriff. She had found a young Mozambican woman, a cleaner in the old tourist lodge, given her some cash borrowed from Steve and sent her to the local markets in search of some other clothing.

'You were nearly killed in Cape Town,' Emma said. 'We're back together again, at last, and we're here with all these armed guys around. Please, can you just stay here with *me*?'

'It's a quick pick-up mission. I'm only providing security for the choppers and looking after any panicking women and children.'

'Right,' Emma said, hands on hips, 'because you're a model of empathy and kindness.'

'I'll ignore that.' She turned to Kelvin. 'Look after this one while I'm gone.'

'You got it, ma'am.'

'I do *not* need looking after. Who was that man you were talking to? I saw him at the fight in Cape Town, with some girl with weird eyes?'

Sonja frowned, then recounted her talk with David.

'They're cops?'

'*Ja*,' Sonja said. 'Get on the phone to Hudson. Tell him to tell his police buddies in Botswana what's been going on here. David says he's going to help us clear our names. He needs help here, though.'

'It's not your war, Mum.'

Sonja sighed. 'It never is.'

'What are we supposed to do?' Emma asked.

'Go to the beach. Have a piña colada. A walk on the sand. Whatever the fuck people do on holiday.'

'I'll look after your daughter, Mrs Kurtz,' Kelvin said. 'Trust me.'

She glared at him. 'It's Ms, and I don't need to tell you what will happen to you if something happens to her.'

'No, ma'am.'

She gave Kelvin a small smile; he had helped rescue her. Sonja went to a group of men, including Wynand from the aircraft. He handed her the AK-47 with the drum magazine. It felt reassuringly weighty in her hands.

*

Emma strode away from her mother, towards the bungalow Steve had said she could use.

Inside, the room smelt musty. She opened a window facing the ocean; a warm breeze blew in. Kelvin stood in the doorway while Emma sat on the bed, shoulders slumped. The emotions of the last few days, visions of the people whose lives she'd taken, or those she had seen killed, welled up inside her and her lower lip started to tremble.

Kelvin walked across the tiled floor and sat down beside her. He put an arm around her and she crumpled into him. Her tears flowed and she sobbed into his shirt as Kelvin stroked her hair. 'It's OK, I've got you, Emma.'

Emma clung to him. She looked up into his eyes. They kissed and Emma was surprised at just how natural it felt to do so. Her head told her this was not the time or place to fall for someone, or whatever this was, but her body craved the solace and comfort

303

of another. She lay back on the bed and Kelvin came with her, content, for the moment at least, to just hold her.

After a few minutes she eased herself away from him, got up and stood by the bed. He looked up at her. 'I'm filthy. I need a shower.'

Emma went into the bathroom, closed the door behind her and slumped against it. She took a deep breath, straightened herself up and stripped. The shower water didn't rise above lukewarm, but she didn't care. She'd been on the road since Zimbabwe. Sonja's dried blood washed from her hands and she watched it circle its way around and down the drain.

When she was finished, she wrapped a towel around herself and went back to the room. Kelvin looked up from the bed and Emma realised she should have got changed in the bathroom.

Outside, overhead, there was the sound of an engine and rotor blades and a shadow passed over the window. Emma could hear the helicopter's noise steady and grow as it hovered then landed, somewhere nearby.

Kelvin sat up. 'You want some privacy? Maybe get some sleep, Emma?'

'No.'

Emma came to him, put a knee on the mattress and lifted her other leg, straddling him. She reached for him, her wet hair curtaining his face as she kissed him deeply. She felt his hands on her skin as the towel slid off her. The ocean breeze caressed her back.

Emma rocked back, looking down at him, revelling in the mix of surprise and lust in his face. He reached over to the bedside table, scrabbling to get hold of the drawer. He slid it out and fumbled inside. One thing she had learned from her trips to Africa was that hotels and resorts were never short of protection. Kelvin found and ripped open the foil-wrapped packet as Emma unzipped him.

Her need was basic. After the killing and chaos she had witnessed she had to connect and, if not procreate, at least do something based on creation, not destruction. She leaned forward, rising now on her knees, so she could kiss Kelvin and he could do what he had to do. He lingered, touching her as their lips met.

The urgency overcame her then. Emma lowered herself down onto him and he grabbed her hips, steadying her. She needed him, craved the connection, so hard and urgent that she couldn't let him slow her at all. With her palms on his chest she rode him, feeling her own arousal grow with every moment. His grip tightened, fingers digging into her, and instead of flinching she ground down harder against him.

Emma shuddered, sated, but Kelvin wasn't done. He rolled her, on the bed, taking over where she had left off, looking down at her as he entered her again, this time from above. She could barely catch her breath, but drew him in, hooking her legs around him, holding on until they both tumbled over the edge together.

Kelvin lay beside her, panting, eyes closed.

'Holy fuck,' Emma said, as she exhaled long and loud.

From outside she heard but hardly registered the sound of a helicopter taking off. Her mother heading to work, she thought. To war. She didn't care.

Kelvin turned his head, opened his eyes and looked at her. He was about to say something when the door to their bungalow flew open.

*

Hudson Brand had been given a desk in the Kasane Police Station the morning after he'd met with the two detectives and had dinner with them at the Chobe Safari Lodge. Goodness Khumalo and Poster Mpho had set up an impromptu task force to investigate the related and chaotic crimes straddling their respective borders.

Hudson's phone rang with a WhatsApp call. 'Chris, howzit?'

'*Ja*, fine and you, Hudson? How's Botswana?'

'Quiet.'

'*Lekker.*' Chris Wessels was a former SAPS detective who now headed up investigations for one of South Africa's biggest insurers. He and Hudson had cooperated in the past on a few life insurance fraud cases – busting people who'd faked their own deaths had been part of Hudson's stock in trade as a private investigator. 'You asked me to keep an eye out for claims about late-model Mercedes G-Class wagons.'

'Glad you got the message,' Hudson said. 'One was shot up last night.'

'*Yip*,' Chris said, 'by someone with some serious firepower. Forty-two 7.62-millimetre holes in the bodywork. Sheesh, those Cape gangsters must be packing PKM belt-fed machine guns these days.'

Hudson gave a small laugh. 'AK-47 with a seventy-five-round drum magazine, would be my educated guess. Anyway, it's OK, Chris, I've traced the owner.'

'Sure. No problem, but I think that customer's up for a hell of an excess payment.'

'Say again?' Hudson said. 'Way I heard it, the vehicle's most likely registered to a Chinese dude named Wu or, most likely, a company called Giraffe Holdings.'

'Must be a different vehicle.'

'Shot up at –' Hudson checked the notes he'd made when Emma had called him with the update '– Morningstar Airport.'

'That's the one,' Chris said. 'It's owned by a small luxury car rental company in Cape Town. Very expensive – they generally supply courtesy cars for people whose Porsches or Lamborghinis have been in accidents, or high-end vehicles to visiting billionaires.'

Or, Hudson thought, to someone who wanted to make it look like they were Carrington Wu or his people.

'You got an ID on the customer, Chris?'

There was a moment's pause. 'I guess I owe you, Hudson.'

'That you do. Also, buddy, this is serious. There could be lives at risk.'

Hudson heard a click on the end of the call. 'Just snapped a picture for you, *boet*, I'll send it now. You never heard it from me, OK?'

'Roger that,' Hudson said. They said goodbye and Hudson checked the digital photo Chris had just sent through.

It was a black and white image, a photo of a photocopy of a passport. The document was a British passport, from the EU days; the place of birth of the woman in the picture was listed as 'Belfast'.

Northern Ireland. The woman was, he calculated, 28 years old, good-looking, skin so fair it was almost blank space on the photocopy. There was something familiar about her; he had seen her before.

'Stewart, Fiona Louise,' he said out loud.

'Got something?' Goodness swivelled her office chair to face him. The air conditioner fitted to the window of the small office they were sharing rattled and hummed as it fought the Kasane heat.

'The black four-by-four that was following Sonja and Emma wasn't one of Wu's cars; it was a rental, driven by this woman.' He stared at the washed-out face again, then handed the phone to Goodness. 'She must be the woman who signed into and out of Hwange National Park as "Jane Smith".'

'Could be,' Goodness said. 'She might have known that the border and parks officials don't pay much attention to what people write in those registries, but anyone who looked, like you, would not find her real name.'

'Want me to check her out?' Poster asked.

'Sure.' Hudson stared at the image.

*

Sonja sat on the floor of the Alouette helicopter's cargo compartment, next to the open door.

David Rafferty was beside her and beyond him, grinning like a hyena, was Johnsy, who had also been recruited by

Steve Oosthuizen. Sonja had seen him when she was getting ready to board and recalled him saying he was also heading to Mozambique. Johnsy pulled back the cocking handle of his cut-down RPD machine gun. 'Ready to rock and roll!' he yelled over the engine noise.

As Sonja leaned out to survey the terrain ahead, the slipstream snatched at her ponytail. They were tracking along the coastline, the glittering Indian Ocean off to their right. To the north was Palma, easily recognisable by plumes of smoke from several burning buildings.

Small villages flashed below the wheels. Steve, up front in the co-pilot's seat, pointed slightly off to the left. Sonja saw he was indicating the target, which he'd briefed them on before take-off. There was a cluster of whitewashed buildings, an out-of-town enclave of holiday villas, also used as accommodation for expats working at the nearby natural gas plant.

The pilot pushed the nose down, lowering them almost to palm-top height. Sonja looked around at the sound of gunfire. Johnsy was firing out of the door on his side. Beyond him, Sonja could see the second bird, this one a Gazelle helicopter, peel up and away from the gunfire. The Gazelle was empty of passengers and would be used to transport the people they were going to rescue. Sonja and the others in the Alouette would set up a security cordon on the ground, though Sonja knew that David, still working undercover, would also be meeting with his contact about the stolen guns he was pretending to try to buy.

Sonja scanned the ground on her side and saw green tracer rounds reaching up towards them. She flicked the safety catch of her AK to automatic, lifted the rifle to her shoulder and fired off a burst.

She conserved her ammunition. The drum magazine carried a healthy seventy-five rounds, but each bullet had to be manually slotted into place, rather than using a feeder on a normal thirty-round magazine. She wore denim shorts and a pair of second-hand Converse sneakers the maid had sourced from the local market; the clothes were probably the hand-me-downs of some do-gooder in America or Australia.

Her phone buzzed in the breast pocket of her camouflage shirt; Sonja had also convinced the domestic to sell her the local SIM card from her phone. Quickly, she took the phone out and opened the message from Hudson – she had sent him a message with her number.

You and Emma were being followed by a Fiona Stewart. I am looking at a copy of her passport photo. DOB 16/11/94. Ring any bells?

'Holy fuck,' Sonja said out loud.

*

'You have to come with me,' the woman said, standing in the open doorway of Emma's beachside chalet. 'My name's Fiona, and I need your help.'

Emma clutched the bedsheet, covering her breasts. 'Couldn't you have at least knocked?' Kelvin was trying to discreetly zip his pants up – he hadn't got as far as removing them completely.

'You're a trainee doctor?' Fiona said to Kelvin.

Kelvin got off the bed. 'Third-year med student. How did you know that?'

'There's a man on a boat, bleeding out from a gunshot wound. He needs help, now.'

He ran a hand through his hair. 'I don't know if I can –'

'Come on, you're better than no one.'

'Who are you?' Emma asked, staring at the woman with long black hair tied back in a ponytail.

'I'm one of the good guys,' Fiona said.

'Let me see some ID,' Emma said.

Fiona reached behind her back and drew a pistol. She pointed it at Emma. 'Good enough for you?' Kelvin moved between them. Fiona nodded to him. 'Finish getting dressed, hero. Both of you. You're coming with me.'

'Who are you?' Emma said.

'I work for the UK security service, Emma,' Fiona said. 'I'm undercover and I need you and your boyfriend to help me.'

'Or what, you'll shoot us?'

'I find people listen more carefully when they're looking down the barrel of a nine-mil.'

*

'Fiona *is* MI6,' David said as he and Sonja skirted a man and a woman each carrying a suitcase, 'I can tell you that much.'

'Dump your bags,' Steve Oosthuizen yelled at the civilians over the noise of the other chopper coming in to land. 'We don't have room.' Other refugees were emerging from the buildings, some empty-handed, some trying to bring valuables with them. A woman held a baby in her arms.

'Let's get away from this noise,' Sonja said to David. They moved to the other side of a villa, away from the helicopters. She had at least made David confirm what she thought. 'How did Fiona end up here, in Africa, chasing gun runners? It's hardly a matter in the UK's national interest.'

'Good question. Fiona's been with Six's Africa desk for a few years now, looking for British-born jihadis based on the continent. Africa has become ISIS's new front, since they were knocked for six in Syria and Iraq.'

'What else do you know about her, as a person?' Sonja asked.

'She likes to work solo. Six uses a few coppers, like me, on attachment in the UK, and Fiona said she needed a middle-aged man to play a UVF man and I was given the nod. She's not what you'd call a people person, Sonja. She made it very clear to me that I was just here to be the spare wheel, as it were.'

'And she thinks I'm this X person.'

'Aye. You did seem to fit the profile – female, military service, a beef against the IRA.'

'Bullshit.' Sonja shook her head. 'I'm African. I fight for money, not religion. If Fiona's looking for terrorists then what's she doing getting involved with a Chinese triad boss and a Cape Town gangster?'

'She'd been gathering intel on this X, a former UK military person running guns and with links to the al-Shabab rebels here in Mozambique. We, the police in Northern Ireland and England, picked up the trail from our end when we arrested the South African middleman and the real UVF fella. There was a bit of a debate as to whether the guns would come via Hendricks or Wu – we actually suspected that as well as being in business together, trading abalone for drugs, they were competing with each other for the gun trade. Hendricks pretty much confirmed that to me – he charged me a consultancy fee to be put in touch with X's people and told me Wu would ship the guns for me, but told me not to tell Wu what I was buying. No honour among thieves, eh?'

'So, X or his or her middleman will contact you here, with a load of guns to sell you?' Sonja said.

'That's about the size of it.'

'And Fiona still thinks I'm X.'

David shrugged. 'I've not had contact with her since the cage fight in Cape Town. She went off with Wu.'

'What do you mean, "went off" with him?'

David frowned. 'She's close to him, Sonja, as part of her under-cover work. I worry a bit, to tell you the truth, about just how close she is.'

'You think she's bent?' Sonja asked.

'I think she's determined – ruthless, even. I've seen it in the way she treats me. The mission is everything to her. She'll do whatever it takes to complete it. I've never come across anyone quite like her.'

Sonja thought hard. 'Where did the information come from that indicated X might be a woman?'

'Hendricks told me, but I'd also heard from the MI6 people in the UK, when I received my briefing and orders, that the intel had come from the Americans – something they picked up, monitoring chatter between a couple of jihadis, joking about a woman selling guns, how it wouldn't have happened under the "old Taliban". Apparently, like you, X had served as a contractor in Afghanistan.' David checked his watch, then opened the flap on the cargo pocket of his trousers, reached in and took out a satellite phone. He switched it on and flipped up the stubby antenna.

Sonja thought about the chain of events that had led her to Mozambique, and began to mentally dismantle the elaborate booby-trap that had been laid for her. She could finally work out what had been going on behind the scenes since Emma's altercation with the boy on the beach, and the years of secrets and lies that had preceded that moment.

'Here we go,' David said, reading the phone's screen. 'Two trucks of weapons are on their way for me to inspect, here.'

'Give me your phone.' Her look brooked no argument from David, who handed it over to her. She punched in a number she had committed to memory a few years earlier, while on a freelance mission for the American government. She waited, her AK slung and her spare hand covering her other ear as the call went through.

'Jed Banks,' said the CIA's station chief for southern Africa.

CHAPTER 25

There had been no chance for Emma to ask more as Fiona hustled them out of the room, across the beach and into a Zodiac inflatable boat. The noise of the outboard motor and the slap of waves on the hull had precluded conversation. Offshore, Fiona rendezvoused with a luxurious motor cruiser, which looked to Emma to be nearly twenty metres in length.

A Chinese man in a black T-shirt and matching jeans, accessorised with an MP5 machine pistol, tossed a rope to Kelvin, who reluctantly took it. Fiona had kept a pistol trained on them during the voyage. Kelvin and Emma went aboard via the diving deck at the aft of the vessel and the guard ushered them downstairs into a large cabin.

'Carrington Wu?' Emma said. It was the man she had glimpsed in the warehouse, running away. He lay on a bed, his eyes half closed, naked except for a pair of boxer shorts. His midriff was wrapped in a blood-soaked bandage.

'Fix him,' Fiona said to Kelvin. She did not deny it was Wu.

Emma glanced around as Kelvin moved tentatively towards Wu. The man with the gun was watching their every move and there was now another man in the corridor. A large medical kit was lying half open on the bed next to Wu. Kelvin began undoing the bandage and inspected Wu's wound.

'Why should we help him?' Emma asked.

Fiona stared at her, deadpan. 'Your mother shot him when she brassed up our Mercedes at that airport.'

Kelvin looked over his shoulder to Emma. 'It's my duty, Emma, as a doctor – well, future doctor, to preserve life.'

'Come with me,' Fiona said to Emma, and pointed to the cabin door. They eased past the armed guard. Fiona kept her pistol at the ready as they moved out onto the rear deck.

'What's going on here?' Emma asked. 'If you're a spy or whatever, why are you trying to keep that gangster alive? Why didn't you just let him die?'

Fiona lowered her voice to a whisper. 'I've been working him for months, undercover, gaining his trust. Wu knows the identity of a major international arms dealer who's supplying terrorist organisations around the world with the surplus of guns and other high-tech weapons and equipment left by the Americans when they pulled out of Afghanistan.'

'But you've been following us,' Emma said.

'Your mother is the arms dealer. She's known as X.'

Emma laughed. 'Rubbish. She might be a bit of a psycho killer, but she's no gun runner.'

'It's true. She supplied guns to Vincent Hendricks for his gang activities in Cape Town, and heroin to Wu, from Afghanistan. She made contact with Afghan warlords when she served there as a military contractor and even though those same chiefs have changed sides and are now aligned with the Taliban, they still need access to cash.'

'But both Wu and Hendricks wanted her dead, in that sick cage fight.'

Fiona nodded. 'Even though she had done business with both of them, as X, they made the cardinal error of hurting those your mother loves – you and her boyfriend, Hudson Brand.'

'You know a lot about my mother.'

'I've been watching her. For a long time. She's gone off the rails, Emma. She killed anyone who she thought might be a possible witness against her.'

Emma shook her head. Her mother had plenty of faults, but Emma knew she would never become involved with drugs, and had clearly had no idea of who Hendricks and Wu were before meeting either of them. 'I'm not buying it.'

*

The last of the civilians clambered aboard the Alouette helicopter, which lifted off. The Gazelle had already departed and Sonja and the other mercenaries had to wait for one of the choppers to offload the refugees at a nearby safe haven, and then return for them.

Sonja kept watch out through the fence that surrounded the compound. Beyond were farmers' fields and a line of palm trees to the rear of the complex. The beach and ocean were on the other side.

Steve came to them. 'Right, we sit tight, wait for the pick-up, then we're out of here. Home in time for peri-peri prawns and Dois M beers on the beach.'

'Steve?' Johnsy called.

Sonja looked to her right; Johnsy came around the corner of the villa. 'There's movement in the shateen, my side,' he pointed to the scrubby bushland on the far side of the compound. 'Armed men, fighting age. I scheme they're al-Shabab.'

'Well spotted, Johnsy,' Steve said. 'Go keep an eye on them.'

'Affirmative.' Johnsy returned to his post.

Sonja heard a beep and saw David, next to her, take out his satellite phone again. He read the screen then looked to her. 'Sonja, I've got a message from Fiona. She says she's on Wu's boat a couple of kilometres off the coast, heading north. She's got Emma and her young friend with her, says they're both safe.'

'My ass, they're safe,' Sonja said. 'I didn't want her anywhere near my daughter.'

Sonja looked around. She needed to get out of this place. Just then, Wynand walked over to Steve. 'Boss,' he said, 'two trucks approaching from the south.'

'They'll be for me,' David said.

Steve looked at him. 'What do you mean?'

Sonja stepped between them. 'Steve, David's an undercover police officer, from the UK – Northern Ireland.'

'What the –'

'Relax, Steve.' Sonja held up a hand. 'He's a good guy. He's posing as a buyer for some guns. David, we've got to watch our backs and get out of here as soon as that chopper lands.'

'Sonja,' David said, 'I can't let those guns stay in circulation. I've got to get a lead on X.'

'Who?' Steve said.

'I'll explain later,' Sonja said.

What a fucking mess, Sonja thought. 'I need to get back to my daughter, Steve. David's partner has a grudge against me and I'm not happy knowing she's on a boat with Emma, somewhere off Pemba.'

'What?' Steve said again.

'Too complicated,' Sonja said. 'Let's talk later.'

At that moment there was gunfire, close by. Sonja felt blood spatter her face and thought for a moment she was shot. Then she saw that two bullets, single shots fired in rapid succession, had exited David's chest. He fell to the ground.

'Contact! Contact!' Johnsy's warning, too late for David, was punctuated by a long burst from Johnsy's RPD machine gun.

Sonja dropped and leopard-crawled towards the perimeter. She saw men advancing through a field of young, straggly maize. One had stopped in the open, an AK-47 at his shoulder. He fired a burst. Sonja took aim and squeezed the trigger on her rifle. The man fell.

Sonja looked over her shoulder from where she lay. Steve was bending over David. 'Get that fucking chopper back here, now!'

Sonja fired again then got up and ran around the building to where Johnsy was. Wynand had run up to reinforce him and they were both firing. Empty casings spat from the ejection point of Johnsy's gun as he raked the cornfield.

'What happened to those trucks?' Sonja asked Wynand.

'Stopped, as soon as the fighting started. I think we might be surrounded. The drivers got out. Last seen hiding in the storm-water drain there by the road.'

Sonja looked out over the field. The jihadis – if that's what they were – had been temporarily halted by Johnsy's sustained fire and had gone to ground. One stood, perhaps hellbent on showing his bravery, and Sonja saw the long, pointed protrusion of an RPG-7 rocket-propelled grenade launcher on his shoulder.

'Drop him,' Sonja said, 'and cover me.'

'What? Sonja, no . . .' Johnsy's protest was lost on her as she slung her AK-47 over her back and scaled the cyclone mesh perimeter fence, rolled over the top and let herself fall.

As Sonja started running across the open ground, she was pleased to hear the two men, at last, open up, giving her covering fire. She swung her AK around and fired a burst from the hip at a man in camouflage fatigues and a black headdress who stood and took aim at her. He fell, either hit or scared.

There was no sign of the man with the RPG launcher, but Sonja ran towards where she had last seen him. Her chest was pounding, her knee sending an electric shock of pain to her brain with every heavy, uneven footfall in the farmer's field. *Do not give out on me now*, she prayed. Bullets crack-thumped over her head. Their fire was ill-disciplined and inaccurate, but it didn't take much to get lucky with an assault rifle on full auto.

The gunfire from the villas had slowed. Sonja dropped and crawled, figuring Johnsy must be changing magazines. More rounds scythed the plants on either side of her. She popped up onto one knee, saw a man running her way, and fired two single shots at him. There was no doubt she had hit him – he was checked in mid-stride and swatted backwards.

Sonja went forward on knees and elbows and came to a body dressed in grubby, now-blood-soaked fatigues. The RPG-7 lay next to him. Sonja rolled the man over and slid a canvas pack, tailored to carry two spare rocket-propelled grenades, from his back. She shrugged it on, slung her own rifle and picked up the launcher.

'Come on, Johnsy.'

The noise of the Alouette's blades chopping the humid tropical air reached her across the field. That and the sound of a long stream of bullets leaving Johnsy's machine gun were her cue. Sonja planted a fist in the ploughed dirt to steady herself, and forced herself to her knees, then stood.

She ran, burdened with the launcher, grenades and her own rifle. A few rounds chased her, but Johnsy and Wynand were turning on the heat. Sonja's breath came in long, ragged gasps. Jacob had done a good job on her ribs and each inhalation felt like a knife into her torso. She had no hope of scaling the perimeter fence of the villa complex with the load she was carrying, and in any case her target was on the opposite side. She ran along the fence line.

Steve was yelling and waving, but the blood pounding in her ears and her ragged breathing drowned out his words. Sonja heard gunfire, and puffs of dust appeared in front of her. She weaved and then dropped to her knees. The two trucks carrying the guns were on the road leading to the holiday villa complex. One of the drivers was firing at her.

Sonja lifted the RPG onto her shoulder. She flipped up the iron sights and the front and rear of the launch tube, then pushed down the hammer at the rear of the pistol grip with her right thumb. Sonja took aim at the lead truck – the driver was between her and the vehicle, still firing at her. Bullets were getting closer to her, even if he was a lousy shot. Sonja pulled the trigger. The firing pin shot upward, connecting with an igniter on the propellent charge, and the rocket-propelled grenade left the tube with a whoosh of smoke out the rear of the launcher.

When the projectile was a few metres away from her, its integral rocket charge ignited and it sailed across the field, trailing dirty grey smoke. Sonja dropped the launcher and unslung her AK-47.

The grenade missed the truck, landing short and detonating against the raised embankment on which the road sat. The blast was enough, however, to either kill or stun the driver. Sonja saw the second driver half crouch, seeming to be deliberating whether or not to join the fight. She fired a burst of rounds at him, which made him dive for cover.

She needed to get closer, within two hundred metres of the vehicles. She picked up the launcher with her left hand and set off. When she had covered a football field's length she stopped, took a rocket out of the backpack, and slid it into the tube. Again, she took aim.

One arm, then another, appeared from under the canvas siding covering the back of the truck. The canopy was thrown upwards, onto the roof, and Sonja saw at least half a dozen armed men inside. All at once, they started firing.

Ambush, she thought. They'd been waiting, like Trojans inside the horse, to get into the compound, but her first RPG round had flushed them out. Bullets zinged around Sonja as she held her nerve and her aim, and fired again.

The grenade slammed into the crush of men in the back of the truck and detonated among them. Smoke, blood and wounded and dying men erupted from the vehicle as the canvas cover caught fire. She heard the welcome chop of rotor blades in the heavy tropical air.

To her left, above the villa complex, the pilot of the Alouette flared the nose of his helicopter as he came in to land. Sonja kept her head down and loaded the last rocket into the RPG-7 launcher. Bullets were landing around her. A quick peek over the foliage confirmed that more men were exiting the second truck, now that their surprise attack was blown.

Steve must have hustled his men, carrying the wounded David, onto the chopper in record time, because a couple of minutes later it was airborne again. There was the chatter of a machine gun firing and Sonja looked up again, after cocking the RPG-7. The Alouette was circling. Johnsy was sitting in the door and laying down fire on the tree line. Sonja guessed the insurgents were moving to try and capture the trucks or outflank her.

She stood, aimed, and fired. Her last grenade was a direct hit on the second vehicle. The explosion sent a shockwave that knocked her off her feet. Sonja rolled over, retrieved her AK-47 and looked above the shredded maize plants. The truck she had just hit must have been packed with explosives – perhaps another surprise for her, David and the other contractors.

The Alouette came towards her. The rotor downwash caught the oily black smoke from the burning trucks and pushed it across the fields opposite Sonja. It also provided a smokescreen for twenty or more jihadis, who emerged from it.

'Allahu-Akbar!' the lead man called. Others started firing on the run.

Johnsy leaned out and aimed backwards. Two men on the ground fell, but others, including one carrying a black flag with white writing, charged on.

Sonja had discarded the launcher and pack. She dropped to one knee, took aim and started firing at the advancing men. One fell. She felt the blast of grit, sand and leaves wash over her as the Alouette flared above her. She fired a long burst of fifteen rounds then hooked the rifle's sling over her head.

The pilot swung his machine around to give Johnsy and Wynand clear fields of fire. Steve opened up from the co-pilot's seat. Sonja grabbed onto a wheel strut as soon as it was in reach. The insurgents kept coming, whipped up into a fervour, firing on the run at full auto. Sonja heard the *ping* of a bullet punching through the chopper's flimsy skin.

'Go, go, go!' she yelled.

The pilot needed no further encouragement and started to lift off. Sonja's legs were bicycling in the air as she fought to lift her own body weight, which was multiplied by the forces of gravity. Wynand reached a big hand out and she grabbed it in a monkey grip. He hauled her up, dragging her inside until she lay sprawled on the cargo floor.

David Rafferty was lying next to her, on his back. His face was white and the hastily applied wound dressings on his chest were soaked with blood. He seemed to be breathing, though – just.

*

Emma stared at Fiona. Her head was reeling as she looked into the other woman's eyes. This spy was hellbent on bringing Sonja in on some trumped-up charge. Assuming Sonja had not gone full psycho and started assassinating witnesses, then perhaps it was Fiona, who admitted she had been tailing them, who had been leaving the trail of death in their wake.

'You want to kill my mother,' Emma said as the realisation sank in.

'I want justice,' Fiona said.

'She's not some ISIS terrorist on an international hit list, Fiona.'

'She's dealing arms from warlords who are now serving the Taliban and selling guns to terrorists and criminals.'

Kelvin came out onto the deck, drying his hands with a white towel. The Chinese gangster with the MP5 covered him.

'He needs surgery.'

'Can't you do it here?' Fiona said.

Kelvin shrugged. 'I'd need anaesthetic, properly sterilised instruments. You've got a glorified traveller's first aid kit in there and a staple gun. I've cleaned his wound as best as I can – the bullet carried shirt fabric in with it – and dosed him with pain-killers and antibiotics, but he needs a hospital.'

'Is he lucid?' Fiona asked.

'Groggy, but, yes, more or less.'

Fiona took out a phone. 'I'm getting a chopper for him, but it's your job to keep him alive until it gets here.'

'I can't guarantee that,' Kelvin said.

Fiona finished sending her message. 'Well, I suggest you give it your best shot . . . or else.'

Fiona left them under the guard of the Chinese man. Emma looked through a porthole into Wu's cabin. She watched as Fiona bent over him, and kissed him on the lips.

'That woman's crazy,' Kelvin whispered.

'No,' Emma said. 'Worse. She's a believer.'

'How many men on this boat?' Kelvin asked, looking quickly around.

Emma had already been assessing their odds of escaping or taking over the boat. 'Crew of three that I've seen so far – the skipper, a deckhand, and our friend with the gun.' Their guard had backed off, keeping watch over them from the shade, sitting on the stairs that led to the wheelhouse, above, where the captain was at the helm.

'Got to figure at least a couple of them are armed,' Kelvin said. 'What are we going to do?'

'I don't know,' Emma said. She nodded to the porthole – Fiona had fetched an iPad and was sitting with it, beside Wu on the bed. 'She wants my mother to come to her, here.'

Kelvin looked through the porthole again. 'What *is* she up to?'

CHAPTER 26

Steve Oosthuizen turned back from the co-pilot's seat and shouted: 'Wu's vessel's up ahead.'

Sonja got up, stepped over the barely breathing David, and peered out through the Plexiglass cockpit. 'No wake.'

Steve checked with a pair of binoculars. 'Nope, he's static.'

The sun was a red ball, low on the horizon. Sonja tapped the pilot on the shoulder. 'Come in from the west. Drop to wave height, three hundred metres short of the boat, then do a slow pass over them.'

The pilot looked to Steve for confirmation.

'Do as she says,' Steve said.

The pilot nodded. 'You're paying the bill, man.'

The chopper banked. Sonja unslung her AK-47. She knelt beside Johnsy. 'Give me your pistol.'

'What?'

'Hand it over, Johnsy.'

'*Eish*,' he yelled back at her over the engine noise, 'you're always losing my guns, girl.'

'Don't call me a fucking girl.'

Johnsy put his RPD machine gun, which he had been cradling in his lap, on the floor of the Alouette. He unholstered his pistol

323

and handed it to her. She pushed the release button and the magazine slid into her left hand. The magazine was not full; it was, as she suspected, missing two rounds. She slapped it back into the butt.

Johnsy smiled at her, but she twisted her gun hand and slammed the butt of the pistol into Johnsy's face. He moved one hand to his shattered nose, but instinctively, his other towards the RPD. Sonja was quicker – she kicked the machine gun out of the open door. It tumbled away in the slipstream and splashed into the Indian Ocean.

'Restrain him,' Sonja ordered Wynand, and the big man did as she ordered.

Steve looked back over his shoulder. Sonja held up the pistol. 'He shot David. I saw Johnsy loading this pistol before we took off and now it's two rounds lighter. He set us up to be ambushed – he's a gun runner and somehow he must have known earlier that David was an undercover cop.'

Sonja looked to Johnsy; he glared back at her and spat blood out the door. 'I could have left you to die or be arrested in the Matetsi,' he said to her, nose and eyes streaming.

'Then why didn't you?' she said over the noise of the helicopter's engine. He just stared back at her.

'What now?' Steve yelled.

'Get David to hospital and keep Johnsy on ice – I want to talk to him. For now, tell the pilot to take her down and do as I say.' The pilot banked and put the Alouette into a gradual turn, losing altitude at the same time.

He bled off speed. The sun was behind them, which meant it would be right in the eyes of anybody on board the vessel. Sonja sat in the open door of the helicopter, legs in the slipstream.

Steve looked back at her again. 'What are you playing at?'

The water flashed below them, the helicopter low enough for its rotor wash to leave ripples on the ocean's surface. 'Circle the boat a couple of times,' Sonja called to Steve. 'Keep them busy.'

'What?'

Sonja launched herself out of the rear of the helicopter and into the sea.

*

The boy Kelvin came into the cabin. Fiona could see what Emma saw in him.

'What do you want?' Fiona said. She tapped the screen of her iPad then put it in the side pocket of her cargo pants.

'There's a helicopter overhead, circling us,' he said. 'Maybe he's come to pick up this guy.'

Wu blinked up at him. 'Please . . .'

Kelvin moved to check on his patient.

Fiona pulled a Makarov pistol from the waistband of her pants, took aim and shot Wu between the eyes. The Chinese man with the MP5 appeared in the cabin doorway. Fiona swung the pistol and fired two shots; both hit the man in the chest and he fell backwards, over the railing and into the sea.

Kelvin ran for the door. Fiona raised her pistol and aimed at his back. Then she hesitated, just for a moment, remembering Emma's dishevelled state, the half-smile on Kelvin's face that had disappeared the moment she entered their room and disturbed their afterglow. Kelvin burst through the door and dived over the railing, into the water.

'Coward,' Fiona said.

Outside, she held up a hand to the late-afternoon sun. The helicopter did a low-level circuit around the boat, then headed west, towards the shore. That told her two things: Johnsy was not in control of the Alouette, as per the plan, and Sonja Kurtz was somewhere nearby.

Fiona called to the two Chinese crewmen who had emerged from the wheelhouse; both now carried pistols. She said in Mandarin: 'Everything is fine. Watch the ocean – someone may try to board the boat.'

They moved to the railings and set off, in opposite directions, to check the perimeter. Fiona had learned Mandarin for her posting to Beijing, as a covert MI6 agent based in the embassy. Prior to that she'd added Pashto to her A-Level French as a third language in time for the first of her three rotations to Kabul.

Before joining the security service, Fiona had served as an officer in the British Army. After excelling at school she had gained acceptance to Sandhurst, the army's military academy, and graduated with the Sword of Honour, the award given to the highest-performing officer cadet. She had been posted to Afghanistan as a lieutenant in the intelligence corps, where she had excelled. MI6 had come looking for her after that. The Secret Intelligence Service had been a perfect fit for Fiona. It allowed her to pursue two things she was privately obsessed with – money, and Sonja Kurtz.

'Ow!' Emma yelled.

Fiona followed the screech to the aft of the boat. One of Wu's men had Emma by the arm.

'Let her go,' Fiona said in Mandarin.

The man nodded and did as he was told, then stepped back.

'You shot Wu in the head,' Emma said.

Wu's man must have understood English, because his eyes widened and he started to raise his pistol. Fiona shot him and he fell overboard.

'What are you,' Emma asked, 'a licensed serial killer?'

Fiona pursed her lips. 'Hmm. That's one way of looking at it.'

'Where's Kelvin?'

Fiona laughed. 'Abandoned ship like a rat. No happy ending with that one, Emma.'

*

Sonja trod water for half an hour, waiting for the sun to set. Every now and then a hand-held spotlight swept across the gentle swell and she ducked her head below the surface to escape detection.

Her pounded, bruised body protested and she drew on every last reserve of strength she had to stay afloat. The light came past her again. As it did, she saw, for a fraction of a second, a head above water. When the beam had passed she swam slowly, much of it underwater, towards where she'd seen the other person.

'Kelvin,' she hissed.

The young man's head spun around. 'Hey . . .'

'Shh.'

He swam towards her.

'What the fuck is going on?' Sonja said.

'That crazy Irish woman . . .' Kelvin's head went half under water and he sputtered sea water.

'Fiona.'

'Yes,' he coughed. 'She said she's a British spy, but she executed Wu, the gangster, in cold blood, then killed one of his men. I just heard more gunfire and a splash, so maybe she killed another one. That would leave Fiona and one other man. I took this from the first man Fiona killed.' Paddling with one hand and both legs, he held up a Heckler and Koch MP5.

'Give that to me.' Sonja swapped Johnsy's pistol for the machine gun. It was harder to tread water with the heavier weapon, but she felt better equipped. 'I need a diversion.'

'I'll call out to them, ask her to take me back on board,' Kelvin said.

Sonja saw the light coming towards them again. 'Down!'

They both let themselves sink, then kicked back to the surface once the spotlight had passed them.

Sonja spat. 'You know they might just open up on you – use you for target practice?'

'If it will give you a chance to get on board and save Emma then I'll take that risk. I was just waiting for dark in any case, to try and get to her.'

Sonja looked him in the eyes. Whatever else he might be, he was certainly no coward.

'Give yourself a fighting chance. Swim to a point about two hundred metres from the bow of the boat before you start making a noise. If they do try and shoot you then you'll be a smaller target at that range.'

'Thanks.'

Sonja checked her watch and made sure Kelvin had one as well. 'Start making a racket in ten minutes.'

'Will do. Ms Kurtz?'

'What?'

'I think I might be falling in love with your daughter.'

Sonja shook her head and swam away into the darkness.

*

'Help me! Help me!'

Fiona sat on a leather-upholstered couch on the rear deck of the cruiser, pistol pointed at Emma, who sat opposite her. Emma had been staring at her, saying nothing. If Emma thought she could unnerve Fiona, she was wrong.

'It's the boy,' the captain called in Mandarin.

'Kill him,' Fiona called back, then translated the brief conversation for Emma.

'Please, what do you want?' Emma said. 'I don't understand. It was you who killed Denzel, at Silver Sands, and that hunter in Victoria Falls, and the guy driving the truck full of drugs in Botswana, wasn't it?'

Fiona smiled. 'I told you – it's your mother I want. I expect she'll be coming up here, at the rear of the boat, any time now. Sending Kelvin to the front is a classic diversionary tactic, but also fairly predictable. Won't be long now.'

Shots rang out, from the boat's captain, and incoming rounds.

Emma got up. Fiona stood and grabbed her by the shoulder. Emma swung around, but Fiona dodged the wildly thrown punch. Fiona clubbed Emma on the side of the head with the butt of her pistol. The other woman sank back into the couch. Fiona was surprised – Emma had risked being shot to go and see what had happened to her young man.

'You didn't shoot me,' Emma said, rubbing her head.

'I need you alive, at least for the short term. But if you try that again, I'll just have to kill you.'

'Madam!' the captain called out. 'Lee is dead. His body is floating in the water.'

Fiona stood. The captain was still unaware Fiona had killed his two shipmates, so she at least had him on her side – for now. 'How annoying.'

Fiona grabbed Emma by the arm and pressed the pistol into her back. 'This time I *will* shoot you if you try anything foolish.' She propelled Emma ahead of her.

A burst of three rounds, fired from an automatic weapon rather than a pistol, sent the boat's captain sprawling back onto the deck. Fiona realised that Kelvin, rather than fleeing for his life, had followed Wu's loyal foot-soldier over the railing into the water and had taken his MP5. But where was Sonja? Had she been wrong?

*

Sonja knew that anyone with half a military brain would expect an attack from the rear of the boat if a diversion was created from the front. For that reason, she had swum to the pointed bow and waited there, hiding, until Kelvin started yelling.

She had heard Fiona give the order to kill Kelvin and waited until the last living crewman showed himself. She knew she was risking the boy's life, but it was the last ordeal she would put him through, hopefully.

When the man began shooting at Kelvin – she had been correct, at the range he was aiming at it would be very hard for him to hit Kelvin with pistol fire – Sonja had quietly kicked out from under the front of the boat in a backstroke. Looking straight up, she had dropped the Chinese man with a single shot from the MP5.

There was no sign of Fiona, so Sonja had then fired a burst on full automatic to draw her out. Kelvin, bravely or stupidly, thought this was a signal for him to swim closer to the boat. Now, Fiona appeared in a pool of light on the side deck, Emma in her grasp. Sonja seethed at the sight. Fiona took aim at Kelvin and fired. The boy yelled out, then disappeared under the water. Emma screamed.

Sonja slung the MP5, dived, and swam the length of the cruiser underwater. She bobbed up at the aft end and hauled herself up onto the diving platform. She unslung her weapon and advanced, silently, on Emma and Fiona from behind.

Emma was gripping the boat's railing, looking out to sea. Fiona was next to her, close, but far enough away for Sonja to take a clean shot with no risk to Emma. Sonja brought the folding stock of the machine pistol up into her shoulder, flicked the selector to single shot and took aim through the sight. She placed the crosshairs over the rear of Fiona's heart, then took up the slack on the trigger.

With one little squeeze, this would all be over – not just the chase, but years of torment. So many problems in her life had been solved with a gun; a bullet would end this one, too.

Sonja drew a breath. She gritted her teeth, her hands tightening on the stock and pistol grip.

As if sensing her presence, her hesitation, both the girls turned as one. It was the first time she'd seen them standing next to each other, the first time she'd seen them close, in twenty-eight years.

'Hello, Mum,' Fiona said.

CHAPTER 27

'Twins?' Emma said, looking at her sister. 'What the absolute fuck?'

Sonja kept the MP5 trained on Fiona though she knew, in her heart, she could not and would not pull the trigger. 'Fraternal twins, but, yes.'

'How . . .?' Emma began.

'Yes, how, Sonja?' Fiona said. 'How could you do what you did?'

Fiona's words pierced her more painfully than any bullet or shrapnel ever could. She could carry the burden of her terrible secret no longer, and now there was no taking it back.

'I slept with the target, Danny Byrne, an IRA quartermaster, as part of an undercover operation in Northern Ireland,' Sonja said. The words spilled from her, now the dam was finally breached. 'Danny wanted out of the struggle; his heart wasn't in it; and the fact that the last lot of explosives he had sourced was used to blow up a bus-load of schoolkids did his head in. I was working with the British SAS, and they were using me to lure Danny into a meeting with his brother, Patrick, who had ordered the bombing. Danny drew a gun during the raid and was about to shoot a soldier I'd been working with – so I shot your father in the back, killed him.'

Emma and Fiona were both looking at her now and though they obviously knew versions of this story, just hearing it in all its sordid details was as shocking for them as it was bitter on Sonja's tongue. 'I was twenty-two and pregnant. Word soon leaked out that I'd slept with the enemy, probably aided by my bastard of a commanding officer who had manipulated me into having sex with him. I'd seen enough death by then, so I couldn't bring myself to have an abortion.'

'So, you gave us up for adoption instead,' Fiona said.

Emma looked to her twin sister. 'Us?'

'There's nothing special about you, Emma,' Fiona said. 'She was as ashamed of you as she was of me.'

Sonja shook her head. 'My mother pushed me to have you both adopted. I was confused. I was kicked out of the army for assaulting a sergeant; my head was a mess. When you were born I became depressed. I changed my mind almost every day about what I should do, but in the end I listened to my mother. I put you both up for adoption. I went away for six months, backpacking, to try and drink you both out of my mind, but I couldn't.

'When I came back to the UK, I found out that you, Fiona, had been adopted by a couple in Northern Ireland, but they only wanted one baby. In those days, unlike now, there was no rule that twins had to be taken together. I was able to get Emma back, but as you, Fiona, had been legally adopted, I had no right to change my mind. I got a lawyer, but it was hopeless. The law was the law. No one else knew, not even my CO – he disappeared and didn't come back into our lives until Emma was three. I never even told Sam, my late husband, Fiona. Only my mother and I knew, and I know she regretted forcing my hand. When I brought Emma home we tried to pretend the whole thing never happened, and at my request my mother took that secret to her grave. I'm sorry.'

Fiona laughed. 'Sorry?'

'Bloody hell, Mum,' Emma said.

Emma reached out to Fiona, but her sister raised her pistol, pointing it between Emma's eyes. 'Don't you dare touch me.'

'You're X, aren't you, Fiona?' Sonja said.

Fiona said nothing.

'Fiona told me you were X, Mum.'

Sonja shook her head. 'I spoke to Jed Banks, from the CIA. He said the Americans did pick up some online chatter, some disaffected Taliban complaining about warlords dealing with a foreign woman who had served in Afghanistan and was now dealing arms and drugs. They said she had been in the British Army, but there was no word of her serving in the 1990s – you made that part up, Fiona, in order to point the investigation towards me, and away from you.'

Fiona sneered. 'You fit the profile well enough.'

'Did you have Johnsy try to kill David Rafferty just to cover your tracks?'

'What?' Emma said.

'Johnsy shot David twice,' Sonja said to Emma, 'and tried to make it look like part of a firefight by opening up straight after with his machine gun. I took Johnsy's pistol from him and noticed two bullets missing from the magazine, even though he had supposedly not used it.' She turned her attention back to Fiona. 'We'll have to see what Johnsy tells the police. Was he supposed to hijack the chopper and come for you – kill all of us on board?'

Fiona gave a small smile. 'I didn't want him to kill you, or the pilot. Are you trying to make a deal with me?' Fiona asked Sonja.

'I want you to tell me what you did, and why. What happened to Wu?'

'Fiona shot him, Mum,' Emma said. 'He was wounded. She was . . . with him.'

Fiona gave a laugh. 'Don't be a tattletale, Emma. I was sleeping with the target. I had to keep him alive long enough to get his bank account details. After that, the world was well shot of him. Shooting the enemy after screwing him – sound familiar, Sonja?'

Sonja ignored the taunt. 'You were playing Wu off against Hendricks. Why? Was it all about money, is that what you got from Wu before you killed him? Access to a bank account or something like that?'

'I owe you nothing,' Fiona said.

Sonja nodded. 'True. I watched you grow up, Fiona, as often as I could. I knew you were with good parents – the Stewarts were lovely people. I, on the other hand, was a crap mother. Emma will tell you that.'

'*Mum*,' Emma said, trying to be brave though her voice was wavering, 'this is *not* the time for jokes.'

'No joke, and you know it, Emma. Fiona, I was so proud of you – your achievements at school and at Sandhurst. I followed your military career. We were even in Afghanistan at the same time at one point. It was so hard for me not to come and find you and tell you, but I knew, under the law, that when you turned eighteen you would have the right to find me, assuming the Stewarts did the right thing and told you that you were adopted.'

Fiona turned on her, the gun now pointed at Sonja. 'The *right thing*? What would you know about that? Yes, they told me, because they are good people, but I was not a good person. Oh, I achieved the marks and the prizes all right, but I always knew, from a young age, that there was something wrong with me. It wasn't until I learned for myself who you were, what you did for a living, how I'd come into the world, that I realised what my problem was. Some of the old hands still talked – joked – about you and your methods, and when I reached a high enough security clearance in the intelligence corps, I was able to access your old case file.'

'Any problem you have is my fault,' Sonja said, 'not yours. I lost track of you after you left the army – no wonder, since you went to MI6. Let's put the guns down and talk.'

'No way,' Fiona said, her pistol still pointed at Sonja, even as Sonja lowered her MP5. 'I was attached to the Americans for a while, in Afghanistan. As an intelligence officer I helped with interrogations. The things I did, to humiliate those men . . . were even worse than anything one of the CIA or US Army guys could do, because I was a woman.'

'I'm sorry you had to do that,' Sonja said.

Fiona shook her head and smiled. 'I fucking loved it.'

'Fiona . . .'

'No, hear me out, Sonja. If Six hadn't recruited me, I would have transferred to the infantry when they started accepting female platoon commanders, or signed on to be a contractor, like you. Guess why, *Mum?*'

'Please . . .' Sonja said. She wanted to open her arms to her poor, broken daughter. What hurt her, especially in that moment, was that she knew what Fiona was going to say next.

'Because I wanted to be like you. I wanted to know what it was like to kill someone, to watch them take their last breath and know that I'd been responsible. The Americans didn't shock me with their renditions – flying terrorists to countries that allow torture and waterboarding, Sonja! They had to hold me back. I wanted to kill those bastards for what they were doing to women and little girls in Afghanistan, to people around the world.'

'So, what,' Emma interrupted, 'you, like, killed all these people here in Africa just to set me and Sonja up?'

Fiona turned to Emma. Despite her cold demeanour and words, Sonja could see now that Fiona's lip was trembling. 'How do you think it felt, when I saw Sonja step in on the beach and punch that abalone poacher, to protect you? How do you think it felt when I saw each of you, time and again, risking your lives to save each other? I *put* you in half those situations, just to watch, just to . . . feel.'

Sonja let go of her weapon so that it hung from her shoulder by its sling. Nearly three decades of pent-up, poisoned emotions threatened to burst from her. So much of what she had done, how she had led her life, how she had struggled in her relationships, was tied to the decisions she had made when the twins had become part of her. Right now, she didn't care what Fiona had done, or who she had killed or robbed. For the first time since their birth Sonja finally, truly . . . felt. She opened her arms and took a pace forward. 'Fiona, my love . . .'

Fiona squeezed the trigger.

*

Emma kept Sonja afloat, one arm around her, as the blood flowed out of her and into the warm water of the Indian Ocean. Sonja had fallen backwards into the sea and Emma, not caring if Fiona opened fire on her as well, dived in after her mother.

Kelvin swam to them, and Emma saw that he, too, had been shot.

'It's not much more than a scratch,' he said. He took off his T-shirt, ripped and stained from where the bullet had grazed his upper arm, balled it up and pressed it against the wound in Sonja's chest. The two of them held her.

The motor cruiser accelerated away into the night, its navigation lights becoming dimmer and more distant as each long minute dragged by.

'Mum, stay awake, please,' Emma said, tears running down her cheeks.

'I'm . . . sorry, Emma. I love you.'

'Shit, you must be delirious,' Emma said.

Sonja tried to smile. 'Tell Fiona . . . I'm sorry . . . and that I love . . .'

'That bitch,' Emma said.

'No,' Sonja said. 'She let you live.'

'We have to try for shore,' Emma said.

'Too far,' Sonja said. 'Leave me.'

'No way, Ms Kurtz,' Kelvin said.

She tried another smile. 'You hurt my daughter, I'll come back and haunt you.'

'Mum!'

Emma held her mother close, clinging to her tighter than she could ever remember, even as a child, as Kelvin trod water to keep them all afloat.

'Tell Hudson, I do love . . .' Sonja began.

A light appeared from above, and its beam raced towards them, across the still waters. Emma heard the rotor blades and thought it the sweetest sound ever. The Alouette settled into a hover above them. A man was waving to them from the open hatch, and another was dangling from a winch cable, being lowered down to them.

'Mum!' Emma yelled over the noise. 'It's your friend Steve; he's come back for us.'

Sonja closed her eyes and went limp in Emma's arms. Her face was serene, washed white by the spotlight and blood loss, and it almost looked to Emma as though she was a different person. She was smiling.

EPILOGUE

Intensive Care Unit, Mediclinic Nelspruit, South Africa

Emma left the ICU and walked out into the hospital corridor, her shoes squeaking on the polished floor.

Hudson Brand was walking up the hallway, on crutches. Emma ran to him and enfolded him in a hug. She started crying again.

'Mum died on the chopper, Brand,' she sobbed into his chest, 'in front of me.'

Hudson held her at arm's length. 'What? I thought . . .?'

Emma wiped her nose with the back of her hand. 'Sorry. Kelvin resuscitated her, gave her mouth-to-mouth in the helicopter, and plugged the hole in her chest with a piece of plastic bag. He was amazing.'

'But she's alive, now, right?'

She saw the panic in his eyes. 'Yes, yes. She is. I'm sorry, that came out the wrong way. It's just that – we came so close to losing her, Brand.'

He held her close again. 'I prefer Hudson, for the record. Can I see her?'

'Yes.' Emma sniffed, composing herself as she showed Hudson the way.

'Who's Kelvin?' Hudson asked.

They reached the entry to the ICU, where Kelvin was sitting on a row of chairs; he had a fresh bandage on the wound on his arm. He stood and put out his hand. 'Kelvin Hendricks, Mr Brand. Emma's told me about you. A pleasure to meet you, sir.'

They shook. 'Pleasure's mine, son, sounds like we owe you.'

'It was just good to use my training, sir.'

Emma put a hand on Kelvin's arm and beamed. 'He's studying medicine, Hudson.'

Hudson nodded, then pushed open the swinging door. 'You joining us, Kelvin?'

'The patient should have no more than two visitors at a time, sir.'

'Listen to you,' Emma said, kissing him on the cheek, 'you sound like a doctor already. I'll be out soon.'

Emma followed Hudson into the ICU. He made his way to Sonja, hopping on one foot as he sat on the edge of the bed. Emma took his crutches and rested them against a lounge chair.

'She hasn't said much, she only came out of surgery an hour ago. She's drugged up, still coming to,' Emma said.

Hudson took Sonja's hand, gently; there was an IV line coming out of her, connected to a bag overhead. She had a chest tube, and an array of other wires, attached to her; an ECG monitor beeped softly.

Sonja licked her lips. 'She . . . has a name.'

Emma rolled her eyes. 'Yes, and she must be getting better.'

Sonja blinked and looked up at Hudson. 'I love you, Hudson Brand.'

From behind, Emma saw Hudson's broad shoulders rise as he took a sharp intake of breath. 'Told you,' Emma said, 'high as a kite.'

Hudson leaned forward and kissed Sonja, reverently, on the lips, then whispered in her ear. When he raised himself again,

Sonja flicked her chin up – a sign, Emma thought, that she wanted Emma to come to her side. She walked around the bed and sat opposite Hudson.

Sonja looked up at Emma. 'Fiona?'

Emma sighed. The news was still sinking in and she didn't know how to feel about having a twin sister, nor the fact that having just regained consciousness, one of Sonja's first thoughts was about the daughter who had shot her in the chest. 'She got away, Mum, in Wu's cruiser.'

Sonja nodded. She took Hudson's hand and squeezed it. 'You look broken. When did you get here?'

'I'm fine. I just arrived,' Hudson said. 'As soon as Emma called me, I got a lift to Victoria Falls and caught the direct flight to Nelspruit. While I was waiting for my flight, and then in the car on the way here, I've been getting updates from Jed Banks. The CIA and MI6 have launched a joint operation to track down Fiona – they both want to talk to her. The British are sending people from their embassy to question a David Rafferty, Fiona's partner, who's apparently here in the Mediclinic as well and doing OK – seems y'all had the same aeromedical evacuation insurance. They've figured out Fiona's whole undercover operation was a ruse to divert attention away from the fact that she was X, the international arms and drug dealer the Americans and the Brits have been after for some time. Jed's going to want to question you when you're up to it.'

Sonja gave a small nod then rocked her head to look at Emma again. The small movement seemed to exhaust her and she closed her eyes for a moment, then opened them.

'Where's your boyfriend, or whatever he is? How is . . .?'

'Kelvin, Mum. He's fine. He saved your life. I'll tell you all about it later.'

'All right,' Sonja took a deep breath, then exhaled. 'I wanted to tell you, both of you, about Fiona, for so long. I was so ashamed of the decision I made and it's been eating me up. Emma, I think it was finally being able to spend some time with you, just doing normal stuff, that made all those feelings come back to the surface again. I was thinking what life could have been like, if I'd raised you both properly, if we'd been a family, the three of us, and . . .'

Emma swallowed. 'It's OK, Mum. You raised me just fine.'

'Liar.' Sonja gave a little smile. 'Give me your hand.'

Emma reached out, took her mother's hand and gave it a weak squeeze.

'I fucking love you as well,' Sonja said.

Emma sniffed. 'I want whatever you're on.'

'Don't joke,' Sonja whispered. 'I want to go on holiday with you.'

Emma wiped her eyes, and started to laugh.

ACKNOWLEDGEMENTS

Several people over the years had suggested to me that I write a novel exploring abalone poaching in South Africa. One, in particular, Brenton Scott, a passionate advocate for these endangered creatures, continually kept me updated with media and scientific reports about the state of the species.

As crazy as some of the observations I've made in this novel seem, they are based on fact. Abalone is poached from South Africa's waters and illegally shipped to neighbouring countries, where it is then legally exported to markets in Asia.

Figures for 2016 give a snapshot of the trade and the problem. The quota for legally harvested abalone that year was 96 tons. However, that year 1,700 tons of abalone, worth more than US$100 million, was imported into Hong Kong. In other words, according to journalist Kimon de Greef, the illegal trade in abalone is 30 times the size of the legal trade.

I started my research by reading an excellent book on the abalone trade, *Poacher: Confessions from the Abalone Underworld* by Kimon de Greef and Shuhood Abader. The authors tell Abader's confronting story of the risks and rewards of diving for abalone.

On the ground in South Africa, I was helped by several people. Dr Tony Cunningham, who also helped me with the research for my last novel, *Blood Trail*, showed me around Silver Sands and gave me a fascinating insight into the current state of poaching. Likewise, Garth Jenman and his mother, Barbara, provided invaluable first-hand information and images about the brazen activities of poachers (the conga-line of divers and carriers that Sonja encounters happens in real life). Brett McDonald, Cape Town resident and managing director of Flame of Africa tours, filled in the gaps in my knowledge of his city's waterfront areas. Thank you, all.

As usual, I must thank my eagle-eyed Afrikaans-speaking friend Annelien Oberholzer, who checked and corrected my incorrect use of her language and, as a keen diver, also helped me fix the underwater scenes, and a few other errors. Thanks, once again, to my go-to firearms expert, Fritz Rabe, and also to pilot guide, Izzy Mok, who taught me how to take off from a darkened airstrip at night.

As in my previous books, good people paid good money to good causes to have their name, or the name of a friend or relative assigned to characters in this story. Thank you to David Rafferty, who made a donation to the International Fund for Animal Welfare; and Pat Musick, who donated to the Conservation and Wildlife Fund in Zimbabwe on behalf of Fiona Stewart. I hope you enjoy your fictitious selves.

Thanks also to my tireless team of unpaid first readers and editors: my wife, Nicola, mother, Kathy, and mother-in-law, Sheila. And to my wonderful publishing team in Australia and South Africa: Alex Lloyd, Danielle Walker, Brianne Collins, Terry Morris, Andrea Nattrass, Veronica Napier, Eileen Bezemer and Gill Spain.

Last, but not least, if you've made it this far then thank you. You're the most important person in this business.

Tony Park
www.tonypark.net